NINETY-FIVE THESES

FOR A NEW REFORMATION

NINETY-FIVE THESES

FOR A NEW REFORMATION

A

—— ROAD MAP ——

for

POST-EVANGELICAL CHRISTIANITY

Donald T. Williams, PhD

Ninety-Five Theses for a New Reformation
A Road Map for Post-Evangelical Christianity

© 2021 Donald T. WIlliams
www.donaldtwilliams.com

ISBN: 978-1-7366761-0-3

Prepared for publication by www.greatwriting.org

All rights reserved. No part of this publication may be reproduced, stored in a retrieval system or transmitted in any form by any means, electronic, mechanical, photocopy, recording or otherwise without prior permission of the publisher, except as provided by USA copyright law.

Cover design: www.greatwriting.org
Book layout and design: www.greatwriting.org

Unless noted otherwise, Scripture quotations are taken from the New American Standard Bible® (NASB), Copyright © 1960, 1962, 1963, 1968, 1971, 1972, 1973, 1975, 1977, 1995 by The Lockman Foundation Used by permission. www.Lockman.org

SEMPER REFORMANDA PULICATIONS
Tocoa Falls, Georgia / www.srpublications.org

About the Author

Dr. Donald T. Williams (BA, Taylor University; MDiv, Trinity Evangelical Divinity School; PhD, University of Georgia) is Professor Emeritus of Toccoa Falls College. An ordained minister in the Evangelical Free Church of America with many years of pastoral experience, he has spent several summers doing pastoral training in East Africa and India for Church Planting International. A past president of the International Society of Christian Apologetics and an internationally known Inklings scholar, he is the author of twelve other books, most recently *Deeper Magic: The Theology behind the Writings of C. S. Lewis* (Baltimore: Square Halo Books, 2016), *An Encouraging Thought: the Christian Worldview in the Writings of J. R. R. Tolkien* (Cambridge, OH: Christian Publishing House, 2018), *Mere Humanity: G. K. Chesterton, C. S. Lewis, and J. R. R. Tolkien on the Human Condition,* 2nd ed. (Chilicothe, OH: DeWard, 2018), *The Young Christian's Survival Guide: Common Questions Young Christians are Asked about God, the Bible, and the Christian Faith Answered* (Cambridge, OH: Christian Publishing House, 2019), and *Stars through the Clouds: The Collected Poetry of Donald T. Williams* (Lantern Hollow Press, 2020). He is also the author of numerous articles, poems, and reviews in publications such as *Christianity Today, National Review, Touchstone, Modern Reformation, Christian Research Journal, The Journal of the Evangelical Theological Society, Philosophia Christi, Christian Scholar's Review, SEVEN: An Anglo-American Review*, etc.

Dedication

I was privileged to have many great mentors in the Faith, but five men stand out as people who not only taught, but incarnated, the idea that the Reformation (and its successors, the Puritans of the Seventeenth Century and the revivalists of the First Great Awakening) could still be a living force today.

- Francis A. Schaeffer, Director, L'Abri Fellowship, who could see the forest for the trees;
- John H. Gerstner, Visiting Professor, Trinity Evangelical Divinity School, who embodied the thought and the spirit of Jonathan Edwards;
- Alan Dan Orme, Pastor, University Church, Athens, Georgia, who translated the theology of the Reformers into life and ministry;
- J. I. Packer, Visiting Professor, Trinity Evangelical Divinity School, who knew the great Puritan fathers as if they were his personal friends;
- John Warwick Montgomery, Professor, Trinity Evangelical Divinity School and Director, The International Academy of Apologetics, Evangelism, and Human Rights, who still brings the mind and the spirit of Martin Luther into the Twenty-First Century.

To these men,
their memory, and their legacy,
this book is dedicated.

Chapter Contents

Appreciations 9
A Synopsis 12
Foreword 19
Introduction 23
Prelude 27
Five Theses on *Sola Scriptura* 28
Five Theses on *Sola Gratia* 52
Five Theses on *Sola Fide* 74
Five Theses on *Solus Christus* 92
Five Theses on *Soli Deo Gloria* 110
Five Theses on Hermeneutics 128
Five Theses on Church Ministry 146
Five Theses on the "Worship Wars" 168
Five Theses on Gender Roles 186
Five Theses on Charismatic Phenomena 202
Five Theses on Evangelism 222
Five Theses on Apologetics 244
Five Theses on Christianity and Culture 264
Five Theses on Pietism 290
Five Theses on the Christian Mind 312
Five Theses on Christian Education 330
Five Theses on Renaissance 350
Five Theses on Reformation 372
Five Theses on Revival 392
Excursus I: The Integrity of the Organized Church 409
Excursus II: Discerning the Times 416
Conclusion 424
Bibliography 428
Index of Names 441
General Index 446
Scripture Index 454
Index of Latin and Greek Terms 458

Appreciations

This book is a distillation of years of reflection on the central doctrines of the Reformation and their practice in our world. It is both a needed corrective to a weakening evangelicalism and a welcome tonic as we go into the future. It is direct, challenging, and worthy of careful study.

DAVID F. WELLS

Distinguished Senior Research Professor, Gordon-Conwell Theological Seminary, and the author of many books, including *No Place for Truth, or Whatever Happened to Evangelical Theology?*

It goes without saying that anyone familiar with Donald Williams's writings will want to acquire his latest book on 95 theses for a new Reformation. But this book is so important for our present generation that it needs to be read by everyone who has a regard for biblical Christianity and the current state of Evangelicalism (and hopefully also by those who have no such concern). The book has but one major thesis; "Only a new reformation can save us from ourselves." Williams presents his case with clarity, vigor and conviction.

EDGAR ANDREWS

Emeritus Professor and former Dean, University of London, England, and author of *Who Made God? Searching for a Theory of Everything.*

We desperately need "a new reformation," and this book can help get us there, God willing. Professor Williams is an articulate man of the Reformation, of the Scriptures, and of the Humanities. As such, he calls us to an intelligent and biblical way of thinking, living, and thriving.

DOUGLAS GROOTHUIS

Professor of Philosophy at Denver Seminary and the author of *Truth Decay* and *Christian Apologetics*.

Having myself prepared a set of 95 theses (for the 450th Anniversary of the Reformation—an incredible half-century ago), I am always fascinated by new takes on Luther's manifesto. Donald Williams is faithful to the spirit of the Great Reformer, and his theses are particularly valuable by way of their lucid organisation—in units of five, covering not only the standard theological topics but also such contemporary issues as apologetics, "worship wars," Charisma, gender, culture, and the Christian mind. Dr Williams's book is replete with valuable insights, old and new, and it deserves an important place in the thinking believer's personal library.

JOHN WARWICK MONTGOMERY

Professor Emeritus of Law and Humanities,
University of Bedfordshire, England
Professor-at-Large, 1517: The Legacy Project, Irvine, CA, USA
Director, International Academy of Apologetics, Evangelism and Human Rights, Strasbourg, France

When the Reformation figures said the church should be "*semper reformanda secundum verbum Dei*," they willed the entire life of believers to be one of continual reformation under the authority of Scripture. This historic Reformation slogan cannot be understood as calling the church to change according to the dictates of sinful men, the whims of culture, the traditions of men, or just for the sake of change, but according to the Word of God. In our day, too many Christians are hastily calling for changes inside the church without considering the long-term implications of their cries. In *The Lord of the Rings*, Treebeard warns us, "We must not be hasty . . . . I must cool myself and think; for it is easier to shout stop! than to do it." Dr. Donald Williams gives the church a call to reformation that is not a hasty treatment of its subject, but a discerning and reflective analysis of our current situation. These are signs of biblical wisdom and maturity from a faithful theologian. Williams's *95 Theses for a New Reformation* does not just shout to the church, "Reform!" Rather, it provides a comprehensive treatment and the means, under the authority of Scripture, to actually accomplish reformation in our day.

WILLIAM C. ROACH

President of the International Society of Christian Apologetics and professor at Veritas International University and Columbia Evangelical Seminary.

I picked up this book because I was interested in learning more about Martin Luther, but I discovered that more than anything else, it kept speaking to me about my own heart. Williams has written a clear, informative, and immensely practical guide to cultivating a more balanced spiritual life. I learned a lot. I was genuinely moved, nourished, and challenged by this wonderful book.

DIANA PAVLAC GLYER

Professor of The Honors College, Azusa Pacific University, and the author of *Bandersnatch, The Company They Keep,* and *Clay in the Potter's Hands.*

A Synopsis

INTRODUCTION
1. Five Theses on *Sola Scriptura*
- *Sola Scriptura* does not mean that Scripture is the only authority.
- *Sola Scriptura* does mean that Scripture alone has "magisterial authority."
- Reason, Tradition, and Experience have "ministerial authority."
- *Sola Scriptura* does not mean that the individual can interpret Scripture alone.
- Proper submission to Scripture as the highest expression of God's authority under Christ is a necessary prerequisite for a faithful individual or church.

2. Five Theses on *Sola Gratia*
- Salvation is by God's grace alone, apart from works.
- Grace is not a spiritual *substance* or force, but an *attitude* on God's part, whereby He grants unmerited favor to poor sinners.
- Good works are *excluded* as *grounds* of salvation but are *required* as its fruits.
- Any admixture of good works *as the grounds* of salvation subverts and destroys the whole biblical plan of redemption.
- Works are necessarily both excluded as ground *and* required as fruit because the end of salvation is the glory of God.

3. Five Theses on *Sola Fide*
- Salvation, wrought by grace alone, is received by the empty hands of faith alone.
- Saving faith is personal trust in God's promise of salvation and in His proffered Redeemer, Jesus Christ.
- Saving faith is not simply holding correct opinions about doctrine; it is personal trust in the saving power of the Christ who is accurately described by biblical truth.

- Because Christ's Person and His Work are what they are and not something else, some major doctrinal errors are inconsistent with a claim to have saving faith.
- The sacraments are inducements to, enablers of, and expressions of saving faith; they have no power to save apart from faith.

4. Five Theses on *Solus Christus*
- Christ stands supreme as the perfect image of the Father.
- Christ stands supreme as the Second Adam, the perfect template of unfallen human nature.
- Christ stands supreme as the Lamb of God who taketh away the sins of the world.
- Christ stands supreme as the only Mediator between God and man.
- Christ stands supreme as the King of Kings and Lord of Glory.

5. Five Theses on *Soli Deo Gloria*
- God's ultimate purpose in the salvation of sinners is His own glory.
- God's glory is the manifestation of His perfect and holy character in all its awesome and majestic splendor throughout the whole of creation.
- Salvation is not primarily for our benefit.
- God's pursuit of His own glory is not selfish, because the glory of God is not just His greatest good; it is *the* greatest good (and therefore ours).
- The vision and manifestation of God's glory should be our highest purpose and deepest joy.

6. Five Theses on Hermeneutics
- Context is everything.
- The original meaning has primacy.
- Interpretation must use the *Analogia Fidei*.
- Interpretation must recognize that all Scripture is profitable in the way it claims to be.
- Interpretation must recognize that Christ is the key to all.

7. Five Theses on Church Ministry
- God means people to be whole persons.
- The ministry of the church should rebuild those whole persons

- out of the fragments created by sin.
- Expository preaching is essential to authentic Christian ministry.
- A sacramental cast of mind is essential to authentic Christian ministry.
- The New-Testament pattern of participatory worship is essential to authentic Christian ministry.

8. Five Theses on The Worship Wars
- The texts sung must reflect biblical truth.
- The texts sung should reflect theological profundity.
- The texts sung should reflect poetic richness.
- The settings of the texts should manifest musical beauty.
- There should be a good fit between the text and its musical setting.

9. Five Theses on Gender Roles
- The Bible is an inescapably hierarchical book, but not as modern man understands (or thinks he understands) hierarchy.
- Headship is unavoidably a leadership position, but not as modern man understands leadership.
- The husband is not given the position of head because he is necessarily more qualified for it.
- The husband's leadership (Eph. 5:22) must be seen in the context of Eph. 5:21.
- We do this to picture the relationship between Christ and His church.

10. Five Theses on Charismatic Phenomena
- It cannot be proved from Scripture that gifts such as tongues have ceased.
- It does not follow that such manifestations as experienced today are *ipso facto* of the Holy Spirit.
- The mission of the Holy Spirit is to glorify the Son.
- The practice of gifts must be evaluated Christocentrically: Do they edify the Body by pointing it toward and concentrating it on the Son?
- No gift should be used contrary to the express instructions for its use in the New Testament.

11. Five Theses on Evangelism
- Evangelism and mission exist because worship does not (John Piper).
- The Great Commission is to make *disciples*, not converts. (Conversion is only the first step in making a disciple—the beginning, not the end, of fulfilling the Great Commission.)
- A "convert" who does not become a disciple is presumed not to be a true convert.
- A disciple is not made until the convert is at least stumblingly trying to learn and do all things whatsoever Christ has commanded us.
- A disciple is not made until the convert is a committed and functioning member of a Bible-believing local church.

12. Five Theses on Apologetics
- We are commanded to be always ready to give a defense (Grk. *apologia*) to anyone who asks a reason for the hope that is within us (1 Pet. 3:15).
- Apologetics is therefore an essential part of Christian discipleship.
- God purposes to save whole persons, which includes their minds as well as their hearts.
- Apologetics seeks to win people, not arguments; nevertheless, sound arguments should be employed because not to do so is to insult and blaspheme the God of truth.
- Apologetics, like every other aspect of evangelism, is impotent apart from the convicting power of the Holy Spirit; and that is a reason to *do* it, not to avoid it.

13. Five Theses on Christianity and Culture
- Human beings are creative because they are made in the image of the Creator.
- Culture is the material, social, and symbolic matrix that results from the full range of their creative activity.
- Culture is not and cannot be spiritually neutral or irrelevant.
- Francis Schaeffer was right to insist that part of Christian discipleship is living out the Lordship of Christ over the total culture.
- The Christian subculture in any society should bring salt and light to that society through its own cultural activity.

14. Five Theses on Pietism
- Pietism, as the word is used here, is the theory that the Christian life consisteth in the multitude and depth of emotions that a person possesseth.
- Pietism arose as a natural and healthy corrective to the dead orthodoxy of eighteenth-century European state churches.
- When not rooted in a holistic biblical anthropology and psychology, pietism cannot be healthy, and it has thus contributed to the superficiality, irrelevance, and corruption of American conservative Christianity.
- Emotions are byproducts of true biblical spiritual life, not the thing itself.
- Horses should be kept in front of carts.

15. Five Theses on the Christian Mind
- Anti-Intellectualism is a heresy because it requires us to disobey a part of our Lord's Great Commandment.
- Study is therefore an essential part of Christian discipleship.
- Every Christian, because he is a Christian, is called to be a life-long learner.
- The content, nature, and commission of Scripture require it of us.
- There are practical steps to the acquisition and wise use of the Christian mind.

16. Five Theses on Christian Education
- Secular education is an oxymoron.
- You cannot educate a human being unless you know what a human being is and what it is for.
- Human beings were created in the image of God to enjoy Him through fellowship with Him and to glorify Him by serving Him as His deputies and regents in the rule and care of the earth.
- Christian education develops the whole person to glorify God in every area of a whole life; it thus includes, but cannot be limited to, mere training for employment.
- Therefore, Milton was right to say that a complete and generous education is that which fits a man to perform justly, skillfully, and magnanimously all the offices, both public and private, of peace and war.

17. Five Theses on Renaissance
- Renaissance is a recovery of the life of the mind.
- God used the historical Renaissance to prepare the way for the Reformation by developing the *ad fontes* ("back to the sources") tradition.
- In the providence of God, the elaboration of grammatico-historical exegesis by Renaissance humanist scholars in the *ad fontes* tradition made *sola Scriptura* a viable response to the crisis of religious authority of the time.
- Our day faces a similar crisis of authority, in the church as well as outside it.
- We need a new Renaissance to make possible a new Reformation.

18. Five Theses on Reformation
- Reformation is a recovery of sound doctrine, especially as it relates to the Gospel itself.
- Historically, Reformation was a fruit of Renaissance and a prerequisite to Revival.
- Many so-called Evangelicals are letting the sound teaching recovered by the original Reformers slip through their fingers.
- These ninety-five Theses represent areas in which a new Reformation is required.
- The only way to be faithful to the original Reformation is by continuing to pursue the ongoing Reformation of the church.

19. Five Theses on Revival
- Revival is a recovery of vital spirituality.
- Revival is a desperate need of the contemporary church, especially its Evangelical wing.
- Revival cannot be scheduled or arranged by human action however well intentioned, conceived, or executed, but can only come through a strong, supernatural reassertion of God's grace.
- That strong movement of God's grace can be prepared for by prayer and faithfulness on the part of the Remnant, but it still waits on God's sovereign action.
- Historically, a deep and long-lasting revival must be preceded and prepared for by Renaissance and Reformation.

Excursus I: The Integrity of the Organized Church

Excursus II: Discerning the Times: Why We Lost the Culture War, and How to Make a Comeback

Foreword

My friend, Professor Donald Williams, and I are kindred spirits—or so I like to think—except he knows more about most things than I do. He is a Renaissance man who, in this wide-ranging and wise book, advocates for a true renaissance in Christian learning, discipleship, formation, worship, and outreach. He is a rational pietist who loves the Bible, theology, apologetics, and literature. His tribe is small but will grow if people read and heed this book. And that tribe needs to grow, given the spiritual torpor and moral barbarism of our day.

He writes with passion, precision, and power about things that matter most—the reformation of the Church for the glory of God and for the good of the city to which we Christians are exiled (Jeremiah 29:7). He covers a lot of territory, but none of it on the cheap. His range is deep and wide. His prose is forceful, but not hectoring.

As Christian thinkers age (as Don and I seem to be doing), they either (1) retire from their former advocacies and yawn on the sidelines, (2) become bitter and issue (if anything) jeremiads, or (3) keep fighting with a wisdom that comes only from years of Christian devotion, research, writing, teaching, preaching, suffering, and overall ministry. Don is in the third category. He is like Duke Ellington, who was asked later in life, "Duke, when are you going to retire?" To which the great jazz pianist, composer, and bandleader extraordinaire replied, "Retire to what?" Duke could only make music. Don can only give expression to the fire in his bones (Jeremiah 20:9). We are the better for it.

The readers of *Ninety-Five Theses for a New Reformation* will grow in their knowledge of the Five Solas of the Reformation (about each of which Don has five theses) and their application today. A further feast awaits the reader in Don's five theses on hermeneutics, church ministry, worship, gender roles, charismatic phenomena, evangelism, culture, pietism, the Christian mind, Christian education, renaissance, reformation, and revival. It all adds up to a tidy ninety-five theses (in honor of Martin Luther's 1517 manifesto). I have not done the math, but I am sure that I agree on more than 95 percent of these theses.

Since I am a philosopher and an apologist, let me comment on his five theses on apologetics, which I have italicized.

1. *We are commanded to be always ready to give a defense (Grk. apologia) to anyone who asks a reason for the hope that is within us (1 Pet. 3:15).* Yes! This is not optional—something only for eggheads like Don and me. This command was given to the whole church for the whole world. If the church begins to heed the call and take full advantage of all the unprecedented resources available to us, we could see the world turned upside down again (Acts 17:6). As Walter Martin used to ask, "What would happen if the sleeping giant of the church awoke?"

2. *Apologetics is therefore an essential part of Christian discipleship.* Since this is true, apologetics should be integrated into the whole educational ministry of the church and not limited to a few apologetics sermons once in a while. We should offer adult education classes in apologetics and be sure to teach apologetics to teenagers about to go off to secular colleges and universities. And so much more, as Don explains.

3. *God purposes to save whole persons, which includes their minds as well as their hearts.* As I often tell my students and anyone else who will listen, "We need to out-think the world for Christ!" We can be transformed through the renewing of our minds to take every thought captive to Christ (Romans 12:1-2; 2 Corinthians 10:3-5). Then we take it to the streets (1 Peter 3:15).

4. *Apologetics seeks to win people, not arguments; nevertheless, sound arguments should be employed because not to do so is to insult and blaspheme the God of truth.* We need to be smart, knowledgeable, and savvy ambassadors for Christ—neither pedantic or pugnacious, but winsome and loving. In this, Don and I have been influenced deeply by the ministry of Francis and Edith Schaeffer. We must speak the truth in love for the honor and worship of our God (Ephesians 4:15; Colossians 3:17).

5. *Apologetics, like every other aspect of evangelism, is impotent apart from the convicting power of the Holy Spirit; and that is a*

reason to do it, not to avoid it. Frederick Nietzsche (1844-1900), the infamous atheist, said, "Live dangerously!" By that he meant that we should pursue truth, come what may. Sadly, Nietzsche failed to stay true to the truth, but Christians can appropriate that adventurous spirit in the power of the Holy Spirit, who is the Spirit of truth (John 16:13). When we study, we ask the Holy Spirit to teach us. We ask the Holy Spirit to lead us to minister where the gospel is not known or believed (Romans 15:20; see also Ecclesiastes 11:1-6). When we do apologetics (writing or speaking), we ask the Holy Spirit to guide and empower us. When we fail, we lick our wounds, and ask the Holy Spirit to correct us, to further instruct us, and to give us courage and wisdom in witness.

I am fired up just writing this introduction to Donald Williams's superb book, since he so adroitly addresses so many crucial themes in living for Christ, the King, in this broken, needy, and guilty world. *Soli Deo Gloria!*

DOUGLAS GROOTHUIS
Professor of Philosophy, Denver Seminary and the author *Christian Apologetics: A Comprehensive Case for Biblical Faith* (InterVarsity Press, 2011).

Introduction

When Martin Luther nailed his ninety-five theses to the Wittenberg church door on October 31, 1517, he changed the world. It was not the dramatic act of vandalistic defiance it seems today. Those massive wooden doors of the church were the university bulletin board. People nailed notices to them all the time. Luther was simply challenging other scholars to debate him on ninety-five points he had composed against the theological legitimacy of the sale of indulgences, certificates for the forgiveness of sin that the church was using to finance the construction of the new St. Peter's Cathedral in Rome. Luther had learned from his study of Romans and Galatians that salvation is a free gift given by God's grace alone and could not be bought with money or even good works, so he was troubled by the actions of Johan Tetzel, the sixteenth-century equivalent of a televangelist, who was hawking those certificates in the neighborhood. He wanted to raise a few polite questions about the propriety of Tetzel's "ministry" and the theology behind it.

So imagine a theology professor thumbtacking a note to the bulletin board in a modern faculty lounge—nothing more dramatic than that. Luther wanted to encourage reformation in the church in the small way a professor could: by discussing ideas. He had no idea he would turn the church upside down and no intention of starting a rival denomination. But the time was ripe, the new technology of the printing press let the message spread like wildfire, and God had His own ideas. So, unfortunately, did the Pope. The, ahem, conversation that Luther started that day is still going on today. We celebrated the 500th anniversary of its beginning just a few years ago. I'm a little late to the party with this volume, but it is kind of hard to finish and publish a book in the year that inspired you to start it. Better late than never.[1]

---

1 If you can only read one book about the original Reformation, I recommend Roland H. Bainton, *"Here I Stand": A Life of Martin Luther* (N.Y.: Mentor Books, 1950). The classic work is J. H, Merle d'Aubigne, *History of the Reformation of the Sixteenth Century* (1846, rpt. Grand Rapids: Baker, n.d.). Also worth reading are Roland H, Bainton, *The Reformation of the Sixteenth Century* (Boston: Bea-

The Reformers—Luther, Calvin, Zwingli, and others—were flawed men who made many mistakes. But I am convinced that they were essentially right about their main thing: the Gospel of salvation by grace alone through faith alone in Christ alone, revealed in a Bible that stands alone as our only inspired and infallible authority about that Gospel. Their most faithful followers in that message in America had been conservative Evangelicals[2]: that movement which came down to us from the original Reformation of the Sixteenth Century through the Puritans of the Seventeenth Century[3] and the First Great Awakening of the Eighteenth.[4] But as I look at Evangelicalism today, I see a movement that has lost its way. Despite having produced glorious consensual documents like *The Chicago Statement on Biblical Inerrancy*[5] and *The Lausanne Covenant*[6] four decades ago, the movement now seems to have no memory of them and no clear idea who it is or what it stands for. Experience trumps Scripture, health and wealth trump grace and sacrifice, and it seems like every week some prominent megachurch pastor or some well-known theologian feels a need to "rethink" or "reimagine" a doctrinal position that has always been part of the Evangelical heritage or an ethical position that has

---

con Press, 1952), Timothy George, *Theology of the Reformers* (Nashville: Broadman, 1988), and Alister E. McGrath, *Reformation Thought: An Introduction*, 2nd ed. (Grand Rapids: Baker, 1993). On the Reformation in England, see A. G. Dickens, *The English Reformation* (N.Y.: Schocken Books, 1964) and Philip Edgecumbe Hughes, *Theology of the English Reformers* (Grand Rapids: Baker, 1980). A newer study that helpfully relates the Reformation to the Renaissance is William R. Estep, *Renaissance and Reformation* (Grand Rapids: Eerdmans1986). And of course there is no substitute for original writings of the Reformers themselves, especially John Calvin, *Institutes of the Christian Religion,* trans. Henry Beveridge. 2 vols (Grand Rapids: Eerdmans, 1975). An excellent reference work is Hans J. Hillerbrand, ed., *The Oxford Encyclopedia of the Reformation*, 4 vols. (Oxford: Oxford University Press, 1996).

2 For an excellent collection of essays on classical Evangelicalism, see David F. Wells and John D. Woodbridge, eds. *The Evangelicals: What They Believe, Who They Are, and How They Are Changing* (Nashville: Abingdon, 1975). A fascinating take on the history of the movement in the Twentieth Century from the ultimate insider for that period (and a perceptive witness) is Carl F. H. Henry, *Confessions of a Theologian: An Autobiography* (Waco, TX: Word, 1986).

3 For excellent treatments of the contributions made by the Puritan fathers to a healthy Evangelical spirituality, see Leland Ryken, *Worldy Saints: The Puritans as They Really Were* (Grand Rapids: Baker, 1986), David Martyn Lloyd-Jones, *The Puritans: Their Origins and Successors* (Carlisle, Pa.: Banner of Truth, 1987), and J. I. Packer, *A Quest for Godliness: The Puritan Vision of the Christian Life* (Wheaton: Crossway, 1990).

4 For an excellent overview of the best of the First Great Awakening, see David Lyle Jeffrey, *A Burning and a Shining Light: English Spirituality in the Age of Wesley* (Grand Rapids: Eerdmans, 1987).

5 *The Chicago Statements on Biblical Inerrancy and Biblical Hermeneutics*, available online at http://www.danielakin.com/wpcontent/uploads/old/Resource_545/Book%202,%20Sec%2023.pdf.

6 *The Lausanne Covenant* is available online at https://www.lausanne.org/content/covenant/lausanne-covenant.

always been part of Christendom's.[7]

I want to reform the Evangelical movement, to call it back to its roots as defined above. But can Evangelicalism be saved, or will God have to create something new that arises out of its ashes in order to preserve a remnant faithful to the New-Testament and Reformation Gospel? I don't know. My provocative subtitle, *Post-Evangelical Christianity*, might be taken to imply an answer, but I actually think it is still an open question. Either way, radical change is needed (though not the kind we have been seeing). We spend a lot of energy praying for Revival, and rightly so. But I have come to believe that something even more fundamental is needed. Only a new Reformation can save us from ourselves. Well, that is very consistent with the original Reformation, one of whose principles was *Semper Reformanda*—the church should always be reforming itself. That American Evangelicalism is no exception to that principle should not be shocking. I am not alone in thinking that the need is reaching a point of crisis.

This book started some years ago with a sermon of five theses that has evolved into the chapter on church ministry. I joked then that with a mere five theses I was only one nineteenth the Reformer that Martin Luther was, but that was enough for me. Well, it isn't enough for me any more. Here are my ninety-five theses for the church in the Twenty-First Century, conveniently laid out in groups of five that address nineteen areas in which I think the Evangelical movement is in desperate need of regrounding and reform.

Those familiar with the original Reformation will see many of its emphases and even much of its language repeated here. I want to confirm its work, not abandon it—and I want to continue it, not just repeat it. So we start with its five slogans, reaffirmed and updated to address contemporary concerns: *Sola Scriptura*, Scripture alone is the only final and infallible authority for doctrine and practice; *Sola Gratia*, salvation is by God's grace alone; *Sola Fide*, it is received by the empty hands of faith alone; *Solus Christus*, Christ alone is the only and the all-sufficient Mediator between God and men; and *Soli Deo Gloria*, glory to God alone is the final end and purpose of it all. Then

---

7 Four prophetic voices that saw the current situation coming were Carl F. H. Henry, *Evangelicals in Search of Identity* (Waco, TX: Word, 1976), Francis A. Schaeffer, *The Great Evangelical Disaster* (Westchester, Il.: Crossway, 1984), James Davison Hunter, *Evangelicalism: The Coming Generation* (Chicago: The University of Chicago Press, 1987), and David F. Wells, *No Place for Truth, or Whatever Happened to Evangelical Theology?* (Grand Rapids: Eerdmans, 1993). A recent work that confirms their diagnosis and charts the progress of the disease is Stephen Cable, *Cultural Captives: The Beliefs and Behavior of American Young Adults* (Dallas: Probe Ministries, 2012).

we move on to other issues that are either dividing us or distracting us or otherwise diverting us from our mission. We need not so much to rethink or reimagine as to regroup, reground, and recommit to the Gospel of grace which is our heritage.

It is hardly to be hoped that very many people will agree with me on all ninety-five of my theses. That is a lot of points of agreement! But I hope that many people will recognize many of them as issues that need to be addressed if we are to remain faithful to our calling, and I hope to do in all of them what Luther hoped to do: get the discussion started. Then, as with Luther, what proceeds from that is in God's hands.

This book aims at a practical Reformation of the church. In fact, it is so practical that it tries to promote contemplation. Unless otherwise credited, the poems embedded in the chapters and the ones that give space for pause and reflection between chapters are from my book *Stars through the Clouds: The Collected Poetry of Donald T. Williams*, 2nd ed. (Lantern Hollow Press, 2020). Those who find them helpful can find many more where they came from.

Prelude

Martin Luther

Can one lone monk be right, and all the rest
    Of Christendom for near a thousand years
    Be wrong? The question brought him close to tears
And troubled Luther sorely, he confessed.
But other problems had to be addressed,
    Like, shall the Gospel reach the waiting ears
    Of people whose good works were in arrears
And had no chance but grace to pass the test?

He meant by that just simply every man
    And thought of men who'd lived by faith before—
    And doubted then his Gospel's truth no more.
With Athanasius *contra mundum*, and
    With John the lone disciple at the Cross
    He clung to Christ and viewed all else as loss.[8]

---

[8] All the poems by the author in this book are from Donald T. Williams, *Stars through the Clouds: The Collected Poetry of Donald T. Williams*, 2nd ed. (Toccoa, GA: Lantern Hollow Press, 2020). This one appears on p. 210.

1

Five Theses on *Sola Scriptura*

These theses come first because if we do not relate rightly to authority and to God's revealed truth, we wander in darkness and every other point is moot.

A. Sola Scriptura does not mean that Scripture is the only authority. (It means it is the only final and infallible authority.)

B. *Sola Scriptura* does mean that Scripture alone has "magisterial authority." (*Magisterial* is from the Latin word for "master." Scripture has ultimate authority to command us and it rules over every other authority.)

C. Church Elders, Reason, Tradition, and Experience have "ministerial authority." (Ministerial authority means that they serve under the Scriptures; they have a certain authority but cannot contradict or overturn what Scripture teaches.)

D. *Sola Scriptura* does not mean that the individual can interpret Scripture alone. (He interprets it in the context of and in the light of the consensual tradition of the universal church. But that tradition is not allowed to contravene Scripture itself; see thesis 1c.)

E. Proper submission to Scripture as the highest expression of God's authority under Christ is a necessary prerequisite for a faithful individual or a faithful church. (Christ is the absolutely highest authority—and Scripture is His word.)

Sola Scriptura, "Scripture alone," is probably the most misunderstood, indeed, caricatured, of all the principles of the Reformation. Even Protestants rarely understand it, and you frequently hear them either misapplying it or even rejecting it as impossible to practice—and almost always it is a straw-man version of it that they are rejecting, a caricature skewed by Roman Catholic or Eastern Orthodox apologetics into something that can be easily dismissed. Yet if we don't have our authority—more accurately our structure of authority, our hierarchy of authorities—clear, we cannot answer any other question. So let's get a running start at a fresh look at Scripture Alone through our first five theses.[1]

---

1   For the philosophical foundations of the Protestant view of Scriptural revelation, see Ronald H. Nash, *The Word of God and the Mind of Man: The Crisis of Revealed Truth in Contemporary Theology* (Grand Rapids: Zondervan, 1982). For the biblical foundations of it, see John W. Wenham, *Christ and the Bible* (Downers Grove, IL.: InterVarsity Press, 1972). For its historical context, see John D. Woodbridge, *Biblical Authority: A Critique of the Rogers/McKim Proposal* (Grand Rapids: Zondervan, 1982). For answers to some apologetic questions related to it, see Donald T. Williams, *The Young Christian's Survival Guide: Common Questions Young Christians are Asked about God, the Bible, and the Christian Faith Answered* (Cambridge, OH: Christian Publishing House, 2019), esp. chp. 1-4. On *Sola Scriptura* specifically as an aspect or implication of the doctrine of Scripture and its inspiration, see R. C. Sproul, "*Sola Scriptura*: Crucial to Evangelicalism," *The Foundation of Biblical Authority*, ed. James Montgomery Boice (Grand Rapids: Zondervan, 1978), pp. 103-119, and J. I. Packer, "*Sola Scriptura* in History and Today," *God's Inerrant Word: An International Symposium on the Trustworthiness of Scripture*, ed. John Warwick Montgomery (Minneapolis: Bethany, 1973), pp. 43-62. See the relevant sections in the standard Evangelical systematic theologies, such as Hodge, Berkhof, Erickson, and Grudem. Most importantly, see *The Chicago Statements on Biblical Inerrancy and Biblical Hermeneutics*, available online at http://www.danielakin.com/wp-content/uploads/old/Resource_545/Book%202,%20Sec%2023.pdf.

Thesis 1a:
Sola Scriptura Does Not Mean That Scripture Is the Only Authority.

Scripture is not the only authority, period; it is not even the only authority on matters of faith. Nobody who had anything to do with the Reformation ever said that it was. It is astonishing that so many people actually believe the Reformers capable of such a ridiculous claim. Scripture stands "alone," not as the only authority, but as the only *infallible* and *final* authority—whatever the topic under discussion.

It is easy to see that Scripture is not and cannot be the only authority on anything at all. It is nevertheless important to make this point because Scripture itself does not recognize any distinction between how we know about "matters of faith" and how we know about so-called "secular" subjects. As Jesus said to Nicodemus, "If I told you of earthly things and you do not believe, how shall you believe if I tell you of heavenly things?" (John 3:13). We are dependent on a network of authorities for our knowledge of the world, and not all of them are equal. We should believe nothing from any of them that contradicts what Scripture says about the world, but we do have to pay attention to the others.

I have never been to Moscow, for example, but I believe it is the capital of Russia on the authority of maps and globes. The Bible says nothing about it. I believe that water is two parts hydrogen and one part oxygen on the authority of science. The Bible offers no such analysis. I believe that I had granola for breakfast this morning on the authority of my memory. The Bible is silent on the subject. I believe that these words are appearing on the screen of my computer as I type them on the authority of my eyes. The Bible somehow fails to contain this information. Nobody can function—and nobody thinks we can function—without a complex matrix of authorities to whom we submit, each in their own proper spheres.

When we add "matters of faith" to the mix, nothing changes. We don't believe Scripture outside of the context of what we know from experience, reason, and tradition. I would not even be able to read

Scripture without what I learned about phonics from my first-grade teacher, Miss Collins; nor would I be able to read the New Testament in the original language without what I learned from J. Gresham Machen's *New Testament Greek for Beginners*. The New Testament itself has no lessons on Greek grammar (though it does have quite a bit of Greek grammar). I am helped to read and understand it by commentaries, and I do not ignore the understandings of it passed down through tradition by wiser men than I who read it in the past. Scripture is not therefore "alone" as the only authority, not even in religious matters, and nobody ever claimed it was—except people using a straw-man argument against *Sola Scriptura*. Martin Luther acknowledged this truth explicitly: "There has never been a great revelation of the word of God unless He has first prepared the way by the rise and prosperity of languages and letters, as though they were John the Baptists" (Letter to Eoban Hess, 29 March 1523).[2]

How then is Scripture "alone"? What were the Reformers trying to say? There are several ways we can put it. We can say that Scripture is alone at the top of a hierarchy of authority. It is alone in the position of having authority that trumps every other authority whenever they come into conflict. This is because it is alone as the only authority that is inspired by God and hence infallible. It is alone as the only authority with which I can never legitimately disagree. How does this work in practical terms?

I properly depend on my eyes and generally believe what they tell me, but they are not infallible. There is such a thing as an optical illusion. Sometimes they make mistakes. But I believe that what they show me is there unless I am given a good reason not to. I properly depend on my memory and believe that what it tells me about the past actually happened. But it is not infallible either. Old memories can get jumbled or confused or become unclear. I've noticed that, as I age, my memories of recent events are still pretty reliable, but my sense of how long ago they took place is not so reliable any more. If I say something happened last year it might very well have been two to five years ago. If I initially think it was five years ago, it was probably ten. Nevertheless, I properly treat my memory as an authority for what I believe about the past—but not an *absolute* authority. When I have good reasons (one of which I just gave), I question what it says

---

2 Matrin Luther, Letter to Eoban Hess, 29 March 1523; qtd. From Wallace K. Ferguson, *The Renaissance in Historical Thought: Five Centuries of Interpretation* (NY: Houghton Mifflin, 1961), p. 54.

and might correct it or even overturn it. If the calendar says I got the year wrong, I treat the calendar as, on that point, a higher authority than my memory. If my eyes tell me that a student on the back row has only a pink blob instead of a face, I treat my eyes corrected by my glasses as a higher authority on that point. We all have to do this kind of thing all the time.

So here's the point. Protestants believe that the Bible is "alone" because, as the written Word of God, who is the highest Authority in existence, it is the only authority in our lives that ought never to be overturned by another one which is, on that point, higher. It is alone as the highest. Its inspiration makes it the only authority that is infallible. My eyes are not infallible; my memory is not infallible. I trust them, but with sufficient reason they can be overturned. My pastor is not infallible; my church tradition is not infallible. I trust them too, and they have a certain authority, but with sufficient reason they can be overturned. My parents were very wise in many ways, and they were certainly in a legitimate position of authority over me under God; but they were not infallible. Neither were any of my other teachers. Francis Schaeffer was a great authority on the Christian worldview and cultural apologetics from whom I learned an awful lot, but I think that in his emphasis on the contrast between the Renaissance and the Reformation he missed what the Reformation owed to the Renaissance. (See chapters 17-18). C. S. Lewis was a great authority on apologetics, mere Christianity, and English literature, but he rejected the doctrine of total depravity in terms that clearly show he misunderstood it.[3] The most basic laws of logic are infallible, but *my* reason, my own application of them, is not. I most certainly am not.

Bottom line: Every merely human authority is wrong about something, and therefore, though many of them should and must be followed, none can be followed completely and without any reservation at all. The Bible is alone simply and precisely as the only exception to that rule. We follow other authorities in their spheres, but there are higher authorities that can overrule them and sufficient reasons to accept those authorities as higher in a given instance. There *is* no higher authority in a position to overturn what the Bible teaches; there is for faithful Protestants no sufficient reason to reject what it says.

---

3   Donald T. Williams, *Deeper Magic: The Theology behind the Writings of C. S. Lewis* (Baltimore: Square Halo Books, 2016), p. 115; cf. Williams, "'For the Sake of the Story': Doctrine and Discernment in Reading C. S. Lewis," *Modern Reformation* 18:3 (May/June, 2009): 33-36.

Faithful Protestants believe this because they believe that the Bible was inspired by the Holy Spirit in a way that makes it, not just words about God, but *the Word of God*.[4] Paul tells us in 2 Tim. 3:16 that *all* Scripture is inspired by God, and that this makes it "profitable for doctrine." He was of course talking about the Old Testament, but Peter extends that claim to the then growing New Testament by listing Paul's apostolic writings along with "the other Scriptures" (2 Pet. 3:16). In Paul's statement the *graphe*, the actual writings, are described as *theopneustos*, which means literally "breathed out by God." And Christ Himself teaches us that the Scriptures, even down to the jots and tittles (Hebrew marks like our crossing of the *t* and dotting of the *i*) cannot be broken (Luke 16:17, John 10:35b). We cannot independently corroborate every statement Scripture makes, nor can we perfectly harmonize them all (though we can come amazingly close). But we feel justified in treating Scripture as what Christ and His apostles told us it is: not just words about God but the Word of God.

Therefore, when we have understood what Scripture teaches on any subject, as faithful followers of Jesus Christ we do not feel at liberty ever to dissent from it or disregard it or disobey it. It is the Word of God! Scripture is then "alone" as the only authority that deserves *that* kind of loyalty and devotion from us—not as something separate from Christ but *because it is the Word of Christ*. It has the same authority He would have if He spoke to us directly. Scripture is not therefore our only authority, but it is our only infallible and final authority—on "matters of faith" and on everything else.[5]

---

4 See my treatments of this doctrine in *The Person and Work of the Holy Spirit* (Nashville: Broadman & Holman, 1996; reprint Wipf and Stock), pp. 22-37, and *Deeper Magic*, op cit., pp. 59-73. Cf. the chapter on the doctrine of inspiration in any standard Evangelical systematic theology.

5 This makes Scripture supremely valuable. Martin Luther rightly said, "No greater mischief can happen to a Christian people, than to have God's Word taken from them, or falsified, so that they no longer have it pure and clear." *The Table Talk of Martin Luther* (Grand Rapids: Baker, 1979), p. 10.

Thesis 1b:
Sola Scriptura Does Mean That Scripture Alone Has "Magisterial Authority."

※

Magister is the Latin word for "master." It combines the senses of master as ruler and master as schoolmaster or teacher. The background to its use in the context of the authority of Scripture in the Reformation is the Roman Catholic use of the word *magisterium* to refer to the collective teaching office of the Catholic church, considered to be authoritative and infallible.

When the Reformers granted "magisterial authority" only to Scripture, they did not of course mean that the church has no teaching office, nor that said office has no authority. It is a requirement of the office of elder that a man be "apt to teach" (1 Tim. 3:2). The office of pastor and that of teacher are considered grammatically one and the same (Eph. 4:11, best translated not "pastors and teachers" but "pastor-teachers"). And the church is supposed to call faithful men to that office and submit to their teaching. But their authority is derivative; they derive it from their agreement with Scripture, and their flock is expected to be like the nobler people of Berea and "search the Scriptures daily to see whether these things be so" (Acts 17:11). The teaching office of the church gains its authority from Scripture, which has its authority because it was given by God—not because it was given by the church. The church did not "create" the New Testament, as Roman Catholics often argue; it *received* it and *recognized* it as having been given by God.

The church then needs teachers and is supposed to have them and listen to them. But it does not treat them as infallible in themselves, but follows them in so far as they faithfully follow the Scriptures. The Text, not the teacher, is the final court of appeal. The Text *is* the teacher, of the teachers as well as of the churches, and the post-apostolic teachers are the servants of Christ, His Text, and His flock. As Calvin put it, "If true religion is to beam upon us, our principle must be that it is necessary to begin with heavenly teaching, and that it is impossible for any man to obtain even the minutest portion of right and sound doctrine without being a disciple of Scripture."[6] The cumulative teaching of our human teachers as handed down from one generation to another is what we call the Christian *Tradition*. So it relates to Scripture in the same way: We trust it in so far as it agrees with the Text. And so do the two other important authorities, Reason and Experience. We will understand better how they function in relation to Scripture if we move on to the next thesis.

---

6   John Calvin, *Institutes of the Christian Religion*, 2 vol., trans. Henry Beveridge (Grand Rapids: Eerdmans, 1975), p. 1:66.

Thesis 1c:
Reason, Tradition, Church Elders, and Experience Have "Ministerial Authority."

Scripture then is our highest authority under Christ Himself, and only Scripture has magisterial authority. But if we pretend that we do not read Scripture in the light of reason, tradition, and experience, we simply deceive ourselves. The point is not to ignore them but to use them rightly, as ministers or servants. Hence they are accorded what we call "ministerial authority."[7]

Without using our minds, we could neither understand Scripture nor interpret it nor apply it. Scripture itself commands us to use basic laws of logic such as the law of non-contradiction. We are to reject prophets who contradict previously given revelation or who are contradicted by reality when their prophecies fail to come true (Deut. 13:1-5, 18:20-22). The law of non-contradiction also tells us when we have taken one passage in a way that disagrees with another, so that we know that we must have gotten one of them wrong. Interpretation would be so handicapped by our inability to do this that it would practically grind to a halt. Reason is not allowed to dictate what Scripture can be allowed to teach, in the sense that we would use our own thinking as a pre-test for what we can accept (as classical theological liberals automatically filter out the supernatural because it does not fit with their secular worldview). But reason is indispensable to our use of Scripture in the sense that the Bible is addressed to our minds as well as our hearts, and we cannot receive what it teaches us without using them both. Reason is a very useful servant as long as it does not try to be the master.[8]

If we seek to understand and apply Scripture while remaining igno-

---

[7] Augustine, the greatest of the church fathers, shows good awareness of this distinction between "our writings, which are not a rule of faith and practice, but only a help to edification," and the writings of the apostles. "Reply to Faustus the Manichaean," *Augustin: The Writings against the Manichaeans, and against the Donatists*, ed. Philip Shcaff (Peabody, MA: Hendrickson, 1994), p. 180.

[8] Luther is infamous for calling reason "the Devil's whore," but he meant reason abused. His actual view is this: "Before faith and the knowledge of God, reason is mere darkness; but in the hands of those who believe, 'tis an excellent instrument. All faculties and gifts are pernicious, exercised by the impious; but most salutary when possessed by godly persons." *The Table Talk of Martin Luther*, op. cit., p. 49.

rant of the work of wise Christians who lived before us and unaware of the consensus they achieved on many points (Tradition), we will at best waste time reinventing the wheel and at worst repeat mistakes that have already been well corrected. *Tradition* is not a bad word. It might seem like one because so many traditions of men had to be rejected in the Reformation's recovery of the biblical Gospel. But it simply means that which has been handed down or handed on. Accepting Christ due to the witness of your parents or of a friend then is a form of Tradition; they received the Gospel from someone else and then handed it on to you. The teaching ministry of elders and pastors in the local church is likewise a form of Tradition, and we want it to represent a handing down of the faith once delivered that has been going on longer than one generation! Part of the job of church leaders is to be a conduit of the best of the wisdom of the Christian past.[9]

Tradition then is unavoidable and can be a positive good. It is an authority whose voice we need to hear. It only becomes a problem when it takes the place of Scripture or is allowed to determine how we read Scripture in ways that go against Scripture or pit one part of it against another. Like Reason, Tradition is helpful as long as it remembers that it is a servant (ministerial authority) and that the Holy Spirit speaking for Christ in the text of Scripture is the Master.

Even Experience cannot be excluded. It is in many ways the most unreliable authority because it is the most subjective and can be the most insistent—especially, it seems, when it is wrong. Too many people have mistaken their own inner impulses for the voice of the Spirit. Neither the fact that my charismatic friend has experienced what he takes to be the gift of tongues nor the fact that I have not should be allowed to predetermine how we read the statements about that subject in the New Testament; rather, its teaching should determine how we interpret our experience. But if we do not think our interpretation of the Scriptures is influenced by our experience, we are simply deceiving ourselves.

Sometimes appealing to experience is right and even necessary. When Jesus speaks of the lilies of the field or of leaven hidden in dough, He assumes that we will bring our experience of such things to bear as we try to understand Him. And of course we are necessarily

---

9 T. S. Eliot reminds us that Tradition "cannot be inherited, and if you want it you must obtain it by great labour." We cannot avoid tradition, but if we want to know reliably that we have it in its fullness and can discern the best parts of it in order to be that conduit, we must *study* church history. "Tradition and the Individual Talent," *Selected Essays of T. S. Eliot* (N.Y.: Harcourt, Brace, & World, 1960), p. 4.

dependent on experience for our understanding of the world in which Scripture has to be applied. Again: Scripture has *magisterial* authority, and Reason, Tradition, and Experience have *ministerial* authority. They are servants, and Christ speaking through the Apostles and Prophets in the Scriptures is the Master.

Albert Outler summarized John Wesley's teaching in this area and came up with what has come to be called "The Wesleyan Quadrilateral":[10] Scripture, Reason, Tradition, and Experience. As beautifully expressed in the Methodist *Book of Discipline*, the Quadrilateral says that "the living core of the Christian faith was revealed in Scripture, illumined by tradition, vivified in personal experience, and confirmed by reason."[11] It is a very good formula if understood rightly, but becomes problematic if someone assumes that the four authorities are equal, like the four legs of a stool (an analogy that has unfortunately been used), or if one of them *other* than Scripture is given the magisterial role.

Indeed, we could analyze any number of heresies or unhealthy theological tendencies as resulting from improper relationships between these four authorities. When Scripture is master and the others are properly functioning ministers, then I would say you get wholesome biblical Christianity. If Reason tries to usurp the magisterial role, you get Arianism, Socinianism (Unitarianism), or modern theological Liberalism. When Tradition gets too much power you get Roman Catholicism or Eastern Orthodoxy. With Experience in the chair, you get the less healthy forms of the Pentecostal or Charismatic movements. With Reason and/or Tradition too *weak*, on the other hand, you are looking at the less biblical and more legalistic and anti-intellectual forms of Fundamentalism. Let Experience fail to do its job and you get Dead Orthodoxy.

Evangelicalism today seems to be splintering into all these directions at once. If we want to restore it to spiritual health, if we want it to see a new Reformation leading to Revival, then it needs to remember that *Sola Scriptura* means that only Scripture has magisterial authority *and* that Reason, Tradition, and Experience have ministerial authority. This Committee needs all its members, and it needs them in their proper places. May God enable it to be so once again.

---

10   Albert C. Outler, ed., *John Wesley* (Oxford: Oxford University Press, *1964*), p. iv.
11   *The Book of Discipline of the United Methodist Church* (Nashville: Abingdon Press, 2004), p. 77.

Thesis 1d:
Sola Scriptura Does Not Mean That the Individual Can Interpret Scripture Alone.

※

A principle common to all the churches of the Reformation but particularly beloved by Baptists is known as "the right of private judgment." Each individual has the right to read Scripture for himself and the responsibility to interpret it accurately so he can receive and follow its message faithfully. He cannot let someone else do his Bible reading for him or understand it for him. It is something he must do himself. Specifically, he cannot simply accept without question what any human teacher or church tells him the Bible says—or what it means. He is to emulate the nobler citizens of Berea who "searched the Scriptures daily to see if these things be so" (Acts 17:11) even when they were hearing them from an Apostle. So the right of private judgment positively asserts each individual's responsibility to receive God's written revelation and negatively denies the claims of the Roman Catholic Church to be the only indispensable and infallible interpreter of it. Indeed, as has often been pointed out against that claim of Rome, the exercise of private judgment is inescapable. The person who accepts the Church of Rome as the only authoritative and infallible guide to the Bible's interpretation has at some point to make the judgment that the Bible is God's Word and that the claims of Rome to be its only legitimate interpreter are valid. Who is to make that judgment other than the individual himself? If he has not made it, he has not accepted the claim. So Rome's very denial of the right of private judgment rests on asking people to exercise it. The only alternative is a vicious circularity.

This principle, though, however necessary and unavoidable it may be, is really very poorly named. It should be called the *responsibility* of private judgment. The other designation too easily degenerates into the idea that each individual is free to interpret the Bible for himself, *however he likes*. He thus becomes his own pope. But the truth is not just a matter of "me and my Bible." It is an objective and public thing that has its own unity and integrity and is not reducible to as many opinions as there are believers. Catholic apologists see anarchy as the only possible result of the right of private judgment, and Protestant believers give them way too much excuse for holding that view. Let us then speak of the *responsibility* of private judgment and consider how to maintain that responsibility without reducing Christian truth to the chaos of the Book of Judges, in which "Every man did what was right in his own eyes" (Judges 21:25).

Each person then has the responsibility to receive and interpret the message of the Bible *for* himself, but not the privilege of doing it *by* himself. It is the Holy Spirit speaking for Christ in the text of Scripture, not the individual, who has magisterial authority (see Thesis 1b). And the individual is subject not only to the magisterial authority of Scripture but also to the ministerial authority of Reason and that of the universal church and its Tradition. How does this work in practice?

Good Protestants do not interpret Scripture in a vacuum. They are aware of a consensual tradition on the major doctrines of the faith derived from Scripture that cuts across denominations and the roots of which can be traced back practically to the Apostles themselves. It is summarized in the Apostles', Nicene, and Athanasian Creeds, and in the Christological definitions of the Council of Chalcedon. Faithful Christians in all three major branches of Christendom—Roman Catholic, Eastern Orthodox, and Protestant—agree on practically every word of that material. The West does add one word to the Nicene Creed that the East does not go along with, but that is still a pretty remarkable body of material on which there is agreement.[12]

Now, the Creeds are part of Christian *Tradition*, and as such have only ministerial, not magisterial, authority. Only Scripture is infallible. But if all faithful Christians for two thousand years, including the church's greatest saints, have agreed that Scripture teaches A and you think it teaches B, what are the chances that you are the only one to have finally gotten it right? In other words, if you discover that Augustine, Aquinas, Luther, Calvin, Wesley, and Spurgeon all agree on something and you are the odd man out, it is *theoretically* possible that you are right and they are all wrong, but before you conclude so you ought at least to go back and check your work one more time. You will almost certainly discover your mistake if you do (at least if you do so teachably), and thus the "ministerial" authority of Tradi-

---

12 For more on the content and meaning of the Nicene Creed and its proper function as a basis for Christian unity, see Donald T. Williams, *Credo: Meditations on the Nicene Creed* (St. Louis: Chalice Press, 2007).

tion will *minister* to you like it is supposed to. It will keep you from making stupid mistakes on the one hand and from reinventing the wheel on the other. That is why every credible Protestant seminary requires courses in church history of its ministerial students. Before you run out and start proclaiming your new doctrine, you have a responsibility to *know* that it is new and to know how it differs from the consensus of the church universal so you can give it a second thought. Scripture is the only infallible source with magisterial authority, but it is not the only thing you need to know. You bow to Scripture only, but you do not read Scripture only, nor should you be (always) alone when you do so. You ultimately do it with all the saints, your brothers and sisters in the Lord.

The Reformers did not depart from this principle, by the way, even though they were accused of "innovation," of departing from the universal Tradition, by their contemporaries in the Church of Rome. They saw themselves as departing from a local and aberrant tradition to get back to the continuity with the early church and its understanding of the Gospel that had been lost over the centuries. And they were great students of the early church Fathers, to whom they appealed in their controversies with Rome to show that it was Rome, not they, who was guilty of innovation.[13] Their modern heirs would do well to follow in their footsteps in that area as well as in their doctrine itself.

Sola Scriptura then, far from giving us *carte blanche* to ignore Christian Tradition, *requires* us to read the Bible with as much awareness of it as we can muster. It is precisely because Scripture is alone as uniquely authoritative and important that we must read it in the right context where it can best be understood, and that context is the Christian Tradition.[14] On those matters where there is not a universal consensus, Tradition sometimes departs from Scripture and needs to be corrected by it—but we will never know where those places are unless we are good students of both.

---

[13] See for example John Jewel's" Challenge Sermon," preached at Paul's Cross, November 26, 1559, challenging his Roman Catholic opponents to "cite any specific sanction for Roman doctrine or discipline from the Scriptures, the fathers, the councils, or the practice of the church during the first six centuries after Christ," Hyder E. Rollins and Herschel Baker, eds., *The Renaissance in England: Non-Dramatic Prose ad Verse of the Sixteenth Century* (Lexington, MA: D. C. Heath, 1954), p. 168. For an excellent recent treatment of the roots of the Reformation in ancient Christian tradition see Kenneth J. Stewart, *In Search of Ancient Roots: The Christian Past and the Evangelical Identity Crisis* (Downers Grove: InterVarsity Press, 2017).

[14] "Someone once said: 'The dead writers are remote from us because we *know* so much more than they did,'" observed T. S. Eliot—and then gave the perfect reply. "Precisely, and they are that which we know." "Tradition and the Individual Talent," op. cit., p. 6.

There is also a second way in which we do not read Scripture alone. We read it not in isolation from Tradition and not in isolation from our fellow believers in the Body of Christ. Much of Scripture is addressed in fact not primarily to individuals but to churches. It was intended to be received and read as part of the covenant community of faith. We do not so much read the Bible to practice individual speculation about abstract truths; we read it as the guide to how to believe the Gospel, follow Christ, and function in the community of faith. Only when we read it that way do we have the best perspectives even on its more speculative truths. As C. S. Lewis put it, "The one really adequate instrument for learning about God is the whole Christian community waiting for Him together."[15] We bow only to the Bible, but we do not do it alone, and consequently we should not always be alone when we do it.

---

15 C. S. Lewis, *Mere Christianity* (N.Y.: MacMillan, 1943), p. 144. For more on Lewis's excellent advice about reading Scripture, see my book *Deeper Magic* (Baltimore: Square Halo Books, 2016), pp. 70-71. For more on his view of the church as the Christian community, see chapter 8 of that book.

Thesis 1e:
Proper Submission to Scripture As the Highest Expression of God's Authority under Christ Is a Necessary Prerequisite for a Faithful Individual or a Faithful Church.

If God has revealed Himself in nature, in history, and supremely in His Son; if He has given us in inspired Holy Scripture the definitive, authoritative, and infallible interpretation of that revelation so that the Bible actually becomes the verbal form of that revelation; if that inscripturated revelation thus rightly has unique magisterial authority in the lives of believers and of the church, supported by the ministerial authority of Reason, Tradition, and Experience; if that hierarchy of authority humbly and teachably followed in the context of the church universal allows us to have, not perfect, but sufficient understanding of that revelation; then proper submission to Scripture as the highest expression of God's authority under Christ is a necessary prerequisite for being a faithful individual or a faithful church. I don't suppose many Evangelicals would want to dissent (out loud) from that logic or its conclusion. But solid evidence of the practice of that submission is getting harder and harder to find.

We all give lip service to the authority of Scripture. But do we really derive our theology and our practice from the teaching of Scripture understood in the context of the church and its history and in the light of Reason, Tradition, and Experience, or are we actually doing something else? Is it possible that we really just find an accommodation to the Spirit of the Age that we are comfortable with and then squeeze Scripture into whatever mold is necessary for us to use it to justify that accommodation? Depending on how conservative or radical our mindset is, some of us may have to squeeze harder than others; but can any of us really say that we are not squeezing at all? Do any of us really allow Scripture to correct us when it calls us to take an unpopular position or do an uncomfortable thing that does not come naturally to us? I hope so. I am sure there are individuals who do, with at least some integrity. But looking at the Evangelical movement considered as a whole . . . I wonder.

As early as 1984, Francis Schaeffer saw the direction in which the Evangelical movement was headed. His book *The Great Evangelical Disaster*[16] warned against the tendency to accommodation that he saw emerging then. That accommodation started with a weakening of theoretical commitment to the full authority of Scripture: It was often being considered inerrant only on "spiritual" matters[17] (What are they?), and higher-critical methods of Bible study were being increasingly accepted even by Evangelical scholars as the price of admission to academic respectability and defended (at first) as not necessarily incompatible with inerrancy. But this weakening of biblical authority could not remain merely theoretical; it flowed on to "certain moral absolutes in the area of personal relationships" being relegated to being merely part of ancient culture and not part of the Bible's "spiritual" message. In the mid-eighties Schaeffer focused on a rising Evangelical acceptance of easy divorce and remarriage and of views incompatible with "the clear biblical teaching regarding order in the home and the church."[18] Today the Bible's teaching on homosexuality is being added to the list of what is considered negotiable.

The problem was not so much that such views were advanced (that is always going to happen), as that there was a strong reluctance on the part of Evangelical leaders and institutions to call them out as not validly Evangelical. That unwillingness no doubt partly flowed from bad memories of the legalism and separatism of earlier Fundamentalism, the extreme and unloving forms of which had rightly left a bad taste in our mouths. Nobody wanted to go back to those bad old days! But the end result was an inability to draw lines in the sand even lovingly, even when they were necessary. The borders demarking what was acceptable were thus extended one inch at a time until they have today almost ceased to exist altogether. "There is no end to this,"[19] Schaeffer warned over three decades ago. If there is, we do not appear to be at all close to reaching it.

Schaeffer seems particularly prophetic in his discussion of gender and sexuality. The Bible views men and women as equal in person-

---

16 Francis A. Schaeffer, *The Great Evangelical Disaster* (Westchester, Il: Crossway, 1984).

17 Contrast Calvin: "The unerring standard both of thinking and speaking must be derived from the Scriptures; by it *all* the thoughts of our minds and the words of our mouths should be tested." John Calvin, *Institutes of the Christian Religion*, trans. Henry Beveridge, 2 vol. (Grand Rapids: Eerdmans, 1975), p. 1:111.

18 Schaeffer, *Disaster*, op. cit., pp. 59-60.

19 Ibid., p. 60.

hood and value, but not identical. But now increasingly even professing Christians read biblical statements about what Schaeffer called biblical "order in the home and the church" through the lens of a modernist understanding of equality, which conflates any distinctions at all with distinctions of value. But that paradigm has "tragic consequences for society and human life."

> If we accept the idea of equality without distinction, we logically must accept the ideas of abortion and homosexuality. For if there are no significant distinctions between men and women, then certainly we cannot condemn homosexual relationships. And if there are no significant distinctions, this fiction can be maintained only by the use of abortion-on-demand as a means of coping with the most profound evidence that distinctions really do exist.[20]

The consensus on these matters that the church had known for two millennia has now almost completely dissolved in Evangelical circles. It is not that complementarians (the traditional view) no longer exist. The "great Evangelical disaster" is that it is now in many circles considered a greater crime to question the Evangelical *bona fides* of a person who sees everything through this secular lens than it is to turn Scripture into a wax nose to justify that vision. (See chapter nine for further discussion of gender roles.)

"But wait," I can imagine someone protesting. "Are you saying there are no issues of interpretation?" Well, no, I'm not. Of course there are. We have gotten to the place where appeals to the "clear teaching" or "plain meaning" of Scripture just induce eye-rolling. That is in itself part of our problem. We got there because so many people used those phrases when they had no business doing so. But from the fact that those phrases have been abused too often by the naïve and ignorant, it does not follow that Scripture has no clear teachings or plain meanings, nor that every question of interpretation or every method of interpretation is a valid one. (We will have a whole chapter of theses about hermeneutics, the science of interpretation, in chapter six.)

How do we navigate our way out of this impasse? Here is a principle that to me seems hard to avoid if we want to be faithful: We should be suspicious of interpretive gambits that bend what Scripture

---

20 Ibid., p. 136.

says in the direction of the Spirit of the Age, that conveniently absolve us from giving any offence to our secular contemporaries. We are not suspicious of such gambits. We embrace them with open arms. That is the problem.

Augustine of Hippo gave a very astute warning sixteen hundred years ago. "To believe [the biblical author] when you wish it, and then disbelieve him when you wish it, is to believe nobody but yourself."[21] Or, more fully, "Your design clearly is to deprive Scripture of all authority, and to make every man's mind the judge of what passage of Scripture he is to approve of, and what to disapprove of. This is not to be subject to Scripture in matters of faith, but to make Scripture subject to you."[22] We must now seriously ask ourselves if this is not where we are as a movement. But neither an individual, nor a church, nor a denomination, nor a parachurch ministry, nor a school can be faithful to Christ without practical submission to the Scriptures as the highest expression under Christ of God's authority. Devoted reading and sound interpretation leading to loving obedience is the very definition of faithfulness. If *Sola Scriptura* does not lead to that, it means nothing.

---

21 Augustine, "Reply to Faustus the Manicheans," *Augustine: The Writings against the Manichaens, and against the Donatists*, ed. Philip Schaff (Peabody, MA: Hendrickson Publishers, 1995), p. 337.

22 Ibid., p. 339. Calvin adds his own sagacious warning: "So long as your mind entertains any misgivings as to the certainty of the word, its authority will be weak and dubious, or rather it will have no authority at all. Nor is it sufficient to believe that God is true, and cannot lie or deceive, unless you feel firmly persuaded that every word which proceeds from him is inviolable truth." *Institutes*, op. cit., p. 1:474.

Conclusion

Sola Scriptura: It is not enough that Scripture be alone. It must be alone in the right place, at the top of the hierarchy of authorities that govern our thoughts and our lives, and in the right way, properly related to the ministerial authorities that surround and support it. That was the "formal principle" of the Reformation, the one that generated and gave shape to all the rest. If we have restored it, we are ready to look at the "material principles" of the Reformation, which constituted its substantive content. They point us to a salvation that is by grace alone through faith alone in Christ alone, to the glory of God alone. Thanks be to God through Jesus Christ our Lord!

Interlude

The Socratic Method at Work:

Michael Bauman Teaching Milton

"The first rule: Don't trust anything I say
    (I might be speaking for the Enemy),
      But when *Truth* calls to you, you must obey."
The student body shuddered in dismay,
    With pens arrested in mid-note, to see
      The first rule: "Don't trust anything I say."
"For there is Truth, though narrow is the Way,
    And few that find it." (But they will be free
      If, when Truth calls to them, they just obey.)
"Do *you* think that, or is it just O. K.
    Because I said it?" This, persistently.
      The first rule: "Don't trust anything I say."
"And what *is* Truth? And what the Good? To play
    The game, you have to know the rules—the key—
      So when Truth calls to you, you can obey."
His every wink and word was to convey
    The simple skill of doubting faithfully.
      The first rule: "Don't trust anything I say,
But when Truth calls to you, you must obey."[23]

---

23 Donald T. Williams, *Stars through the Clouds*, op. cit., p. 364.

1 Peter 1:24-25

All flesh is like the meadow grass,
Her glory as its flower;
Sun beats, wind blows, the seasons pass;
They wither in an hour.

The petals fade and fall and die;
Their fate, like ours, is sure.
Not so the Word of God! For aye
It lives and shall endure.[24]

---

[24] Ibid., p. 170.

2
Five Theses on *Sola Gratia*

Sola Scriptura is the formal principle of Reformation; *Sola Gratia*, etc., are the material principles. In other words, *Sola Scriptura* creates the stage and builds the set on which the other four *Solas* enact their parts; *Sola Scriptura* is the grammatical structure of the sentence, and the other four fill it with substance; *Sola Scriptura* builds the house, and *Sola Gratia*, etc., are the family that fill it with life.

A. Salvation is by God's grace alone, apart from works. ("... being justified as a gift by His grace," Rom. 3:24; "By the works of the law shall no flesh be justified,: Rom. 3:20; "For by grace are ye saved through faith, and that not of yourselves; it is the gift of God, not as a result of works, that no one should boast," Eph. 2:8-9.)

B. Grace is not a spiritual *substance* or force, but an *attitude* on God's part, whereby He grants unmerited favor to poor sinners. (We reject the notion that grace is "infused" through the sacraments. It is rather the free granting of God's favor to faith—see Theses 3b, 3e.)

C. Good works are thus *excluded* as the *grounds* of salvation, but they are *required* as its *fruits*. (This is because true justification never occurs in a vacuum, without regeneration and sanctification accompanying it.)

D. Any admixture of good works *as the grounds* of salvation subverts and destroys the whole biblical plan of redemption. ("I do not nullify the grace of God; for if righteousness comes through the Law, then Christ died needlessly," Gal. 2:21.)

E. Works are necessarily both excluded as ground *and* required as fruit because the end of salvation is the glory of God. (God is not glorified by a salvation that produces no fruit, nor by one in which credit for the fruit can be taken by the sinner rather than the Savior.)

The Reformation was all about the recovery of the biblical Gospel. The Gospel is the Good News about what God has done in Christ to save us from our sins. It is the Good News that God so loved the world that He gave His only begotten Son, that whosoever believeth in Him should not perish, but have everlasting life (John 3:16). It is the Good News that Christ died for our sins according to the Scriptures, and that He was buried, and that He was raised on the third day, according to the Scriptures (1 Cor. 15:3-4). It is the Good New that, because of that death and resurrection, if you confess with your mouth Jesus as Lord and believe in your heart that God raised Him from the dead, you shall be saved (Rom. 10:9).

Well, why did this Good News need to be recovered? The medieval church had never stopped teaching that Christ was God, that He had died for our sins and been raised from the dead, and that this made salvation available to men. It had, however, subtly and gradually over time, begun to add other layers to that biblical message, dilutions and adulterations of it that ultimately changed it into something not biblical at all. Without denying justification it changed the meaning of justification from a forensic declaration of righteousness on God's part to an attainment of it on man's part. As a result of that change, without denying grace it gave human works a role they were not supposed to have—which in effect undermined the role of grace. Without denying faith it gave the sacraments and the priesthood a role they were not designed to have—which in effect obscured the role of faith. Without denying Christ it added other mediators to confuse and complicate the path to reconciliation with God that the Bible had set forth—which in effect hid that path from many people. The end result was a theology that was used to justify the selling of indulgences—certificates for the forgiveness of sin and remission of time to be spent in Purgatory—for money. That was the practice that provoked a reevaluation of where that whole theology was going that led to the Protestant Reformation.

The clarity on these matters that the Reformation recovered is in danger of being lost once again. Sometimes the doctrines of grace are not so much denied (at first) as ignored in favor of other interests—whether material prosperity, ecstatic experience, social "justice," or seven steps to a better marriage. But ignoring leads to ignorance, and ignorance to denial. We now have Protestant leaders who ought to know better questioning whether Luther really understood Paul on justification by faith. So we will try to get some of that clarity back in the next few chapters, beginning with *Sola Gratia*, salvation by grace alone.[25]

---

25 For further reading on *Sola Gratia*, see the following: on the biblical basis of the atonement, James Denney's classic work *The Death of Christ* (London: Tyndale Press, 1951); on the theological implications of that biblical teaching, John Murray, *Redemption Accomplished and Applied* (Grand Rapids: Eerdmans, 1955); on contemporary Protestant waffling on *Sola Gratia* and its implications for justification, John Piper. *The Future of Justification: A Response to N. T. Wright* (Wheaton: Crossway, 2007) and William C. Roach, *Sola Fide: A Primer on Paul's Doctrine of Justification in Romans* (Matthews, N.C.: Bastion Books, 2018). See also the relevant sections in the standard Evangelical systematic theologies, such as Hodge, Berkhof, Erickson, Grudem, and Oden. For a secular treatment that deals with the empirical evidence for the doctrine of sin that makes the atonement necessary, see Karl Menninger's brilliant book *Whatever Became of Sin?* (N.Y.: Hawthorne, 1973).

Thesis 2a:
Salvation Is by God's Grace Alone, apart from Works.

⊘

There is little in the New Testament that is taught so clearly and unmistakably as salvation by grace alone. What is grace? Grace is God's unmerited favor toward lost sinners. As mercy is His love expressed to the needy, grace is His love expressed to the unworthy. Lost sinners are of course both. And the New Testament is clear that salvation from sin is something that is not—cannot be—earned or merited. Paul says we are "justified as a gift by His grace" (Rom. 3:24). The world *gift* should be enough to make this point all by itself. A gift is not something that one earns. A gift is not a reward. Specifically, one cannot merit salvation by keeping the moral law, whether the law written on the hearts of Gentiles by general revelation or the law written on the tablets of Moses by God himself. "By the works of the law shall no flesh be justified," that is, found or declared righteous ("just") before a just and holy God (Rom. 3:20). We see the unmerited nature of grace by the way it is so often contrasted with works. As Paul explains again, "For by grace are ye saved through faith, and that not of yourselves; it is the gift of God, not as a result of works, that no one should boast" (Eph. 2:8-9). Salvation is not of works, and even the faith by which we receive it is not anything we can take credit for: It too is the gift of God.

This Pauline understanding of salvation by grace *alone* makes perfect sense if we understand what sin is and who God is. Sin is rebellion against His sovereign rule; it is any deviation from His perfect law, which flows from His stainless character. Because God is just, the wages of sin is death (Rom. 6:23). Because He is holy, only perfect righteousness can stand before His burning purity. Because He is God, these realities are absolute and non-negotiable.

If we left things here, human beings would be lost without any hope at all. Good luck trying to make yourself perfectly righteous again, even with help from above! And none of the works of righteousness you performed—even if you could perform them, and did it heroically for the rest of your life—would erase the guilt of the sins you have already committed. (It is not just that you have committed certain isolated acts that happened to be sinful, by the way—the rebellion, the desire to be your own God that is the heart of sin, is actually part of you.) But fortunately God's love is just as absolute as His justice, and so is His wisdom, which found a way for both to be expressed fully despite the conflict between them seemingly created by our rebellion. That is where grace comes in.

Instead of asking of you the impossible task of paying for your own sin and reforming yourself, God did something more radical than anything any human religion outside of biblical faith ever dreamed of. In the person of His Son, He became a man—a perfect man without sin, like Adam was before the Fall. As such He was able to stand in for us and pay the full penalty of our sin by dying on the Cross. Based on that substitution and that sacrifice, God was able to count our sins as Christ's and His righteousness as ours. He therefore judicially and forensically declares us innocent and counts us as perfectly righteous and offers this new status to us as a free gift received simply by faith. (This in theology is known as *justification*.) With our relationship to God thus restored, He sends the Holy Spirit to help us start becoming in actuality what He has already declared us to be and accepted us as being—perfectly righteous. (This in theology is known as *sanctification*.) That process continues throughout our earthly life and is completed only when we reach the next life.

The genius of this brilliant divine scheme is that it makes salvation possible for fallen sinners—and it is the only plan of salvation that succeeds, or can succeed, in doing so. For we do become righteous, but we are not saved by our attainment of that righteousness. Rather, our attainments in righteousness are the result of our salvation. And that salvation is based one hundred percent on the merit of Christ, and zero percent on our own merit. Rather than asking us to do what would for us be impossible (reform ourselves sufficiently to merit salvation), God does what is gloriously possible for Him alone (provide a full and finished atonement that comes completely from His side). That is the sense in which salvation is, and must be, by grace, by grace supremely, and by grace *alone*.

This would all be pretty plain sailing were it not for one passage in the book of James which seems to contradict it by saying that Abraham was justified by works (James 2:18-24). This passage has been used to try to find a role for our works in providing salvation—but that effort comes from misunderstanding. Tortured attempts have been made to reconcile Paul and James, but the actual solution is fairly simple. The Greek word translated "justify" (*dikaiozo*), like many English words, has more than one possible meaning. It can mean to declare righteous, to make righteous, or to demonstrate or prove to be righteous. Paul uses the word in the first sense, as we can tell from its place in the train of thought in Romans: God declares us righteous. James uses it in the third sense, as we can tell from his context: "I will *show* you my faith by my works" (2:18, emphasis added). Works for James demonstrate our righteousness (but they do not cause it). So there is no real disagreement between Paul and James—the apparent conflict is only verbal, not substantive. Both affirm that works demonstrate our justification, and James does not really say that they cause it.

Paul was very careful to distinguish the *grounds* of salvation (grace alone) from the *fruits* of salvation (works) because of his controversies with the Judaizers, who wanted to impose the Mosaic law on Gentiles. James used the language differently but says essentially the same thing. You can see Paul's basic agreement with James in the way his great affirmation of grace alone and denial of works in Ephesians 2:8 flows out toward verse ten. "For by grace are ye saved through faith, and that not of yourselves, *not of works*, lest any man should boast. For we are His workmanship, created *unto good works* which God hath prepared beforehand that we should walk in them" (emphasis added). We are not saved by works, but we are saved for works. (See Thesis 2c.) Luther had the same idea. "God forgives sins merely out of grace for Christ's sake; but we must not abuse the grace of God. . . . It is also needful that we testify in our works that we have received the forgiveness of sins."[26] Those works are then the evidence or demonstration of a salvation that was a free gift provided by grace alone and received by faith alone in Christ alone.

---

26 *The Table Talk of Martin Luther* (Grand Rapids: Baker, 1979), p. 154. Cf. p. 177. "Now, when the mind is refreshed and quickened again by the cool air of the gospel, then we must not be idle, lie down, and sleep. That is, when our consciences are settled in peace, quieted and comforted through God's Spirit, we must prove our faith by such good works as God has commanded."

Thesis 2b:
Grace Is Not a Spiritual *Substance* or Force, but an *Attitude* on God's Part, Whereby He Grants Unmerited Favor to Poor Sinners.

In the scheme of salvation the Reformers were trying to correct, it was rightly understood that in order to go to heaven people had to be righteous. But as sinners they cannot become righteous enough on their own; they need help. In this false view, that help comes to them in the form of grace, which flows into them through the ministry of the church, especially through the sacraments. With that help they are able to pursue righteousness and obtain enough of it to merit salvation. If they do not obtain enough merit in this life, that's OK; they can go to Purgatory and finish the job there.

This understanding of salvation is embedded in the language of Roman Catholic theology. Grace is spoken of as "infused" through the sacraments, as if they were a kind of spiritual hypodermic. That is why the mass is so crucial in that scheme: With the bread and wine literally transformed into the actual body and blood of Christ, He is being sacrificed for us afresh, as it were, and by literally eating His broken body and drinking His shed blood, we are taking the spiritual power of that sacrifice into our very being. That is "grace" "infused" at its most potent.

The purpose of this grace was to help sinners earn the merit they need to be saved. And that may be the most serious misunderstanding of all. For it leads to statements that are blatantly Pelagian. Here is the most winsome exponent of this theology explaining the way it works in his great allegory, *The Divine Comedy*: "Its subject is 'Man, as by good or ill deserts, in the exercise of his free choice, he becomes liable to rewarding or punishing justice.'"[27] It is all about the merit ("deserts") of the individual; that, not the merit of Christ, is what makes the individual liable to "rewarding justice." And it is justice, not grace, that *rewards* him with salvation. Grace has not given it to him as a gift, as Paul teaches; justice has awarded it to him because

---

27 Dante Alighiere, *The Divine Comedy 1: Hell*, trans. Dorothy L. Sayers (Baltimore: Penguin, 1940), p. 15.

grace has helped him come to deserve it. It is no wonder that this process usually has to be completed in Purgatory. Who would claim to have gotten there in this life?

This understanding of grace led inevitably to horrible abuses. If grace helps *us* to merit salvation, then we become focused on our own merit, not Christ's. A saint is someone who has attained enough merit to skip Purgatory and go straight to heaven. Indeed, some of them had more than they needed. This extra merit goes into a celestial bank account known as the "treasury of merit." And guess what? The Pope has the authority to draw on those funds and apply them to your account—which he will be happy to do for a slight fee, using the proceeds to pay for the renovation of St. Peter's Cathedral. That can let you off any amount of your time in Purgatory, which you would otherwise have spent continuing to atone for your sins which you had not sufficiently purged in this life. But wait—had not Christ already paid for our sins in full on the Cross? Luther raised a few polite objections to the vending of salvation and the rest, as they say, was history.

Luther of course realized that all of this apparatus of "grace" that we have just described is not only completely absent from Paul's descriptions of it in Romans, Galatians, and Ephesians; it is completely foreign to the development of the concept in the New Testament. Notice for example how grace in Ephesians 1:6 is paralleled with "the kind intention of His will" in 1:5. Grace is not something that can be "infused"; it is part of God's character which inclines Him to be merciful to the undeserving, to lost sinners, and to find a way to do so that does not compromise His justice (which He achieves in the atonement). So the misunderstanding of the nature of grace is tied to the perversion of its purpose. It does not help us "merit" anything. It substitutes Christ's merit for ours completely so that justification can be received as a gift (Rom. 3:24). To say that salvation is all of grace then is to say that it is entirely a gift and not at all an attainment—so that no man can boast (Eph. 2:8-9). But it is a gift that has consequences: the good works that are its fruits in Eph. 2:10. So the fear that *Sola Gratia* will lead to "sinning that grace may abound" (Rom. 6:1) is completely unfounded. (More on this in Theses 2.c-e.) Salvation is seen to be by grace alone when we understand what grace is and how it functions. The Reformers' corrections to the medieval paradigm here then were crucial and should not be forgotten.

Thesis 2c:
Good Works Are Thus *Excluded* As the *Grounds* of Salvation, but They Are *Required* As Its *Fruits*.

It is impossible to read the New Testament with open eyes without realizing that there runs through it a consistent dichotomy between grace and faith on one side and works and boasting on the other. "Where then is boasting?" in the plan of salvation? "It is excluded" (Rom. 3:27). If Abraham had been justified by works he would have had something to boast about—"but not before God" (Rom. 4:2). The idea is, if you think you can boast of anything in the presence of God, you can think that salvation is by works. Not going to happen: You have been saved by grace through faith, and this is not of works, "lest any man should boast" (Eph. 2:8-9). That is why salvation is by grace alone: Works are inherently incapable of providing a basis for it, being by their very nature incompatible with a salvation that is the expression of God's unmerited favor.

This motif is so important to faithful Protestants who understand the dynamics of their theology that they have managed to get the reputation of being opposed to good works. Whether from caricatures by their enemies or their own lack of clarity (or of good works!), the reputation exists. I hope to show in this thesis that it does not flow from their theology, rightly understood.

Because the Gospel of salvation by grace alone through faith alone in Christ alone is the power of God for salvation to those who believe (Rom. 1:16), Satan has a vested interest in obscuring it, perverting it, and casting it in a negative light. One of his ways of doing this is by disseminating gross caricatures of it: God will send an upright, moral philanthropist who never harms anyone and does self-sacrificial good to everyone to Hell because he has the wrong opinions on theology, and take a horrible, antisocial, and downright mean person to Heaven because he once assented to the right words after an altar call. If once you accept Christ as Savior, you can commit any sin you want after that and you will still go to Heaven. No matter how badly you might want to serve Him, if God hasn't elected you, you are just out of luck. Justification by faith is just a legal fiction that leaves people as wicked as it found them, so it is no surprise that people who believe this silly Protestant Gospel tend to stay that way. Or so the enemies of *Sola Gratia* seem to think.

These distortions of the Gospel flow from two mistakes: a hasty assumption about what Grace alone means and a failure to see its role in justification in the context of the fullness of what redemption means.

The assumption is that because works are denied any role as the ground, or basis, or cause of salvation, they must therefore have no role in it at all. But that conclusion simply does not follow. The key passage here is Eph. 2:8-10. In the every same breath in which he denies any role to works, "lest any many should boast," Paul makes them the goal of the whole process: "For we are His workmanship, created unto good works, which God has prepared beforehand that we should walk in them." Good works are excluded precisely in order to be included! They are excluded (as grounds) so that they can be included (as fruit). Their exclusion is precisely the only way in which their true presence can ultimately be guaranteed. The final reason we cannot be saved *by* works is that we *are* a work.

This might sound like a paradox until we remember the difference between causes and effects, or between grounds and fruits. We are absolutely forbidden to think of our own works as in any sense the cause or ground of our salvation: That is the grace of God and the work of Christ, period. But if that grace has actually encountered us, if that work has actually been applied to us, it is not without certain effects and consequences—amongst which are a changed life and good works.

Here is an analogy that might help. Imagine that I throw a rock into a pond. This will result in ripples moving out in concentric circles from the point of impact toward the shore: cause and effect. The pond cannot ripple itself. Only the rock can do that. But the rock is not going to impact the pond without making ripples. Alright, the pond is the human soul, the rock is God's grace, and the ripples are a transformed life issuing in good works. To think of the pond rippling itself to try to attract a rock—being saved *by* good works—is utter nonsense. But so is the idea of a rock hitting the water with no effect—being saved *without* good works. If I look at the surface of the water and it is absolutely smooth, what do I conclude? The rock never hit the pond.

Thus it is perfectly logical to conclude that good works can be totally excluded as the ground or cause of salvation and simultaneously considered necessary as its fruit. Judging individuals is tricky, and we should be slow to do it. Sometimes the effects are subtle, they do not always appear immediately or at the same pace, and we can be fooled by counterfeits. But the principle is clear. God wants you to do good works, and His method of producing them is to eliminate them completely from your consideration as something you must produce by your own efforts to gain His favor. He does this so that you are thus thrown completely into the position of trusting wholly in His grace and the work of Christ rather than in your own righteousness. When we understand this dynamic, and when it is working, the result is good works indeed, streaming from a fountain of gratitude and joy that is kept freshly flowing from above.

The second mistake people make is that of looking at justification in the abstract, divorced from its context in the fullness of the salvation God aims to grant us. Justification is the joyous moment when we realize that our sins have been completely covered by the blood of Christ and we hear ourselves pronounced innocent in the court of God's justice.[28] This is a legal sentence. It is tremendously important in itself, because without it nothing else that God wants to do for us can happen. But by itself, it leaves us just as messed up by sin as we were before. That is actually the beauty of it! We do not have to make ourselves worthy of this gift. We simple receive it as a free gift of pure grace, by faith (Rom. 3:24).

Nevertheless, that very beauty of justification by faith can seem to be a problem. I have a dear friend who once said, "I'm not interested in a mere legal fiction. I want to be made *really* righteous!" And she was absolutely correct to feel that way. What she could not yet see was the way that the apparent legal "fiction" of justification by faith is the key—and the only key—that opens the door to where she so rightly wanted to go.

Justification *by itself* leaves us just as messed up in our lives as

---

28 Calvin summarizes the doctrine of Justification beautifully: "A man is said to be justified in the sight of God when in the judgment of God he is deemed righteous, and is accepted on account of his righteousness.... A man will be said to be *justified by works* if in his life there can be found a purity and holiness which merits an attestation of righteousness at the throne of God.... A man will be *justified by faith* when, excluded from the righteousness of works, he by faith lays hold of the righteousness of Christ, and, clothed in it, appears in the sight of God not as a sinner, but as righteous." *Institutes of the Christian Religion*, op. cit., 2:37-8. Clearly justification by works as described is not possible for fallen men. It is justification by faith or nothing.

we were when it found us. Fortunately, justification does not come by itself. Justification is only one part (though a crucial and critical part) of redemption or salvation. It is part of a package that includes regeneration and sanctification. Regeneration, or the new birth, takes one who was spiritually dead in his trespasses and sins and makes him alive again in Christ (Eph. 2:1-5). Sanctification is the lifelong process by which this new spiritual life is strengthened and developed until it becomes increasingly dominant in our experience—the process by which we start actually to become in experience what God declared us to be and accepted us as already being in justification. At the very moment of regeneration, the Holy Spirit who effected it is sent to indwell us and by His presence and influence move forward the process of sanctification.

Here is the point. Nobody is justified who is not regenerated and who is not beginning to be sanctified—all of which is the work of God. And the legal declaration in justification is precisely what makes possible this restored relationship with God that allows regeneration and sanctification to happen. Without it, our sins are still a barrier between us and God which would prevent that relationship from being actualized. Justification does not *require* good works on our part, in other words; it *enables* them because it is the door to regeneration and sanctification. And that is part of what it means to say that salvation is by grace alone.

Thesis 2d:
Any Admixture of Good Works *As The Grounds* of Salvation Subverts and Destroys the Whole Biblical Plan of Redemption.

Why do these emphases of the old Reformation need to be part of a new one? Because they are what make the Gospel the power of God for salvation for those who believe, and because we are losing our grip on them. My friend who was confused about justification by faith had spent her life in conservative Protestant churches. Some of them had created that confusion, some had fed it, and others had done nothing to alleviate it. She is still in the process of emerging from that fog to enjoy what she delightfully calls "a less worried obedience." And she is not an isolated case. She is joined by many who commit the opposite error, which is sometimes called "cheap grace" or "easy believeism": They divorce justification and sanctification by treating sanctification as almost optional. Either way, Satan rejoices as the biblical Gospel is distorted and disfigured. People with possibly false hopes of salvation and people with unnecessarily frustrated Christian lives are the result.

Therefore, like the original Reformers, we need to recover not only the content but also the logic of the biblical Gospel. In the wisdom of God it is precisely calibrated to apply the fullness of His character in all its majestic splendor to the particularities of our need in all its hopeless degradation. Not moral reform but spiritual transformation; not turning over a new leaf but turning on a new life; not winking at sin but a full pardon completely paid for; not a compromise between His mercy and His justice but a full reconciliation of all their inexorable claims: Nothing less than the wisdom of God could have devised it; nothing less than the love of God could have chosen it; nothing less than the power of God could have accomplished it. And no less a Person than the incarnate Son of God could have embodied it. Blessed be He!

Let us then try to understand the logic of the Gospel. We started to see how it works in the thesis above. Our sinfulness is a barrier that separates us from God and His mercy; it necessarily does so because of His justice (Is. 59:2). We naturally think, "OK, I will try to do better. Maybe I can make myself worthy enough so God will accept me. Then He will forgive my sins and everything will be OK." So we discipline ourselves, we try to do good deeds, we give money to the church, we attend its services and avail ourselves of its rituals. But when have we done enough of this? We can *never* know that we have. Never! But it is much worse even than that. We can actually be sure that we have *not* done enough and can never do enough, because we are trying to do the impossible.

The natural man's approach to salvation is doomed to unavoidable failure by at least four fatal flaws. First, it does absolutely nothing to erase the guilt of previous sin. The question is not how nice a person you are or can become; it is whether or not you are guilty of rebellion against God, of treason against the Kingdom of Heaven. Imagine that the evidence shows you to be guilty of high treason and the judge asks you what you have to say for yourself. "Well, from now on I promise to go to church, give ten percent of my money, and do all the good deeds I can." Such a response would be ludicrously inadequate because it is not just disproportionate to the seriousness of the charge against you; it does not even address it.

The second flaw is that the natural man is utterly failing to address not only the issue of what he has done but also the problem of what he is. Our sin does not just consist of a list of various arbitrary rules that we have somehow managed to break along the way. Our rebellion, our desire that we rather than God should be sovereign over our lives, is the essence of sin, and it is something we inherited from Adam. It is encoded into our very spiritual DNA. And we can no more change that fact by trying to be better persons or by practicing religion than the Ethiopian can change his skin or the leopard his spots (Jer. 13:23). You might succeed in making yourself a less egregious sinner by this method (by human standards, anyway)—but you would still be a sinner.

Third, whatever your religious leaders may tell you about how they are conduits of grace from God that can help you, you are trying to achieve this goal of moral improvement on your own. Your sins are still a barrier that separates you from God, and hence from any help He might offer you. You can only appeal to Him *after* you have already become acceptable to Him, after you have already gotten rid of those sins, which is the very thing you are trying to accomplish—by a method which has no hope of success. You are trying to lift yourself by your own spiritual bootstraps. You might achieve a life that is in some ways admirable, but you will still be a sinner. There is no escape from this Catch-22 by your own efforts.

Finally and most importantly, good works done with the idea that by doing them you can merit or earn God's approval would not even *be* good works—not in any spiritually relevant sense. The hidden assumption that by doing this I can in any way *make myself* righteous, *make myself* acceptable to a holy God, carries with it an element of spiritual pride that taints these very good works—outwardly beneficial and noble though they may be—with sin. This is why Scripture tells us that without faith it is impossible to please God (Heb. 11:6) and that whatever is not of faith is sin (Rom. 14:23). Good works done with the idea that they will let you take any credit at all for your own salvation, therefore, are themselves sins. You are then trying to overcome your sins by committing more of them; you are trying to overcome your sinfulness by reinforcing it! The person trying to dig himself out of the hole of sin with the shovel of good works is only digging himself in deeper.

The Gospel of salvation by grace alone cuts this Gordian knot and breaks this impasse by flipping the tables. Instead of putting the conquest of sin at the end of the process, it moves it to the beginning. Jesus' relationship with us as the Second Adam and His sacrifice as our substitute make it legitimate for God to *count* our sins as completely covered and therefore *treat* us *now* as if we were already the righteous people we would never be able to become if He did not do this. Thus our absolution and our adoption come at the beginning, and are complete and whole *before* we are worthy of them—while we are (in one sense) still sinners. And this is the very thing that lets us spend the rest of our earthly lives growing into this new identity which we have been freely and gratuitously given. We are enabled to do that because, with our relationship to God restored, based wholly and completely on *Christ's* merit and not at all on our own, God is able to send His Holy Spirit to indwell us as Christ's personal agent and representative to complete in us the work that has been begun.[29] This is given to us as a free gift which we do nothing to earn but simply receive by faith. So, like Abraham, we believe God and it is *counted* to us as righteousness

---

29 See the fuller treatment of these matters in Donald T. Williams, *The Person and Work of the Holy Spirit*, op. cit., esp. pp. 63-78.

(Rom. 4:3). The counting or reckoning of righteousness (the theological word is *imputation*) is so important because it is the necessary first step to the *reality* of righteousness. Indeed, it is the only foundation on which it can be built.

The sole graciousness of this plan of salvation, with its resulting rigid distinction between works as ground and works as fruit, is not incidental; it is essential to its ability to function. It is only by rigorously excluding works as the ground or cause of salvation that God preserves truly spiritual good works, oriented to God's glory and not our own and therefore acceptable to Him, as the fruit of it. That is why any reintroduction of works as in any sense the ground or basis or cause of salvation subverts the whole scheme and reduces it back to the futility of manmade religion. So it is not the desire to absolve themselves of the necessity of an amended life producing good works that causes faithful Protestants who understand their theology to cling so strongly to the Gospel of grace alone. They do it because they "do not nullify the grace of God; for if righteousness comes through the Law, then Christ died needlessly" (Gal. 2:21). And they do it because the love of God shed abroad in their hearts make them appreciate that Gospel as the only path to those things—and to the God who so graciously gives them. Amen.

Thesis 2e:
Works Are Necessarily Both Excluded As Ground *and* Required As Fruit Because the End of Salvation Is the Glory of God.

※

In Thesis 2d we saw how the Gospel of salvation by grace alone elegantly achieves God's purpose of restoring sinners to the good works which He had prepared beforehand that they should walk in them (Eph. 2:10). Now we shall see that it is just as elegantly designed to achieve the even deeper and more ultimate purpose of salvation: the glory of God.

God's ultimate purpose in everything He does is His own glory. (More on this in chapter five.) He says, "I am the Lord; that is my name. I will not give my glory to another" (Is. 42:8). He declares, "For the sake of my name I delay my wrath, and for my praise I restrain it for you. . . . For my own sake, for my own sake I will act, for how can my name be profaned? And my glory I will not give to another" (Is. 48:9-11). In the first chapter of Ephesians Paul gives a summary of all that God has done for the salvation of His people. Three times he breaks into the exposition with a purpose statement: It was all done "for the praise of the glory of His grace" (1:6), "to the end that we who were the first to hope in Christ should be to the praise of His glory" (1:12), and "with a view to the redemption of God's own possession, to the praise of His glory" (1:14). Everything moreover was done with a view to "the summing up of all things in Christ" (1:10).

So, to summarize: God's ultimate goal in all that He does is the glory of His Son, and the most profound way in which this is achieved is through the salvation of sinners. The Cross is a figure of two lines meeting: God's justice demanding the death penalty for sin, and His love, wishing to avoid the carrying out of that sentence without the slightest compromise to His justice, taking that penalty on Himself in the Person of His Son. Thus God's inner nature as it relates to fallen humanity is made manifest to all of creation in the most profound way conceivable, and thus He is glorified.

God is glorified in His Son that He might return glory to His Son by every aspect of the plan of salvation, from the accomplishment of the atonement to its application to sinners. Salvation *by grace alone* is beautifully designed to accomplish this goal, and one of its most elegant features to that end is its radical exclusion of human works from being the grounds of salvation so they can be included as its fruit. Jesus said, "Let your light so shine before men that they may see your good works and glorify your Father who is in heaven" (Mat. 5:16). He thus set us an interesting problem. Normally when I see someone doing a good deed, I praise that person, the doer of the deed. But we are supposed to do our good works in such a way that they are seen, but the glory for them goes not to us but to God. This happens only as we proclaim *and become personally identified with* the Gospel that makes God the source of all good, including anything that is good in us.

That understanding, that proclamation, and that identity must be compromised to the extent that I see my good works as contributing in any way to my standing as a redeemed child of God and not a condemned sinner. For my salvation to bring glory to God in the most complete and efficient way, my good works must be seen, yet they must *not* be seen as anything for which I can take the credit. My growth in Christlike character must be seen, and it must be seen as coming from (and pointing to) Him and not me. God is not glorified by a salvation that produces no fruit, nor by one in which credit for the fruit can be taken by the sinner rather than the Savior.

Conclusion

For God to receive glory for our salvation before men, we must live lives that reflect His grace, and we must *come across* as people who know we are saved by *nothing* in ourselves but only by His all-sufficient grace. Do we? For us to live this way, salvation must be by grace alone, operating with the holy, liberating, and life-changing dynamic I have tried to describe above. And for us to come across this way, the Gospel of *Sola Gratia*, of salvation by grace alone, must not be a relic of the historic Reformation but a present reality that is ground into the very marrow of the marrow of the bones of our bones.

Soli Deo Gloria!

Interlude

The Commendation
(Rom. 5:8)

In all mankind no greater love can be
Than to lay down
One's life for a good friend. But look around,
And you will see
A man, to save his spiteful enemy,
Lie down to die—
No other reason why.

And does God then commend His love in this?
While we were yet
Sinners, in our sins still firmly set,
With Judas' kiss
Still warm on our lips and His cheek, the hiss
Still ringing, "Crucify!"
He willingly did die.

And so we hear the glorious decree,
"Reconciled!"
And I, who would have stood there and reviled,
Now on my knee
Search in vain for something that could be
A fit return
For grace I did not earn.

And I, who solely by His sacrifice
Now live,
Will never find a single thing to give
That would suffice
To pay back one ten-millionth of the price
He freely gave
To save me from the grave.

Ah, well, I must give all; my grateful heart
Could do no less.
Yet, in so doing, freely I confess
There is no part
To give He has not purchased from the start.
Before His throne,
I give Him but His own,

And worship Him for grace beyond my art
To think or tell:
By death and love a double debtor made,
I find all debts in Him forever paid.
He doeth all things well![30]

---

30 Donald T. Williams, *Stars through the Clouds*, op. cit., p. 166-7.

3

Five Theses on *Sola Fide*

Luther rightly held that justification by faith alone is the indicator of a standing or a falling church. In this chapter we will see why.

A. Salvation, wrought by grace alone, is received by the empty hands of faith alone. ("For by grace are ye saved through faith," Eph. 2:8.)

B. Saving faith is personal trust in God's promise of salvation and in His proffered Redeemer, Jesus Christ. (Faith is not ticking off the right boxes on an opinion poll; it is not repeating a formulaic prayer; it is personal trust in and commitment to Christ.)

C. Saving faith is not simply holding correct opinions about doctrine; it is personal trust in the saving power of the Christ who is accurately described by biblical truth. (We are saved by God's grace, not by having correct opinions; nevertheless, see 3d.)

D. Nevertheless, because Christ's Person and His Work are what they are and not something else, some major doctrinal errors are inconsistent with a claim to have saving faith. (Scripture specifies that denying the incarnation [1 John 2:22, 4:2-3] and affirming salvation by works [Gal. 5:2-4] are incompatible with saving faith, which must positively affirm the Lordship of Christ and His resurrection [Rom. 10:9]. We are not saved by perfect understanding of doctrine, but some serious errors are *prima facie* evidence of lostness.)

E. The sacraments are inducements to, enablers of, and expressions of saving faith; they have no power to save apart from faith. (If salvation is by grace alone through faith alone, then the sacraments are the servants of faith, not magical substitutes for it.)

Sola Gratia and *Sola Fide*, salvation (more specifically, justification) by grace alone and by faith alone, are coordinated concepts that go together. The first deals with how salvation is provided, the second with how it is received. And it is gloriously appropriate that a salvation given to us as a free gift by grace alone should be received by faith alone; for that is just to say that it is simply *received*, as a gift is. It does not need to be accessed through an elaborate apparatus of conduits, intermediaries, and practices. Some of those things are indeed there as aids to faith—but faith itself is the key.[31]

---

[31] The classic work is J. Gresham Machen, *What is Faith?* (Grand Rapids: Eerdmans, 1962). For further reading on contemporary Protestant waffling on *Sola Fide* and its implications for justification, see John Piper. *The Future of Justification: A Response to N. T. Wright* (Wheaton: Crossway, 2007) and William C. Roach, Sola Fide: *A Primer on Paul's Doctrine of Justification in Romans* (Matthews, N.C.: Bastion Books, 2018). See also the relevant sections in the standard Evangelical systematic theologies, such as Hodge, Berkhof, Erickson, and Grudem.

Thesis 3a:
Salvation, Wrought by Grace Alone, Is Received by the Empty Hands of Faith Alone.

To say that salvation is received by faith alone is simply to echo the consistent message of the New Testament. When asked, "What must I do to be saved?' the Philippian Jailer was told, "*Believe* on the Lord Jesus Christ and thou shalt be saved" (Acts 16:30-31). Righteousness comes "through *faith* in Jesus Christ" (Rom. 3:22). The atonement makes God able to be "just and the justifier of the one who has *faith* in Jesus" (Rom. 3:26). "A man is justified by *faith* apart from works of the Law" (Rom. 3:28). Abraham "*believed* God, and it was counted to him as righteousness" (Rom. 4:3). "Having been justified by *faith*, we have peace with God" (Rom. 5:1). "For by grace are ye saved through *faith*" (Eph. 2:8). And in what may be Paul's most definitive summary of his answer to the Jailer's question, "If you confess with your mouth Jesus as Lord and *believe* in your heart that God hath raised him from the dead, you shall be saved" (Rom. 10:9).

This testimony to salvation by faith alone is even more impressive in Greek than it is in English. All the italicized words in the summary above represent the same root in Greek: *pistis*, the noun form, translated "belief" or "faith," and *pisteuo*, the verb form translated "I believe" or "I trust in." Probably the best translation is "trust." "Believe" might imply to some people that faith is just a matter of holding a certain opinion. Romans 10:9 alone shows it was more than that. Merely entertaining the opinion that God raised Jesus from the dead is one thing. But this kind of belief involved *confessing* His lordship in an environment where such a confession could get you killed. You would have to believe in His lordship pretty strongly to do that. This is not "I think on balance this is probably true." Nor is it the opposite, if that is "I am certain beyond the shadow of a doubt that this is true." The level of subjective confidence is not the point.

It's more like "I am staking my eternal soul and everything that makes life meaningful now on this truth." That makes sense in the light of Ephesians 2:8-10. Saving faith is only possible as a gift from God. We do not need any such divine intervention merely to entertain an opinion that costs us nothing. Faith is the trust that commits.

There are a few passages that might seem to complicate the picture we just gave. Sometimes people are told to *repent* and believe (Mark 1:15) or believe and *be baptized* (Mark 16:16) or even repent and be baptized (Acts 2:38). But baptism and repentance are not steps to salvation or requirements for salvation in addition to faith; rather, they are best understood as expressions or declarations of faith. "Repent" is *metanoeo*, literally to change your mind. It is best understood as a 180-degree turn: You turn from trusting in your own works to trusting in the blood of Christ, from following your own will to bowing before Christ as lord, from a life of sin to one of discipleship, lived not perfectly but with a measure of integrity. If your "faith" doesn't cause you to follow through in that way, it is not a very serious belief. It is only an opinion, not biblical faith, the trust that commits. Repentance is simply faith in action.

Baptism is also best understood not as a ritual added to faith as another hoop to jump through on the way to salvation but as an expression of faith. You can see this in the fact that in several cases people were clearly already saved (by faith) before they were baptized. Peter ordered the baptism of Cornelius's household because the Holy Spirit had already come upon them in regeneration (Acts 10:44-48). Clearly it was their salvation that made them eligible for baptism, not the other way around. Baptism is a graphic and dramatic public statement of one's identification with Christ in His death, burial, and resurrection (Rom. 6:3-7) and with His people, the church. A faith which drew back from that identification would be less than biblical faith. But the baptism from which saving faith does not draw back is an expression and demonstration of that faith, not an addition to it.

So we see then that we are saved by faith, and by faith alone. Faith is the empty hand with which we receive the free gift of salvation that God offers us. We are saved then by faith: not by faith plus works, not by faith plus church rituals, not by faith plus confession, not by faith plus the sacraments. We are saved by grace alone through faith—alone.

Thesis 3b:
Saving Faith Is Personal Trust in God's Promise of Salvation and in His Proffered Redeemer, Jesus Christ.

෴

We have already begun to see what saving faith is: it is personal trust in God's promise of salvation and in His proffered Redeemer, Jesus Christ. When we fully understand what faith is, we will understand its sufficiency as the means by which we receive God's work of salvation. It is not that the other things offered by some as requirements in addition to faith are not good things. Many of them are valuable helps in the Christian life, or even things we are commanded to do. But they are not how we are saved, and indeed they are valuable precisely as aids to faith itself. Faith is the key.

If faith is how we receive salvation, we had better be clear about what faith is. Some people add things to biblical faith, and others seem to subtract part of its very essence from it. We have heard evangelists, eager for converts and trying with perhaps the best of intentions to smooth the path into the Kingdom, reduce faith to an opinion, an experience, or a "decision." "Come down to the front, agree to the basic facts of the Gospel, pray the sinner's prayer, repeating after me, and you will be saved and can never be lost again!" Well, I hope that many of the people who have responded to that kind of appeal are indeed saved, and I am pretty sure that some are. But the number of them who follow through with any serious attempt to lead the Christian life is, shall we say, disappointing. I've been in too many churches that boasted of inflated numbers of "converts," hardly any of which were in the church at the end of the year when such reports are typically given. Where were they? Are such "converts" lost? Of course I do not know. But there is no positive evidence that they are saved. One is saved by having faith, not by once having made a profession of it.

Biblical faith is not agreeing to a summary of basic Gospel facts, even if it is a good summary (though of course it involves commitment to the truth of those facts). Biblical faith is not an impulsive emotional response to an appeal (though it may well involve emotion and will lead to a response). Biblical faith is not having a set of orthodox opinions which one would be willing to check off on a poll (though it does involve commitment to the truth of the Gospel). Biblical faith is personal trust in God's promise of salvation and in His proffered Redeemer, Jesus Christ. Saving faith casts one's soul wholly and unreservedly onto the finished work of Christ as one's only hope of meaning in this life and salvation in the next. It is not something you can just up and decide to have or not; it is a work of God in your heart that changes it, that makes you a new person, that brings you from spiritual death to life and makes you a disciple, a follower, of Jesus Christ. Calvin well emphasized its aspect as a work of God by calling saving faith "a firm and sure knowledge of the divine favor toward us, founded on the truth of a free promise in Christ, and revealed to our minds and sealed on our hearts by the Holy Spirit."[32]

You can see the true nature of saving faith by meditating on the conversions that the New Testament presents to us. We know them to be real conversions because their results are history. We know them to be paradigmatic and exemplary conversions because they are given to us as instructive examples in the New Testament. Matthew did not walk away from a profitable career as a tax collector just because Jesus gave him warm fuzzies in his heart. Zacchaeus did not offer to give away half his wealth just to satisfy a nagging conscience. The Ethiopian Eunuch did not stop his chariot and ask to be baptized in the middle of nowhere just because he had had his idle curiosity satisfied about the interpretation of Isaiah. The Philippian Jailer did not ask what he must do to be saved because he was caught up in the hype of other people (half of whom he did not realize were counselors) "going forward" around him. Saul of Tarsus did not go from being the most zealous persecutor of Jesus' disciples to being their most articulate spokesman and zealous recruiter as a result of a midlife crisis.

Something happened to these people that changed them, turned them around, and sent them off in the opposite direction from the one they had been taking before. Something changed them from skeptics to believers, from people wandering in darkness to people who reflected the Light of the World, from people going their own way to devoted disciples and servants of the King of Kings and Lord of Lords. They had experienced the Gospel as the power of God for salvation to those who believed. They had been regenerated by the Holy Spirit.

---

32 John Calvin, *Institutes of the Christian Religion*, 2 vol., trans. Henry Beveridge (Grand Rapids: Eerdmans, 1975), p. 1:475.

They had believed the Gospel and put their faith in Jesus, not as a passing fancy or a superficially held opinion or a passive acquiescence in the faith of their parents, but as a response to the work of God's grace in their lives. Because of the faith God had given them, they had come to know the truth of Paul's claim: "If any man is in Christ, he is a new creature. The old things passed away; behold, new things have come" (2 Cor. 5:17). They had been saved—by grace alone, through faith alone.

I am not trying to create a stereotyped model of a conversion experience for believers to try to conform to. That was an error of a previous generation that we gladly leave in the past. Saving faith comes to people in a thousand different ways. It may or may not be dramatic at the outset; it may or may not involve intense emotion. Some people only realize it has happened in them after the fact. What I am trying to do is get us back to a more biblical set of expectations that saving faith in Jesus Christ is something that makes a difference in your life. It is personal trust in God's promise of salvation and in His proffered Redeemer, Jesus Christ, that causes you to follow Him. You cannot cook this faith up in yourself, but you are exhorted to believe anyway. If you find yourself responding to that exhortation with a trust in Jesus that makes you want to follow Him, rejoice! That is saving faith. If you do not have it, ask for it. The very desire to do so is the first sign of its being given. A mustard seed of the real thing is all you need. Confess with your mouth Jesus as Lord, believe in your heart that God raised him from the dead, and you shall be saved. I am authorized to promise you that!

Thesis 3c:
Saving Faith Is Not Simply Holding Correct Opinions about Doctrine; It Is Personal Trust in the Saving Power of the Christ Who Is Accurately Described by Biblical Truth.

&

Thesis 3d:
Nevertheless, Because Christ's Person and His Work Are What They Are and Not Something Else, Some Major Doctrinal Errors Are Inconsistent with a Claim To Have Saving Faith.

☙

Theses 3c and 3d are separate ideas, but they are so closely related that they need to be discussed together. Most Christians instinctively realize that there must be some connection between saving faith and sound doctrine. It makes no sense to say you are trusting Christ for your salvation when what you actually believe in is something else. On the other hand, there are lots of doctrinal points that genuinely saved people disagree on. We are saved by the grace of God, not by the clarity of our thinking. We are saved by the power of the Christ about whom those biblical statements tell the accurate truth—by the power and the merit of that *Christ*, that is, not by the statements themselves. But unless those statements are true, there is no Christ to save us. So there must be a relationship between right doctrine and saving faith, even if it is not a simple one. Sound doctrine is a sign (one of many) of genuine faith, but we must not make it into a new form of merit, as if it could save us itself. People who check all the right doctrinal boxes can be lost, and people with a surprisingly high level of confusion about doctrine can be saved. What doctrinal affirmations then are actually necessary for salvation? Unfortunately, that is one of the things Christians disagree about!

The New Testament draws at least three doctrinal lines in the sand such that crossing them is presumed to put a person outside of the Faith. We are not saying that these are the only essential beliefs. There is very little in the Apostle's and Nicene Creeds that one could disbelieve while claiming with any credibility to be a faithful Christian. But these three ideas are specifically singled out by an apostle as boundary markers, so they are clearly very important. And most of the other essential affirmations flow from them. We must confess that Jesus came in the flesh, that God raised Him from the dead, and that the salvation He provided comes to us by grace through faith alone, apart from works.

John in his first epistle makes the confession that Christ has come in the flesh an indicator of whether one serves Christ or Antichrist. "By this you know the Spirit of God: Every spirit that confesses that Jesus Christ has come in the flesh is from God, and every spirit that does not confess Jesus is not from God; this is the spirit of the antichrist" (1 John 4:2-3). What is the context of this statement? One of the more popular forms of religion at the end of the First Century was Gnosticism, which taught, among other things, that spirit was good and matter was evil. People influenced by that idea would have had a hard time seeing how Jesus could be divine and sinless if he had a material body, which must necessarily, by that thinking, have tainted Him with evil. So one of the early doctrinal errors was the idea that Jesus must have been a purely spiritual Being who only *seemed* to have a real physical body. John said no: A real incarnation is absolutely essential to Christian faith. In Paul's terms, a Christ who was not a real human being could not be the Second Adam whose substitutionary death could save us. So the full deity of Christ on the one hand and a real incarnation on the other are non-negotiable. If your faith is not in *that* Christ, it is not in the Savior of the world.

Paul adds two more boundary markers. The key facts of the Gospel as it is proclaimed at any point in the New Testament are that Christ died for our sins according to the Scriptures and was buried and raised from the dead on the third day, according to the Scriptures. If that is not true in cold, hard fact, then we are yet in our sins and are of all men most miserable (1 Cor. 15:17-19). So there is no forgiveness of sin—no salvation—without the resurrection. The simplest form of the Gospel is "Believe on the Lord Jesus Christ and you shall be saved" (Acts 16:31). But of course that inevitably leads to the question, "Believe *what* about the Lord Jesus Christ?" The answer must include the facts that He died for our sins and was raised from the dead according to the Scriptures (1 Cor. 15:3-4). Moreover, the resurrection is specifically what comes to the fore as needing to be believed in the heart in Paul's classic summary of the Gospel in Rom. 10:9-10. No one who disbelieves in the historical, bodily, physical resurrection of Jesus in objective space and time can credibly claim to be a Christian in any sense recognized by the New Testament.

Paul etches the other line in the sand, drawn in no uncertain terms, deeply across the pages of Galatians. Any compromise of the proposition that "A man is not justified by the works of the Law but through faith in Jesus Christ" (Gal. 2:16) is treated as a "different Gospel" which is no Gospel at all (Gal. 1:6-7)—and people who teach such a false Gospel are to be considered accursed (1:9). It is impossible to avoid the conclusion that salvation by works is absolutely condemned as a doctrine that is inconsistent with the Gospel and incompatible with faithful Christian teaching. Grace and works (when discussing the grounds of salvation) are like oil and water: They just do not mix.

Now, the purpose of these theses is not to satisfy our curiosity about who is or is not in Heaven, still less to let us make pronouncements on such a thing that is quite frankly far above our pay grade. Did John Milton's Arianism (a compromised view of Christ's full deity) land him in Hell despite his excellent understanding of most of the rest of theology and his obviously sincere desire to honor Christ and glorify God for the salvation He had wrought through Him? I hope not. Have we just consigned every Roman Catholic to eternal punishment for their church's official denial of *sola fide*, justification by faith alone, despite the Nicene orthodoxy and genuine love of the Lord shown by many of them? God forbid! We are saved by faith, and faith is personal trust in God's promise of salvation and in His proffered Redeemer, Jesus Christ. This is a faith which, despite the false teachings they have received, we hope that many such people genuinely have.

We are saved by *trust* in these Realities, in other words—not by a perfect understanding of them. Only God sees the heart, and He will respond graciously to that trust when it is present, despite many and serious confusions about many things that may accompany it. When those confusions are serious enough, they do compromise our confidence that the faith being professed is indeed saving faith. In such a case it is our responsibility to express our concern, with loving clarification and even sober warning; but it is not our business to indulge in final judgments. So we call churches like Rome that have strayed from a pure grasp of the biblical Gospel of grace back to it while hoping that many of its adherents may be saved by grace through faith in spite of its soteriology. It is of course better that your theology be an encouragement to saving faith rather than a hindrance to it!

Judging doctrines is not the same thing as judging people. We must do the former forthrightly while being much slower to do the latter. It is appropriate to say, "The Gospel you are preaching is not the biblical Gospel; and a false Gospel puts your own soul, and the souls of those who listen to you, in jeopardy." We must sometimes say this of people's *doctrine*, because doctrine is objective and public and its influence if it is false must be counteracted. Without being able to see their hearts, we should leave pronouncement on the people themselves to God.

Sound doctrine is important because it teaches us to put our trust in the right things, the ones that truly save us. False doctrine obscures those realities and encourages us to trust in false hopes instead. It is crucial for our churches to call people clearly to faith in Christ as their all-sufficient Redeemer and in His completed work as the only and all-sufficient expression of God's grace, and not encourage them to put their trust in anything else—whether other than grace alone or in addition to grace alone. That is why *sola gratia* and *sola fide* are still matters of concern for the Reformation we need today. Meanwhile, God sees our hearts as well as our heads, and the ideal is for them to match. When they do not, it is our place to warn of the possible consequences, and His to decide, with reference to individuals, what those consequences need to be.

Thesis 3e:
The Sacraments Are Inducements to, Enablers of, and Expressions of Saving Faith; They Have No Power to Save apart from Faith.[33]

If salvation is given by grace alone and received by faith alone, then this has implications for every element of Christian worship and practice. If salvation is given by grace alone and received by faith alone, then we cannot conceive of the sacraments as magical rites that pour grace into us or in any other way magically alter our status or our standing before God. This does not make them trivial or unimportant. If we are saved by faith, then anything that feeds and enables faith, anything that strengthens it by expressing it and by reconnecting us with the Realities in which our faith is placed, must be very important to us indeed. And so we are commanded to make two such expressions central to our worship: Baptism and Communion, or the Lord's Supper.

Protestants sadly disagree about the time and mode of Baptism. Should it follow a self-conscious profession of faith made with understanding ("adult baptism" or "credobaptism"), as all of the recorded baptisms in the New Testament do? Or should it be administered to children by believing parents in faith that they will come to faith when they are able so that in the meantime they are already marked out in advance as part of the believing community ("infant baptism" or "paedobaptism"), in parallel with the way circumcision functioned in the Old Covenant? And should Baptism be administered by dunking in water (immersion), pouring it over the candidate (effusion), or sprinkling it (spargation)? Probably nothing has more tragically divided Christians trying to be faithful to the Scriptures.

These disagreements persist because the New Testament never clearly settles them. There are passages that adherents of the various positions take as indications one way or the other, but they are all based on inferences. There is no definitive passage that actually gives detailed instructions for how Baptism is to be conducted. I have my

---

33 For more on these points, see Thesis 7d. See also Alan Dan Orme, *God's Appointments with Men: A Christian's Primer on the Sacraments* (Athens, Ga.: The University Church Press, 1982).

own opinions and preferences on these matters, but I am not going to defend them here. I am seeking a new Reformation of the church *universal* centered on the biblical Gospel of salvation by grace alone through faith alone in Christ alone. The original Reformation was greatly hindered when its leaders could not agree on their theology of the Lord's Supper; more accurately, it was hindered when they could not agree to disagree. This time, I would rather see Evangelical Baptists unified with their Evangelical Presbyterian, Lutheran, Anglican, and Methodist brothers and sisters around the Gospel and the Lord while remaining lovingly committed to a stance of agreeing to disagree on their denominational distinctives. I will confine myself then to a discussion of how the sacraments should function in relation to the Gospel—that is, in relation to faith.

Baptism: When I see someone professing his own faith and his identification with Christ and His people in such an arresting fashion, or parents claiming it for their children, I am challenged afresh with the Gospel they profess. People who were baptized when they were able to confess their own faith are reminded of and can renew the commitment they made then, and those whose parents made that commitment for them can reaffirm that faith as now their own possession. For the person who is being baptized as a believer, the water should feel like a Rubicon from which there is no going back. Those who have their infant children baptized are expressing their most cherished hopes for those children in terms of the Gospel promises they claim for them. For both candidate and congregation, then, baptism is a profound expression of their faith and their commitment to Christ and His church that reinforces both the faith and the commitment. Without faith baptism will do nothing to save you; it will not save those baptized as infants if they do not come to confess with their own mouths Jesus as Lord and believe in their own hearts that God raised Him from the dead. With faith it becomes as meaningful an act as can well be imagined.

The Lord's Supper functions in much the same way, except that instead of commemorating one's initiation into the community of faith once and for all, it serves as the ongoing celebration of our relationship to Christ and His people. It is a memorial of the atonement and a visible proclamation of it, for the broken bread and poured wine remind us of Christ's body and blood and thus we "show forth the Lord's death until He comes" (1 Cor. 11:26). But it is more than that:

It is a fellowship meal in which the Lord is present to us in a special way through the elements which symbolize His body and blood. We do it "in remembrance" of Him (Luke 22:19). The wine represents His blood "of the covenant" (Mat. 26:28), the New Covenant being the basis of the restored relationship we have with God as our Father through the merit and the mediation of the Son who is our Redeemer and our Lord.

A covenant meal may be the best way to understand how the Lord's Supper is meant to function in the believer's life. It is a reaffirmation of the New Covenant. It is like the custom in which some married couples will renew their wedding vows on their fiftieth anniversary. "Do you still take this woman to be your lawful wedded wife? Do you still mean to honor and cherish her and forsaking all others to keep you only unto her until death do you part?" "Oh, yes!" So as the minister offers you the bread and the wine, God is saying (in a visible and tactile manner, as it were), "I still offer you Jesus, my only begotten Son, as your Savior and Redeemer. I am still counting the sacrifice of His broken body and shed blood as the all-sufficient payment for your sin; I am still counting your faith as righteousness on that basis, just as I did for Abraham and for all the saints. I still take you as my adopted child, my beloved, the apple of my eye, for Christ's sake." And by receiving it you reply, "I still believe in Jesus as my Savior and bow before Him as my Lord. I still confess Him as Lord and believe in my heart that you raised Him from the dead. I still identify myself with Him in His death and resurrection, and with His people, the church. I receive the reality of these things afresh in these elements which speak so eloquently of them." Thus we draw near to the Lord, and He to us, in ways too deep for words. It is little wonder that one of our names for this meal is Holy *Communion*. For that is precisely what it can be when it is received *by faith*.

Most Protestants do not think that the bread and wine are literally transformed into the actual body and blood of Jesus. They are metaphors. It would have been pretty obvious which was which when His literal body was handing his symbolic body to the disciples at the Last Supper. But they are not *mere* metaphors. We believe that the reality of what they represent comes to us spiritually through the consecrated bread and wine that represent them. And we should believe that this communion in the context of such a reaffirmation of the New Covenant should be central to our worship as it was to that of the early church. Yet in many of our churches it is celebrated only once a month or even more seldom, and often tacked on to the end of another service into which it was not really integrated. There is no more profound expression of our faith than when we take that which represents it and literally make it part of our own bodies. And thus there is nothing that, received in faith, can do more to deepen, strengthen, and renew that faith. And that is why people who believe that salvation is received by faith alone should be much more focused on the Lord's Supper than they seem to be. Restoring it to the place it had in the worship of the first Christians should be a major plank in the Reformation the church needs today.

Conclusion

Why then is justification by faith the mark of a standing or falling church? Saving faith is personal trust in God's promise of salvation and in His proffered Redeemer, Jesus Christ. By it we receive the Gospel of salvation by God's grace alone; without it we either delude ourselves that we are saved because we are relatively nice people or labor under a crushing burden of performance that can never be enough. With it, rightly understood, we receive God's forgiveness and His favor and are liberated into the "less worried obedience" that is the Christian life. Thus we discover the Gospel to be what Paul said it was: the power of God for salvation for those who believe.

Personal trust in God's promise of salvation and in His proffered Redeemer: A church that fosters that faith and enables that discovery is a standing church, however imperfect it might be. One that hinders that faith and discourages that discovery is fallen or falling. Find a church that lets you stand with the Gospel. That is all.

Interlude

There Then Abide These Three

And what is Faith? Not simply to believe
    Unless Hope is no more than wishful thinking
    Or Love a cynical disguise for lust.
Evidence and reason can relieve
    All valid doubt, and yet still leave us shrinking
    From what we do not love and will not trust.

Reason is necessary, not enough.
    Soul-conquering Love must come alongside, linking
    The mind in Hope to One who felt the thrust
Of all our hate and still looked back in love.
    In *Him* we trust.[34]

---

[34] Donald T. Williams, *Stars through the Clouds*, op. cit., p.185.

4

Five Theses on *Solus Christus*

Salvation can be by grace alone through faith alone because of who Christ is:

A. Christ stands supreme as the perfect image of the Father. ("And He is the radiance of His glory and the exact representation of His nature, and upholds all things by the word of His power," Heb. 1:3.)

B. Christ stands supreme as the Second Adam, the perfect template of unfallen human nature. (He is not only Son of God but also Son of Man, i.e., representative man, ideal man, and as the Second Adam, the Head of restored humanity.)

C. Christ stands supreme as the Lamb of God who taketh away the sins of the world. ("Without the shedding of blood there is no remission of sin," Heb. 9:22; "But God demonstrates His own love toward us in that, while we were yet sinners, Christ died for us," Rom. 5:8.)

D. Christ stands supreme as the only Mediator between God and man. ("For there is one God and one mediator also between God and men, the man Christ Jesus," 1 Tim. 2:4.)

E. Christ stands supreme as the King of Kings and Lord of Glory. ("He who is the blessed and only sovereign, the king of kings and lord of lords," 1 Tim. 6:15.)

The central reason why *solus Christus*, Christ alone, was one of the slogans of the historic Reformation was the need to counteract the tendency of medieval religion to multiply mediators, when Scripture says plainly that "There is one God and one mediator also between God and men, the man Christ Jesus" (1 Tim. 2:4). The Virgin Mary, saints, and angels, who are all asked to intercede for us, and the priest, who is needed both for confession and to consecrate the bread and wine and transform them into the literal body and blood of Jesus for the mass to work: the New Testament knows nothing of such a complex bureaucracy of intermediaries between the believer and his God. Contemporary Evangelicals need to be reminded of those issues, but even more perhaps they need to be reminded that their faith is faith in *Jesus*, not in a set of techniques for achieving a better earthly life. We will therefore look at five ways in which the supremacy of Christ fully justifies the Christocentric nature of biblical religion and of historic Evangelical faith.[35]

---

35 For further reading on the supremacy of Christ, you could not do better than John R. W. Stott, *The Incomparable Christ* (Downers Grove, Il.: InterVarsity Press, 2001) and John Owen's classic works *Christologia: Or, A Declaration of the Glorious Mystery of the Person of Christ* (1679) and *Meditations and Discourses on the Glory of Christ* (1648), both reprinted in vol. 1 of *The Works of John Owen*, ed. William H. Goold (Edinburgh: Banner of Truth, 1965). See also the relevant sections in the standard Evangelical systematic theologies, such as Hodge, Berkhof, Erickson, and Grudem.

Thesis 4a:
Christ Stands Supreme as the Perfect Image of the Father.

When the first Christians really wanted to boil the Gospel down, they could get it into two words: *Kyrios Christos*, "Jesus is Lord." And just in case you might miss the significance of that claim, He was not just Lord but "King of kings and Lord of lords" (1 Tim. 6:15). It might not be clear why it is Good News that there is such an absolute sovereign with whom we have to deal—until you realize that it is *Jesus* who holds this exalted position. We will look at five ways in which Jesus stands supreme, each of which makes it exceeding Good News that He does. And the first is that He stands supreme as the perfect image of the Father.

If God is the supreme Good and the source of all that is Good, True, and Beautiful, then the *summum bonum*, the ultimate good for which we were made and which alone can deeply fulfill us, is the beatific vision: to see Him face to face. But therein lies a problem: In our fallen state, that vision is so high and holy, so awful and majestic, that we could never handle it. No man has seen God at any time (John 1:18). Moses had to be protected by the cleft of a rock just to survive a glimpse of the backside of His glory (Ex. 33:19-23). Old Testament saints who saw even the Angel of the Lord—a *representative* of Yahweh appearing as a man—marveled that they were still alive afterwards. Isaiah, granted a Mosaic-type vision of the Lord's glory filling the Temple, responded with "Woe is me, for I am ruined! Because I am a man of unclean lips and live among a people of unclean lips, for my eyes have seen the King, the Lord of Hosts" (Is. 6:5). Only a coal from the altar applied to his lips allowed him to survive that vision. Hence the dilemma our Fall has created: Without that vision life would not be worth living for eternity, but with it in its fullness it cannot be lived by sinful men at all.

As a result of this reality, one of the unique features of Israelite religion in the Old Testament was the absolute prohibition of graven images. They were a staple of Canaanite worship, but they were forbidden to the Israelites by the Ten Commandments (Ex. 20:4-6), and the children of Israel were constantly being reminded of this fact. They were reminded that at Sinai when they had heard God's very voice speaking to them from the fire, they had seen no form (Deut. 4:12). They were not to think of God as something they could picture, because any image they formed of Him would be a diminution of His transcendent and holy Reality. Any image they were capable of creating would be a domestication of the divine Reality that would have the effect of corrupting their concept of God and desecrating His true Image. To avoid this, the Old Testament was very much a Dispensation of Distance.

Yet even in the old order there was another reality that hinted of a resolution of this impasse. There was one image of God that had been authorized by the Lord Himself: mankind. But Adam had fallen into sin, and so this image was not really usable any more either. It was a corrupted image like all the others, of four-footed beasts and creeping things. Nevertheless, One was coming who would restore this possibility. We do not understand it until we get to the New Testament, but when God the Son is incarnate as man, everything changes. We realize that God had not prohibited graven images because He did not want to be seen, but because he wanted to be seen only for who He is. Therefore, He cut us off from graven images in order to shut us up to the given Image: His Son Jesus Christ.

The depths of this truth are laid out for us in the prologue to John's Gospel. God expressed Himself fully, and that word—that *logos*—was born as the man Jesus and so made flesh and dwelt among us (John 1:1, 14). *Logos*, the Greek word translated "word," means not just a single isolated bit of vocabulary but word in the sense of a *message*, a rational discourse. It implies that the Son was full disclosure, as it were. Everything God wanted to tell us and show us about Himself, everything He *could* show us about Himself, was in Jesus; and that changes everything. No man has seen God at any time, but the uniquely begotten God who came from the Father has now revealed Him (1:18). And what He revealed was grace and truth (1:18). The image defaced by Adam's disobedience has now been restored. A clearer and fuller revelation of God than the smoke of Sinai or the cloud that filled the tabernacle or that shook Isaiah's Temple, a vision you can see without being blinded or slain, once walked among us. If you want to know who God is, look at Jesus.

Jesus stands supreme as the only answer to our need to see God, made otherwise impossible by our sins. He answers that need both by His deeds, by dying for our sins, but also simply by being who and what He is. "In Him all the fullness of God dwells in bodily form" (Col. 2:9). "And He is the radiance of His glory and the exact representation of His nature, and upholds all things by the word of His power" (Heb. 1:3). There is nothing greater or more exalting that can be said about Christ than this: "He who has seen me has seen the Father" (John 14:9). Amen.

Thesis 4b:
Christ Stands Supreme As the Second Adam, the Perfect Template of Unfallen Human Nature.

We have just seen that part of what makes it possible for the incarnate Christ to be the ultimate revelation of God, the perfect representation of His nature and His character, is the fact that Adam and Eve were originally created in God's image and likeness (Gen. 1:26-7). So the second aspect of Christ's supremacy is related to the first. He stands supreme not only as the perfect image of the Father but also as the Second Adam, the restoration of what Adam was meant to be, and thus the perfect template of unfallen human nature.

Jesus' favorite self-designation was not Messiah but "Son of Man." The full meaning of that elliptical phrase centers around two foci: an Old-Testament reference and a Hebrew idiom. The Old-Testament reference is Daniel 7:13-14.

> I kept looking in the night visions,
> And behold, with the clouds of heaven
> One like a Son of Man was coming,
> And He came up to the Ancient of Days
> And was presented before Him.
> And to Him was given dominion,
> That all the peoples, nations, and men of every language might serve Him.
> His dominion is an everlasting dominion which will not pass away,
> And His kingdom is one which will not be destroyed.

This is clearly a messianic figure. It combines the idea of the Davidic (messianic) kingdom with the promise to Abraham that his descendants would bless *every* family on earth (Gen. 12:3).

But who is this messianic king who will be granted a rule both universal and eternal? Here the Hebrew idiom comes into play. The phrase "son of X" means "one who has the characteristics of X in an exemplary or maximal way." When Jesus called James and John "sons of thunder" (Mark 3:17), he meant they were thunderous people, loud and boisterous. Judas, the "son of perdition" (John 17:12) is the quintessentially lost person; if you look up the word *lost* (a synonym of perdition) in the dictionary, Judas's picture should by all rights be next to the definition. Often the idiom is obscured by our modern translations. In Deuteronomy 25:2, the wicked man who in the NASB "deserves to be beaten" is literally "a son of stripes."

"Son of Man," then, means one who is the ideal human being, one who exemplifies the essential characteristics of humanity perfectly. If you look up the word *man* in the dictionary, you should by all rights see Jesus' picture next to the definition. We can't build a doctrine on an idiom alone, but the implications of this idiom combined with the Danielic reference are wonderfully consonant with the way the doctrine of Christ is developed in the New Testament, as we shall see. Indeed, the whole orthodox Christology as it would later be developed, "fully God and fully Man," is gloriously hinted at by the phrase "Son of Man" as Jesus used it.

Where this designation really becomes interesting is when we set it next to Paul's explanation of Christ as the Second Adam in Romans chapter five. There a parallelism is set up between Adam and Christ that aids us greatly in understanding why the plan of salvation works. Sin came into the world and brought death to all men through Adam's one act of disobedience, and righteousness comes to men in like manner through Christ's one act of obedience. The best explanation for this parallel is that underlying it is a relationship that both Adam and Jesus sustain to the human race, which theologians call "federal headship." Adam was not just the father of the human race but also its king and head, who thus stood before God as its *representative*, with full authority to make decisions in its behalf. Thus when he rebelled against God and chose to sin, he did it not as a private individual but as the head and king, *representing* all of us. He really had a kind of organic relationship to the race as a whole that made such a representative act completely legitimate, so that there is a sense in which we were actually there in him and are thus rightly condemned by his eating of the forbidden fruit. That is the reason why we are all born into sin. It is not that we inherit it genetically; it would be more accurate to say we inherit sin *dynastically*. "In Adam's fall / We sinned all."

And here is the beauty of the plan of salvation. Christ was a fresh start for the human race—a new dynasty, as it were. He is a new Head, who is thus, also by virtue of His unique relationship to us, fully authorized and able to act as our Representative—to act in our place, to act for us. Just as Adam's sin counted for all of us, so can Christ's sacrifice. When we confess Him as Lord—as our new federal Head—we are given the opportunity to replace Adam in that position so that we are now represented before the Throne not by Adam's rebellion but by Christ's loyalty, not by Adam's disobedience but by Christ's obedience, not by Adam's sin but by Christ's righteousness. That is the basis on which *Christ's* sacrifice can be accepted by God as paying for *our* sins, the basis on which, like Abraham, when we believe God it can be counted for us as righteousness. It is not just an arbitrary act when God counts Christ's death as having paid for our sins. He has the kind of relationship to us as the New Adam that makes that act of imputation perfectly rational, perfectly appropriate, and perfectly legitimate. This is the only way that can God be at the same time both just and the justifier of the one who has faith in Jesus (Rom. 3:26).

To see Christ as the Second Adam is to see more deeply into the rationale that qualifies Him to function as our Substitute. It helps us to understand what He did. It also gives us a new window into the beauty of who He is. When you look at Jesus you see the perfect image of the Father; you also see a picture in His human nature of what mankind was supposed to be. You see what Adam might have been like had he never fallen. You see the perfect template for human nature as it was designed to be, and as in Christ it will become. This vision is practical, for it shows us the goal or end at which our sanctification aims. It is also profound because it gives us a new way to appreciate the ways in which He is the One who is altogether lovely, the One who doeth all things well. He stands supreme not only as the perfect image of the Father but also as the Second Adam, the restoration of what Adam was meant to be, and thus the perfect template of unfallen human nature.

Thesis 4c:
Christ Stands Supreme As the Lamb of God Who Taketh Away the Sins of the World.

The third facet of the jewel which is the supremacy of Christ is His all-sufficient work as our Savior and Redeemer. He was, in the words of John the Baptist, "The Lamb of God who taketh away the sins of the world" (John 1:29). Like the idiom "Son of Man," this metaphor is rich with Old-Testament associations. It recalls the Passover lamb, who had to be "an unblemished male a year old" (Exodus 12:5). Its blood sprinkled on the doorposts caused the angel of death to pass over the Israelites and spare their firstborn in the last and climactic plague by which God delivered them from bondage in Egypt. Passover then is a picture of the atonement, with the lamb's blood covering the firstborn and protecting his life just as the blood of Christ functions in the propitiation He wrought on Calvary.

Calling Jesus the Lamb of God also speaks to the nature of the sacrificial victim: an unblemished male from the flock. Indeed, of every kind of sacrifice that requirement was repeated. "It must be perfect to be accepted" (Lev. 22:21). So the picture of Christ as the Lamb of God speaks eloquently of His sinlessness. He who knew no sin became sin for us (2 Cor. 6:21). "We do not have a high priest who cannot sympathize with our weaknesses but One who has been tempted in all things as we are, yet without sin" (Heb. 4:15).

We have already called Christ the perfect template for unfallen humanity, and this new affirmation refers to a specific aspect of that reality. He is pure and spotless, a completely sufficient sacrificial victim. As the Second Adam, Christ was qualified to stand for us as our Substitute. As the Lamb of God, He was qualified to do so as a Sacrifice for our sin. As the Son of Man, He was eligible to die for us. And as the Lamb of God, He was worthy to do so. One who was tainted by sin would have had his own payment to make, and could not make ours. As the Son of Man, Christ's death was relevant to our sin as a human death. As the infinite and divine Son of God, His death was of sufficient value to counterpoise all the sins of those who would come to believe in Him.

We can never fully appreciate what Jesus did for us by dying on the cross, because that would require an infinite capacity for appreciation. But we can take a step closer to fully appreciating it by fully absorbing the meaning of His titles. How absurd it is to say, "God could never forgive *my* sins!" Do you not understand who it was who died for them? Of course you don't. But can you begin to grasp the first inklings of the indescribable worthiness of this Life that was laid down for you? The perfection of His character, the beauty of His personality, the depths of His love, all multiplied beyond comprehension by the divinity of His Person: The Son of God was the Son of Man, and the Son of Man was the Lamb of God who taketh away the sins of the world. *That* Sacrifice was powerfully sufficient, yes, even for me and for you! Blessed be He.

Thesis 4d:
Christ Stands Supreme As the Only Mediator Between God and Man.

To begin to appreciate the worthiness of the One who made atonement for us is to begin to appreciate the completeness of that atonement. What could be added to a sacrifice so worthy? What could be left out of account by wisdom so unsearchable? What could be left undone by love so great? Some appreciation of these realities lay behind the Reformation's rejection of the corruptions of the church of their day. They made extorting a further payment for sin, whether of money or of penance, not only unbiblical but impious. And they made the multiplication of mediators not only unbiblical but blasphemous.

One of the realizations that comes across to us as we truly begin to grasp what God has given us in Christ is a dizzying vertigo at the unimaginable gap that has been spanned. From Heaven to earth, from holiness to fallenness, from infinity to finitude: It is all contained in the very Person of Christ Himself. "For in Him the fullness of deity dwells in bodily form" (Col. 2:9). It is there in the very dual designation: Son of God and Son of Man, both somehow encompassed in one Person. What we get simultaneously is the exaltation of Christ that we have been trying to hint at here and an equally amazing humility. In the beginning was the Word, and the Word was with God and the Word was God . . . and the Word was made flesh and dwelt among us (John 1:1, 14). "What manner of man is this that even the winds and the sea obey Him?" (Mark 4:41). "Suffer the little children to come unto me" (Mark 10:15). "And His face shone like the sun, and His garments became as white as light" (Mat. 17:2). "Come unto me, all ye that are weary and heavy laden, and I will give you rest" (Mat. 11:28).

The point is that Jesus as He is narrated in the Gospels is simultaneously high and humble, awe-inspiring and accessible, exalted and approachable. It is His exaltation that makes His approachability so astonishing and wonderful. Jesus as He is explained in the Epistles has both of those qualities, and we are exhorted to forget neither while making full use of the latter. Because we have a high priest who can sympathize with us, having been tempted in all the ways we are but without sin, "Therefore let us draw near *with confidence* to the throne of grace" (Heb. 4:16, emphasis added). On that throne Christ now sits at the Father's right hand to make intercession for us (Eph. 1:20, Heb. 7:25), and from there He sends the Holy Spirit who enables us to cry, "Abba! Father!" (Rom. 8:15) with supreme confidence in our adoption as sons and daughters of God. It is *Jesus* who represents us there! It is the Jesus about whom we have been speaking throughout this chapter. What else could we possibly need?

In late medieval piety, Jesus was considered high and lifted up, and rightly so, but He had lost the accessibility that shines through the Gospels, and His people had lost something of the understanding that He had come precisely to grant us that kind of accessibility to the very throne of God. That role had somehow gotten transferred to his mother, Mary. I have read many devotional works from that period. In all of them Mary gets twice as much space allotted to her and three times as much emotional energy expended on her as Christ Himself does. A slightly less blatant version of the same sentiment still exists in certain quarters today. Such devotion is well meant and sincere, but it is a little off—disproportionate and misdirected. It is ultimately sub-Christian.

We should honor Mary as a great woman of faith whose sacrificial obedience should be an example to us all. Protestants should not overreact to her elevation to an improper status by fearing to say so. But she herself, precisely as that woman of faith and obedience, would be the first one to demur at being elevated to a position where she rivals her Son in our affections or shares the stage with Him as our Intercessor. No. Paul had it right all along: "There is one God and *one Mediator* between God and men, the Man Christ Jesus" (1 Tim. 2:5). It is Jesus. Nothing else and no one else is needed. It is He, and He alone, who enables us and encourages us to approach the throne with confidence. He stands supreme as the only Mediator between God and man.

Thesis 4e:
Christ Stands Supreme as the King of Kings and Lord of Glory.

Most Evangelicals are not tempted to Mariolatry. They have made idols out of far less worthy objects: health, wealth, success, popularity, political power, comfortable emotions . . . sound doctrine. Even right doctrine can become an idol, when you care more about winning arguments than you do about the Lord those arguments are allegedly about. I shall waste no time exposing the unworthiness of these substitutes for what is supposed to be our deepest love and highest pursuit. I shall simply continue trying to exalt the One who so preeminently deserves all our worship, all our devotion, and all our obedience. If we truly desire a new Reformation of the church, we must begin by putting Him back in the center of it.

We started the first thesis of this section with the reminder that when the first Christians really wanted to boil the Gospel down, they could get it into two words: *Kyrios Christos*, "Jesus is Lord." The very word *Messiah* (Hebrew—in Greek, *Christos*) means "anointed one," and the anointing in question was that by which a man was prophetically set aside to be king of Israel (1 Sam. 9:16, 10:1, 16:12-13). That Jesus is Lord is Good News, the Gospel, precisely because He is the Jesus we have been attempting so inadequately to describe in these last theses. But apparently some Evangelicals have missed this connection between the Gospel and Jesus' lordship. It seems so because they are capable of arguing about whether Jesus can be accepted first as Savior without being accepted as Lord, and they accuse those who deny this strange proposal of teaching a new doctrine called "lordship salvation."

There is not a single New-Testament passage over which this overlay of accepting Jesus as Savior now and Lord later can fit without terrible distortion. What was the Philippian Jailer told in the most succinct summary of the Gospel? "Believe on the *Lord* Jesus Christ and thou shalt be saved" (Acts 16:30-31, emphasis added). What about Paul's more definitive summary? "If you confess with your mouth Jesus *as Lord* and believe in your heart that God has raised

Him from the dead, you shall be saved" (Rom. 10:9, emphasis added). There is simply no Jesus narrated or described or expounded or proclaimed anywhere in the New Testament who is not Lord, nor is there one whose Lordship is ever presented as optional. To seek salvation by believing in such a Jesus is to put your faith in a false Christ, a Christ who does not exist. Why is His Lordship essential to the Gospel? Because it is *as the King* that He has the authority to pardon your rebellion against God's Kingdom and restore you to citizenship. Recognizing Him as the true King is not an extra requirement in addition to believing in Him; it is simply part of believing in Him. You simply cannot ask for the pardon without acknowledging His authority to grant it. You believe on the *Lord* Jesus Christ to be saved by grace alone through faith alone.

Opponents of what they call "lordship salvation" fear the reintroduction of works as a ground of salvation (cf. theses 2c-e), as if we were demanding perfect obedience as a kind of precondition before faith can save us. That fear is healthy, but its application in this case is unwarranted, misguided, and unbiblical. None of us has any such perfect obedience to offer, nor will have until we see Christ face to face. We all stumble, sometimes rather badly. No one is saved by achieving a good enough performance at not stumbling; we are saved by grace and by grace alone. But the question remains, on what road are we stumbling? What are we stumbling toward? If you do not believe in the *Lord* Jesus Christ, if you do not confess Him *as Lord*, you are not yet on the right road at all.

Part of the reformation needed by many Evangelicals today is a restored commitment to the Lordship of Christ. Some of us need to proclaim it more forthrightly, not fearing that it is somehow in tension with *sola gratia* any more than the Apostles did. And some of us need to forsake our idolatry. Jesus is Lord. He is not the servant of our agenda. He is not a means to our ends, whether health and wealth or a better marriage or emotional serenity. He is the absolute sovereign over Heaven and earth. He deserves to be. Every knee is going to bow before Him and every tongue is going to proclaim that He is Lord to the glory of God the Father (Phil. 2:10-11). Ours should be doing so already. He stands supreme as King of Kings and Lord of Lords. And we are His servants. Amen.

Conclusion

Christ stands supreme as the perfect image of the Father, as the perfect template for restored humanity, as the Lamb of God who taketh away the sins of the world, as the only Mediator between God and man, and as the Lord of Lords and King of Kings. The Reformers needed to counteract the tendency to multiply mediators, but even if there had never been any such tendency, Christ would deserve to be exalted because of who He is, first, and what He is to us as well. It is impossible to express all that we owe to Him, but Calvin comes close:

> When we see that the whole sum of our salvation, and every single part of it, are comprehended in Christ, we must beware of deriving even the minutest portion of it from any other quarter. . . . If we seek redemption, we shall find it in his passion; acquittal in his condemnation; remission of the curse in his cross; satisfaction in his sacrifice; purification in his blood; reconciliation in his descent into hell; mortification of the flesh in his sepulcher; newness of life in his resurrection; immortality in his resurrection; the inheritance of a celestial kingdom in his entrance into heaven; protection, security, and the abundant supply of all blessings in his kingdom. . . . In fine, since in him all kinds of blessings are treasured up, let us draw a full supply from him, and none from any other quarter.[36]

Praise Him!

---

36 John Calvin, *Institutes of the Christian Religion*, 2 vol., trans. Henry Beveridge (Grand Rapids: Eerdmans, 1975), p. 1:452.

Interlude

Hymn: Spiritual Vision

To the tune of "Amazing Grace"

The gaping sockets blankly stare
   Beneath the bony crown,
Skull-like, always grinning there:
   The Hill outside the town.

A lonely sentinel, it stands
   With shadow grim and chill
Above the landscape it commands:
   The Tree upon the Hill.

The very Sun would hide its face,
   Not strong enough to see
The blight now brought to such a place:
   The Man upon the Tree.

But sunlight never could have showed
   Nor eye of flesh have scanned
The grievous Burden of the Load
   That rested on the Man.

Only weakness could have won,
   Only frailty freed
Us from the Burden laid upon
   The Man upon the Tree.[37]

---

37 Donald T. Williams, *Stars through the Clouds*, op. cit., p. 153.

"Surely, This Man Was..."

The Centurion Speaks

"Things are not always what they seem: we drove
    The spikes through wrist and ankle bones to bind
    The criminals up on the cross. We spliced
Their flesh to wood with iron; thus we strove
    To make secure what fates the gods had twined—
    And generally that view of things sufficed.

But that last Jew clean put me at a loss
    To tell what held up what. Have I gone blind?
    No! I would swear that, when he paid the price,
I saw the world suspended by the cross
    From Christ."[38]

---

38 Ibid., p. 152.

5

Five Theses on *Soli Deo Gloria*

Every false view of salvation and every corrupted practice of the Christian life flows from the worship of a lesser god. These may be the most crucial theses in the book, then, for every problem in the church eventually finds its way back to them.

A. God's ultimate purpose in the salvation of sinners is His own glory. (Salvation is "to the praise of the glory of His grace," Eph. 1: 6; cf. 1:12, 1:14.)

B. God's glory is the manifestation of His perfect and holy character in all its awesome and majestic splendor throughout the whole of creation. (It is the sum of His attributes, and the work of Christ in the salvation of sinners its highest expression.)

C. Salvation is not primarily for our benefit. (We benefit from it greatly, but something much larger is at stake.)

D. God's pursuit of His own glory is not selfish, because the glory of God is not just His greatest good; it is *the* greatest good, and therefore our greatest good. (It would be wrong, hence inconceivable, for God *not* to make His own glory His highest aim.)

E. The vision and manifestation of God's glory should be our highest purpose and deepest joy. (This is what makes life worth living for all of eternity.)

There was a fifth slogan of the historic Reformation, a fifth *sola* that is often forgotten today: *Soli Deo Gloria*, "glory to God alone." Johan Sebastian Bach remembered it. The great Lutheran church musician, universally recognized as the greatest contrapuntalist, and by some as simply the greatest composer who ever lived, wrote endless anthems and cantatas for church worship ("Jesu, Joy of Man's Desiring"), a number of "secular" concert pieces (*The Brandenburg Concertos*), and a popular keyboard primer (*The Anna Magdalena Bach Book*). He treated all of them the same. At the top of the first page of the manuscript he started with the Latin initials for *Jesu juva*, "Jesus, help me." And at the bottom of the last page he finished with *Soli Deo Gloria*, "glory to God alone." What did Bach understand that we need to recapture if we want to see a new Reformation today?[39]

---

39   For further reading on the centrality of God and His glory in salvation, see J. I. Packer's classic *Knowing God* (Downers Grove, Il.: InterVarsity Press, 1973 and the first volume of D. Martyn Lloyd-Jones's collection of sermons on Ephesians, *God's Ultimate Purpose: An Exposition of Ephesians 1* (Grand Rapids: Eerdmans, 1978).

Thesis 5a:
God's Ultimate Purpose in the Salvation of Sinners Is His Own Glory.

God's purpose in the salvation of sinners is His own glory? That is not the first answer most of us would give if we were asked why God saves sinners. We would probably respond that it is out of love, and we would not be wrong. "For God so loved the world that He gave His only begotten Son, that whosoever believeth in Him should not perish, but have eternal life" (John 3:16). But there is something else going on too: God works in everything, and especially in salvation, supremely for His own glory; or the Father does it with the glory of the Son, and the Son with the glory of the Father, in mind: "Father, the hour is come. Glorify thy Son, that the Son may glorify Thee" (John 17:1).

This is a perspective that is conspicuously absent from much contemporary preaching and evangelism, but it is essential to an accurate understanding of the Gospel, and even of why the Gospel is good news. It is emphasized three times in the opening section of Paul's epistle to the Ephesians as a kind of refrain for emphasis. Paul there is giving a summary of the plan of salvation, of all that the whole Trinity has done to save us. Why did God the Father conceive the plan of salvation and elect us to sonship? To the praise of the glory of His grace (v. 6). Why did God the Son redeem us through His blood? That we should be to the praise of His glory (v. 12). And why did God the Holy Spirit seal us for redemption as a pledge of our inheritance? To the praise of His glory (v. 14b).

But we find this doctrine not just here; it is a major theme of the whole Bible You find it implied or stated in passages such as Ex. 3:12, 7:3-5, 9:16, 40:34, Ps. 19:1, 79:9, and Is.48:9-11. Israel was brought out of Egypt that she might *worship* in the wilderness. The purpose of the plagues was so that Pharaoh would know that Yahweh is God, and He alone. By allowing Pharaoh to live, God will demonstrate His power and proclaim His name through all the earth. The glory of the Lord filled the Tabernacle, and then the Temple, at their dedications. The very heavens broadcast His glory, as the firmament shows His handiwork. Why does God delay His wrath? For the sake of His own name! "For my own sake, for my own sake I will act; for how can my name be profaned? And my glory I will not give to another" (Is. 48:9-11). But the climax of the theme appears in the Lord's great high priestly prayer, in John 17:1. What was foremost in the mind of Christ as He was facing the great crisis of His life, at the fulfillment of His purpose for coming into the world? What was foremost on His mind as he was facing the Cross and spiritually preparing Himself for it? "Father the hour is come. Glorify thy Son that the Son may glorify thee."

Yes, God loves us, and yes, salvation has our good in mind. But the emphasis is inescapable: God's ultimate purpose is His own glory. We see it first in in the creation of the universe: What God ultimately achieves in the existence of the universe, is His own glory. The universe accomplishes this purpose simply by existing in all its intricate design and glorious splendor, but it accomplishes it even more profoundly as the setting for a Narrative through which God's glory achieves even more piercing clarity: the creation, fall, redemption, adoption, and glorification by grace alone of God's ultimate creation, made in His very image. God's greatest glory comes from His greatest work; His greatest work is the salvation of sinners. And so God's *ultimate* purpose in the salvation of sinners, what He ultimately achieves in their salvation, is His own glory—not incidentally but by design. God's glory is the ultimate purpose of every atomic particle, every creature, every event that has providentially been allowed to happen. It all works together for His glory as much as for the good of those who love Him.

Thesis 5b:
God's Glory Is the Manifestation of His Perfect and Holy Character in All Its Awesome and Majestic Splendor throughout the Whole of Creation.

Thesis 5a makes the glory of God an awfully important concept. We had better get it right. What then do we mean when we talk about God's glory? What does it mean to say that it is the ultimate purpose of creation, culminating as the ultimate purpose of salvation? If we were to trace the word "glory" through the Bible, we would find it associated with the presence of God and the nature of God. It burns from the top of Sinai so that people have to be warned not to touch the mountain (Ex. 19:16-25, 24:9-18). Moses has to be protected even from the trailing edge of it by the cleft of a rock—as God passed by and proclaimed His name, that is, the essence of His nature, of who He is (Ex. 33:18-23). His glory fills the Tabernacle and then the Temple so that the priests cannot stand to minister (Ex. 40:43-38, 1 Kings 8:10-13). It shakes even the heavenly Temple in Isaiah's vision as he hears the Seraphim crying out, "Holy, holy, holy is the Lord God of Hosts! Heaven and earth are full of His glory!" (Is. 6:1f). It shines from the face of the ultimate revelation of God, Jesus Christ (2 Cor. 4:3-6) because it was the fruit of the climax of His saving work at the Cross (John 17:1).

How do we put all of this together? I would define the glory of God as the manifestation of His perfect and holy character in all its awesome and majestic splendor throughout the whole of creation. This definition is already in bold in the thesis above, but it is so important that I'm going to repeat it a third time to make sure we do not miss it. *God's glory is the manifestation of His perfect and holy character in all its awesome and majestic splendor throughout the whole of creation.* Manifestation: Angels and men were created so that God's glory could be seen, understood, marveled at, and worshipped. His perfect and holy character: It is His very nature and essence, His personality and His heart, in so far as they are sharable at all with finite beings, which are to be revealed. Awesome and majestic splendor: Words fail to capture how great, how weighty, how shatteringly good this revelation is. Throughout the whole of creation: No canvass could be sufficient for this painting, no screen for this film; but all the vast reaches of space and time are there to impress us small ones with as much of it as we can grasp. From the mightiest super-galaxy cluster to the smallest quark, it all has the same message: Behold the glory of the Lord!

Alright, then, what does it mean to say that God's glory is the purpose of salvation? It means that for God's character to be revealed to men and angels is the greatest good conceivable; that it is the highest value imaginable; that it is the ultimate reason for which the world was made. That is why Creation glorifies God: the heavens declare His glory and the firmament shows His handiwork (Ps. 19:1). "For since the creation of the world His invisible attributes, His eternal power and divine nature, have been clearly seen, being understood through what has been made" (Rom. 1:20). The world's stubborn persistence in existence despite its utter contingency; its elegant design; its fine tuning for life: All speak eloquently not just of the existence but of the dynamic creative energy and incomprehensibly brilliant intelligence of its Maker.

As impressive as the voice of the universe is, the most profound way God is glorified in the history of this creation is through the salvation of sinners. First is the very existence of persons created in the image of that inscrutably glorious Maker, capable of their own derivative creativity which made possible art and culture and even gave them the capacity to depart from His commandment and fall. Then comes the utterly unpredictable response to that fall: the history of Abraham and the People of faith who followed him, who were redeemed from slavery, received the Law, and gave the world a Hope that could overcome even the depths of its fall.

And then we have the fruition of that Hope. The virgin birth, sinless life, atoning death, and triumphant resurrection of Christ; the work of the Holy Spirit in calling out of the Gentiles a people for His name, regenerating them, sanctifying them, uniting them in one body, the Church, and keeping them for final union with Christ: All this reveals the nature and character of God and writes it indelibly on the pages of space, time, and history in the fullest and deepest manner conceivable. At the Cross we see the justice of God demanding the death penalty for sin, the love of God taking that penalty on Himself, the wisdom of God reconciling the apparently contradictory claims of love and justice, and the power of God in the resurrection of the crucified Savior. What could manifest the depths of God's character, the heart of who He is, more profoundly? Nothing. But it does not end there. The fullness of the provision for His own, the work of the Spirit in behalf of the Son to convict them of sin, call them to faith, regenerate them, sanctify them, keep them, and finally unite them to the Son in such a way that they share his glory forever: "Please, Aslan," said Lucy, "can anything be done to save Edmund?" "All shall be done," said Aslan.[40] In all of this, then, God is glorified. For God's ultimate purpose in the salvation of sinners is His own glory.

---

40 C. S. Lewis, *The Lion, the Witch, and the Wardrobe* (1950; N.Y.: Harper Collins, 1978), p. 141.

Thesis 5c:
Salvation Is Not Primarily for Our Benefit.

A sobering fact follows from this realization. Salvation is nor primarily for our benefit. Now, do not misunderstand me. God does love us, and salvation does bless us, designedly so. But that can no longer be viewed as the *primary* consideration, as if salvation were all about us. Yet we think it is. Just listen to our typical testimonies: "*My* pardon, *my* exemption from the flames of Hell, *my* adoption, *my* personal peace (and health and wealth?) here and now, and *my* final fulfillment in Heaven—Wait a minute! What are you saying? I thought salvation *was* all about me!" But while those things are all involved in salvation (well, maybe not health and wealth), they are not the primary thing. The primary thing is that we begin to catch glimpses of the glory of God and that we live to see more of them and to make them visible to others. *That* is what makes salvation worth having. That is what makes God worthy of our love. That is what makes the Christian life worth living here and now. That, and nothing less than that, could make it worth living for all eternity. But there, for some, lies a problem.

The definition of this doctrine then leads us inevitably to its difficulty. This emphasis on God's glory as His own ultimate purpose makes many modern Christians profoundly uneasy. I suppose that is understandable. After all, it evicts us from the center of things; it is a frontal attack on our human pride. Rather than being the apple of God's eye, we might feel like mere pawns in a cosmic chess match. But there is a more noble reason for objecting to it than that. It might seem to make God appear selfish, less than altruistic; it might appear to be a blot on His character. We would rather think He did everything purely out of love for us, with no concern for Himself or His own glory at all. We don't mind His receiving glory from our salvation. We're even rather glad that He does. But we want that to be a pleasant side-effect, a fortunate afterthought, not the end that was aimed at in the very beginning.

Why don't we like the idea that the end of salvation is the glory of God? It's as if we discovered that a millionaire who had given much money to charity and spent hours volunteering in the community had done it only for the good publicity it brought his company. Rather than flowing from his unselfish concern for his fellow citizens, his acts really flowed from and fed his ego. In such a case, the very good deeds that had once brought such polish to the fellow's name would now seem rather to tarnish it. It would leave a bad taste in our mouth. Motives matter, and we don't think good deeds done for an unworthy motive are really all that admirable. And we are right to think so, as far as human beings are concerned. Therefore, when it comes to salvation, we would prefer to think of God as purely altruistic, motivated only by love for us. We don't want to think of Him as selfish in any way. Again, we are not wrong. So if we are not careful, this very emphasis on God's glory might seem to detract from His glory rather than promote it. Therefore, having grasped the definition of the doctrine and looked squarely at its difficulty, we need to look carefully at the defense of the doctrine. It is found in the next thesis.

Thesis 5d:
God's Pursuit of His Own Glory Is Not Selfish, Because the Glory of God Is Not Just His Greatest Good; It Is *the* Greatest Good, and Therefore Our Greatest Good.

The first line of defense for the idea that God purposes His own Glory as the end of salvation is that the Bible teaches it. We have already sufficiently demonstrated that this is inescapably true in Thesis 5a, and that ought to settle the matter. But it is always useful, if we can, to understand *why* the Bible teaches something. The rationale behind a doctrine may be as important as the fact, especially when we start trying to apply it practically. Besides, we will not fully and wholeheartedly be able to ascribe to God the glory coming to Him from our own salvation unless the objection is met and any stumbling block to our full embracing of the idea removed. Therefore, there is a second line of defense against the charge of divine "selfishness." Why does God seek His own glory? *A proper understanding of who God is demands it.*

Our uneasiness with the idea of God seeking His own glory is based on a false analogy. You see, it would be wrong for us to seek our own glory, and we know that. So we mistakenly transfer that feeling to God. We look at Him seeking His own glory as we would look at our fellow creatures doing it, and it leaves a bad taste in our mouths. But it is *not* wrong for God to do so, because He is not like us; more importantly, He occupies a very different position in the scheme of things than we do. He is the Creator; we are the created. He is eternal and infinite and dwells in unapproachable light; we are weak sinners who dwell in dolorous darkness. He is completely self-sufficient; we are utterly dependent on Him. Therefore, all glory *belongs* to Him as an inalienable right; it does not belong to us. He belongs in the center; we do not.

Seeking my own glory is idolatry when I do it, because I am a creature. My purpose is to serve the Creator, not to serve myself. It is to worship the Creator, not to take to myself the honor that belongs to Him and to Him alone. But for the One who *is* the Creator, manifesting His own glory is just telling the truth. It is just God being true to reality. It is just God being God. Therefore, the falseness that is inherent in attempts to seek our own glory does not apply to God at all. And the feeling of "selfishness" we get from this doctrine does not apply to God at all either. The glory of God is not just His greatest good; it is *the* greatest good—period—and therefore it is *our* greatest good. There is nothing better, more loving, more unselfish, more generous, more altruistic, more magnanimous that God could do for us than allow us to glimpse His glory and participate in its revelation to others. To see the glory of God in the face of Jesus Christ and to have it manifested in and through us as a result of that vision: What greater gift could there be? If we could imagine a salvation which did not include that gift, it would, in comparison, hardly be worth having. If we want to maximize the value of the salvation we have been given, God's making His own glory central to it is the best thing He could have done.

Do you see? A proper understanding of who God is demands this understanding of His motives, His purpose in all that He does. The glory of God is not just His greatest good; it is *the* greatest good. If God is morally perfect, then He must always pursue the greatest good. Because He is perfectly wise, He will never confuse it with lesser goods, as we often do. Because He is perfectly good, He will never choose those lesser goods over the greatest good. Because of who He is, therefore—because He is God—It would be wrong for Him *not* to seek His own glory. To seek His own glory is not then an act of selfishness at all; it is precisely the most loving thing God can do for us. And that is why God's ultimate purpose in the salvation of sinners is His own glory. This defense of the doctrine leads us then to the delights of the doctrine.

Thesis 5e:
The Vision and Manifestation of God's Glory Should Be Our Highest Purpose and Deepest Joy.

Ironically, evicting ourselves from the center and putting God's glory there enhances all the benefits *we* derive from salvation. In other words, forgetting our own profit from it as being what salvation is all about is actually the shortest and surest path to our own joy and blessing. This is so in at least three ways.

First, remembering that salvation is mainly about the glory of God gives us a new perspective on pain and affliction. For the Christian life does not exempt us from pain and suffering in this life. In fact, while it brings great joy, in certain ways it may actually increase our opportunities to experience suffering, as it certainly did for the martyrs. Being fed to lions or burned at the stake is not exactly the most pleasant experience one could have. But life in a fallen world has sorrow enough even if we are never called upon to suffer in that way. So if our Christianity is man-centered (really, self-centered) rather than God-centered, if we cling to the erroneous view that God's work is primarily about us and our benefit, then the pains, sorrows, and frustrations of living in a fallen world must inevitably appear to us as defects in our salvation. The inexorable logic of a self-centered salvation must eventually cause us to doubt God's benevolence and kindness toward us, which can only lead to a vicious cycle of spiritual defeat. But if our Christianity is God-centered, then suffering becomes an opportunity to fulfill our purpose by glorifying Him rather than an occasion for doubt.

When Francis Schaeffer was dying of cancer, he was asked if he prayed to be healed. Of course, he replied, in the taped interview that was appended to the film series *How Shall We Then Live*? But even more he prayed that God would be glorified in his illness. Whether God received glory by healing him or by letting him show how a Christian faced death was immaterial to Schaeffer, and completely up to the Lord. This is the right attitude for us to have—and what a liberating attitude it is! How so? It is undeniable that when the Holy Spirit enables a believer to show Christlike character in the midst of suffering, God is glorified. Suffering is going to be part of life in a fallen world until Christ returns. It is inescapable. To understand the purpose of salvation as God-centered is to be spared the agony of compounding that suffering with doubt. It has a double benefit: We are spared the difficulties of doubt and we are set free to experience the ultimate fulfillment of our natures by living to the glory of God.

Second, seeing God's glory as the ultimate end of salvation gives us, paradoxically, a greater enjoyment of the benefits of salvation. For a secondary purpose of salvation *is* our benefit. But those benefits can only be fully enjoyed when they are not our primary focus. This truth becomes obvious when you think about it. A focus on yourself will kill your enjoyment even of earthly pleasures. A person who asks himself, "Am I enjoying this concert? Am I having an esthetic experience here?" is not. If he were, he would not be thinking about himself or his enjoyment at all, but rather about the music. We even say of a person who is truly enjoying the concert that he has "lost himself" in the music. We might say he has been "taken out of himself" by it. Curiously appropriate expressions! Those are our moments of greatest joy.

The same principle holds true on the spiritual level. Do you want the joy of salvation? Don't try to be joyful; worship God. Do you want more faith? Don't focus on your faith or your lack of it; just serve the Lord with what little you have. Do you want Christian fellowship? Stop thinking about whether you are having fellowship and love the brethren. Do you want to know the blessings of salvation? Forget about your own benefit and focus on the glory of God.

Finally, to see God's central purpose in salvation as His own glory is to gain a greater grasp of spiritual victory. Diluted Christian living flows from belief in a diluted Gospel. Therefore, examine the Gospel you believe in. Is it a man-centered Gospel? Does it contain the subtle assumption that all this is done just for our benefit? Brothers and sisters, there is something far greater at stake in our salvation than that! The Gospel is the power of God for salvation for those who believe (Rom. 1:16) Let us then believe it in all its full, unmitigated, theocentric potency—to the eternal glory of the living God.

Conclusion

It is the forgotten *Sola* in the Reformers' classic summary of the biblical Gospel. Not only *Sola Scriptura*, Scripture alone, *Sola Gratia*, Faith alone, and *Sola Fide*, Faith alone; there is also *Solus Christus*, Christ alone, and the greatest truth of all, *Soli Deo Gloria*, glory to God alone. It is the apex and climax of the series. It is the meaning and rationale of them all, without which the others are incomplete. Calvin expresses the whole connectedness of the relation between every aspect of salvation and God's glory beautifully:

> For what accords better and more rightly with faith than to acknowledge ourselves divested of all virtue that we may be clothed by God, devoid of all goodness that we may be filled by Him, the slaves of sin that He may give us freedom, blind that he may enlighten, lame that he may cure, and feeble that he may sustain us; to strip ourselves of all ground of glorying that he alone may shine forth glorious and we be glorified in him?[41]

If we long to see real Reformation in the church again, let us return to the God-centered Gospel of the Bible and make His glory our greatest good. And if you do not yet know the Lord as your personal Redeemer and King, receive Him today, and begin to experience in your life the greatest good of all: the glory of God.

---

41 John Calvin, *Institutes of the Christian Religion*, trans. Henry Beveridge, 2 vols. (Grand Rapids: Eerdmans, 1975), p. 1:6.

Interlude

Conjunction

At the fulcrum of the Cross
A host of concepts meet:
The Profit hidden in the Loss,
The Victory in Defeat.

The Acceptance, the Rejection;
The Worship and the Jeers;
The Freedom in Election,
The Ecstasy in Tears.

The Mercy and the Justice;
The Human, the Divine;
Pilate; Judas; Jesus—
The broken Bread, the Wine.

The Maker of Orion,
The Victim of the Scam;
The Meekness of the Lion,
The glory of the Lamb.[42]

---

42 Donald T. Williams, *Stars through the Clouds*, op. cit., p. 163.

Commentary, 1 Cor. 13:12

The Southern Appalachians
  In their autumn glory dressed
Are all the beauty we can bear,
  Or in which we can rest.

The mighty hills of Heaven,
  With their oppressive weight,
Would crush our spirits into dust,
  Seen in our present state.

But when they burst upon us
  In sudden majesty,
We will be given souls to match
  And purer eyes to see.[43]

---

43 Ibid., p. 96.

6
Five Theses on Hermeneutics

If Scripture is our norm, then all right practice flows from the right use of Scripture, enabled by grace. Therefore, nothing is more important than sound interpretation, because sound interpretation allows the Word to speak for itself.

A. Context is everything. (Context is *immediate*, related to the surrounding passages in the work; *generic*, participating in a particular form or style of writing; *canonical*, related to the progressive unfolding of revelation in the Bible as a whole; *linguistic*, related to the original language; *historical*, related to the time and situation of the document's original composition; *cultural*, related to the culture of the original writer and audience; *ecclesiastical*, related to the understanding and use of the passage in the history of the church; and *personal*, related to its application to the reader. The personal must be in line with the other forms of context.)

B. The original meaning has primacy. (The passage means what it would have meant to the audience for which it was originally written. Application to current issues can begin only after that original meaning has been ascertained.)

C. Interpretation must use the *Analogia Fidei*. (All Scripture ultimately agrees. Therefore, no passage should be interpreted in such a way that it contradicts any other passage, nor should any doctrine be based on a single passage in isolation.)

D. Interpretation must recognize that all Scripture is profitable *in the way it claims to be*. (All our teaching should be "profitable for doctrine, reproof, for correction, and for training in righteousness," 2 Tim. 3:16. It should "further the administration of God which is by faith" and promote "love from a pure heart, a good conscience and a sincere faith," 1 Tim. 1:4-5. Therefore, any interpretation that is merely speculative or which leads only to wrangling about words is either faulty or incomplete.)

E. Interpretation must recognize that Christ is the key to all. (As Martin Luther said, "The whole Scripture is about Christ only, everywhere." The Old Testament prepares for His coming and predicts it; the New Testament narrates it, explains it, and applies it. Therefore we must always ask, "How does this passage teach us to love Jesus, to trust him, to glorify his Name, to proclaim his Gospel, to advance his Kingdom, to edify his Church, or to please him by doing his Will?")

I have spent several summers over the last decade and a half training rural pastors in places like Uganda, Kenya, and India, where the church is growing faster than it can train leaders. These men have great zeal but no formal schooling in Bible, theology, homiletics, etc. With each trip I take, I am led to spend more time on hermeneutics, the science and art of interpretation. Why? Every cult you have ever heard of and two hundred more that don't have a name are swarming all over those countries—and they all come quoting Scripture. The pastors I am teaching know the Gospel, and they sense that something is wrong. But they do not know how to explain *why* one use of Scripture is legitimate and another is not. As teachers of the church, that is one thing they definitely need to know how to do—and they realize it. I have never seen eyes light up the way theirs do when I explain some of the simple principles in this chapter. They know I am giving them ammunition they desperately need for the spiritual warfare that confronts them.

Many American Christians have the same weakness—only, unlike my African and Indian pastors, they are blissfully unaware of their need. In the Bible we have the truth—in the Bible as it was written, which is not necessarily the Bible as you understand it. The truth is what the Bible says, not what you feel like it says. So if the Bible alone has magisterial authority (thesis 1b) and if we have the responsibility to hear it correctly (thesis 1d), then there can be no faithful Christianity and no reformation of the church without a recovery of commitment to sound procedures of Bible study, based on the nature of the revelation that God gave us in Scripture. This chapter then is necessary. But it is only a brief introduction to hermeneutics, not a complete course in it. Nevertheless, here are five critical principles to help us be faithful to what Scripture actually teaches.[44]

---

44 For further reading on hermeneutics, excellent resources include Louis Berkhof, *Principles of Biblical Interpretation* (Grand Rapids: Baker, 1950), E. D. Hirsch, *Validity in Interpretation* (New Haven, Ct.: Yale Univ. Pr., 1967), Walter C. Kaiser, Jr., *Toward an Exegetical Theology: Biblical Exegesis for Preaching and Teaching* (Grand Rapids: Baker, 1981), J. Robertson McQuilkin, *Understanding and Interpreting the Bible* (Chicago: Moody, 1992), J. I. Packer, *God Has Spoken* (Downers Grove, Il.: InterVarsity Press, 1970), Bernard Ramm, *Protestant Biblical Interpretation* (Grand Rapids: Baker, 1970), and James W. Sire, *Scripture Twisting: Twenty Ways the Cults Misread the Bible* (Downers Grove, Il.: InterVarsity Press, 1980). Most importantly, see *The Chicago Statements on Biblical Inerrancy and Biblical Hermeneutics*, available online at http://www.danielakin.com/wp-content/uploads/old/Resource_545/Book%202,%20Sec%2023.pdf.

Thesis 6a:
Context Is Everything.

Words have meaning. Meaning is a relationship, a relationship between a speaker, an audience, a word, a concept, and a thing or referent. So words have meaning in their relations to those elements of the act of communication, all of which must be taken into account. Does the word *house* for example mean a dwelling ("my house"), a family ("house and lineage"), the people present in a room debating a proposition ("Be it resolved that his house believes . . ."), or a branch of congress ("the house of representatives")? The answer depends on factors like who is using the word, to whom it is being said, in what circumstances, at what period of history, and in what kind of combination with what other words, in what grammatical structures. The general term for all those relationships is *context*. By etymology from its Latin roots, context refers to all the things the "text" is "with." If you get all those relationships right, you will probably get the meaning right.

There are at least eight different relationships, eight different contexts, that have to be considered when we want to be sure about the meaning of a passage of Scripture. The first is IMMEDIATE CONTEXT: How do the words and sentences we are reading relate to the words and sentences immediately around them? Here we must remember that the chapter and verse divisions in our modern Bibles were not part of the original text. They were added later to help us find passages more easily, and they certainly work well for that purpose. But they were not inspired and can sometimes be misleading and obscure the immediate context. For example, in Mat. 16:28, Jesus said that "There are some of those standing here who will not see death until they see the Son of Man coming in His kingdom." This is a problem if it refers to the Second Coming because all of the Disciples died long ago and we are still waiting for the Kingdom to come. But in the very next verse, we read that "Six days later Jesus took with him Peter, James, and John" to a high mountain where he was transfigured and revealed to them in His glory. It is very likely that this was the fulfillment of the statement in the previous verse, especially since the connection between them ("six days later") had no chapter break to make the original readers stop and start over and therefore miss it.

The next context to consider is generic: How does what we are reading relate to various established kinds or *genres* of writing? Is it History? Poetry? Law? Sermon? Epistle? Parable? Proverb? Prophecy? Apocalyptic? Polemic? Something else? Each of these kinds of writing has its own rules, its own expectations, its own conventions, its own way of expressing things. Poetry, for example, is more likely to use figurative language than history, and Hebrew poetry structures itself with parallel statements. A parable is a story made up to illustrate a point. Though it typically appears in a historical narrative (i.e., it is literal history that Jesus told such and such a story in answer to such and such a question), it is not itself history, but fiction. It is an illustration, not an allegory. That is, it probably is there to make one basic point, and we should not try to find a special spiritual meaning in every detail.[45]

Next, the passage will have a CANONICAL CONTEXT: How is it related to the rest of the Bible? What particular role does the book which contains it play in the progressive unfolding of God's revelation of Himself and His plan of salvation to mankind through history? Everything centers around Christ. The Old Testament is the preparation for His coming. It gives us the history of mankind's fall and of God's working to bring us a Redeemer through the call of Abraham and the creation of a people through whom that Redeemer would come. It reveals God's Law and our failure to keep it, and it describes the sacrificial system that dealt with that failure until the Messiah it foreshadowed would come to atone for sin once and for all. It has prophecy to deal with the practicalities of Israel's failure and to predict what that Redeemer would be like when He came to restore us to faithfulness and fellowship. The New Testament narrates that coming (the Gospels) and explains and applies it (the epistles). Every book has its own contribution to make to the unfolding of that revelation.

Then there is the LINGUISTIC CONTEXT: What does the original language tell us about the meaning of what we are reading? How does it relate to the translation we are using? We cannot all learn Greek and Hebrew, or course, but we need faithful people who do (and we should require our pastors to be among them) because it is the *original* text that is the Word of God and the final court of appeal. A good

---

45 "Allegories ought to be carried no further than Scripture expressly sanctions; so far are they from forming a sufficient basis to found doctrines upon." John Calvin, *Institutes of the Christian Religion*, 2 vol., trans. Henry Beveridge (Grand Rapids: Eerdmans, 1975), p. 1:291.

modern translation (KJV, NASB, ESV) is the Word of God to the extent that it captures accurately the meaning of the original, which for all practical purposes they reliably do. But they are the Word of God because the original stands behind them. We occasionally need the original to settle a dispute, and often it provides insight that even a good translation has a hard time capturing. For example, our New Testaments are full of words like faith, trust, believe, and belief. To fully understand the role of faith in the Gospel and the Christian life is it useful to know that all of these words have the same root in Greek (See the fuller discussion of this point in chapter 3). That realization allows us to connect passages that an English concordance would never have told us to put together.

Indispensable of course is the HISTORICAL CONTEXT: How does this document relate to what was going on at the time of its composition? When was it written, by whom, to what audience, in what circumstances, to achieve what purpose with that audience? Romans is Paul's most systematic exposition of the theology of the Gospel because he was writing to a church he had not yet visited and been able to teach in person. Galatians was written to deal with the Judaizers who were troubling the churches of Galatia with the demand that they must keep the Jewish ceremonial law in order to be saved. First and Second Timothy were written toward the end of Paul's life to prepare his protégé to continue as a leader of the church in the time that was apparently coming when the Apostles would no longer be around. We cannot fully understand any of those letters without being aware of the circumstances in which they were written.

We cannot ignore the CULTURAL CONTEXT: What do we know about the cultural practices and assumptions of the author and his original audience and how they differ from our own? What does it mean to "cut" a covenant (Gen. 15), for example? What is a suzerainty treaty, and how does that concept function in the relationship of Israel to its neighbors—and to God? "The Jews have no dealings with the Samaritans" (John 4:9). Why not? The Bible often does not explain such things itself because its authors assumed that everybody they were writing to knew them just by being part of that society. So we need people who are students of the cultural background of biblical times and peoples to help us bridge that gap as modern readers. You can get the gist of the biblical story without knowing about such things, but the better you understand them the more the meaning of the biblical text becomes richer and clearer.

There will also be an *ECCLESIASTICAL CONTEXT:* How has this passage been understood and used by the church throughout its history? Roman Catholics, for example, base their claims for Petrine supremacy and papal infallibility on Mat. 16:18-19. If Protestants do not accept those claims, they need to know why not. What passages are your own denominational distinctives based on? Are they an adequate basis? How far should they be issues that divide Christians from one another? Has anybody in church history agreed with your own interpretation of a passage? Who has disagreed with it? Why? It behooves us to have informed views about such matters as we interpret Scripture today. (See thesis 1d.)

Finally there is the *PERSONAL CONTEXT:* How does this passage relate to me as an individual, the one who wants to understand it, believe it, and apply it in my current life here and now? It is a folly all too common in our generation to jump to this context first, when it can only be profitably pursued after the other seven considerations have all been factored in. Otherwise I will just be talking to myself, not really receiving the message the biblical writer was trying to give me. The Bible becomes a mirror that reflects my own preconceived notions back to me rather than a message from God that can challenge them. But once we have understood what the passage is really saying, personal application—what does God want *me* to *do* about this?—is a necessary final step, and our understanding of the text is incomplete without it.

Thesis 6b:
The Original Meaning Has Primacy.

When we study a biblical book in context—all the contexts mentioned above, but especially historical context—we are asking what the book would have meant to its original audience in its life circumstances (what scholars call *sitz im leben*, "situation in life") at the time. They were the people the writer had in mind, whose minds he was trying to instruct, whose questions he was trying to answer, whose problems he was trying to solve, whose wills he was trying to move to repentance, and whose hearts he was trying to inspire with faith. His words have an application to us, of course. But what we are applying to ourselves are the words he wrote to *them*. The starting place for our discussion of the meaning of those words must be what they would have meant to that original audience. What would *they* have gotten out of those words?

What we are trying to discern, in other words, is authorial intent. What was Matthew or Mark or Luke or John or Paul trying to say? The words and phrases he used mean what he *meant* (i.e., intended) them to mean. We are trying to recover the mind of the author—the mind, that is, that the Holy Spirit inspired him to have as he was writing those particular words to those particular people. So we don't ask, "What does this mean to *me*?" before we have asked "What does it *mean*?"

Many literary critics question whether the search for the author's intended message is not an exercise in futility. We cannot recover the author's alleged intention, they argue; we only have his words. He is not available to tell us what he intended to communicate by them, so we just have to do our best with them as they are. The New Critics of the middle Twentieth Century coined the phrase "intentional fallacy" to describe the misguided quest for the author's original meaning. It is a fallacy even to talk about the author's meaning, they said. They still thought the text could have a meaning on its own apart from its author, but the more skeptical theorists who followed them no longer have confidence even in that.

But wait a minute. Did the New Critics *intend* for us to think of the search for the author's intention as a rabbit trail when they wrote about the intentional fallacy? Did they *mean* for their students to forget about the author's purported intention and just focus on the text? I think they did, and I think we can know that they did. We cannot even receive their message casting doubt on authorial intention unless they were wrong to cast that doubt. What a paradox!

When you cannot apply your philosophy of interpretation to your own words without creating a contradiction, I think that is a problem. Instead of living with that contradiction, we should reject it and boldly seek the author's original meaning by applying the hermeneutical golden rule. If you want your readers to care about what *you* actually are trying to say to them (and you do, or else you would have no reason to write), then you have to extend the same courtesy to other authors, living or dead.[46] Authorial intention is inescapable.[47]

O.K., so authorial intention is inescapable. How then do we discern what it was? The author has given us clues that are normally sufficient to let us recover his meaning with reasonable moral certainty. They are found in the eight forms of context we introduced above. With the help of the Holy Spirit who inspired that author, they make it possible to understand what the Bible is trying to communicate to us. Thus they make devoted reading, faithful interpretation, and loving obedience possible. Otherwise, we are only obeying our own ideas about the text, not the text itself. In other words, we are obeying ourselves. But there is no Reformation in just talking to ourselves, no real Reformation without devoted reading, faithful interpretation, and loving obedience of what the Scriptures actually say.

---

46 For more on this point see Kevin J. Vanhoozer, *Is there a Meaning in this Text? The Bible, The Reader, and the Morality of Literary Knowledge* (Grand Rapids: Zondervan, 1998), pp. 240-63.

47 The same paradox even more fiercely bedevils the later and more radical Postmodern critics who have followed the New Critics to influence in English departments today. Ask this question: If Jacques Derrida and Roland Barthes really believe in "the death of the author," why are their own names on the spines of their books?

Thesis 6c:
Interpretation Must Use the *Analogia Fidei*.

The phrase *Analogia Fidei* means "the harmony of faith," or, practically, the consistency of our faith as it is derived from Scripture. If Scripture alone has magisterial authority because it was inspired by God, then we can trust it to teach us only the truth. And if God is a God of reason, then that truth will be a unity that is always ultimately consistent. So we factor that prior commitment to the ultimate consistency of God's self-revelation in the Bible into our interpretation of it. Therefore, no passage of Scripture should be ever be interpreted in such a way that it contradicts another passage. When it does, we know that we have gotten at least one of those passages wrong. Ninety percent of biblical hermeneutics is just the same set of procedures we use rightly to understand any other book. This is one place where it is different. If you think I have contradicted myself, it is theoretically possible (though, I assure you, not very likely) that you are right. If you think God has contradicted Himself in His Word, you can be confident that you are the one mistaken, not Him.

A second implication of our commitment to the *Analogia Fidei* is that we are oriented toward the way God has revealed Himself and His will in the *total consistency* of the biblical message rather than in isolated statements. Therefore, we base our understanding of doctrine on that total consistency. God only needs to say something once for it to be true. But if we are basing a doctrine on a single statement rather than on the consistent message of the whole Bible, the chances that we might be taking that passage out of context or otherwise misunderstanding it go up exponentially. There is safety in numbers, and God has so inspired the text that all the major doctrines that are important for us to believe are revealed "in many portions and in many ways" (Heb. 1:1). For this feature of Scripture we should be humbly grateful, and to it we should be obedient.

The *Analogia Fidei* is a practical procedure in interpretation that flows from a right orientation of the heart. We must be willing to treat the Bible as really being what Jesus said it is: the Word of God that stands above all human traditions (Mat. 15:6), whose very jots and tittles are authoritative (Mat. 13:18), and which will outlast heaven and earth (Mat. 24:35). We must be willing to treat the Bible as really being what Paul said it is: inspired by God and profitable for doctrine (2 Tim. 3:16). We must be willing to treat the Bible as really being what Peter said it is: a light shining in the darkness which is not reducible to human will but rather comes from men being moved by the Holy Spirit to speak from God (2 Pet. 1:19-21).

The outcome of that willingness is that we submit to the text completely and approach it with a firm policy of always ascribing any problems we have with it to our own ignorance or error rather than to error in the Bible. Where we don't understand the Bible, we admit our ignorance. Where we do, we follow it. If we do not follow it, we make a mockery of our faith by claiming that we are in any meaningful sense right with God. Repenting of that mockery is an indispensable prerequisite to the desperately needed Reformation of the contemporary church.

Thesis 6d:
Interpretation Must Recognize That All Scripture Is Profitable *In The Way It Claims To Be.*

⌀

Faithful Christians believe that the Bible is inspired, and that its inspiration makes it "profitable for teaching, for reproof, for correction, for training in righteousness" (2 Tim. 3:16). Their interpretation and application of the Bible should therefore be in accord with its purpose. Paul shows us what that looked like in his own ministry: The goal of his instruction was "love from a pure heart and a good conscience and a sincere faith." This goal caused him to avoid "mere speculation" which did not further "the administration of God which is by faith" (1 Tim. 1:4-5). We must follow suit if we are to be faithful today.

If we are to get out of Scripture the lessons which its divine and human authors put in it for us, in other words, we have to pay attention to what they thought those lessons were. We must recognize Scripture as being profitable in the precise ways it claims to be. There is no better summary of those claims than what Paul wrote in his two letters to Timothy, written to help prepare him to be Paul's successor as the pastor at Ephesus. What is the Bible good for? It is good for teaching. The word could be translated *doctrine*: The Bible teaches us what to believe about God and His purposes for our redemption. We do not learn these beliefs primarily so we can speculate about them or win arguments about them (though the latter is sometimes necessary when false doctrines are proclaimed), but more to be reproved and corrected by them. Reproof is showing us where we are wrong, and correction is setting us right. This is to the end that we be trained in righteousness so that we will be completely prepared for every good work in our service of God and the advancement of His Kingdom.

Part of what informs our interpretation of Scripture then is the use we are supposed to make of it once we have understood it. And that use is to promote in ourselves and in others "love from a pure heart and a good conscience and a sincere faith" (1 Tim. 1:5). In English that could be read as three things: first love from a pure heart, second a good conscience, and third a sincere faith. But in Greek it is clear that it is one thing with three sources: love—which comes from having a pure heart, a good conscience, and a sincere faith. This is love, in other words, that comes from the Gospel, which through faith gives us the justification which is the only foundation for a good conscience and a pure heart. Overcoming our guilt in justification and our sinfulness in sanctification unleashes the love of God to be shed abroad in our hearts.

If your study of Scripture then does not cause you to have a growing love for God, for your fellow Christians, and for a lost world, you are doing something wrong. If your teaching of Scripture does not cause your disciples to have a growing love for God, for their fellow Christians, and for a lost world, you are doing something wrong. The only conclusion we can draw is that a lot of us are doing something wrong. Interpretation must recognize that Scripture is profitable in precisely the way it claims to be, or Reformation will continue to tarry.

Thesis 6e:
Interpretation Must Recognize That Christ Is the Key to All.

☙

The Bible is not an encyclopedia of miscellaneous theological truths. It is the written form of the self-revelation of the God who is the Creator of heaven and earth, who was the God of Abraham, Isaac, and Jacob, and who is the Father of our Lord Jesus Christ. He reveals Himself in miracles, in prophecy, in poetry, in *cultus* (prescribed worship), but most of all in history. And it is a history that was going somewhere, so strongly moving on the trajectory of its story arc that it pulls everything else along with it. The miracles are building up to something even bigger; the prophecy predicts, and the poetry praises, One who is coming; and every drop of blood sprinkled on every Jewish altar for two millennia was one more tick of the clock driving the story inexorably forward . . . to what? The God of the Old Testament was a hidden deity, but One who kept sending the prophets, trying ever to come into clearer focus, until

> The smoke of Sinai slowly clears away
> To show a Baby lying in the hay.[48]

Everything points forward to or back to Jesus. Everything. As Martin Luther said, "The whole Scripture is about Christ only, everywhere." The Old Testament prepares for His coming and predicts it; the New Testament narrates it, explains it, and applies it. That was the perspective of the author of Hebrews: "God, after He spoke long ago to the Fathers in the prophets in many portions and in many ways, in these last days has spoken to us in His Son, whom He appointed heir of all things, through whom also He made the world. And He is the radiance of His glory and the exact representation of His nature" (Heb. 1:1-3). It was the perspective of the Apostle Paul: The Law (the Old Testament) was our schoolmaster or tutor "to lead us to Christ" (Gal. 3:24). But not just the Law: this is true of all of

---

48 Donald T. Williams, "Martyres," *Stars through the Clouds: The Collected Poetry of Donald T. Williams* (Toccoa, Ga.: Lantern Hollow Press, 2020), 117.

history. "But when the fullness of time came, God sent forth His Son" (Gal. 4:4). "The fullness of time" means of course when time was ripe, when everything was ready. It implies that all of time was in fact a preparation, a process to produce the readiness for this event.

That implication becomes explicit when the same phrase appears again in Ephesians. Everything God has done was done "with a view to an administration suitable to the fullness of the times, that is, the summing up of all things in Christ, things in the heavens and things on earth" (Eph. 1:10). The word translated "summing up" was a term from Greek rhetoric for the moment in a discourse that pulls all of its points together. Paul is saying that Jesus was in God's eternal purpose the thesis statement for the universe. Everything in heaven and earth finds its meaning in relation to Him. If this is true of heaven and earth and all their history, how much more is it true of the more focused form of that revelation which is Scripture!

Not every word of the Bible relates to Christ *directly* of course. But everything in the Bible relates to Him, leads to Him, eventually, and He is therefore the key to the understanding of it all. It is the job of interpretation to find out *how* it relates to Him. Therefore we must always ask, "How does this passage teach us to love Jesus? How does this passage teach us to trust Jesus? How does this passage teach us to glorify His Name? How does this passage teach us to proclaim His Gospel, to advance His Kingdom, to edify His Church, or to please Him by doing His Will?" If we can answer those questions for ourselves and our disciples, we will be good servants of our Lord Jesus Christ who can foster the kind if Reformation the church truly needs in our day.

Conclusion

Context; original meaning; the analogia fidei; the intended profit; the Christocentric focus: These five criteria are important because they enable the Text of Scripture to function with the magisterial authority its divine Author wants it to have in our lives. They are important because they enable the devoted reading and faithful interpretation leading to loving obedience that Scripture is designed to foster in us. Without them no reformation of the individual or the church is possible. With them, empowered by the Holy Spirit, it is inevitable. Let us pursue them, then, to the glory of God and the salvation of the world. Amen.

Interlude

The Lindisfarne Gospels
The British Museum, London
(Since Moved to the British Library)

The monks of Lindisfarne illuminate,
    In brilliant tones of gold and blue and red,
    A text. That beckons us to meditate
On what could lead such men to dedicate
    Such long, painstaking labors to the dead?
    The monks of Lindisfarne illuminate
A lot of things, if we but ruminate
    Enough to follow out the knotted thread.
    "A text that beckons us to meditate
Deserves such honor; so we celebrate
    The truth it teaches us," they might have said,
    The monks of Lindisfarne. "Illuminate
Our hearts, restore our souls, and elevate
    Our minds that we may read the way they read
    This text that beckons us." To meditate
Like that before the Lord might be the gate
    That leads us back to where the flock is fed.
    Thus, monks of Lindisfarne illuminate
All texts that beckon us to meditate.[49]

---

49 Donald T. Williams, *Stars through the Clouds*, op. cit., p. 302.

7

Five Theses on Church Ministry

With our message and its authority in place, the next thing requiring attention is the ministry of the church.

A. God made people to be, and means people to be, whole persons. (We have bodies as well as souls, minds as well as hearts.)

B. The ministry of the church should rebuild those whole persons out of the fragments created by sin. (It is not to reinforce that fragmentation by valuing souls over bodies while aiming only at hearts and disparaging minds.)

C. Expository preaching is essential to authentic Christian ministry. (It is the application of the whole counsel of God to the whole person in the whole of life, with Christ at its center; "And we proclaim Him, admonishing every man and teaching every man with all wisdom, that we may present every man complete in Christ," Col. 1:28.)

D. A sacramental cast of mind is essential to authentic Christian ministry. (Christianity is all about the Incarnation, and its worship should reflect that fact. Not sacramentalism—but the New-Testament church appears to have celebrated Communion weekly, making it central to its worship. Most of us don't. Why not?)

E. The New-Testament pattern of participatory worship is essential to authentic Christian ministry. (We are to avoid neglecting our assembling together so we can "stimulate one another to love and good deeds," Heb. 10:24-5. *One another?* When does that happen in the typical American church?)

I spent most of the 1990's trying to plant an Evangelical Free Church in the sleepy little backwoods Southern town of Toccoa, Georgia, near the college where I teach. It was hard, time-consuming work on top of what was already more than a full-time job. I never got a substantial salary or attracted more than a handful of followers. The few we had were passionate about our vision, but lacking in time and resources. By the early spring of 2001, reality had set in, and they reluctantly voted to disband.

Why did I persist in this quixotic endeavor? All the church planting experts (including my own District Superintendent) told me it was demographically doomed from the outset, and I figured from the beginning myself that they were probably right. Toccoa did not need another church. She might have needed a church of a different kind, but she was culturally unlikely to recognize that need or to support such a thing if it were offered. But I had to try. For I had become convinced that the conventional Evangelical, Fundamentalist, Charismatic, and Catholic congregations surrounding me had bits and pieces of the Truth but were failing to offer—and were in fact actually hostile to—the spiritual wholeness of full-orbed biblical Christianity. Each of them had things they needed to learn from the others.[50]

That is a claim that takes some substantiating. So let me nail these five more Theses to the virtual Church Door, as it were. I write as a committed Evangelical Protestant who has not abandoned that tradition but who has come to realize how much he stands in need of things his own tradition is weak at providing.

I tried to summarize what we had been about in my final message to Trinity Fellowship on that last Sunday when we finally laid her to rest. I took as my text on that solemn occasion 2 Tim. 1:13-14. *"Retain the standard of sound words which you have heard from me, in the faith and love which are in Christ Jesus. Guard through the Holy Spirit who dwells in us the treasure which has been entrusted to you"* (NASB). I took these words as

---

[50] An idea of what that wholeness might look like could be discerned from my critique of C. S. Lewis's theology in *Deeper Magic: The Theology behind the Writings of C. S. Lewis* (Baltimore: Square Halo Books, 2016), or from a church which has made some strides toward achieving it, University Church in Athens, Ga. (website http://theuniversitychurchathensga.blogspot.com/).

my final exhortation not because I think I am the equal of Paul, but because our situations seemed parallel. And so I had been asking myself that week, "What is the treasure that I have been trying to entrust to this congregation for the last ten years?" I tried to summarize it in these theses.[51]

---

[51] For more on the role and ministry of the church in general, see Francis A. Schaeffer, *The Church at the End of the Twentieth Century* (Downers Grove: InterVarsity Press, 1970). What he said at the end of the Twentieth Century is just as applicable in the early decades of the Twenty-First. For more on the nature and necessity of expository preaching, see D. Martyn Lloyd-Jones, *Preaching and Preachers* (Grand Rapids: Zondervan, 1972) and John R. W. Stott, *Between Two Worlds: The Art of Preaching in the Twentieth Century* (Grand Rapids: Eerdmans, 1982. For more on the sacramental cast of mind recommended here, see Alan Dan Orme, *God's Appointments with Men: A Christian's Primer on the Sacraments* (Athens, Ga.: University Church Press, 1982).

Thesis 7a:
God Made—and God Means—Human Beings To Be Whole Persons, Including Not Only Spirit but Also Body, Not Only Emotion and Will but Also Mind and Imagination.

※

And one of them, a lawyer, asked him a question, testing him, "Teacher, which is the greatest commandment in the Law?" And he said to him, "You shall love the Lord your God with all your heart, and with all your soul, and with all your mind"
(Mat. 22:35-38).

To love the Lord your God with all your mind: This principle comes from no less an Authority than our Lord Himself, who went out of His way to insert the mind into His answer to the question about the greatest commandment. Why is that fact significant? Because popular Evangelical piety has tended to drive a wedge between the mind and the heart. (See chapter 14.) "Head knowledge" is disparaged even if it is shared by the heart. And this rhetoric is employed in complete ignorance of the biblical usage it is supposedly referencing. The "heart" symbolizes the emotions in post-Victorian English, and so biblical references to the heart are used to justify an emotion-based faith. But in the Bible, the heart does not refer to the emotions at all. A biblical writer who wishes to symbolize the emotions will use the bowels, not the heart. (The King James translates this idiom literally and hence does not miss the point; our modern translations tend to substitute the heart as more communicative to modern readers and so do miss the point completely.) In biblical culture the heart when it is referenced in the original language meant not the emotions but the central core of the inner personality, the place where the three faculties of intellect, emotion, and will find their unity. To "believe in your heart" means to believe *there*, with the whole of your being, not just to feel the truth emotionally. It means a belief that is embraced by and affects the whole personality, including the mind as well as the emotions and the will. Following the Bible's actual usage here would produce a very different kind of piety indeed from the one we typically have.

Seeing head and heart as in opposition rather than as unified has contributed to additional forms of fragmentation that have prevented us from the wholeness God designed for human beings to experience. Fallen human philosophies lead to fragmentation; biblical Christianity (properly understood) fosters unity. Thus, secular thought treats Man as a body alone, while many human religions treat him as a spirit trapped in or burdened by the body—and too much Evangelical rhetoric follows that pattern, which is actually more Gnostic than Christian. But Christianity uniquely among all religions and philosophies teaches the Incarnation of Spirit in our Lord and the Resurrection of the Body in Him and in us. Thus, Body and Spirit are supposed to be integrated rather than opposed, cooperative rather than antagonistic, unified rather than fragmented, as Gerard Manley Hopkins captures in his glorious sonnet:

The Caged Skylark

Like a daregale skylark scanted in a dull cage,
    Man's mounting spirit in his mean house, bone house, dwells.
    That bird beyond the remembering his free fells,
This in drudgery day-laboring out life's age.
And yet on turf or perch or poor low stage,
    Both sing sometimes the sweetest, sweetest spells.
    But both sometimes droop deadly in their cells,
Or wring their barriers with bursts of fear or rage.

Not that the sweet fowl, song fowl needs no rest.
    Why, hear him as he babbles and drops down to his nest—
    But his own nest, wild nest, no prison.
Man's spirit will be flesh-bound when found at best,
    But uncumbered. Meadow down is not distressed
    By a rainbow footing it, nor he for his bones risen![52]

As with the Spirit and the Body, so with the Mind and the Emotions: Integration rather than opposition, unity rather than fragmentation is the goal. A Christianity that is content to be merely emo-

---

[52] W. H. Gardner and N. H. MacKenzie, eds., *The Poems of Gerard Manley Hopkins*, 4th edition (London: Oxford University Press, 1967), pp. 70-71.

tional (or merely intellectual) is simply inauthentic Christianity. So how then do we end up in a religious subculture which believes that the human mind is the only part of our nature which is so fallen that Christ can't redeem it, the Holy Spirit can't sanctify it, and God can't use it? That its only legitimate function is that of thinking up clever arguments against its own use?

Anti-Intellectualism is not just an error; it is a heresy, a denial of the faith, if we take seriously our Lord's very own definition of the Greatest Commandment. (For more on this see chapter 15.) We at Trinity had not just been eggheads wanting a style of worship we liked; we had been people who long for wholeness struggling against a false spirituality that would deny it to us. "God," said Thomas More in Robert Bolt's play *The Man for All Seasons*, "made the Angels to show him splendor, as he made the animals for their innocence and the plants for simplicity. But Man he made to serve him wittily, in the tangle of his mind."[53] So we must not just repudiate Anti-Intellectualism as false spirituality and false religion; we must incarnate the opposite (unity and wholeness) for all the world to see. Otherwise, we become implicated in a false spirituality which is ultimately a denial of the faith.

---

53 Robert Bolt, *A Man for All Seasons* (NY: Vintage Books, 1960), p. 73.

Thesis 7b:

If thesis no. 1 is true, then

Church Ministry Should Reconstitute, Reunify, and Rebuild Those Whole Persons God Intended out of the Fragments Created by Sin.

☙

> *And he gave some as apostles, and some as prophets, and some as evangelists, and some as pastors and teachers, for the equipping of the saints for the work of service, to the building up of the body of Christ until we all attain to the unity of the faith and of the knowledge of the Son of God, to a mature man, to the measure of the stature which belongs to the fullness of Christ. As a result, we are no longer to be children, tossed here and there by waves and carried about by every wind of doctrine . . . but speaking the truth in love, we are to grow up in all aspects unto Him who is the head, even Christ, from whom the whole body, being fitted and held together by that which every joint supplies, according to the proper working of each individual part, causes the growth of the body for the building up of itself in love*
> (Eph. 4:11-16).

In this classic description of ministry from Ephesians, the goal is to grow up into Christ; the method is by speaking the Truth in Love. And we are to grow up into Christ "in all aspects" (v. 15). *In all aspects?* How did those words get left out of the Bible of American Evangelicalism, whose fragmented view of spirituality leads to a compartmentalized approach to spiritual life? In the churches in which I was raised, the whole spiritual life had been reduced to four "decisions": get saved, be baptized, join the church, and rededicate your life. Some of my preachers certainly believed there was more to it than that, but the approved liturgy borrowed from revivalism defeated their better intentions: Everything in the service was geared to getting people down to the "altar" sufficiently motivated emotionally to do one of those four things. So will as well as emotion got isolated from intellect. We were actually working pretty hard to create fragmented persons. And you could only rededicate your life so many times before it became an exercise in futility. Certain decisions are necessary, and I am certainly in favor of these; but one could easily lose discipleship in the decisions to the point that one's faith became compartmentalized from real life. It had to be so compartmentalized because the faith as thus taught had very little to do with real life outside the church's walls. What would it look like, then, this alternative *biblical* vision that Paul had?

Growing up "In *all* aspects . . . into *Christ*" can mean nothing less than that the Church is trying to grow people who think like the One who designed the stars, who astounded the rabbis, and who defeated the Pharisees. It is trying to grow people who imagine the world like the One who wrote the parables. It is trying to grow people who make choices like the One whose meat and drink was to do the will of his Father. It is trying to grow people who serve like the One who washed his disciples' feet. And it is trying to grow people who love like the One who died on Calvary. It is trying to grow people who see all these acts as essential parts of an indissoluble unity whose Center is the very character of its Lord. Getting saved, accepting Christ as one's Savior and Lord, means setting out on *that* road. What else could it mean?

If then we are satisfied simply to teach people to follow a set of rules or train them to buy the approved style of kitsch or move them to cry at altar calls, our ministry is less than authentic Christianity. It is a false spirituality which has denied the faith.

How then do we rebuild this unity out of the fragmentation caused by sin? We have to start by recognizing that rebuilding as the goal of Christian ministry. Currently we do not hit this target because we are not even aiming for it. Once we repent of that sin and get our aim properly focused, we will discover that three aspects of ministry mandated by the New Testament are indispensable to its pursuit. We will deal with them in theses 7c-e.

Thesis 7c:

If both of these things are true, then
Expository Preaching Is Essential To Authentic Christian Ministry.

※

From childhood you have known the sacred writings which are able to give you the wisdom that leads to salvation through faith which is in Christ Jesus. All Scripture is inspired by God and profitable for teaching, for reproof, for correction, for training in righteousness that the man of God may be adequate, equipped for every good work
(2 Tim. 3:15-17).
And we proclaim Him, admonishing every man and teaching every man with all wisdom, that we may present every man complete in Christ
(Col. 1:28).

If indeed we are trying to grow whole people as followers of Christ, as we described that wholeness above, then we must begin with the preaching and teaching ministry of the church. We dare not end with it, but we must begin with it. People no longer come to us with any prior knowledge of the content or the meaning of Scripture, and the worldview of the Bible is a foreign country to them. Preaching that merely exhorts them to spiritual decision or moral action no longer even begins to meet their needs. There must be systematic teaching addressed to the head as well as the heart, and it must apply the whole counsel of God to the whole of life. No other approach can even begin to meet the need of the hour. Such teaching cannot be limited to the pulpit. It requires a coordinated effort by the pulpit, the home, the Sunday School, Christian schools and colleges, and Christian literature. But it begins with the pulpit, the formal and official proclamation of the Word of God by the called leaders of the church. Expository preaching is essential to authentic Christian ministry.

Exposition is not just a preferred style of preaching. It is the mandated approach to preaching. For God has spoken in Christ and in Scripture, and this—not the opinions of men—is the only spiritual food worth offering people. Surely speaking the Truth in Love is essential to ministry. And our primary access to this Truth which transforms is through a Text (the *graphe*, or writings, inspired or "breathed out" by God according to 2 Tim. 3:16). This text, as we saw in the chapter on hermeneutics, was made of a certain series of words arranged in particular grammatical structures in a certain context, aimed at a particular audience at a certain time in history. So preaching is not expository just because it works its way systematically through a biblical book (though such an approach will naturally be a staple of an expository preaching diet). Unless the Text is understood in terms of its Author's and its authors' intent, discernible only by prayerful attention to these details—unless it is thus understood and applied, we build on sand and have nothing to offer.

Homiletics 101: Villanelle no. 18

Nothing less can speak to our condition,
    Not prooftexts, pretexts; we must have the *Word*.
    There is no power but in exposition.
The Text is captain of the expedition,
    The Apostles' accents are what must be heard,
    For nothing less can speak to our condition.
The finger on the verse, the fair rendition,
    Then, not to brandish but to thrust the Sword:
    There is no power but in exposition.
When heralds mind the message and the mission,
    Not feelings only—mind and heart are stirred,
    And nothing less can speak to our condition.
Can mere opinion lead to true contrition
    When bone and marrow splitting's not incurred?
    There is no power but in exposition.
Such splitting, like the atom: in that fission
    The power is unleashed, the faith conferred.
For nothing less can speak to our condition;
    There is no power but in exposition.[54]

I do not hesitate to say it: to accept anything less from our pastors denies the doctrine of Inspiration and implicates us in a false spirituality which has ultimately, whatever its intentions, denied the faith.

---

54 Donald T. Williams, *Stars through the Clouds*, op. cit., p. 385.

Thesis 7d:

If these things are true, it also follows that
A Sacramental Cast of Mind Is Essential To Authentic Christian Ministry

> *For I received from the Lord what I also delivered unto you, that the Lord Jesus in the night in which he was betrayed took bread; and when he had given thanks, he broke it, and said, "This is my body, which is for you; do this in remembrance of me." In the same way he took the cup also, saying, "This cup is the new covenant in my blood; do this, as often as you drink it, in remembrance of me." For as often as you eat this bread and drink this cup, you proclaim the Lord's death until he comes.*
> *(1 Cor. 11:23-26)*

Understand me carefully here. I said a *sacramental* cast of mind—not *sacramentalist*. What is the difference? A sacramentalist sees the sacraments as working by a kind of magic. The Latin phrase is *ex opera operato*—baptism and the Lord's Supper, rather than faith, become the way God's saving grace is brought to man, with saving power in themselves because the bread and wine of Communion are actually physically transformed into the literal body and blood of Jesus. That is not the understanding of the covenant meal we laid out in Thesis 3e. But one need not accept a medieval or even "high-church" view of the nature of the Lord's presence in the elements to see that Communion has a very different place in typical Evangelical approaches to worship today than it did in the first-century church. Why is this?

Part of the answer is an over-reaction to perceived Roman Catholic abuses. But less than fully biblical understandings of doctrine also have a lot to do with it. The fragmentation we have accepted, the wedge between spirit and flesh, leads us to an understanding of how spirit works through matter that is more gnostic than Christian. It leads to lots of Christians who essentially reduce the sacraments to nothing more than rather elaborate object lessons and then naturally wonder why they are all that big of a deal. How do we counteract that tendency without falling into the opposite error? We do it by remembering some very basic theology.

Two of the most unique doctrines of Scripture are Creation and Incarnation. There is no Christianity if they are denied. Creation sets the whole Christian story in motion. We saw in Thesis 3d that one of the non-negotiable doctrinal affirmations was that Jesus had come *in the flesh*. In both creation and incarnation, the Spiritual expresses itself in and through the Material. For historic, biblical Christianity, matter (or the body) is not the tomb or the prison of spirit but is the *medium* of the spirit, the material in and through which it works. For Man is, as Sir Thomas Browne said, "that great and true Amphibium, created to live not in divers elements but in divided and distinguished worlds."[55] We are the place where Spirit and Matter most crucially come together, the place where they meet. Therefore, any ministry which flows from that Spirit—the God who created the physical world and made us in his image—to that Man—the one who was made to bear the image of God as a spiritual *and* a physical, material creature—is going to partake of this incarnational pattern.

It is precisely in The Lord's Supper that we find that incarnational pattern most profoundly presented to us, as the spiritual significance of the Lord's person and his sacrifice, his New Covenant, is expressed by—in and through—the physical elements of bread and wine. (One does not have to affirm either transubstantiation or consubstantiation to see and appreciate this reality; indeed, insisting on such definitions goes beyond Scripture in unhelpful ways.) The Lord's Supper therefore is a paradigm (a foundational and defining model or pattern) not only for the Content of the Gospel (as we show forth Christ's death until He come) but also for the Method of Ministry (incarnation). This incarnational way of thinking helps us understand why the sacraments are important, and it should color our thinking not only about them but also about all of life.

When the makeup of the congregation permits, this incarnational, i.e., sacramental, cast of mind should be expressed by the Church returning to its historic role as the great Patron and Nurturer of the Arts. For the arts create physical objects (or auditory ones, but always presentations to the senses) that incarnate a spiritual vision, whether it be of goodness, truth, and beauty or chaos and despair. The recov-

---

55 Sir Thomas Browne, *Religio Medici*, Alexander M. Witherspoon and Frank J. Warnke, eds., *Seventeenth Century Prose and Poetry*, 2nd ed. (N.Y.: Harcourt Brace Jovanovich, 1982), p. 339.

ery of that role had certainly been part of our identity at Trinity. One of our ministries, which still survives the dissolution of the church itself, was a writers' and artists' support group known as Inklings II, in honor of the group that met with C. S. Lewis twice a week in Oxford in the middle of the twentieth century. Here the church was actively discipling future writers and artists as if that were an actual calling for God's people for which they needed to be spiritually prepared. Where the makeup of the congregation permits, this cast of mind should be expressed by nurturing budding artists; in every congregation, it should be expressed through a culture that values the arts and their role in life and by that understands the centrality of the sacramental in worship. Here the Spiritual is expressed in and through the Material, bread and wine.

As Man was created to have a Mind, authentic Christian ministry must be based on the sound exposition of the Word; as he was created to be a Spirit expressing itself through a Body, authentic Christian ministry should be centered on the Lord's Supper.

Eucharist

Once again the Lord of Heaven
Stoops with towel around his waist,
Breaks the Bread made without leaven,
Watches Judas leave in haste.

Once again the Lord of Glory
Lifts the Cup to bless the Wine.
We who reenact the Story
Seek the Savior in the Sign.

More than just an illustration
Though it is but Wine and Bread:
This, the Spirit's proclamation
Of the holy One who bled.

It is more than just a symbol
Though it is but Bread and Wine;
For the Spirit flows, as nimble
As the sap within the vine.

More than just a silent letter
Lying dormant on the page,
This is Truth that breaks its fetters,
Vaults the intervening age.

Words like Transubstantiation?
Too precisian to define
How the Lord takes up his station
In the Bread and in the Wine.

Although we, like doubting Thomas,
Need to see the Hands and Side,
He is gracious with the Promise:
"Come, behold them where they hide."

It is more than just a token,
More than just a word about;
With this Bread we must be broken,
Like this Wine, our lives poured out.

In that mysterious oblation
Faith is strengthened and restored.
With refocused adoration,
Saints rejoice to meet the Lord.

So again the Lord of Glory
Lifts the Cup to bless the Wine.
We who reenact the Story
See the Savior in the Sign.[56]

Communion therefore should not be occasional and peripheral but continual and central to our worship. Dare we say it? Anything less than this is a failure to understand the most basic doctrines of Christianity (not to mention our Lord's instructions). It is a false spirituality which has denied the faith.

---

56 Donald T. Williams, *Stars through the Clouds*, op. cit., p. 150-51.

Thesis 7e:

If all these things are true, then

The New Testament Pattern Of Worship Is Also Essential To Authentic Christian Ministry.

What then is the outcome, brethren? When you assemble, each one has a psalm, has a teaching, has a revelation, has a tongue, has an interpretation. Let all things be done for edification
(1 Cor. 14:26).
Let the word of Christ richly dwell within you, with all wisdom teaching and admonishing one another with psalms and hymns and spiritual songs
(Col. 3:16).
Let us consider how to stimulate one another to love and good deeds, not forsaking our own assembling together, as the habit of some is, but encouraging one another
(Hebrews 10:24-25).

"*Each one*," according to these verses, comes with a teaching, an exhortation, a psalm; we assemble together to stir up "*one another*" to love and good deeds. Yet Evangelical Protestant worship in America has typically consisted of a large number of people sitting passively in their pews and watching the Performance that happens up at the front of the auditorium. So how did these words fall out of the Bibles used by American Evangelicals? When do these things happen in their "worship" services? As Man is a Mind, *Exposition* is foundational to Christian worship. As Man is a Spirit expressing itself through a Body, the *Sacraments* are central to it. And as Man was made to be a social animal, *Mutuality* is essential to true Christian worship and ministry. Look back to Eph. 4:16 again: the body grows through what is supplied by *each individual part*. Only as ministry is mutual can we grow as we are designed to; only as ministry is mutual can Christ fully be made manifest in and through the Congregation.

What would this look like if we were actually practicing it? It does not mean chaos or lack of structure. It simply means letting the New Testament set the agenda for what happens when the church gathers. There should be a planned and structured service. It can even be liturgical, and it should definitely include formal preaching of the Word. But it is deliberately planned in such a way as to foster participation rather than passivity. Opportunities for people to share testimonies of what God is doing in their lives, to share prayer requests and pray for each other, for example, should be a normal part of worship, not an occasional special event. Those opportunities create expectations. We might have to abandon the idea that the agenda for the church can be pursued in one hour, and we might decide that megachurches are not the best format for creating a real community of faith as opposed to just a venue for a rock concert with a lecture attached. Go back to the descriptions of how the New-Testament church was actually supposed to work, and program *that* instead of just the boring entertainment you are used to.

Practical Ecclesiology

Villanelle no. 17

Each member has a place; each one belongs
    As seen when, gathered as a congregation,
    They sing their psalms and hymns and holy songs.
Whether two or three or mighty throngs,
    The Lord is in their midst. A priestly nation,
    Each member has a place; each one belongs.
The Lord himself with love eternal longs
    For them; each one by special invitation
    Is singing psalms and hymns and holy songs.
A pincer movement, ministry. The prongs?
    A verse, a prayer, a word of exhortation.
    Each member has a place; each one belongs.
How beautiful the feet, the sandal thongs
    Which go to every tongue and tribe and nation
    Singing psalms and hymns and holy songs.

> Spectators passive in their pew? It wrongs
> > The vision, suffocates the celebration.
> > Each member has a place; each one belongs,
> Singing psalms and hymns and holy songs.[57]

The "entertainment model" for ministry, in which everybody sits passively in their pews watching the performance provided for them up on the stage, is simply disobedient and inauthentic Christianity, a false spirituality that has implicitly denied the faith. The combination of strong expository preaching, a sacramental cast of mind, and mutual ministry gives the church a much stronger platform for accomplishing its purpose: to glorify and worship God in a holistic way that rebuilds whole persons out of the fragments created by sin.

---

57 Ibid., p. 384.

Conclusion

Well, these are my five theses on church ministry: God made and meant us to be whole persons, including mind and imagination; church ministry must reflect this fact by restoring that wholeness and unity out of the fragmentation created by sin; therefore, Expository Preaching, a Sacramental Cast of Mind, and the NT pattern of Mutual Ministry are essential to authentic Christianity. Not desirable; not ideal; not preferable; *essential*. For otherwise we deny by implication if not outright the most unique and fundamental doctrines that make the Christian faith what it is.

Trinity Fellowship was founded for one reason: out of the conviction that these principles are indeed essential to Authentic Christianity. They are not a matter of style, or of preference, or of taste. They are a matter of obedience. And therefore, if those who were touched by that ministry—or who read this chapter about it—ever become comfortable in the pew of a church that is satisfied with the false spirituality of conventional Christianity, then truly we shall have existed and striven in vain. But if you can never again be content without insisting that any church which names the name of Christ that you are a part of must reckon with these realities and be transformed by these truths—then, though Trinity Fellowship is no longer here, we may be able to say without dishonesty that she accomplished her mission. Amen.

Interlude

1 Timothy 3:15

The Lord's Work

In the name of the Father,
For the sake of the Son,
By the aid of the Spirit
All the is worthy is done.

All that's a boon to the Body,
Knitting its sinews in love,
Taking the News to the nations,
Born on the wings of the Dove.

For the increase of the Kingdom,
Unto the glory of Grace,
By the means of the Mercy,
Longing to look on the Face.[58]

The Founding of Trinity Fellowship

Hard the path of men who live alone:
Outcasts, Eliot's Magi with their race
Uncomprehending, staring, blank of face;
Seeking—those who ought to be their own,
Easily the hardest, hard as stone;
Hearts that claim and mouths and hands that trace
Outwardly the elements of Grace—
Lacking life, corruption over bone.

---

58 Donald T. Williams, *Stars through the Clouds*, op. cit., p. 167.

Daring to believe the Message still,
Onward plodding, leaving Hope behind,
Forgetting hunger for the kindred mind.
Grace has not forgotten all its skill:
Onward plodding, shows us in the trip
Delights unlooked for: founds the Fellowship.

Supper of the Lamb together shared;
Useless baggage seen and laid aside;
Prayer from deepest need—the need supplied;
Preaching from the Text—the Text declared;
Odes of ancient praise renewed and aired;
Royal priesthood serving side by side,
Tasks imposed by Scripture not denied;
Old and new, the treasures are prepared;

Flock responding to the Shepherd's fife;
Truth digested into will and heart,
Realized in acts—at least a start;
Unction of the Spirit bringing life;
Together finally, Boaz and Ruth:
House of God and pillar of the Truth.[59]

---

59 Ibid., p. 383.

8
Five Theses on the "Worship Wars"

What often passes for "worship" today would not have been recognized as such by our ancestors. We could have just one thesis here: Christian worship in its music should preserve the best of the old and support the best of the new. But we need criteria to discern what that best is. Here are five. (None of them is that the music be new or old!)

A. The texts sung must reflect biblical truth. (This is the simple application to worship of *sola Scriptura*; see theses 1.a-e and 6.a-e.)

B. The texts sung should reflect theological profundity. (They should be neither simplistic nor unnecessarily difficult, but should promote the worship of a transcendent and holy God understood in the specific terms in which He has revealed Himself to us—focused on Him, not our feelings.)

C. The texts sung should reflect poetic richness. ("My God must have my best, even all I had," George Herbert.[60])

D. The settings of the texts should manifest musical beauty. (As Luther pertinently is supposed to have asked, "Why should the Devil have all the good music?")

E. There should be a good fit between the text and its musical setting. (These are the criteria of excellence in worship music. If contemporary hymns meet them, so be it; but to ignore the heritage of the church that has already been sifted and weeded is folly. Preserve the best of the old and support the best of the new.)

---

60 George Herbert, "The Forerunners," *The Works of George Herbert*, ed. F. E. Hutchinson (Oxford: Clarendon, 1941), p. 176.

The "worship wars" that rage in the church today are nothing new. They go back at least as far as ancient Israel when David was despised by Michal for dancing before the Ark. In the patristic period St. Ambrose was considered an innovator (horrors!) for writing hymns and teaching his people to sing them. The controversy over melismatic textual elaboration in the Middle Ages was (according to legend) settled by Palestrina's *Pope Marcellus Mass*. The Reformation started debates over exclusive psalmody and the use of instruments that continue among some Protestants to this day, though now overshadowed by heated arguments over contemporary "praise-and-worship" music versus traditional hymnody.

No pastor, minister of music, or institution which trains people for ministry can afford to ignore these controversies today. For the drastic shift to what is called "contemporary" worship too often carries with it a disastrous shift in the very concept of what worship is. The problem is not when the music was written or how it is played. It is a shift from the ascription of worth to God to the cultivation of a particular emotional state in the congregation. Emotions are no longer the byproduct of worship; they have become, in effect if not in intention, the end of it. Getting back to a more biblical understanding of what worship music is and how it should function would be a big step in the right direction.[61]

I am under no illusion that I can settle the current disputes. But I am concerned that they are often conducted more on the basis of personal taste than principled teaching. A positive step toward peace would be to recognize what the biblical principles that should govern our practice are. Then there are some lessons from history that can help us apply them constructively.

The Lessons of Scripture

I suggest that at least the following passages of Scripture are relevant. We are commanded to "Sing to Him a *new* song; play *skillfully* with a shout of joy" (Ps. 33:3, NASB, emphasis added). It is discouraging to find the first phrase of that verse quoted often while seldom hearing the second. One effect of being filled with the Holy Spirit is "speaking unto one another in psalms and hymns and spiritual songs, singing and making melody with your heart to the Lord" (Eph. 5:19-20). And we are also told to use discernment and "approve the things that are excellent" (Phil. 1:9-10).

As one thinks about these passages, it is hard to see that the Lord is on either "side" in the current squabbles. Neither a slavish adherence to the old music nor a total abandonment of it for the new has any warrant in Scripture. God apparently wants us to preserve the best of the traditional music that connects us to our forefathers in the faith, for the New-Testament church was still using the psalms, the hymnbook of the Old Testament, in their worship. On the other

---

61 Four important books on worship that will repay study are Horton Davies, *Worship and Theology in England*, 3 vols. (Grand Rapids: Eerdmans, 1996), *Christian Worship: Its History and Meaning* (N.Y.: Abingdon Press, 1957), Donald P. Hustad, *Jubilate! Church Music in the Evangelical Tradition* (Carol Stream, Il.: Hope Publishing, 1981), Ronald Allen and Gordon Borror, *Worship: Recovering the Missing Jewel* (Portland: Multnomah, 1982), and Calvin R Stapert, *My Only Comfort: Death, Deliverance, and Discipleship in the Music of Bach* (Grand Rapids: Eerdmans, 2000).

hand, they were also led by the Holy Spirit to sing new hymns (songs of praise addressed to God in the second person) and spiritual songs (first-person statements of personal testimony or spiritual truth) of their own composition, some of which scholars believe are actually quoted in the New Testament (e.g., 1 Tim. 3:16). In doing so they were following the Old Testament exhortation of Psalm 33:3. If they followed all of it, they sang and played those songs, old and new, with all the skill as well as all the exuberance they could muster. (Presumably this meant that their lyre players knew more than three chords.) And if they followed the New Testament exhortation of Philippians 1:9-10, they would have been concerned to discern in their new music what was truly excellent and cleave to it, adding it gradually to the rich stock of resources for worship that they were building so they could pass it on to us.

If this reading is correct, it gives us a good general guideline for the church at all times: Preserve and honor the best of the old; encourage and support the best of the new. If that is right, then the Christian college and seminary should be providing the kind of training that would help future church leaders to be in a position to do just that. The question then becomes, how is this training best to be achieved?

The Lessons of History
Part of the answer to that question was inscribed over the door to the old Ayres Memorial Library at Taylor University, a door I passed through almost daily when I was an undergraduate: "What is past is prologue; study the past." We study the past precisely because we live in the present and look toward the future. We study the past not because the present is unworthy of our attention but because only by studying the past can we learn the criteria by which to discern that which is worthy in the present. No one has explained this principle better than Dr. Johnson:

> To works, however, of which the excellence is not absolute and definite, but gradual and comparative; to works not raised on principles demonstrative and scientifick, but appealing wholly to observation and experience, no other test can be applied than length of duration and continuance of esteem. What mankind have long possessed they have often examined and compared, and if they persist to value the possession, it is because frequent comparisons have confirmed opinion in its

favour. As among the works of nature no man can properly call a river deep or a mountain high without the knowledge of many mountains and many rivers; so in the productions of genius, nothing can be styled excellent till it has been compared with other works of the same kind.[62]

In literature and art, Johnson argues—which would include choral literature and musical art—the ultimate test of excellence is staying power. We recognize classics as works of genius that probably still have something to say to us because they have stood the test of time. This does not mean of course that we exclude contemporary works. If it did, Johnson himself could never have addressed his own generation so that he could still be pondered by ours. But we have to know those works of the past in order to discern what made them excellent so we can seek for the same features in the works of our peers. Thus we study the past for the sake of the present and the future.

Criteria of Excellence

How do we apply these principles to the Worship Wars, as pastors, as ministers of music, or as those who train them? We do it partly by recognizing that ninety percent of today's music is very poor. Well, that shouldn't be too surprising; ninety percent of the music of the past was, too. The difference is that with the past the weeding-out process described by Dr. Johnson has already taken place. Therefore, we cannot find, encourage, and preserve the best contemporary music without knowing those marks of excellence that made the best of the past stand out and survive so long. What are those marks? There are at least five, and they are my five theses on the Worship Wars: 1, Biblical Truth, 2, Theological Profundity, 3, Poetic Richness, 4, Musical Beauty, and 5, the Fitting of Music to Text in ways that enhance rather than obscure or distort meaning.

These five qualities are the marks of excellent worship music in any age. These marks are not arbitrary but are derived from biblical teaching about the nature of worship (it is to be in spirit and in truth, and involves loving God with our whole person including the mind) and from an understanding of the nature of music and how it can support those biblical goals.

---

62 Samuel Johnson, *Preface to the Plays of William Shakespeare* (1765); qtd. in Geoffrey Tillotson, Paul Fussell, Jr., and Marshall Waingrow, eds., *Eighteenth Century English Literature* (N.Y.: Harcourt, Brace, & World, 1969).

Thesis 8a:
The Texts Sung Must Reflect Biblical Truth.

This thesis should go without saying for people committed to the magisterial authority of Scripture. God wants people to worship Him in spirit and in truth, and Scripture is our primary and most trustworthy source of truth about Him. Therefore, the faithful church has always insisted on biblical truth, and Protestant hymnody started out with a special emphasis on it. The earliest congregational songs for the churches of the Reformation were paraphrased Scripture texts, especially the Psalms. The metrical Psalms of Thomas Sternhold and John Hopkins (1549) was one of the most popular books in Elizabethan England. What those versified psalms lacked in literary elegance they made up for in biblical faithfulness:

> The man is blest that hath not gone
> By wicked rede astray,
> Ne sat in chair of pestilence,
> Nor walked in sinner's way;
>
> But in the law of God the Lord
> Doth set his whole delight,
> And in that law doth exercise
> Himself both day and night.[63]

By the Eighteenth Century, writers such as Isaac Watts, William Cowper, John Newton, and the Wesley brothers felt at liberty to compose freely words of praise that were not strict paraphrases of Scripture. In this, they were following the example of their first-century brothers. But they still felt strongly the obligation of being sure that their words were Scriptural if not Scripture. In that, they were following the example of their first-century (and sixteenth-century) brothers as well. Often in those early days, hymns were printed with the biblical references that justified their content appended at the end of

---

63 John Hopkins, ed., *All Such Psalms of David as Thomas Sternhold Did in his Lifetime Draw into English Meter* (1549); qtd. in Hyder E. Rollins & Herschel Baker, eds., *The Renaissance in England: Non-Dramatic Prose and Verse of the Sixteenth Century* (Lexington, Mass.: D. C. Heath & Co., 1954, p. 161.

every verse or even every line. Even when that was not done literally, the mentality behind it was healthy. It goes back to the way the Psalter functioned as the first hymnbook of the First-Century church. Exclusive psalmody is too limited an application of this principle, for the early church, while using the psalms, also composed its own hymns, and we, like our forebears in the First Great Awakening should follow its example. But the impulse to ensure that the content of hymns be biblical is sound. Indeed, it should be non-negotiable.

One of the healthy trends in contemporary Christian music is the revival of the ancient practice of singing Scripture. Unfortunately, this revival is sometimes limited to the mantric repetition of short and simple phrases rather than enabling the congregation to follow the train of biblical thought through fuller passages, as was more typically the earlier practice.

Thesis 8b:
Texts Should Reflect Theological Profundity.

Theological Profundity is also a mark of the best of past hymnody. It is not that hymn texts were unnecessarily difficult or abstruse; profundity is often confused with difficulty or abstruseness, but it is not the same thing. Reading John's Gospel should convince us that the deepest profundity is perfectly compatible with great simplicity. So the texts I am talking about were not necessarily difficult or academic, but they were theologically informed, and it was good theology that informed them.

St. Ambrose wrote hymns and taught his people to sing them in order to instill good Christology and refute Arianism. As a result you could hear people on the streets of Milan discussing whether there was a time when Christ was not. In the classical age of Protestant hymnody after the First Great Awakening, simple lay persons did not turn their minds off in worship but praised a majestically transcendent Trinitarian God with a graciously incarnated Son who had saved them by grace through faith in Christ. Philip Doddridge asked, "Do you feel in your breast a deeper appreciation of the infinite majesty of the blessed God and of the glory of His perfections?"[64] That was one way in which a good hymn text was evaluated. The best hymnody should still facilitate that kind of worship.

The best texts of the past not only lifted God's people above themselves in worship but also helped them interpret their own religious experiences in biblically sound ways. So we sing to One who is "Immortal, invisible, God only wise, / In light inaccessible hid from our eyes." We give our "Praise to the Lord, the Almighty, the King of Creation." Because He is "A Mighty Fortress" whose Son "must win the battle," we tremble not for the prince of darkness and we can "Let goods and kindred go, / This mortal life also." Has anyone ever done a better job of applying the specifics of the atonement to the process and experience of conversion than Charles Wesley in "And Can it Be that I should Gain?" The doctrine of regeneration is captured perfectly by this verse:

---

64 Philip Doddridge, *The Rise and Progress of Religion in the Soul*, qtd. in *A Burning and Shining Light*, ed. David Lyle Jeffrey (Grand Rapids: Eerdmans, 1987), p. 186.

> Long my imprisoned spirit lay
> Fast bound in sin and nature's night.
> Thine eye diffused a quick'ning ray;
> I woke; the dungeon flamed with light.
> My chains fell off, my heart was free;
> I rose, went forth, and followed Thee.

Stanzas like that, giving equally eloquent attention to the atonement, the incarnation, and justification, fully justify the exultation expressed in the chorus:

> Amazing love! How can it be
> That Thou, my God, shouldst die for me?[65]

Recent choruses sometimes limit themselves by being so simplistic and repetitive that theological reflection never has a chance to get started. But how then can we love and worship God with our minds, as Christ particularly commanded us? Answer: We cannot.

---

65 *Trinity Hymnal*, revised ed. (Atlanta: Great Commission Publications, 1990), p. 455.

Thesis 8c:
Texts Should Reflect Poetic Richness.

Like theological profundity, poetic richness is a virtue that must be pursued carefully, for a text that is too allusive and requires too much literary expertise to unpack will be self-defeating for average lay persons and thus hinder worship rather than enabling and enriching it. Like theological profundity, though, poetic richness is also a virtue that should not be ignored. Appropriate kinds of literary excellence have a role to play. Examples include gems like the use of the questions in "What Child is this?" to create a parallel structure that captures the wonder of the incarnation, the appropriate military metaphors in that great meditation on spiritual warfare, "A Mighty Fortress," or the choice of a simple but evocative word like "wretch" in "Amazing Grace." That one monosyllabic word conveys the helplessness, the misery, and the poverty of life without Christ, Little touches like that which make a text more intellectually suggestive or aesthetically poignant or emotionally powerful without making it unnecessarily difficult will tend to show up in those hymns which have survived the test of time, while texts that are just rhymed prose with tunes attached are, for that very reason, the more forgettable.

How many praise and worship texts today would be worth reading simply as devotional poetry without the music? Many classic hymns rise to that level.

Thesis 8d:
Settings Should Manifest Musical Beauty.

Musical beauty might be thought by many to be in the eye of the beholder (or the ear of the hearer). To a certain extent this is true: *De gustibus non est disputandem* ("There is no accounting for taste"). Nevertheless, those who have studied music also know that there are certain contours, structures, and cadences that make for a sing-able melody and certain harmonic felicities that can make that melody more memorable or even haunting. Think of the way Slane ("Be Thou my Vision") rises and falls like an ocean wave or a sine curve. Think of the gently rolling ABA structure of Ebenezer ("Oh the Deep, Deep Love of Jesus"). Think of the way each phrase of Gift of Love ("Though I may Speak with Bravest Fire") varies the same pattern. Think of the way the men's voices in Diadem (the "complicated" version of "All Hail the Power of Jesus' Name") punctuate the flowing women's line in the chorus, or the way the inner parts move against the still melody in the third measure of Nicaea ("Holy, Holy, Holy").

We offer beauty to the Lord because our musical worship, like the lambs and goats offered in the Old Testament, should be unblemished. Not perfect—then we would have to stop singing altogether—but the best we can give, not a lame, blind, half-dead sheep cheaply tossed onto the altar. And we offer all the beauty we can to each other and to the listening world because we serve a Lord who is altogether lovely, and we want to come across as if we actually believed that He is.

Though some very beautiful pieces have come out of contemporary Christian music ("El Shaddai," much of John Michael Talbot's, Michael Card's, Keith and Kristyn Getty's, and Andrew Peterson's work), too many of the more recent praise choruses seem to ignore all the rules of good composition deliberately, giving us not well-shaped melodies but just one note after another. These "tunes" are not very sing-able, but it doesn't really matter because the "worship team" is playing them so loudly that no one can tell whether the congregation is singing along or not. (I am not against rock-influenced styles or amplified volume as such; I have myself played electric bass in and written songs for a praise and worship band. But we knew that there is a difference between giving a performance and leading a congregation in worship.) And where did so many guitarists get the notion that it is somehow cute to avoid ending a song on the tonic chord (i.e., "home base")? Why would we act as if structure doesn't matter when we believe in a God who grounds meaning in the world and saves us from the chaos that expresses despair of meaning in those who do not know Him? Shouldn't well-structured music in church be part of doing things "decently and in order" (1 Cor. 14:40)? There can be great beauty in contemporary styles, but that is not what we are typically offered.

Thesis 8e:
There Should Be a Good Fit between Text and Setting.

A good fit between the words and their musical setting is essential to great worship music even when text and tune are both excellent in themselves. The most egregious violation of this principle may be A. B. Simpson's "A Missionary Cry." It expresses in graphic terms a salutary concern for the fate of the lost: "A hundred thousand souls a day / Are marching one by one away. / They're passing to their doom; / They're passing to their doom." If ever there was content demanding a minor key and a mournful, dirge-like tempo, this is it. But if you've sung this song you know it is set to a completely inappropriate snappy march tune, as if we were happy about the damnation of the unsaved! It might be a good tune for a different text; it might be a good text to a different tune.

Examples of good fit between message and music are the quietly meditative, plainsong-derived melodies of Picardy in the contemplative "Let all Mortal Flesh Keep Silence" and *Divinum Mysterium* in "Of the Father's Love Begotten" or the sprightly and joyous rhythms of Ariel in "Oh Could I Speak the Matchless Worth." The way the minor key expresses the longing of "O Come, O Come, Emmanuel," the quiet simplicity of "Silent Night," and the way the suspensions and resolutions of the inner voices in Bach's arrangement of Hans Leo Hassler's tune for "O Sacred Head, Now Wounded" encourage us not to hurry past those notes and words but to pause for contemplation of the mystery of the passion, are exquisite. Examples could be multiplied almost endlessly. Contemporary songs with a good fit include Don Francisco's ballads "He's Alive" and "I've Got to Tell Somebody." Michael Card is especially good not only at writing worthwhile texts but also at giving them appropriate settings.

Conclusion

Biblical truth, theological profundity, poetic richness, musical beauty, and appropriate fitness are not matters of style or personal preference. They are the marks of excellence for worship music in any age, but only the comparison of many ages—in other words, a knowledge of musical history—can tell us this. It is therefore shortsighted for a Christian college music department to offer a degree in contemporary worship music which does not require exposure to and immersion in the classic hymnody of the past. I do not say this out of hostility to contemporary music, but out of concern for its health and the health of the church. Only those musicians who are classically and historically (as well as biblically and theologically) trained are in a position to guide the church in a judicious appropriation of the best of the new music as a supplement to the church's rich musical heritage.

The marks of excellence are not absent from all contemporary music. The problem is not that new music is being introduced; the problem is not that it is being written in contemporary styles; the problem is not even that much of it is bad. That was all true in every period. Every hymn in the hymnbook was "contemporary" when it was first introduced! The problem is that, for the first time in church history, there is in many places a wholesale replacement of the old by the new, with a corresponding loss of the old. The hymnbook is thrown out and the new, instead of being added to our heritage, simply replaces it. This is not growth; it is mere change, which is not the same thing. It means a loss of historical continuity, a loss of the riches of our inheritance, and therefore, ironically, a loss of the ability to discern and pursue excellence in the new music. The last thing a Christian college music program should be doing is aiding and abetting that loss. We need to keep the old around not only for its own sake (and ours), but also for the sake of the new.

Every psalm, hymn, and spiritual song in the hymnbook was new (and contemporary) when it was written. The names of some of their authors crop up more often than others do because their work manifested truth, profundity, richness, beauty, and fitness more powerfully and reliably than anyone else's. The church should still cling to their work, both for its intrinsic merit in itself and because only an intimate and informed familiarity with that merit can help us discern and

propagate the best "new songs" that are being written today.
Whom do I mean? Well, these four would be a good place so start:

Quartet

Newton, Cowper, Wesley, Watts
Worked within their garden plots;
Domesticated by their toil
Exotic plants in English soil:
Pungent spices, soothing balms,
Cadences of David's psalms;
Parsley, sage, rosemary, thyme,
Words of God in English rhyme.
Weeded, hoed, the Garden bears
But few of thistles, thorns, or tares—
Rather, carrots, beans, and maize,
Solid sustenance of praise;
Waving grain and curling vine,
Wheat for bread and grapes for wine;
'Most every plant beneath the sun—
But leeks and garlic grew they none.

Much sand now through the glass has spilled;
They lie beneath the ground they tilled.
But still the seeds they sowed abide
And thrive, transplanted far and wide:
Where e'er a congregation sings,
Anew from earth their produce springs.
Such honor still their Lord allots
To Newton, Cowper, Wesley, Watts.[66]

Something old and something new: we need both, but the old has a privileged position because it has already been sifted by time. Thus the wise cling to the best of the old, not to exclude the new, but partly for the sake of nurturing the new. Like the early church, we still need both to be healthy—and to please our Lord.

---

66 Donald T. Williams, *Stars through the Clouds*, op. cit., p. 331.

Interlude

A Plea

To Certain Evangelical "Worship" Leaders

What We Think

What elicits deepest feeling?
What promotes profoundest praise?
That were worship whole and healing,
That would set our hearts ablaze!

What We Do

So we focus on emotion,
Turn our gaze within ourselves.
But does that foster true devotion,
However deep the sinner delves?

What We Need

Truth, He promised, is what frees us.
Fill our cup then to the brim!
Stand aside and show us Jesus:
Let our eyes be fixed on Him.[67]

---

67 Ibid., p. 394.

9
Five Theses on Gender Roles

Is the Bible setting our agenda, or the Spirit of the Age? We started asking that question in thesis 1e. It is not going to go away. And gender is one area where it becomes especially pertinent. Here are five theses that will probably make people mad on both sides.

A. The Bible is an inescapably hierarchical book, but not as modern man understands (or thinks he understands) hierarchy. (We think differentiation in role entails differentiation in value and prestige. Scripture simply does not think that way, and we should beware of imposing our assumptions on to it.)

B. Headship is unavoidably a leadership position, but not as modern man understands leadership. ("Let him who is the greatest among you become as the youngest, and the leader as the servant," Luke 22:26.)

C. The husband is not given the position of head because he is necessarily more qualified for it. (Why would we want to reintroduce human merit here after having excluded it under *sola Gratia*?)

D. The husband's leadership (Eph. 5:22) must be seen in the context of Eph. 5:21. (Wifely submission presupposes mutual submission as brother and sister in Christ. The husband as head is not given the *right* to have his *own* way, but the *responsibility* to lead the family in seeking *Christ's* way together.)

E. We do this to picture the relationship between Christ and His church. (This great mystery is equally but differently obscured and corrupted by chauvinism and by egalitarianism alike.)

> *And be subject to one another in the fear of Christ. Wives, be subject to your own husbands as to the Lord. For the husband is the head of the wife, as Christ also is of the church, He Himself being the Savior of the body. But just as the church is subject to Christ, so also the wives ought to be to their husbands in everything*
> *(Eph. 5:21-24).*

Perhaps no passage of Scripture has been more misunderstood, more disastrously applied, and hence more feared by both congregation and preacher than Eph. 5:22-24. The traditional (hierarchical) understanding is so tainted by misapplication and abuse that it can hardly be heard without distortion; and the new (egalitarian) understanding is so skewed by reaction against the traditional—or against how the traditional account is perceived—that it is equally unable to help us hear the Word of God clearly. Therefore, a new beginning is needed, a fresh start. This we will attempt in this chapter—or at least the beginning of this new beginning. We will attempt to provide a framework, a new paradigm, if you will, that will allow the wise and sane Voice of Scripture to be heard constructively in the Church once again. And we will do this by propounding five theses about this passage.[68]

---

[68] For further reading on Evangelicalism's compromises with the Spirit of the Age when it comes to gender, see Vernard Eller, *The Language of Canaan and the Grammar of Feminism* (Grand Rapids: Eerdmans, 1982), John Piper and Wayne Grudem, eds., *Recovering Biblical Manhood and Womanhood: A Response to Evangelical Feminism* (Wheaton: Crossway, 1991), and Donald T. Williams, *The Young Christian's Survival Guide* (op. cit.), chp. 15.

We now have even more profound confusions about questions of gender and sexuality than this one. For them, see my article "Defending the Biblical View of Human Sexuality: A Socratic0Question Approach," *Christian Research Journal* 50:4 (July/August 2017): 42-46, or chapter 14 of *The Young Christian's Survival Guide: Common Questions Young Christians are Asked about God, the Bible, and the Christian Faith Answered* (Cambridge, OH: Christian Publishing House, 2019).

Thesis 9a:
The Bible Is an Unavoidably Hierarchical Book, But Not As Man Understands (or Thinks He Understands) Hierarchy.

The biblical concept of hierarchy is modeled by the very Trinity itself. In passages such as John 4:34, 5:19-23, 30, 10:30, we see the Father and the Son equal in nature, power, glory, dignity, and honor, but differentiated in role. The Son's meat and drink is to do the will of the Father. The Son obeys the Father; the Father does not obey the Son, though He may grant His requests. The Father and the Son send the Spirit; the Spirit does not send the Son or the Father. Yet the Son and the Father are one. Both their unity and their differentiation are clear. Nevertheless, the "Higher" (Commander, Sender) does not dominate the "Lower" (Obedient, Sent), but rather seeks the honor of its subordinates. The Father wants all people to honor the Son even as they honor the Father (Jn. 5:22-23).

So radically different is this Trinitarian model of hierarchy from anything that we have ever experienced in a fallen world that even our Lord could not express it without seeming to create a paradox: "The Father is greater than I; . . . I and the Father are one." This set of relationships is called by theologians the "economic subordination" of the Trinity—a subordination not of value or nature or dignity or honor, but of function or role only, voluntarily adopted through love. Though all three Persons are absolutely equal in nature, honor, and even rank (being all one God), nevertheless, they are not interchangeable or redundant: The Father initiates, the Son accomplishes, and the Spirit applies. The Son does the will of the Father, the Spirit glorifies the Son, and the Father seeks the honor of the Son. If Adam and Eve as human beings were made in the image of this God, then all our thinking about right order (i.e., hierarchy) needs to start from the way the Bible articulates the inner workings of the triune God.

Equal in nature but different in function or role: The same kind of paradox, based on the nature of God, is reflected in the Church, where there is a universal priesthood of believers, and yet where within this spiritual equality elders are set aside for rule and given double honor if they rule well (1 Tim. 5:17). Likewise, there is in this Church neither male nor female (Gal. 3:28), yet the male is head of the female as Christ is of the male and God of Christ (1 Cor. 11:3). Traditionalists would often like to ignore one of these sets of verses, and feminists the other. But neither of those options is open to us if we want to be faithful to Scripture. There males exclusively serve as elders without being in any way superior to females. And this same paradoxical hierarchy is reflected in the home (Eph. 5:23), where the husband is head of the family, and thus of the wife, whose equality with him in every way is not in the least compromised by that arrangement.

But this biblical picture is unfortunately very different from the human perversions of hierarchy created by man to feed his pride. In these human and worldly hierarchies, a difference in authority or even role implies a difference in value, it is assumed to be based on a difference in ability, and it leads to a difference in prestige. As a result, we lord it over one another like the Gentiles of Mat. 20:25-28. It was forbidden to be so among the disciples.

It was not to be so among the disciples because none of these things is at all true of the biblical model in its Trinitarian original. Nor should they be true, therefore, of its temporal reflections in the church and the home. Christian husband and Christian wife are supposed to be a living portrait of the relationship between Christ and the church. But how can they fulfill that role if they obliterate either side of the biblical order outlined above? How can they do so if hierarchy is either avoided as indistinguishable from oppression or practiced in an oppressive and unChristlike way? Nothing more distorts our presentation of the Gospel, nothing more hinders its credibility, and nothing more undermines our practice of the Christian life than our failure to get back to the place where both sides of this equation can be upheld with full value and complete harmony.

Thesis 9b:
Headship Is Unavoidably a Leadership Position, But Not As Man Understands Leadership.

Some feminists interpreters have tried to read the word translated *head* in Ephesians 5:23 ("The husband is head of the wife as Christ is also the head of the church") as "source" and deny that it even implies a leadership role. The word *kephale* can indeed mean source, as the spring is the "head" of a stream and we think of a river as having "headwaters." But the context is against that meaning here, as there is no point in exhorting someone to be "subject" to a source (vs. 22, referring back to the mutual submission of all believers to each other and applying it to the wife in the marriage relationship). No one would get the idea that being head did not involve leadership from this passage without a prior commitment to avoiding it no matter what. So the husband does have a leadership role. But what kind of leadership is he supposed to exercise?

Our model for leadership is Jesus, and His kind of leadership is defined in Mat. 20:25-28, where He contrasts what we might call the "Gentile Paradigm" of leadership ("lording it over" one's subordinates like the Gentiles do) with Christ's notion that the greatest should be the servant of all. This new Christian Paradigm of leadership is incarnated for us in John 13:1-16, where Jesus washes the disciples' feet and goes out of his way to make the point that this is done in fulfillment of his role as *Lord* and teacher (13:12-16). After washing their feet—the role of a menial servant—he asks the wonderful Socratic question, "Do you know what I have done?" (13:12). Those who continue to lead by the Gentile Paradigm, *and* those who think that male leadership must perforce exemplify the Gentile Paradigm and therefore must be replaced by an egalitarianism foreign to the Scriptures, both show that they do not understand what He had done—not in the least.

Remember this phrase, the "Gentile Paradigm." It is a mode of understanding leadership and headship that has infiltrated the traditional view of male headship in marriage and thus all too frequently caused it to become utterly unChristlike and unbiblical. Physical abuse happens, but emotional abuse is much more common as too many Christian wives are browbeaten by men who think their anatomy somehow gives them the right to get their way. I have counseled many women who have been made to feel guilty for not liking such treatment! One can understand why many secular feminists and their Christian sympathizers have come to *equate* male headship ("patriarchy") with abuse and why they feel compelled to twist the Scriptures into grotesque shapes in order to avoid it. Unfortunately, such twisting is still twisting, and it can only produce twisted results.

So how does Christ lead the Church? Even He does not follow the Gentile Paradigm, though He of all people would have a right to. How does He lead? By loving the Church and giving Himself for her (Eph. 5:25-28). Why do we follow Him? Why do we hail Him as "Lord"? Because He first loved us and gave up His life for us. Even so ought husbands to be the heads of their families. What does this look like in practice?

Headship as leadership is not about the husband getting his way just because he is a man. It is about Christ getting *His* way, and the husband being responsible before God to see that this is what happens in his family. The husband and the wife in a healthy Christian marriage are not in a competition to see who gets his or her way. They both want Christ to get His way, and they both recognize that God has given the husband a special role of responsibility to take the lead in seeing that the family pursues that agenda together. Submission for the wife means encouraging and supporting her husband in *that*. She is responsible for the family following Christ's way too, but one of the most important ways she exercises her responsibility is by supporting her husband in the exercise of his.

Thesis 9c:
The Husband Is Not Ultimately Given the Position of Head because He Is More Qualified for It.

The assumption that the husband is given this role of leadership because he is more qualified for it really flows from the Gentile Paradigm, which, as we have seen, falsely equates role with worth and ability. In studying this topic, it is disappointing to see how many conservative scholars defend male headship by trying to argue that men inherently make better leaders. Even C. S. Lewis fell prey to this mistake in one of the least convincing sections of *Mere Christianity*, the end of chapter six of Book III, where men are portrayed as more objective toward those outside the family than women. No doubt some are. Maybe the majority are. But is that an adequate basis for male headship? Scripture never appeals to it.

Do men make better leaders? I do not care to dispute this claim, but simply to point out its irrelevance. Even if it were true as a generalization, that would still mean that lots of women would make better leaders than lots of men. We all know marriages in which the wife has tons more sense than the husband. Nor does Scripture teach this supposed male superiority as the rationale for its model. It is not mentioned in Ephesians 5, and even the passage often quoted in support of it (1 Tim. 2:12-14) merely says that Eve was deceived in the Garden—not that all women are generally or inherently more gullible than all men. The key to that passage is actually verse 13, referring to Adam's position of *responsibility* before God; Adam, having been made first, was head of the race and therefore had the greater responsibility as its leader. Besides, if the Trinity is our model, there is no way to argue that the Son is any less "qualified" than the Father is to be the Initiator of the plan of Salvation.

So why assume that the wife is necessarily less qualified for leadership than the husband is? Doing so misses the point in ways that are profound. Why would we want to reintroduce merit as a consideration here after rejecting it in favor of grace in chapter two? God has made the husband head of the family, and it is a mantle of responsibility he needs to take up. Trying to believe he is somehow more worthy of this responsibility than his wife is would be a distraction at best and a path to damaging folly if he were not careful. He needs to fulfill this responsibility because it has been given to him. That is really all he needs to know.

Thesis 9d:
The Husband's Leadership Must Be Seen in the Context of Ephesians 5:21.

It has often been said that the Bible was inspired by the Holy Spirit, but the chapter and verse divisions were inspired by the Devil. That is not true of course. The chapter and verse divisions were inserted by well-meaning men as an aid to finding passages, and they have served well in that role for hundreds of years. But those men were fallible, and they did not always put those breaks in the most logical places. We should remember that they were not part of the original text and are not inspired. If we don't, we may miss some very important features of context. We spoke of this already in the chapter on hermeneutics (Thesis 6a).

The passage from Ephesians five is a perfect example. Our translations almost all take their cue from the verse divisions and begin a new sentence in verse 22, "Wives, be subject to your husbands," as if we were starting a new topic. But actually there is no verb in Eph. 5:22, nor is there any period at the end of v. 21 in the original. It should literally read like this: "Being subject to one another . . . [including] wives to their own husbands." The main verb is actually way back in verse 18: "*Be filled* with the Spirit." The marks of the Spirit-filled life are then laid out through a series of participles. (Tongues, by the way, are not even mentioned.) What are the effects of being filled with the Spirit? *Speaking* to one another in psalms, hymns, and spiritual songs; *singing* and making melody with our hearts to the Lord; always *giving thanks* for all things; and *being subject* to *one another* in the fear of Christ (Eph. 5:18-21, emphasis added).

Verse 22 is then a continuation of verse 21, and there is a close connection between them. Wifely submission is not a new topic. There should be no period, only a comma! Wifely submission is a continuation of the discussion of the *mutual* submission to Christ which results from a Spirit-filled life; it is an aspect of that mutual submission, a special application of it. In other words, before there is any submission of wife to husband, both wife and husband must already be submitting to one another in the Lord. It is all about submission to Christ, enabled by the Spirit. This includes the husband submitting to his responsibility to be the spiritual leader of the family and the wife submitting to that godly leadership. They should have practiced for these roles by submitting to each other in the Lord as Christian brother and sister before there was any talk of a wedding. Mutual submission in the fear of Christ means that they have a mutual commitment to follow Christ, which means following whichever one of them first discerns Christ's will in the situation. If you are not already practicing that kind of spiritual friendship in the Lord, you have no business even thinking about getting married.

Wifely submission as an aspect of mutual submission means that the husband and the wife are designed to lead the family as a *team*—but it is a team with a designated *captain*. (Once again we see the two-edged nature of the truth, with both sides of it needing to be kept in balance: It is a team; the team has a captain.) The wife should be consulted as an equal partner, and she may even initiate. Part of the husband's responsibility as the leader is to listen to her and follow her advice when she is right. The bottom line is that if the family is not being led in a godly direction, it will be the husband who is first and most severely called on the carpet by God—just as it happened in Gen. 3:9. The husband and wife are to lead the family together, but God holds the husband primarily responsible for making sure that their leadership takes the family in directions pleasing to God. And, like Christ, he is to do this not by barking orders but by setting an example of loving service, of godly living, of costly sacrifice. Otherwise, he is leading by the Gentile Paradigm, and that is *not* what God is commanding the wife to submit to. (How to handle less than ideal situations is a difficult topic that goes beyond the scope of this Thesis, which is simply to restore an accurate picture of what the ideal is. I will touch on it, though, very briefly and tentatively, below.)

Thesis 9e:
We Do This To Picture the Relationship Between Christ and the Church.

I promised you a new paradigm: Here it is. God wants the family to be a Drama Company in which the husband is assigned to enact the role of Christ, and the wife that of the church, so that the church and the world might understand who Christ is. Why is this role assigned to the husband? Not because he is more qualified for it or worthy of it. Who could be? No doubt it is partly because Christ was male, as Adam was. And, looking at today's church, I cannot help but wonder if it is not partly because the modern male is the least inclined to take this role. I am afraid that the Gentile Paradigm comes naturally to us males. We would not learn to lead like Christ unless we had to. And the ironic tragedy is that Satan has succeeded in so permeating the traditional hierarchical view with the Gentile Paradigm that men do in fact take on the role of Head with results precisely opposite to those that God intended. But Scripture is plainly opposed to this as much as it is to egalitarianism and its erasing of all role distinctions.

What then does submission mean for the wife in the Christian Paradigm? It does not mean the husband has the right to give orders—any orders—and she must simply carry them out. It means she is willing to let the man lead the family in a godly direction. She will in fact encourage him to take on this God-assigned role. Even if she is more qualified for leadership herself, she will not usurp this role but graciously help her husband learn to grow into it, if he is willing.

What if the husband is not willing? What if he is abusive? If he is not willing to be a godly leader, the wife may be forced to take that role herself by default, but that is never her purpose or intention or preference. She will support and encourage her husband whenever he moves in the direction of genuine godly leadership. She will be willing to be the "straight man"—er, person—that he plays off of in developing the part. If on the other hand the situation is even worse, if the husband is abusive and unrepentant, the wife has some difficult decisions to make about protecting herself and her children. Nothing I can say here will make them easier. But she should not compound her situation and make it even more difficult by feeling guilty that somehow the husband's sin is her fault or by feeling that God wants her to "submit" to a situation that was never commanded. Surely the church needs to do a better job of preparing people for marriage by teaching Ephesians 5 correctly so that these abusive situations never get a chance to get started.

Our focus here is not solving all the problems of abuse but rather that of restoring an accurate picture of the ideal as Scripture actually teaches it. So let us focus on these drama companies presenting the biblical pageant of Christ and the church. If both partners are playing the part they have been assigned, the husband will not be imposing his agenda on the wife, but they will be finding Christ's agenda together. For her, it means allowing someone who is her equal, not her superior, to lead in the dance. But it must be the dance tune Scripture is playing, not just any whim the husband happens to have. Now, that would be a powerful Reformation of the life of the church indeed!

Conclusion

Did I model what I am teaching here in my own marriage? Not always. Not as well as I wish I had, especially early on when I was myself more tainted by the Gentile Paradigm than was at all good for the relationship. Where, I can imagine someone asking in despair, do we see such a thing as you are talking about? I would like to say, here. In your house, your congregation, and mine. Already the foretaste, increasingly the fullness. From now on. By the grace of God, let there be a new beginning in this vexed matter, in your family and mine. For this mystery is great: I am speaking of Christ and the Church.

Interlude

Elementary

"And the world was without form and void, and darkness was upon the face of the deep. And the Spirit of God was brooding upon the surface of the waters"
(Gen. 1:2)

Earth, Water, Wind, Fire
Each against the others strain
Until the stronger God, Desire,
Binds them in the Golden Chain.

Water, Wind, Fire, and Earth
Mix in Chaos uncontrolled
Until sweet Order, brought to birth,
Links them in the Chain of Gold.

Wind, Fire, Earth, and Water,
Each of which, in Nature's course,
Would make the world's foundations totter,
Bow before a greater Force.

Fire, Earth, Water, Wind
Perform what they've no knowledge of:
Find their unity and end
Within the Golden Chain of Love.

Harmony in universe;
From cacophony, a Choir;
Thus does Grace redeem the curse
Of Earth, Water, Wind, and Fire.[69]

---

[69] Donald T. Williams, *Stars through the Clouds*, op. cit., p. 100.

10

Five Theses on Charismatic Phenomena

Experience is not an end in itself. It is valuable for what it is an experience of and what it leads us to. What should that be for believers? The glory of God in the face of Jesus Christ; fervent worship and loving service that is faithful to His Word. Is that true of our experiences of grace? How can it be? Let's see.

A. It cannot be proved from Scripture that gifts such as tongues have ceased. (There is no reason to think that "the perfect" in 1 Cor. 13:10 is a reference to the completion of the canon, which is not mentioned in that context, rather than the Second Coming.)

B. It does not follow that such manifestations as are experienced today are *ipso facto* of the Holy Spirit. (They may be genuine; they may be demonic; they may just be emotional hype. They must be evaluated on a case-by-case basis in terms of whether they advance the Spirit's mission as taught in Scripture.)

C. The mission of the Holy Spirit is to glorify the *Son*. ("He shall glorify me, for He shall take of mine, and shall disclose it to you," John 16:14.)

D. The practice of gifts must therefore be evaluated Christocentrically: Do they edify the Body by pointing it toward and concentrating it on the Son? (Or do they focus attention on the gift, the one practicing the gift, or even on the Holy Spirit Himself? The Spirit is not in the business of hindering His own mission.)

E. No gift should be used contrary to the express instructions for its use in the New Testament. (Many modern "tongues" would be very quickly and efficiently eliminated if people simply took 1 Cor. 14 seriously.

For the last couple of generations, the Pentecostal movement and its offspring the Charismatic movement have been the fastest growing segment of the church around the world. Arising in the Azusa Street revival of the early Twentieth Century, the Pentecostal denominations added to the two-stage conversionism of the Wesleyan holiness tradition an emphasis on speaking in tongues (glossolalia) as the definitive sign of the baptism and fullness of the Holy Spirit. The Wesleyan "second experience" of "entire sanctification" was repackaged as the baptism of the Spirit evidenced by glossolalia understood as parallel to the experience of the early Christians on the day of Pentecost in Acts. When the experience of tongues broke out of the historic Pentecostal denominations into mainline churches, the Charismatic movement was born. The emphasis on personal ecstatic experience has certainly resonated in a subjective age, with the result that no one can avoid reckoning with Pentecostal theology and experience in contemporary Christianity.[70]

Pentecostal theology and practice have always been controversial. To traditional Christians in the modern world an outbreak of tongues seemed the very antithesis of doing things "decently and in order." And the doctrinal underpinnings of the experience were even more problematic, picking out one of the spiritual gifts as a sign of superior spirituality with the implication that differently gifted Christians were obviously not filled with the Spirit. Also, it is curious that, while Pentecostal apologists always appeal to the Day of Pentecost in the Book of Acts, that particular experience seems to have disappeared even in the First Century. In Acts, the gift of tongues *did away* with any need for interpreters, for everyone heard the Gospel in his own dialect. By the time we get to First Corinthians, tongues are *creating* a need for interpreters, having become a special language for private devotion. Whatever was happening in Corinth, it was the antithesis of Pentecost, not a continuation of it. And the Corinthian tongues seem to be the

---

70 For a comprehensive view of the theology of the Holy Spirit (pneumatology) as it relates to these movements, see my book *The Person and Work of the Holy Spirit* (Nashville: Broadman, 1994; reprinted by Wipf and Stock). Other excellent and balanced treatments include Frederick Dale Bruner, *A Theology of the Holy Spirit: The Pentecostal Experience and New Testament Witness* (Grand Rapids: Eerdmans, 1970); John R. W. Stott, *Baptism and Fullness: The Work of the Holy Spirit Today* (Downers Grove: InterVarsity Press, 1976); J. I. Packer, *Keeping in Step with the Spirit* (Old Tappan, N.J.: Revell, 1984); and Donald A. Carson, *Showing the Spirit: A Theological Exposition of 1 Corinthians 12-14* (Grand Rapids: Baker, 1987).

only kind we encounter today. I have heard a lot of instances of what passed for the gift of tongues, but none of them involved someone speaking a real language he had never studied to present the Gospel to a native speaker of that language.

The errors of Pentecostal theology, the excesses of Pentecostal practice, and sometimes the overreactions of the traditional response to them have all been sources of difficulty. The controversy has been at best a distraction from and at worst a hindrance to the accurate understanding and clear proclamation of the true Gospel (even as it can also seem to some like a boost to it). As such it deserves its own set of theses to help us see through the clutter and achieve a needed reformation of the church in this area.

Thesis 10a:
It Cannot Be Proved from Scripture That Gifts Such As Tongues Have Ceased.

At the opposite pole from Pentecostal and Charismatic theology is the position known as *cessationism*, which holds that the "miraculous" spiritual gifts, such as tongues, prophecy, and healing, ceased with the passing of the apostles and the closing of the New-Testament canon. There are basically two arguments in favor of this idea: a theological argument and a textual argument. Theologically it is argued that the purpose of miracles was to attest revelation. They are not evenly or randomly distributed even through biblical history but cluster around key revelatory moments like the Exodus and Sinai in the Old Testament or the coming of Christ in the New. Their function is to show who God's true prophets and apostles are so that we can believe their prophecies with confidence. Naturally, then, when the apostolic age comes to an end and the New Testament is no longer being written (say, with John's last book, Revelation, about AD 90), miracles, having accomplished their purpose, fade from history until it is time for the Second Coming. God would not permit true miracles to take place after the apostolic age because this could only confuse us as to what His Word actually is, opening the door to spurious claims of extra-biblical revelation.

The textual argument is based on First Corinthians 13:9-11. In the midst of his discussion of spiritual gifts, Paul says this:

> For we know in part and we prophesy in part; but when the perfect comes the partial will be done away. When I was a child, I used to speak as a child, think as a child, reason as a child; when I became a man, I did away with childish things. For now we see in a mirror dimly, but then face to face; now I know in part, but then I shall know fully, just as I also have been fully known. But now abide faith, hope, and love; but the greatest of these is love.

The context is prophecy, so the "complete" must refer to the completion of prophecy or of God's revelation, right? We know and prophesy in part, but when the perfect comes, the partial will be obsolete and will no longer obtain. So when the canon of Scripture is completed (the word translated "perfect," *telos*, can often mean "complete"), then prophecy and other miraculous gifts, having fulfilled their purpose, will no longer be needed and will disappear from God's economy. History, it is argued, confirms that this is exactly what happened.

It is easy to see why cessationism is an attractive position for people appalled by the errors and excesses of Pentecostalism. It is simple. It upholds the authority and the uniqueness of inscripturated revelation. And it does not require us to use discernment. All Charismatic phenomena can be summarily dismissed as emotional hype at best and demonic delusion at worst. Unfortunately, neither of the two arguments in its favor is completely convincing.

Theologically, it is clear that the attestation of revelation is *a* function of miracles, and an important one. But in order for the cessationist conclusion to follow, we would have to be able to establish that attesting revelation is *the* function of miracles. And this would be very difficult to maintain. Miracles in Scripture attest God's messengers, but they also proclaim His glory and they deliver His people. Christ's miracles of healing are explicitly attributed to His *compassion* for the people on multiple occasions. If God's compassion has not ceased, then we cannot rule out His use of miraculous intervention subsequent to biblical times. The most we could conclude from the theological argument is that a lessening of emphasis on miracles in God's working after the age of revelation might not be wholly unexpected; indeed, it would be consistent with the clustering of miracles that we observe even in biblical times. But it simply does not follow that He cannot or will not ever intervene miraculously once the canon of Scripture is completed. The theological argument at best takes us only part way to where the cessationist wants to go.

John F. MacArthur, Jr., avoids this conclusion and maintains a form of cessationism by giving a technical definition of a miracle as "an extraordinary event wrought by God through human agency," an agency that implies the authentification of that human instrument "to declare a specific revelation."[71] He believes that God still intervenes

---

71 John F. MacArthur, Jr., *Charismatic Chaos* (Grand Rapids: Zondervan, 1992), p. 106.

supernaturally, but does not count such a phenomenon as a medically inexplicable healing as a "miracle" unless it is done by an individual who has the "gift" of healing. He believes that "God can heal people apart from natural or medical remedies," but does not believe "that God uses men and women in the same way He used Moses, Elijah, or Jesus." "The Holy Spirit has not given any modern-day Christians miraculous gifts comparable to those He gave the apostles."[72]

Given MacArthur's narrow technical definition of miracle, I do not disagree with him. But that is not the meaning given to the term in normal usage. It is not the definition used by C. S. Lewis in his classic work *Miracles*: "an interference with Nature by supernatural power."[73] By the normal definition, miracles have not ceased, though their function of authenticating revelation has. We should indeed be suspicious of people claiming to be contemporary prophets parallel to Moses or Elijah. MacArthur gives many needed warnings, and I think his arguments are basically sound, though I do not think they quite justify the dogmatism of his conclusions, for the reasons I give here. Nevertheless, I recommend his book as a needed corrective to the lack of discernment that characterizes our age in these matters. The theological argument from authentication has some validity but does not quite take us with full assurance as far as its proponents want to go.

The textual argument fares no better. It is possible that the "perfect" referred to by Paul is the perfect completion of the New-Testament canon; but a couple of factors make it not very likely. Do we see Christ "face to face" in the New Testament? Surely not; that sounds much more like a reference to the Second Coming. Do we know Him "fully" now that the New Testament has been completed? Is there nothing to be added to that knowledge when we get to Heaven? I will not know Christ *as I am known* until I see Him face to face when He returns. It looks very much as if the future time when tongues will cease is not the completion of the biblical canon at all but rather the return of Christ. Even if you are not convinced by this analysis, it is hard to avoid the conclusion that the completion of the canon can hardly be the *clear and plain* meaning of this text. And if another possible meaning (the Second Coming) is even still on the table (and it is), then the complete cessation of all miraculous operations and gifts

---

72 Ibid., p. 109.

73 C. S. Lewis, *Miracles: A Preliminary Study* (N.Y.: MacMillan, 1947), p. 10.

has not been *proved* by the passage.

I am not arguing that the Holy Spirit either still gives or that He no longer gives the gift of tongues. That is more than I know. But nothing in the New Testament lets me rule out in advance the possibility that He does (or might). There are moments when I wish I could draw such a blanket conclusion. This chapter would certainly be easier to write if I could! But in all honesty I cannot. I believe I have observed miraculous events. I knew a lady whose large, aggressively growing cancer, in response to the prayers of her church, suddenly and mysteriously disappeared in ways that baffled her oncologists. I saw the before-and-after x-rays myself. On the other hand, I have heard many examples of glossolalia, none of which convinced me that it was what we read about in the Book of Acts. This naturally makes me skeptical and suspicious. But I cannot absolutely rule out the possibility that God could still work that way.

Where does this leave us?

Thesis 10b:
It Does Not Follow That Such Manifestations As Are Experienced Today Are *Ipso Facto* of the Holy Spirit.

✠

Many people seem to assume that if the case for cessationism fails, Pentecostal theology and experience are thereby vindicated. Not so fast! From the fact that we cannot prove that, say, a black swan is impossible, it does not follow that it exists. To show that, we would actually have to find one, and see that it matches the criteria: it is a swan, not a goose; it is real, not just an urban legend or a rumor; it is black, not just dark gray. Can we do that with the Charismatic gifts? The answer to that question is going to be messier than anyone would like.

There are at least four logical possibilities when we see one of these manifestations. (Let's just stick with tongues for simplicity's sake.) It might be someone exercising a genuine gift of the Spirit. It might be a demonic delusion. It might in the third case be neither; it might have nothing supernatural about it at all. It might just be the result of someone losing control of his vocal apparatus as a result of overwhelming emotional stimulation. And there is a fourth possibility that definitely has happened. I have had people confess to me that they had actually *faked* tongues to avoid being labeled "unspiritual." You can easily learn to do so convincingly, they said. So each instance has to be judged on a case by case basis. I told you it was going to get messy!

The only way to clean up the mess is to have biblically and scientifically solid criteria by which to discern what is happening. I will start with the scientific because, while it is less important than the biblical, it cannot be ignored. I have a bit of a background in linguistics. As a medievalist, general and historical linguistics was one prong of my doctoral studies because of the radical ways the English language has changed from Beowulf to Chaucer to Shakespeare to us. So I know something about what to listen for: I know the kinds of patterns that occur in a real language, the different strategies by which phonemes and morphemes can be deployed to create meaning. There are isolating, inflective, agglutinative, and incorporative languages. (Don't worry; I won't try to explain the different ways they work.) I have learned several languages and studied more. The point is that every single time I have had the opportunity to hear alleged glossolalia, my conclusion has been that what I heard was not any kind of language at all. It was just somebody stuttering, randomly and rhythmically repeating a few syllables over and over. Others with more expertise than I possess have done careful studies to come to the same conclusion: These are not human languages known by anyone.[74] As for heavenly languages—do we seriously think that angels are *less* articulate than we are?

What can we conclude from this data? Neither the Holy Spirit nor an unholy one was required to produce these effects. A lot of what passes for the gift of tongues is not the manifestation of anything but emotional hype. Surely glossolalia is not a genuine effect requiring the miraculous intervention of the Holy Spirit if people can learn to fake it convincingly! But wait. Should we generalize from these examples to cover *every* occurrence of the phenomenon? That would be a dangerous move to make. Nevertheless, we should not be shocked to discover that Satan is in the business of encouraging counterfeits, nor that he does not even need to exert supernatural power to achieve those deceptions. We are perfectly capable of generating them without any supernatural help ourselves! All Satan has to do is encourage our native tendencies. We should beware of creating environments and expectations that make people more susceptible to his deceptions. To stop doing that is surely a Reformation desperately needed by large segments of the church today.

We are left then with a lot of emotional pressure and with some people responding to it by manifesting a stuttering "tongue" that they have been convinced is real, and others responding by deliberately faking one. Demonic influence cannot be eliminated as a possibility, whether it be directly supernatural or merely the encouragement of cultural expectations. I had a classmate in seminary who was from India. He was taken to a Pentecostal service and was horrified by what he saw. "This is nothing but paganism!" he responded. "I can take you to Hindu temples where people are doing that." And while all the

---

74 E.g. William J. Samarin, *Tongues of Men and Angels* (N.Y.: MacMillan, 1972), 227-8. "There is no mystery about glossolalia. Tape-recorded samples are easy to obtain and to analyze. They always turn out to be the same thing: strings of syllables, taken from among sounds that the speaker knows, put together more or less haphazardly but which nevertheless emerge as word-like and sentence-like units because of realistic language-like rhythm and melody."

above makes me skeptical, I cannot fully eliminate the possibility that the Holy Spirit might use the experience in some people's lives. There are those who speak of a deepened love for Christ and confidence in His Word as a result of speaking in tongues whose testimony is hard to dismiss.

We have no choice but to examine each case on an individual basis. To sort through this mess and evaluate manifestations of these "gifts" on an individual basis, we need biblical criteria. They are provided by the next two theses.

Thesis 10c:
The Mission of the Holy Spirit Is To Glorify the *Son*.

We need biblical criteria by which to evaluate alleged manifestations of the Holy Spirit and His gifts. They need to be *biblical* criteria, derived from the actual teaching of Scripture and not from our experience (or lack of experience). And they need to be *criteria*, capable of helping us use discernment to distinguish the real and the valid from the fake and the abused. How can we find them? We can assume that the Holy Spirit is not in the business of hindering His own ministry. When He is truly at work we would expect to find Him advancing it. So we had better begin by being clear about what His mission is. Fortunately, Jesus Himself gives us a rather long and comprehensive exposition of it, as recorded in John's Gospel.

Starting in the middle of John chapter 14 and running through chapter 16, the Lord gives His disciples an extended treatment of the ministry of the Holy Spirit. Jesus' purpose was to prepare them for the coming period when He Himself would no longer be physically present with them. It will be all right, for He promises to ask the Father to give them another Helper (Grk. *parakletos*) who will be with them forever—"the Spirit of Truth" (Jn. 14:16-18). This Helper will teach the disciples all things and bring to their remembrance all that Jesus had said to them (14:26). This Helper, who proceeds from the Father, will testify about Jesus and enable the disciples in turn to testify about Him (15:26-7). It is to their advantage that Jesus should go away, for then He will send the Helper to convict the world (16:7-8). When the Spirit of Truth comes, He will not speak on His own but will speak whatever He hears from the Father and the Son. The end result of all of this is that "He will glorify me, for He will take of mine and disclose it to you" (16:13-16).

Impressive in this long discussion of the ministry of the Holy Spirit is its Christocentric focus. The Spirit is sent to stand in for Jesus in His coming physical absence as "another" Helper—not a "different" kind of Helper but "another" of the same kind (Grk. *allos*, not *heteros*). He thus keeps the disciples from being left as orphans. He does this by reminding them of Jesus and His words, by testifying about Jesus, by speaking for Jesus, by disclosing Jesus. Everything the Spirit does is seen in relation to Jesus. If there is one phrase that sums it all up it is that He will glorify Jesus. "He will glorify me." The heart of the ministry of the Spirit is to promote the glory of the Son.

This interpretation is confirmed by the Apostle Paul in the prologue to his Epistle to the Ephesians. There he gives a summary of all that God has done for the salvation of His people—election, predestination, calling, redemption, etc.—from the standpoint of its purpose. What that purpose is he reiterates four times. It is "to the praise of the glory of His grace' (1:6). It is oriented to "the summing up of all things in Christ, things in the heavens and things upon the earth" (1:10). It is "to the end that we who were the first to hope in Christ should be to the praise of His glory" (1:12). And finally, all this whole enterprise, this whole project to bring glory to God and to the Son particularly in terms of their grace through the salvation of sinners, is sealed to its recipients in Christ "with the Holy Spirit of promise who is given as a pledge of our inheritance, with a view to the redemption of God's own possession." And, oh, yes, there is one last climactic phrase. Wait for it: "To the praise of His glory" (1:13-14). God's purpose in the salvation of sinners is His own glory, and the Spirit's key role in that salvation is fully focused on that purpose. The ministry of the Spirit is to glorify the Son. It is to serve as His personal Agent and Representative, making Him real to His people by making them one with Him, until His return. The ministry, the purpose, the overruling desire of the Holy Spirit is to glorify Jesus. It is all about Jesus.

This purpose informs every aspect of the Spirit's ministry. All are best understood as the fulfillment of His burning desire to bring glory to the Son. He inspired the Prophets of the Old Testament and the Apostles of the New to write Scripture, and He illuminates our minds to understand it, because it reveals Jesus. He convicts the world of sin to show it its need of Jesus. He calls us to and enables in us faith and repentance to connect us with Jesus. He regenerates us so that we may live in Jesus. He sanctifies us so that we may be like Jesus. He seals us in salvation and preserves us in faith so we can see Jesus face to face. And the ministry of spiritual gifts is no exception. He gives spiritual gifts to the saints in the church so that they may edify each other, build one another up, *in Jesus*. It is all about Jesus.[75]

---

75 I think one of the most critical needs of the church today is a truly Christocentric pneumatology.

Thesis 10d:
The Practice of Gifts Must Therefore Be Evaluated Christocentrically: Do They Edify the Body by Pointing It toward and Concentrating It on the Son?

If the primary purpose of the Holy Spirit and His ministry is to glorify the Son, then we have a fruitful way of understanding that ministry and a useful criterion by which we can evaluate alleged instances of it. How, in any particular aspect of His ministry, does the Spirit glorify the Son by continuing, as the Son's Representative and on His behalf, the Son's ministry? How does this supposed manifestation of the Spirit's ministry edify the Body of Christ by pointing it toward, and concentrating it on, and unifying it with, the Son? If there is no obvious answer to that question, how is it then a manifestation of the Holy Spirit sent by Christ according to the Scriptures? That is the test that any "experience" of the Spirit has to pass in order for people truly in tune with the Spirit and His priorities to get excited about it.

The gift of tongues as it was seen on the Day of Pentecost got high marks on this test. People heard the disciples talking *about Jesus* in their own language so they could *understand* the Gospel of salvation *in Jesus* and believe *in Jesus*. Peter in his sermon on that occasion had to talk about the Spirit at first in order to explain what was happening as the fulfillment of prophecy (Acts 2:17-21). But as quickly as he could he moved on to his main point: talking about Jesus (2:22-36). Peter showed himself to be filled with the Spirit by spending three times as many verses on Jesus as on the Spirit, and by saying as the conclusion and climax of his message, "Therefore let all the house of Israel know for certain that God has made Him both Lord and Christ—this Jesus whom you crucified" (2:36). We know that the Spirit was at work because Luke says so, of course, but also because the focus was right where the Spirit Himself wants it: on Christ. We likewise know that John the Baptist was filled with the Spirit from his mother's room because the Gospels tell us so, but we also know it

---

I tried to take some steps toward providing one in my book *The Person and Work of the Holy Spirit* (op. cit.). See it for further development of these ideas.

from John's own statement about Jesus that "He must increase, but I must decrease" (Jn. 3:30). That is the authentic voice of the Holy Spirit speaking. Three thousand people were baptized in the name of Jesus as a result of Peter's sermon about Jesus and the disciples' clear and articulate testimony to Jesus in their own birth tongues. That is what the ministry of the Spirit looks like!

Contrast this with the tongues that were happening just a few years later in Corinth (1 Cor. 12-14). Whatever that phenomenon was, it was not the same thing, for it had a very different nature and it produced very different results. In Jerusalem, tongues did away with any need for interpreters. In Corinth, they *created* a need for interpreters. In Jerusalem, in other words, the curse of Babel was being reversed. In Corinth, it was being recreated. People were talking, but nobody had any idea what they were saying. They could not have told you themselves. If you want to do that as a private prayer language at home, fine, Paul says in effect—but not in church, unless someone can interpret it. No understanding, no edification; no edification, no glorification of Jesus; no glorification of Jesus, no genuine and valid and not abused ministry of the Holy Spirit. Instead of being glorified, Jesus was being associated with confusion. Why would the Holy Spirit want to promote that? Presumably, He would not. Presumably, He either had nothing to do with it, or the gifts he had given were being grossly abused and misused.

Well, guess which kind of tongue the vast majority heard among Pentecostals and Charismatics today is? To be accurate, we should be calling it the Corinthian Movement, not the Pentecostal or Charismatic Movement. That realization does not automatically invalidate everything that is happening in those churches, but it does mean that Paul's exhortations to the Corinthians are precisely what we need to hear today as we seek to discern where the Holy Spirit is genuinely at work and to reform the church so that it is more open and friendly to His real work as opposed to the various counterfeits of it that Satan uses to distract us from it today. And that leads us to our next Thesis.

Thesis 10e:
No Gift Should Be Used Contrary to the Express Instructions for Its Use in the New Testament.

In chapters 12-14 of his first Epistle to the Corinthians, Paul gives the definitive extended treatment of the work of the Spirit, especially as it relates to spiritual gifts. Those who wish to be faithful to the Lord and to see the Spirit at work in their own ministries should pay special attention to it. It sounds as if it could have been written specifically to deal with our issues, just yesterday. It is a detailed blueprint for the Reformation of the church in this area of its life.

Chapter twelve begins by reaffirming the focus of the Spirit's ministry: People moved by the Spirit do not curse Jesus but avow His lordship (12:3). This is consistent with Jesus' and Paul's emphasis on the role of the Spirit in bringing glory to Jesus. Then Paul introduces the topic of spiritual gifts. Each Christian is given at least one way to manifest the Spirit's work "for the common good," i.e., the edification of the whole Body (12:7). While speaking in tongues is affirmed as part of the Spirit's repertoire of gifts, the Pentecostal theology that makes it the sign of baptism and fullness is radically undercut, indeed, explicitly denied and contradicted. Members of the Body receive different gifts. At the end of the chapter, we have a series of sentences that in Greek grammar are called "questions expecting a negative answer." The New American Standard translates accurately: "All do not speak in tongues, do they?" (12:30—expected answer, "No, of course not"). But if tongues is the definitive sign of Spirit baptism, all Christians *should* speak in tongues. If they don't, there is a problem. According to Paul, though, if they *did* it would be a problem, undermining the complementarity of the gifts which his teaching here upholds. We simply cannot have it both ways. If tongues belong in the list of spiritual gifts in this discourse, then they cannot be the definitive sign of Spirit baptism. We really do have to make up our minds.

Chapter thirteen is the famous digression on love, often quoted separately as "the love chapter." By calling it a digression I do not mean to compromise its importance. Nor do I object to its use as a self-contained discourse on love, as long as we do not forget its actual purpose: It is central to the whole discussion of gifts because it is crucial that the kind of genuine love that comes only from God, the kind that the Spirit is elsewhere described as "shedding abroad in our hearts" (Rom. 5:5), be the motivation that moves and the power that enables our use of spiritual gifts. Apart from that love, they are just an annoying, clanging cymbal (13:1); apart from that love, they are nothing (13:2, 3).

Chapter fourteen then moves on to specific instructions for the use of gifts—particularly tongues—in public worship. The transitional imperative "Pursue love" of 14:1 signals that the point of these instructions is that they will help us do what chapter thirteen had stressed: practice the gifts in love. The one who loves, for example, pursues the edification of the whole Body, and consequently cares more about prophecy, which is addressed to the understanding of the whole Body, than about the Corinthian style of tongue, which is understood only by God and thus edifies nobody except the speaker (14:1-4). The implication is that to intrude Corinthian tongues into the gathered assembly is selfish, not loving.

The bulk of the rest of the chapter is a continuing explanation of the rationale for preferring prophecy to tongues in public worship, focused on the importance of edification and the essential necessity of *understanding* if edification is to happen. Paul cares greatly that the mind be fruitful, which does not and cannot happen as a result of an uninterpreted Corinthian tongue (14:14). (Once again we remember that somehow on the Day of Pentecost this had not been a problem!) Paul claims to be able to speak in tongues himself (14:18), but in the assembly he would rather say five words addressed to the mind than ten thousand in that kind of tongue (14:19). Believers need to be edified, unbelievers need to be convicted, and Jesus needs to be glorified; and love, which wants these things to happen, will gladly follow suit with the rules Paul is about to lay down.

In verses 26-33 we then get the specific rules Paul propounds to deal with the abuses that flow from the Corinthians' lack of love and their lack of understanding of the Spirit's ministry and the purpose of the church in coming together. People may bring psalms, revelations, teaching, tongues, interpretation—but edification is the grand principle that determines their use. Nobody should speak in tongues unless someone can interpret them; no more than two or three should speak in any case; and they have to take turns. The Babel-like chaos that occurs when everyone is praying and speaking different things at once is explicitly forbidden. Prophets may also speak, and the others are to pass judgment on their prophecies (14:29). (This last provision proves, by the way, that New-Testament "prophets" did not have the same gift as Old-Testament prophets. They are not to preface their message with "Thus saith the Lord," but rather with something like "I believe the Lord may be saying to us . . . ." Other mature believers would then confirm their message—or not—as being consistent with Scripture. They were not giving revelation like an Isaiah or Jeremiah, who could indeed say, "Thus saith the Lord . . . for the mouth of the Lord has spoken!") The prophets are also to take turns and not speak over one another, because God is not a God of confusion, but of peace (14:33).

What are we to make of this set of rules? If they were followed, the great bulk of the tongues that are heard today would simply disappear. It looks to me as if Paul wanted to discourage the use of tongues in public worship as far as he possibly could without forbidding it outright. He apparently did not wish to forbid tongues outright because of the possibility that the Spirit might return to the Pentecost-type tongue, or even want to use the Corinthian type with an interpretation at some point. He apparently accepted the Corinthian-type of tongue as something the Holy Spirit could use as a private experience in a believer's devotional life, but found it inappropriate in a public service. So he forbids, not tongues as such, but the conditions and practices that encourage and sustain the counterfeits and abuses of tongues. Thus Paul does not tie the Spirit's hands, as it were, but he does tie ours. Nothing is to be allowed in public worship that does not address the understanding, the mind. The bottom line: "Therefore, my brethren, desire earnestly to prophesy, and do not forbid to speak in tongues. But all things must be done properly and in an orderly manner" (14:39-40).

Conclusion

The conclusion is inescapable: A reform desperately needed by large swaths of the conservative church today is simply to pay attention to these apostolic directives and return to obedience. We can lay it down as a principle without exception and deserving full acceptance: The Holy Spirit of Jesus Christ is not in the business hindering His own ministry of glorifying Jesus; nor is He is the business of promoting disobedience to the Scripture which Jesus commissioned Him to inspire. The true and genuine ministry of the Holy Spirit does not do that. It will not do that. When what passes for the ministry of the Spirit does, something is very profoundly and seriously and fundamentally wrong. There can be no real Reformation without obedience.

Interlude

Pentecost
(Compared with Later Imitations)

Stronger than a hawk, the Dove
Swept by, and in the eddies of
His passing, tongues of flame were fanned
And men fell to the ground unmanned.
They stuttered as their wits were lost
And thought it a new Pentecost:
The merely inarticulate sigh
Of His furious passing by.

But when He stopped to build His nest
First in the Apostolic breast,
A different language was expressed
In fit words, honed and well disposed;
Those were not drunk as men supposed,
But spoke real tongues they had not learned:
Thus the true tongues of fire burned.
Men heard about their sins and grieved;
They heard the Gospel and believed,
For each one heard of Jesus' blood
In his own tongue—and *understood*.

Does that Dove's nesting in the heart
Drive it and the mind apart?
Never! Rather, say He brings
The two together 'neath His wings.
The mind alert was not the cost
Of the primal Pentecost,
Where true wit was not lost, but gained
When the showers of blessing rained.[76]

---

76 Donald T. Williams, *Stars through the Clouds*, op. cit., p. 164.

11
Five Theses on Evangelism

Is the Great Commission really the commission we are following?

A. Evangelism and mission exist because worship does not. (John Piper gets this right.[77])

B. The Great Commission is to make *disciples*, not converts. (Conversion is only the first step in making a disciple—the beginning, not the end, of fulfilling the Great Commission.)

C. A "convert" who does not become a disciple is presumed not to be a true convert. (A person who gives no evidence of regeneration, ongoing sanctification, and commitment to a Bible-believing church, gives no evidence of conversion. We are saved by *faith*, not by once having said the right words or signed a card—see thesis 3.b.)

D. A disciple is not made until the convert is at least stumblingly trying to learn and do all things whatsoever Christ has commanded us. (This is how Jesus Himself defined discipleship when He gave the Great Commission in Mat. 28.)

E. A disciple is not made until the convert is a committed and functioning member of a Bible-believing local church. (The church in the New Testament is not an optional club for believers; it is the Body into which they are grafted *by* their salvation, Acts 2:47b, 1 Cor. 12:13, etc. And a church not committed to the truth of the Faith is no church of Jesus Christ.)

---

[77] John Piper, *Let the Nations be Glad: The Supremacy of God in Missions* (Grand Rapids: Baker, 2003), p. 17.

It is ironic and tragic that the movement in the history of the church most characterized by its commitment to the Great Commission and to conversionism is now being spiritually hollowed out precisely by its failure to pursue the Great Commission. The very name of *Evangelicalism* and its related adjective *Evangelical* are so close to the noun *evangelism* and its adjective *evangelistic* that the two word groups are often confused. The first means commitment to the Gospel (Grk. *evangelium*, "good news," see chap. 2 and 3), and the second refers to commitment to practicing Christian witness to that Gospel, that is, to spreading the Gospel and actively seeking converts to it. The two should go together of course, and for most of the history of Evangelicalism as a movement, they have. Accommodation to a relativistic and pluralistic society has compromised some of that zeal for recent generations. But the additional problem is that even when we were more zealous, we weren't doing it right. The Great Commission is not to do what we mostly tried to do, to make *converts* (though of course they do have to be made in the process of fulfilling the Great Commission). It is to make *disciples* (Mat. 28:19-20).

In its zeal to fulfill the Great Commission, Evangelicalism has largely been satisfied with making converts and failed to finish the job and make disciples out of those supposed converts. That is a major reason why too many of its adherents today have such a generally poor knowledge of the Bible, such a shaky understanding of Christian doctrine, and such spotty practice of Christian ethics.[78] It is a major reason why an increasing number of its institutions are suddenly sporting such a poor track record of fidelity to classical Evangelical (much less Christian) orthodoxy. Therefore, one of the most critical reforms needed by the Evangelical movement today is a return to its historic commitment to the Great Commission—to evangelism rightly understood.[79]

---

[78] James Davison Hunter saw this trend coming a generation ago in *Evangelicalism: The Coming Generation* (Chicago: The University of Chicago Press, 1987). David F. Wells confirms the trend and offers his own analysis in *No Place for Truth, or Whatever Happened to Evangelical Theology* (Grand Rapids: Eerdmans, 1993). A recent work that confirms their diagnosis and charts the progress of the disease is Stephen Cable, *Cultural Captives: The Beliefs and Behavior of American Young Adults* (Dallas: Probe Ministries, 2012).

[79] We have not lacked good (if not perfect) books on the theory and practice of biblical evangelism. They include Robert E. Coleman, *The Master Plan of Evangelism* (Old Tappan, N.J.: Revell, 1963), Billy Graham, *A Biblical Standard for Evangelists* Minneapolis: World Wide Publications, 1984), D. James Kennedy, *Evangelism Explosion* (Wheaton: Tyndale, 1977), R. B. Kuiper, *God-Centered Evangelism* (London: Banner of Truth, 1961), Jon Tal Murphree, *Responsible Evangelism: Relating Theory*

Thesis 11a:
Evangelism and Mission Exist because Worship Does Not.

It is not surprising that as Evangelical Christianity has grown less aware of its heritage in the Reformation it has lost some of its zeal for lost souls. As we become less Evangelical, we naturally become less evangelistic. Why is this so? The glory of the Gospel message and the way it is elegantly designed to meet our deepest needs and meet them completely is compelling just to the degree that we understand it accurately, and the Reformers were the ones, after the Apostles themselves, who most clearly pointed us to the salient points of that understanding.

So it would be a good idea to review chapters two through five at this point. As we said there: Like the original Reformers, we need to recover not only the content but also the logic of the biblical Gospel. In the wisdom of God it is precisely calibrated to apply the fullness of His character in all its majestic splendor to the particularities of our need in all its hopeless degradation. Not moral reform but spiritual transformation; not turning over a new leaf but turning on a new life; not winking at sin but a full pardon completely paid for; not a compromise between His mercy and His justice but a full reconciliation of all their inexorable claims: Nothing less than the wisdom of God could have devised it; nothing less than the love of God could have chosen it; nothing less than the power of God could have accomplished it. And no less a Person than the incarnate Son of God could have embodied it. Blessed be He!

To restore a profound understanding of the Reformation Gospel then is the first step to a new Reformation when it comes to evangelism. To know that human beings are sinners rightly subject to the wrath of a holy God is to be desperately concerned about their plight. To know that, despite our rebellion, God offers salvation through the incomprehensibly generous gift of His only Son is to be overwhelmed by His love and filled with confidence that we have a wonderful solu-

---

to Practice (Toccoa, Ga.: Toccoa Falls College Press, 1994), and John R. W. Stott, *Our Guilty Silence* (Downers Grove, Il.: InterVarsity, 1967). All have good practical advice, and none of them make the mistake this chapter is here to correct. Sadly, we have only followed them rather selectively.

tion to offer to the horrible plight of our fellow men. To realize that this salvation was purchased at the price of Christ's innocent blood, that it pays for all our guilt completely as He dies as our substitute, and that God can on that basis offer a free pardon and eternal life by grace alone through faith alone in Christ alone, is to be inspired with joy unspeakable and full of glory, a joy that is infectious because it flows from a message of News so good that it just has to be shared. To realize the completeness of this provision and the way it perfectly reconciles God's justice and His love and brings them both to full expression is to be compelled to worship because we begin to have an inkling of just how much this God deserves our complete and total submission, adoration, and devotion. And to realize that there are people who do not worship Him is to realize that they are missing out on the most joyous and fulfilling experience of which human beings are capable, indeed, the one for which they were created.

Compassion for the lostness of our fellow men and zeal for God's glory then are not motives in competition. They flow together to make it intolerable to us that He should not receive all the praise, adoration, and devotion of which the human race is corporately capable. This cannot be borne! Something must be done. How shall they worship unless they believe? How shall they believe unless they hear? How shall they hear without a preacher, or at least a witness (Rom. 10:14-15)? As the flow of the logic of the Epistle to the Romans captures perfectly, these are the questions borne in upon us irresistibly by the Gospel itself.

We saw in chapter five, "*Soli Deo Gloria*," that the glory of God is the manifestation of His divine nature in all its majestic splendor throughout the whole of creation. We saw that God's own glory is rightly and properly His ultimate purpose in all that He does, including our salvation, because it is the greatest good that is conceivable. To participate in that purpose and to help others find their purpose in it as well it is the most fulfilling end to which we can come—not just because it is fulfilling to us, but even more because God deserves to be glorified *for His own sake*. Glorification then needs to be done for *its* own sake. And so it is fitting that glorifying God for its own sake and His turns out to be the best thing we can do for *our* own sake and for that of others.

Bottom line: We will never relate properly to evangelism until we relate properly to the Gospel itself, and we will never relate properly to the Gospel until we are granted a fresh vision of the glory and majesty of the One who offers it. The first Reformation pointed us back to all of that with blessed clarity and power, and the Reformation we need today must do exactly the same thing if it is to bring glory to God and salvation to men.

Thesis 11b:
The Great Commission Is To Make *Disciples*, Not Converts.

If we are going to reform our approach to fulfilling the Great Commission, perhaps we had best begin by reminding ourselves of what it actually says.

> The eleven disciples proceeded to Galilee, to the mountain Jesus had designated. And when they saw Him, they worshiped Him; but some doubted. And Jesus came up and spoke to them, saying, "All authority has been given to Me in heaven and on earth. Go therefore and make disciples of all the nations, baptizing them in the name of the Father, the Son, and the Holy Spirit, teaching them to observe all that I commanded you. And lo, I am with you always, even to the end of the age." (Mat. 28:16-20)

In the original Greek of this passage, there is one imperative verb, and it is not "to go." It is *to make disciples*. The other verbs are all participles, actions preparatory to or flowing from the main thrust carried by that imperative: Make disciples! A more accurate translation would be something like this: "As you are going forth, make disciples of [people from] all the nations, baptizing them in the name of the Father, the Son, and the Holy Spirit, and teaching them to keep all the commandments I have given you." Going is part of it, but the command is not to go. It is assumed that we will be going, but the going is for the purpose of disciple making. Likewise, baptizing and teaching flow from that disciple making on our part, and being baptized, learning, and obeying flow from it on the part of those who receive it. Making disciples is the Prime Directive. Going, baptizing, and teaching are part of what that means for the disciple-maker. Being baptized, learning, and obeying are what it means for the disciple.

The key questions we need to confront then are "What is a disciple? What does it mean to make a disciple?" They are questions to which we have given surprisingly little attention. (There are books and teachers who have given it, or course, some of which are referenced in this chapter; but they have been too much ignored in practice.) For if one were to observe our actions, our standard practice, one would get the impression that we thought the Great Commission was to make converts. We treat discipleship as something almost optional, certainly not part of the Commission itself, but an "extra" that is relegated to a separate action called "follow-up," which must not be all that important because it so seldom gets done very well, if at all. After all, our main job is to keep these poor people from going to Hell. It would be nice if they became mature Christians in the process, but surely that is less earth-shakingly important than getting them *saved*, for goodness' sakes, and besides, it is somebody else's job. So we make a lot more converts than we make disciples. What is the difference? And what difference does it make? Ironically, it may actually lead to fewer real *converts*, as we shall see.

The English word *disciple* translates the Greek *mathetes*, which means student, learner, pupil; the closest English equivalent, though, might actually be *apprentice*. A disciple is more than a student, if by a student we only mean someone who sits in a classroom and half listens to a lecture, which he takes down in a distorted form he is pleased to call his "notes," which are not referred to again until the night before the exam when he has forgotten pretty much everything about what they originally were supposed to summarize. A disciple learns by actually following his master and copying him, emulating his life. The disciple learns as much from his master's hands and his heart as from his words. Think of Obi-Wan Kenobi and Qui-gon Jin in *Star Wars: Episode One*, or Luke and Obi-Wan in *Episode Four*, or Luke and Yoda in *Episode Five*. Think of the original disciples of Jesus, who lived with Him and served Him for three years and then in the Great Commission were asked to replicate themselves across the globe. "Become Jesus' *Paduan*" may actually in some senses be a more biblical appeal than "Accept Him into your heart." We as Christ's followers are asked first to have that kind of commitment to Him ourselves, and then to enlist others to share it. We are not asking people to adopt an opinion or join a club but to swear allegiance to a Master. We are not saved by our performance, by how well we follow that Master; but His grace and pardon are promised precisely to those who are *following* Him, however much they may stumble on the Way.

A convert is someone who decides to believe something that he previously did not believe. What kind of change he will make in his life as a result is an open question: It might be trivial or all-encompassing. The commitment the Great Commission is asking for is not, "OK, I'm going to start rooting for the Georgia Bulldogs instead of the Florida Gators." It is to actually show up on campus, move into the dorm, enroll in classes, and declare a major. Obviously you are not going to do that unless you have become convinced that Georgia is a good school. But not everyone who says, "Go Dawgs!" is actually a member (or alumnus) of the student body, just as not everyone who says, "Lord, Lord" will enter the kingdom of heaven (Mt. 7:21). So why are so many evangelists, both professional and amateur, content merely to elicit the words, as if that had accomplished anything?

I am all for making converts, because making converts is the first step in making disciples. But if we pay attention to what Jesus actually asked of us, we must realize that it is only the beginning, not the completion, of the task. We want people to make a "confession of faith." Surely they must do this. But what does it mean when they do? Does it reflect real saving faith, or is the person just saying what you want to hear so he can get rid of you? Does it reflect real, life-changing faith, or is it just a momentary emotional reaction to the emotional manipulation we have used to get the person down to the altar? Time will tell. I have been in too many churches that boasted of the impressive numbers of "conversions" recorded by their evangelism teams over the past year, but then I look around the pews and see the same set of people who were there a year ago. Where are all these alleged converts? I am not saying that none of them were saved—only God sees the heart—but where is the *biblical evidence* that any of them were saved? A person whose heart is truly changed by grace to respond in faith shows it by following the Lord. We only begin to have confidence that his profession meant something as we see him begin to do that, and it is as much our job to guide him in beginning to do that as it was to present the Gospel to him in the first place. Churches that do not do so, churches marked by magical disappearing and ever-after invisible "converts," flatter themselves that they are fulfilling the Great Commission. They are not.

Thesis 11c:
A "Convert" Who Does Not Become a Disciple Is Presumed Not To Be a True Convert.

✎

A "convert" who does not become a disciple is presumed not to be a true convert. This thesis is guaranteed to get me accused of arrogant judgmentalism. But those who make that accusation will not have understood the point. I make no pretensions of knowing who is or is not saved. Unlike God, I see only the outward appearance, not the heart. I have a robust belief in God's mercy, and as with the professing Christians who did not have a perfect doctrinal understanding of the Gospel in chapter three, I hope that many of the people who have been victims of our evangelistic malpractice will still be in heaven, if only by the skin of their teeth. Our business here is not to judge those converts who do not live up to our standards of discipleship. It is to learn to practice the Great Commission faithfully as it was given. We must always leave the results to God. It is our part to see to it that the results in question are the results of our faithfulness and obedience to what was actually asked of us, not the results of our practice of a watered-down version of the Lord's Commission.

We see only the outward appearance, not the heart. But the heart is supposed to have an impact on what we can see. A genuine conversion produces results, and those results tend toward practical discipleship. A real, living faith produces outward works, and those works are evidence of that unseen faith (see thesis 2c). We must be slow to judge because that evidence can be faint at first, and its appearance can be hindered and obscured by poor teaching or by our own failure to practice the Great Commission, i.e., by our having prioritized converts over disciples. But a complete lack of outward evidence (or the presence of outward counter-evidence) is cause for concern. A person who gives no evidence of regeneration, ongoing sanctification, and commitment to a Bible-believing local church, gives no evidence of real conversion, because genuine faith brings with it the new birth and all that flows from it. A person who does give evidence of regeneration (a new nature), ongoing sanctification, and commitment to a Bible-believing local church is on the path of discipleship, however slow and stumbling his journey down that path may be. This continuing journey—not the fact that he once "went forward" or once said the right words—is what gives us confidence that he is a true believer and that the Great Commission in his case has been fulfilled.[80]

Regeneration refers to the transformation that occurs when we are brought from spiritual death to life by the Holy Spirit. The same phenomenon is described in different language by various biblical writers. Jesus told Nicodemus that in order to see the Kingdom of God he had to be "born again" (John 3:3). And John says that Christ gave to believers the right to become children of God, "who were born, not of blood, nor of the will of the flesh, nor of the will of man, but of God" (John 1:13). Paul says that we were dead in our trespasses and sins, but "God, being rich in mercy because of the great love with which He loved us, even when we were dead in our transgressions made us alive together with Christ" (Eph. 2:1, 4-5). And as a result, "If any man is in Christ, he is a new creature. The old things have passed away; behold, new things have come" (2 Cor. 5:17).

A child who is born does not continue to exist or act in the same way he did in the womb. He starts breathing and crying. You can tell a difference. Would a person who is spiritually born not also show it in some way? A person who is alive does not behave in the same way a dead person does. Would this not be true of a person who becomes spiritually alive? What can we say of a new creature (or new creation) who is no different from the old creature? In what sense is he "new"? What exactly has passed away? What exactly has come? To reprise a metaphor we used in our discussion of good works as the evidence of the salvation which is by grace alone through faith alone and not at all by works as a cause, what do you conclude about a pond with an absolutely smooth surface and no ripples? The rock didn't hit the pond. We cannot make an absolute judgment, because the change may be slow in coming and not materialize with the dramatic speed we expect. But a person whose life does not change *at all* as a result of his profession of faith certainly causes one at some point to suspect that he has only made the profession and has no real saving faith. He certainly does not look like any biblical description of a person who is regenerate, born again, made alive, and recreated.

---

80 Iain Murray gives a sad analysis of how spotty the results of even Billy Graham's use of the invitation system (especially when some of those who responded were funneled into liberal churches) proved when his converts were checked on later: *Evangelicalism Divided: A Record of Crucial Change in the Years 1950-2000* (Carlisle, Pa.: Banner of Truth, 2000), pp. 53–8.

The new life that is granted in regeneration, as it is nurtured and exercised and grows, causes a continuing, progressive increase in the visibility of its presence, a progressive growth in grace, a progressive and increasing Christlikeness. It may have setbacks, but the normal arc of the Christian life, because of the powerful dynamic of the Holy Spirit indwelling the individual, is toward godliness. Theologians call this process *sanctification*. It is best understood as regeneration working itself out in time. We, "beholding as in a mirror the glory of the Lord, are being transformed into the same image from glory to glory, just as from the Lord, the Spirit" (2 Cor. 3:18). This transformation is described as laying aside "the old self" and being "renewed in the spirit of your mind," putting on "the new self, which in the likeness of God has been created in righteousness and holiness of the truth" (Eph. 4:22-4). Nobody without the Spirit belongs to Christ (Rom. 8:9), and "the fruit of the Spirit is love, joy, peace, patience, kindness, goodness, faithfulness, gentleness, self-control" (Gal. 5:22-3). These qualities should be naturally (or should we say supernaturally?) increasing where the Spirit is present.

Now, we can easily miss work that the Spirit is actually doing in a person's life. It might progress more slowly than is ideal, and it might experience setbacks. But God does not justify people without regenerating them and sanctifying them. Justification does not depend on our progress in sanctification—it is what makes that progress possible. But these three works of God in the believer's life are coordinated and tied together. If the two that are more visible in terms of their outward effects are not happening, it is cause for concern. The New Testament knows nothing of a "salvation" that does not change the sinner's life. We must then make disciples because we were told to, but also because only then can we have any biblically justified confidence that our supposed converts are actually saved. We are saved by *faith*, not by making an empty profession of faith.

Thesis 11d:
A Disciple Is Not Made Until the Convert Is At Least Stumblingly Trying To Learn and Do All Things Whatsoever Christ Has Commanded Us.

☙

Our job is to make disciples. We have to make converts to do that, but we should not be satisfied to make converts, for reasons both pragmatic and spiritual. We do not know if a convert who has been called to something less than discipleship is actually saved or not. We show a lack of confidence in the saving power of Christ by our low expectations for the difference being saved makes. And we are simply disobedient to the Commission we were given if we are not even trying to make disciples rather than just converts. Let us remind ourselves of the terms in which the great Commission was couched: "All authority has been given to Me in heaven and on earth. Go therefore and make disciples of all the nations, baptizing them in the name of the Father, the Son, and the Holy Spirit, teaching them to observe all that I commanded you" (Mat. 28:18-20).

An unbaptized person is saved the moment he confesses Jesus as Lord, believing in his heart that God raised Him from the dead (Rom. 10:9-10). But what this convert signed up for at that moment includes identifying himself with Christ and His church through baptism and being taught to observe all of Jesus' commandments. If his conversion was genuine, he will follow through on those commitments. Jesus Himself defines a disciple as a person who has been baptized and who is being taught, and by implication is learning, all of Jesus' commandments, to the end that he will follow them. We are not at liberty to substitute another definition of our own for the one given by our Lord.

So sensitive are some Protestants (and rightly so) to any implication that works can play a role as the *cause* of salvation that they will fear that what I am saying here will take us back to that forbidden place. Indeed, one of Satan's most effective strategies for neutralizing the witness of the church and keeping it frozen in superficiality, unreality, and impotence is stoking that fear. The human tendency to reintroduce works into the equation is subtle and insidious and does indeed need to be guarded against with great vigilance. But if we let that vigilance pull us away from confessing the *power* of the Gospel of grace alone to save and *to save mightily*, we play into Satan's hands and produce a church full of carnal and compromised Christians at best, and of many complacent professors of faith who may not even be saved at all. If we let that vigilance undermine our confidence in the power of the Gospel to save and to save mightily so that we ask for cheap conversions so we can multiply the notches in our evangelistic gun belts, we produce the same kind of weakened and compromised churches. It is then hardly to be wondered at if such a church sends forth a muted message at best.

Let me therefore say it again: We cannot be saved *by* works, but we are saved *for* works. We are not saved by our obedience, but we are saved for obedience. Everything that we said in thesis 2c is relevant here. We do not obey in order to merit salvation; we follow the Lord because we have been granted salvation. You will never obey Christ sufficiently to merit salvation. You are not saved by having taken an adequate number of steps on the path of obedience. But if you are not *on* the path of obedience, you are not on the path of salvation. A genuinely saved Christian may stumble, may stumble badly, may fall, may fall often. But in what direction is he stumbling? If the direction has not changed, then by what legerdemain of language can we claim that this person has saving faith? Well, the new direction is not just any new direction; it is *toward Christ*, whom we have accepted *as Lord* because God has opened our eyes to the fact that He is altogether sufficient to save us, altogether worthy of our worship, devotion, and obedience, and altogether lovely.

When Shakespeare's Kent applies to be taken into King Lear's service, Lear asks him why he wants to serve. "You have that in your countenance," Kent replies, "which I would fain call master."[81] A true Christian is one who has been moved to say something like that to Jesus. A true Christian is one who has bowed before Jesus like Merry before Theoden or Pippin before Denethor, offered up the hilt of his sword, and begged, "Command me!" We want to follow Christ and obey Him precisely because He has accepted us as we are, despite our track record of disobedience and rebellion and despite our inability to obey Him perfectly even now. You might be saved without fully un-

---

81 William Shakespeare, Shakespeare: *The Complete Works*, ed. G. B. Harrison (NY: Harcourt, Brace, & World, 1948), p. 1147.

derstanding this, but you are not a *disciple*, by Jesus' own definition, unless this is where you stand. Therefore, the task of the Great Commission has been accomplished with any given individual when, and only when, we have seen this desire for full obedience in that convert and started helping him learn to fulfill it.

If a disciple is a person who is learning to obey all that Jesus commanded, then a disciple is not fully made until the convert himself becomes a disciple-maker—for certainly Jesus' commandments include the Great Commission itself. This point is made by the Commission, and it is confirmed by the instruction Paul gave to his own disciple, Timothy: "The things which you have heard from me in the presence of many witnesses, these entrust to faithful men who will be able to teach others also" (2 Tim. 2:2). Connor Gonzalez has a good analogy for understanding the rationale of this requirement. "It's like a craftsman teaching his trade to an apprentice." If the apprentice doesn't eventually teach the trade to others and take his own apprentice, "then the master hasn't made a successful heir to the trade; he has only made a skilled, yet selfish, craftsman."[82] Sadly, many of our supposed "converts" are not brought even to that level.

---

82 Connor Gonzalez, "Training and Discipleship" (unpublished paper, Toccoa Falls College, 2018), p. 2.

Thesis 11e:
A Disciple Is Not Made Until the Convert Is a Committed and Functioning Member of a Bible-Believing Local Church.

We must be concerned when our converts do not show evidence of regeneration and sanctification by at least wanting to learn to obey their Lord's commandments. A similar concern is justified when the alleged convert never becomes a functioning member of a Bible-believing local church; for doing so is indeed one of Christ's commandments. The church is not an optional club for believers supplied just in case they are interested or feel the need for it. It is the Body of Christ into which they are grafted by salvation (Eph. 1:22-3). God did not send His Son merely to save individuals, but to create a People for His name. The church as that people is indeed central to God's eternal plan for the salvation of sinners. He planned the reconciliation of Jews and Gentiles into one Body from the beginning (Eph. 2:16-22). This was all done so that "the manifold wisdom of God might now be made known through the church to the rulers and authorities in the heavenly places" (Eph. 2:10). That is why Christ gave Himself, not just for isolated individuals, but for the church (Eph. 5:25-7).

It might be possible for an individual to be saved (by the skin of his teeth) outside the church, but it is clearly not possible for him to be a *disciple* who is following the Lord without commitment to Christ's Body. And therefore the Great Commission is not fulfilled until the convert is a member of a genuine, i.e., Bible-believing, local church, attending its services faithfully, participating in its life, and supporting its ministries with his money, time, and energy. An individual might well begin the process of discipling the new convert, but it takes the whole community of faith operating under the faithful leadership of biblically called elders and deacons to continue it. I will not say "complete it," because it will never be completed in this life. It will be completed when the disciple sees his Lord face to face.

In the total absence of any signs of regeneration, sanctification, and commitment to Christ's Body, there is presumably a complete absence of real conversion. Here is one very practical difference it makes: Such people should be treated as lost sinners in need of salvation—not told, as they often are, that because they once said the right words they are eternally secure and can never be lost again![83] We are saved by faith, by *having* faith, not by having once professed to have it. We have to make converts in order to make disciples, but a "convert" who does not become a disciple should not be presumed to be a true convert. He is missing and presumed lost until he shows that he is actually a person of faith by starting to follow the Lord. And you cannot follow the Lord without following Him *into* His church; you cannot follow the Lord without following Him *with* His church.

Let's see if we can head off a couple of potential misunderstandings at the pass. I've been stressing a couple of descriptors almost every time I mention the church: "Bible-believing" and "local." Why are they important, and what do they mean?

"BIBLE-BELIEVING": New converts and beginning disciples may not be aware of the fact that not all organizations that erect steeples and put the name of a church over the door are actually legitimate parts of the true church, the Body of Christ. Many of them once were, but have departed from faithfulness to the point that you cannot join them now without compromising your own commitment to Christ. You also have to look past the local congregation to its relationship to the denomination of which it may be a part. So there are some critical questions that we need to ask when deciding on a church home.

First, does this group have a doctrinal statement? If not, be suspicious. You want a group that is willing to be upfront about what it believes. Beware of people who say they have "no creed but the Bible." That affirmation does not tell you anything about how they interpret the Bible and what they think it teaches. Ask for a doctrinal statement and examine it carefully to see if it is compatible with classical Christian theism as expressed in the Nicene Creed and with the five Reformation *Sola*s as outlined in the first five chapters here. Then try to determine if this church takes its doctrinal statement seriously. Why is this important? Because Paul describes the church as "the household of God, which is the church of the living God, *the pillar and support of the truth*" (1 Tim. 3:15, emphasis added). This role is not incidental to the church's identity or its mission. And how can it act as the

---

[83] I believe in the doctrine of the perseverance of the saints. But it applies to *real* believers only, not to merely professing believers.

Five Theses on Evangelism

pillar and support of the truth if it has no clear idea of what the truth is, or if it is willing to compromise on essential tenets of it?

Particularly crucial at this point is the way the church relates to the authority of Scripture. Everything else it believes and does will flow from that. So be sure that its elders truly believe that the Apostles know more about Christ and Christian faith than they do. Be sure they are fully committed to the magisterial authority of Scripture (Thesis 1b) and that they function credibly under it, responsibly using their own ministerial authority (Thesis 1c) to serve Christ and the congregation. Be sure that they respect the authority and integrity of the Text enough to interpret it in accordance with the hermeneutical principles outlined in Theses 6a-e. Be sure, in other words, that they believe the Bible as truth without exception and teach it as God's Word without compromise. But that is not enough. It is important to be sure that the denomination (if there is one) that they belong to has the same commitment, that it disciplines pastors and does not hire seminary or college professors who deviate from those commitments. You do not want your tithes going to pay the salaries of professors who are undermining the church's commitment to the truth; nor do you want to be in the intolerable position of not being able with any confidence to recommend a church of your own denomination to someone in another city. A church not committed to the truth of the Gospel and to the authority of God's Word is no true church of Jess Christ. You are not looking for perfection. (You won't find it.) But you should demand *integrity* in these matters. Otherwise your own discipleship will be hindered and your witness compromised.

Am I saying that every believer who is in a church compromised by its entanglement in an apostate denomination is going to Hell? No. But such people, however sincerely, are helping to perpetuate error, they are sending a mixed message to the world, and they are in places where their own discipleship will have obstacles to overcome that they do not need. Do not replicate their mistakes.

"LOCAL": You meet people with commitment issues when it comes to actual concrete congregations meeting in a designated place in a specific community. Their reluctance is often understandable. They may have been badly treated by churches in their past (partly due to the pathologies flowing from the very failure to practice the Great Commission that is the subject of this chapter). But bad experiences are no excuse for disobedience. We are commanded not to forsake "our assembling together as is the habit of some" (Heb. 10:25). Some of these people will piously say that they are members of the (universal) "Body of Christ" and hence don't need to limit themselves to one actual congregation. But this is clearly a rationalization. To paraphrase John, we could ask, "How shall we belong to the church universal which we have not seen when we cannot relate to the local church which we have seen?" (1 John 4:20). Clearly it is an expectation of disciples that they be a functioning part of an actual, concrete, local congregation. They are not even trying to follow all of Jesus' commandments if they are in rebellion against this one.

Finding good (in some communities, even minimally acceptable) local churches can be a challenge in many places. For that very reason it is crucially important that we keep searching until we do find one that deserves our support and then be faithful to it. There can be no meaningful Reformation of the church today unless that happens.

Conclusion

Surely the appalling biblical illiteracy documented by Cable among the self-styled "born again" shows how appalling our failure to make disciples has been.[84] It also shows how appalling our failure even to do evangelism has been. People who neither believe Christian doctrine nor have a biblical worldview nor lift a finger to practice the Christian faith can be called "Christians" only in an exercise either of sick humor or self-delusion. Let this delusion come to an end with the Reform of our approach to the Great Commission mandated by the words in which our Lord gave it! Now is the day of salvation.

---

84 *Cultural Captives*, op. cit.

Interlude

Legacy:
Uganda, Near Karikajunga

"I look out from my camp, and I can see
    The cook-fires of a hundred villages
    Where no one even knows the name of Christ."
And I have come to teach theology
    In places where the smoke he saw still is
    Ascending, next to churches that are priced

At Jesus' blood and missionaries' lives
    Who added their own sacrifice to His,
    Since nothing less than that would have sufficed.
They packed in coffins, but their work survives:
    The Church of Christ.[85]

---

[85] Donald T. Williams, *Stars through the Clouds*, op. cit., p. 396-7.

Village Evangelism

"But I'm a teacher, not an evangelist."
"No, the muzungu *must preach at the crusade. That way, everybody will come to hear what the crazy white man gonna say."*

The stars shone on the hills of Africa
And on a sea of eyes that shone in wonder
At the generator-driven cinema,
Another sky of stars that spread out under
The temporary platform we'd erected.
They'd never seen a video before.
The younger ones had never once inspected
A white man. I can't say which held them more
Enthralled, the flashing images or my skin.
It was the skin that made them pay attention
When, once the "Jesus" film was at an end,
I rose to preach. And now, what new dimension,
Stranger than moving pictures on a screen
Or ghost-like skin in health by some strange art
Could possibly be waiting to be seen?
Christ crucified and raised; the human heart
      Made clean.[86]

---

86 Ibid., p. 397.

12

Five Theses on Apologetics

If we treat our own faith as if it were indefensible, how must the world perceive it?

Five Theses on Apologetics

A. We are commanded to be always ready to give a defense (Grk. *apologia*) to anyone who asks a reason for the hope that is within us (1 Pet. 3:15). (An *apologia* is the word for an attorney's final summation in defense of his client; it implies presenting evidence and reasoning to help the jury draw the right conclusions from that evidence.)

B. Apologetics is therefore an essential part of Christian discipleship. (We are not obeying all things whatsoever Christ commanded us unless we are obeying this command given through His apostle Peter.)

C. God purposes to save whole persons, which includes their minds as well as their hearts. (A faith that is held only emotionally is less than fully biblical faith.)

D. Apologetics seeks to win people, not arguments; nevertheless, sound arguments should be employed because not to do so is to insult and blaspheme the God of truth. (We cannot serve truth with lies, or with fallacies.)

E. Apologetics, like every other aspect of evangelism, is impotent apart from the convicting power of the Holy Spirit; and that is a reason to *do* it, not to avoid it. (If it is true that we cannot argue people into the kingdom, it is equally true that we cannot preach or witness them into it either—yet God has ordained those means and promised to work through them. This one is no different.)

American conservative Christians are not as biblical as they think they are. In support of this claim we need look no further than the fact that, while we are clearly commanded always to be ready to make a defense to anyone who asks a reason for the hope that is within us (1 Pet. 3:15), vast swaths of our adherents think it is somehow unspiritual to obey this biblical commandment. Some of them treat questions almost as a spiritual vice.[87] Things are better than they were a couple of generations ago. We now have a veritable Apologetics Industrial Complex and a horde of consumers interested enough to keep it in business. (Full disclosure: I must confess to being a part of it.) But it has virtually no influence on the rank and file in the pews or on the conduct of daily life in the church or on the practice of evangelism outside the relatively closed circle of apologetics nerds. Therefore, a thorough Reformation of the contemporary church requires some theses on this critical and essential but much misunderstood branch of Christian theology and ministry.[88]

---

87 See my article "Doubt as a Christian Virtue," *Modern Reformation* 15:4 (July/August 2006): 19-21 for an alternative view.

88 Further reading on apologetics: For a brilliant analysis of the apologetic situation that is still prophetically relevant, Francis Schaeffer, *The God Who is There: Speaking Historic Christianity into the Twentieth Century* (Downers Grove, Il.: InterVarsity, 1968); for an excellent comprehensive textbook, Douglas Groothuis, *Christian Apologetics: A Comprehensive Case for Biblical Faith* (Downers Grove, Il.: InterVarsity, 2011). Classic works by C. S. Lewis include *Mere Christianity* (N.Y.: MacMillan, 1943), for the moral argument for Theism, the Trilemma, and the Argument from Desire; *Miracles: A Preliminary Study* (N.Y.: MacMillan, 1947) for supernaturalism and the Argument from Reason; and *The Problem of Pain* (N.Y.: MacMillan, 1967) on theodicy. For an evaluation of Lewis as an apologist see Donald T. Williams, "C. S. Lewis: Defender of the Faith," *Christian Research Journal* 40:4 (July/August 2017): -17, and "Answers for Orual: C. S. Lewis as a role Model for Winsome Apologists," (2016 Presidential Address from the annual meeting of the International Society for Christian Apologetics), *The Journal of the International Society of Christian Apologetics* 10:1 (March, 2017): 5-20. For a classic work on the historical argument for the resurrection of Christ, see Frank Morison, *Who Moved the Stone?* (Downers Grove, Il.: InterVarsity, n.d.). A good short work on the trustworthiness of Scripture is F. F. Bruce, *The New Testament Documents: Are They Reliable?* (Downers Grove, Il.: InterVarsity, 1960). See also William Lane Craig, *Reasonable Faith: Christian Truth and Apologetics* (Wheaton: Crossway, 1984) and Donald T. Williams, *Reflections from Plato's Cave: Essays in Evangelical Philosophy* (Lynchburg: Lantern Hollow Press, 2012) and *The Young Christian's Survival Guide: Common Questions Young Christians are Asked about God, the Bible, and the Christian Faith Answered* (Cambridge, OH: Christian Publishing House, 2019). A useful reference work is the *New Dictionary of Christian Apologetics*, ed. W. C. Campbell-Jack and Gavin McGrath (Downers Grove, Il.: InterVarsity, 2006). For advanced students, Stuart C. Hackett, *The Resurrection of Theism: Prolegomena to Christian Apology* (Grand Rapids: Baker, 1957).

Thesis 12a:
We Are Commanded To Be Always Ready To Give a Defense (Grk. *Apologia*) to Anyone Who Asks a Reason for the Hope That Is Within Us (1 Pet. 3:15).

1 Peter 3:15 is often cited as a prooftext in favor of Christian apologetics—rightly so. Often the context is not noted, but it adds a pertinent level of understanding to what is being asked of us. The commandment is part of an ongoing discussion of persecution from chapter 2 that resumes in verse 8. In such times, Christians are to return good for evil and blessing for curses (3:8). They are to be zealous for good, make sure that if they suffer it is for righteousness, and not be intimidated or troubled (3:13-14). Instead of all that, they are commanded to "sanctify Christ as Lord in your hearts, always being ready to make a defense to anyone who asks you to give an account for the hope that is in you, yet with gentleness and reverence" (3:15). Then the discussion continues, circling back to the topic of persecution. The result of this defense is that those who slander Christians will be put to shame by the Christians' good behavior in Christ (3:16).

The context does not lessen the emphasis on rational apologetics but roots it in the realities of life. That is why the actual imperative verb, the command, of verse 15 is to "sanctify Christ as Lord in your hearts." We are to set Christ apart as absolute monarch of our central, inner personality, in other words. In biblical terms, He is to be Lord of the central core of our personality, the unity from which flows the distinct faculties of our intellect, our will, and our emotions. (In biblical usage, the heart is not a symbol for the feelings, as it is in modern English, but rather for that central core of the whole personality.) Then, when people see how we respond to persecution, returning good for evil and blessing for curses, they will be astonished, and they will want to know how and why we do such a thing. (Maybe if we had truly sanctified Christ as Lord on such a deep level we would get more people asking such questions!) When they do, we need to be prepared with a reasoned response, a defense delivered not as a counterattack but rather with gentleness and reverence. So that's what apologetics is supposed to look like! Maybe there would be less resistance to it among believers themselves if it more often did.

The "account" (NASB) or in some translations "defense" we are to be ready for is the Greek word *apologia*, from which we get the English word apologetics. It was a legal term that referred to the final summation a lawyer would make to the judge or the jury in defense of his client. In it he would be expected to present the evidence for his client's innocence along with sound reasoning about that evidence to lead the jury to the correct verdict: acquittal. There is then evidence for why our hope is not misplaced and there are rational reasons for why Christians hold to it that we need to know and be prepared to present. This readiness, this preparedness, is commanded. It is not optional. It is an integral part of making Christ Lord of your heart. It is therefore for every believer, not just for nerds and intellectuals.

No dichotomy is permitted. The commandment includes both message and manner, both substance and style. It is a rational defense requiring preparation (message, substance) which is delivered with gentleness and reverence (manner, style). We are not obeying the commandment if we have mastered every argument and can run posers on intellectual websites or even real scholars who are skeptics through with the rapier of our intellect. Nor are we fulfilling its requirements if we are wonderfully nice people whose courage and hope in the midst of suffering or even persecution makes our neighbors scratch their heads, but then we have nothing to tell them but "just believe." No. What is demanded is the same kind of wholeness that Paul expressed in the phrase "speaking the truth in love" (Eph. 4:15): Not either/or, but both/and. Most of us, including many who actually believe in and think they are practicing biblical apologetics, are simply in disobedience here. And Reformation, if it is to begin with us at all, must begin with obedience.

Thesis 12b:
Apologetics Is Therefore an Essential Part of Christian Discipleship.

If a disciple is a person seeking to be obedient to all of Jesus' commands (Thesis 11d), and if Jesus gave us this one through His Apostle, Peter, then a disciple must be a person who aspires to obey the command to be always ready to make a defense, and to be the kind of person whose response to suffering and persecution invites the questions that this defense is designed to answer. Apologetics is therefore an essential part of Christian discipleship. The mere existence of the biblical commandment is sufficient in itself to make this point, but there is more to be said about why the Lord considers it a commandment important enough to have been given in the New Testament to His church. Christian apologetics is based on a biblical precept, a biblical precedent, and a biblical principle.

THE BIBLICAL PRECEPT is the command of 1 Peter 3:15 that we have just been expounding. It should be seen not as an isolated injunction but as a special application of the Great Commission (Mat. 28:18-20; see Theses 11a-e). It is also a special application of the mandated teaching ministry of the church, which has the goal of "equipping the saints for the work of service" (Eph. 4:12) by grounding them in the divine Word that is profitable for teaching "so that the man of God may be adequate, equipped for every good work" (2 Tim. 3:17). In that teaching ministry "We proclaim Him [Christ], admonishing every man and teaching every man with all wisdom so that we may present every man complete in Christ" (Col. 1:28). The completeness referred to in several of these passages surely includes the preparation called for by Peter's apologetic command. Apologetics is then relevant not only to evangelistic preaching but also to the proclamation of the Word that edifies and equips the saints for ministry that takes place both within and outside of the walls of the church. In all of this we respond also to Jude's appeal that we "contend earnestly for the faith that was once delivered to the saints" (Jude 1:3).

THE BIBLICAL PRECEDENT is the example set by the Apostles, particularly Paul in the book of Acts, of integrating apologetics seamlessly into their proclamation. Luke sets the stage for the disciples' preaching by noting that Jesus had presented Himself to the disciples by "many convincing proofs" (Acts 1:3). Then the early Christians preach as if they had that kind of foundation to build their message on. It is instructive to note how frequently verbs like "reasoned," "argued," and "persuaded" or conjunctive adverbs like "therefore" appear in the narrative. Peter's Pentecost sermon sets the precedent: It appeals to both the disciples' experience and to the Old Testament, concluding with a rousing "*Therefore* let all the house of Israel know for certain that God has made Him both Lord and Christ—this Jesus whom you crucified" (Acts 2:36, emphasis added). They could know of the Messiahship of Jesus with confidence because of the logical connections of the conclusion to the evidence that had been so clearly and powerfully presented.

The Apostle Paul is the Apostle of grace *par excellence*, and he is the Apostle of apologetics *par excellence* too. He began his public ministry after his conversion by "proving" to the Jews in Damascus that Jesus was the Christ (9:23). He did this by "arguing" (9:29). In Thessalonica he "reasoned" and "gave evidence" (17:2-3). Luke calls the Bereans "noble" because they thought Paul's claims through for themselves, "examining the Scriptures daily to see whether these things be so" (17:11). Paul is next found "reasoning" with the Greeks in Athens (17:17:17). At the end of his Areopagus sermon he claims that the historical resurrection is "proof" that God was revealed in Christ (17:31). The Athenian philosophers were a tough audience (in a different way than the Jews had been), but some, including Dionysius and Damaris, were saved.

There are those who criticize Paul for his apologetic approach in Athens, blaming it for his limited success there and claiming that he then returned to just preaching the Word, the "simple Gospel." I think most of us would give our right arm for the assurance that we would have a few converts from even our most skeptical audiences! But the real response to that view is simply to point out that Paul's practice was consistent. He did not start reasoning and persuading in Athens; he had been doing it all along, and he kept right on doing it after he left. We next find him in Corinth, "*reasoning* in the synagogue every Sabbath and trying to *persuade* Jews and Greeks" (18:4, emphasis added). And it's not just Paul. After his further instruction by Priscilla and Aquila, Apollos is described as a big help because he "powerfully *refuted* the Jews in public, *demonstrating* by the Scriptures that Jesus was the Christ" (18:28, emphasis added). Then we move on to Ephesus and the focus switches back to Paul, "reasoning and persuading" (19:8). Back in Jerusalem, he gives an *apologia* before the Jews who had rioted in the Temple (22:1)—the same word used by Peter in 1 Peter 3:15. He uses the verb form of that word to describe his defense to Felix (24:10). And he spends his time under house arrest in Rome at the end of the book "trying to persuade" the Jews about Jesus (28:23). And some of them were persuaded (28:24).

There is a consistent pattern in Paul's arguments. He appeals to premises which he can expect his audience to accept as real evidence and tries to persuade them that this evidence supports the claims of Jesus to be Lord and Christ. With Jewish audiences he appeals to the Old Testament, because they were supposed already to accept it as the Word of God. With Greeks he might appeal to general revelation, the witness of Nature to her Creator. With everyone he appeals to the historical resurrection which "was not done in a corner" (Acts 26:26). There were five hundred eyewitnesses to it, most of whom are still alive (1 Cor. 15:6). Finally he adds his own eyewitness testimony, granted on the Road to Damascus (15:8). The biblical precedent is clear: Peter was not asking us to do anything that the Apostles had not already practiced, setting us an example of faithful witness.

THE BIBLICAL PRINCIPLE is that God wants to save whole people, their minds as well as their emotions, their intellects as well as their wills. Jesus went out of His way to establish this principle in His explanation of the Greatest Commandment: to "love the Lord your God with all your heart, and with all your soul, *and with all your mind*" (Mat. 22:37, emphasis added). Surely when we preach the Gospel we are calling people to love God that way in the light of His glorious grace shown to us in Christ. Therefore, the Gospel should be addressed to the whole person, including the mind. It does not mean we should speak only to intellectuals, or in a way that only intellectuals will be able to understand. It does mean that we present the Gospel as if we actually thought it was true, as something that can be thought about as well as felt, as something that can stand up to the rough and tumble of rational investigation, and as something that will affect the whole life of the person we are trying to reach.

There is then not only a biblical precept but also a precedent and a principle in favor of the proposition that apologetics—being always prepared to give a rational defense of the hope that is within us—is an essential part of Christian discipleship. Not everyone is called to major in apologetic ministry of course, but everyone is called to treat the Gospel as something that is actually true in the real world. We are given a command, good examples of people following that command, and a principle that explains why it is important to do so. And the principle is so basic, yet so little understood, that it deserves a Thesis of its own.

Thesis 12c:
God Purposes To Save Whole Persons, Which Includes Their Minds As Well As Their Hearts.

In a number of these theses we keep coming back to the fact that much of contemporary American Christianity has in many ways absorbed the fragmented view of life that is typical of the modern world. In the chapter on church ministry we argued that God made people to be, and means people to be, whole persons. We have bodies as well as souls, minds as well as hearts. The ministry of the church should therefore rebuild those whole persons out of the fragments created by sin. It is not to reinforce that fragmentation by valuing souls over bodies while aiming only at hearts and disparaging minds (Theses 7a-b). The impact of this fragmented view of human nature makes itself felt in many ways. We refer to effective evangelists as "soul winners" and think of their purpose as "saving souls"—as if God were not interested in saving *people*—whole people, including both soul and body.

As we concluded in Thesis 7b,

> Growing up "In *all* aspects . . . into *Christ*" can mean nothing less than that the Church is trying to grow people who think like the One who designed the stars, who astounded the rabbis, and who defeated the Pharisees. It is trying to grow people who imagine the world like the One who wrote the parables. It is trying to grow people who make choices like the One whose meat and drink was to do the will of his Father. It is trying to grow people who serve like the One who washed his disciples' feet. And it is trying to grow people who love like the One who died on Calvary. It is trying to grow people who see all these acts as essential parts of an indissoluble unity whose Center is the very character of its Lord. Getting saved, accepting Christ as one's Savior and Lord, means setting out on that road. What else could it mean?

If one reform we need is to start thinking of the Christian life and of church ministry in such terms, and if evangelism means inviting people to become disciples of Jesus in such terms, to the end that they might become whole persons, then surely the Gospel should be presented as something relevant to the enquiring mind as well as the searching heart. We start where people are. We do not foolishly burden seekers with a curriculum of answers to questions they are not asking as a set of hurdles they must clear before coming to faith. But at the same time, we are presenting a message that consists of truth claims—claims that need to be pressed. Such claims have the inherent potential to raise apologetic questions, and we are required to be ready to deal with them when they do. Besides, if we are not presenting the Gospel as *truth*, we are not presenting the biblical Gospel at all. The enquiring mind may not be engaged at first in every case, but the very nature of the Gospel is that it will tend to engage it. We are after all asking for allegiance to a Lord who is the Way and the Truth as well as the Life.

We need to present the Gospel as a message that is addressed to the whole person, is relevant to the whole person, promises to transform the whole person, and therefore asks for a response from the whole person—including the mind. This is what the biblical writers mean when they tell us that the Gospel is addressed to the heart and needs to be believed in the heart (Rom. 10:9-10; see the discussions of the heart under Theses 7a and 12a). Therefore, apologetics might not be the central thrust of our dealing with any given person, but it is always lurking just beneath the surface. When the truth question comes up, we need to be prepared to deal with it honestly and with confidence. When it does not come up in a "post-truth world," we may need to bring it up ourselves. Otherwise we are being less than honest about what we are asking people to commit to. Whether we are confronted by believers wrestling with doubts or enquirers raising objections, if we say, or even imply, "Don't ask questions—just believe," we are simply being disobedient to the command of our Lord through His Apostle. To repent of that disobedience is a reform that has been a long time coming to much of American conservative Christianity.

Thesis 12d:
Apologetics Seeks To Win People, Not Arguments; Nevertheless, Sound Arguments Should Be Employed because Not To Do So Is To Insult and Blaspheme the God of Truth.

✇

Apologetics is a necessary aspect of holistic discipleship; it is also a dangerous one. I say this as a practitioner who is fully aware that I am highly susceptible to its pitfalls and have to guard against them vigilantly. Apologetics is especially dangerous to those who are naturally prone to pursue it. We have egos. We like winning arguments. In fact, we relish demolishing our opponents, crushing them into dust, and receiving the accolades and ovations of those who already agree with us as we do so. Oh, wait. That does not actually sound much like the kind of apologetic that the context of Peter's command seems to call for (see Thesis 12a). Oops.

The goal of Christian apologetics of course is not to win arguments; it is to win people. It is to win people to Christ, to remove obstacles to their belief in Him, and to help the faith they will come to have in Him be one that has integrity and flows from their whole personality, not just from an emotional response. We want to remove obstacles to their belief in Him because they are obstacles to seeing Him as He is and *loving* Him. We want their faith in Him to be more than an emotional response because we understand that love is more than an emotional response, and we want them to love Him deeply, with all their souls and all their might and all their minds. They will find it hard to love Jesus that way unless they see something in us as His representatives that does not completely repel them. And guess what? The experience of being defeated and then subjected to a victory dance performed over your supine carcass is not exactly conducive to seeing your conversation partner that way.

The difficulty is of course that we cannot make the case for the truth of our claims about Christ without winning arguments. You have to show that your view is based on a better sampling of real evidence and the other view (the one your potential convert probably picked up from his secular society) is not. You have to show that your view is a logical conclusion reached by valid argument from that evidence, and the other one is not. Your potential disciple has picked up, and may strongly adhere to and zealously defend, ideas that come straight from the Enemy himself. It is easy to forget that this potential disciple is not the Enemy, but rather one his victims. If he is not someone you are trying to reach but rather someone attacking you as a superstitious misleader of the masses, not to mention an idiot (and you are going to attract that kind of attention if your apologetic becomes known), that mistake is especially easy to make. I used to make it all the time, and I am still trying to wean myself from it completely. It is never helpful. So we have to win arguments *in such a way* that we can also win people. It is the old difficulty of speaking the truth in love. I can speak the truth. (I think I'm actually somewhat good at that.) I can be nice to people I disagree with. (That comes a little less naturally, but I can do it.) Doing both at the same time? That takes dependence on the Holy Spirit. And that takes a kind of death to self that does not come naturally at all.

We have to win arguments in such a way that we can also win people.[89] Addiction to winning arguments at all costs is an insidious malady to overcome. It is like food addiction. If you are addicted to alcohol or drugs or gambling or video games and get to the point where you are finally serious about getting your life back, you can go cold turkey and give those things up completely. You learn to live without them. It is (relatively) clean and uncomplicated: You walk away and never look back. It isn't easy, but you have to do it. But if you are addicted to comfort food, you have an even more difficult struggle. You cannot just walk away from food and never look back, or you won't be living very long at all. You have to look back all the time. That is the position we are in with winning arguments instead of people. If you give up arguments altogether, you are no longer doing rational apologetics. We have no choice but to do the dying to self which alone can make it possible for the Holy Spirit to use us.

If we must use arguments, they had better be good ones. The need to present them in love does not absolve us from the responsibility to make them evidentially rich and logically rigorous. "'Logic!' said the Professor half to himself. 'Why don't they teach logic at these

---

[89] For an excellent practical guide to how to do this, see Greg Koukl, *Tactics: A Game Plan for Discussing Your Christian Convictions* (Grand Rapids: Zondervan, 2009).

schools?'"[90] Well, they should. And if the public schools won't, Sunday Schools should. There's a radical reform we could implement in the church!

We serve a God who is the God of truth and whose Son is the Way, the Truth, and the Life (John 14:6). We cannot serve Him with lies. We serve a God whose character is the ground of logic. It is because He cannot lie (Titus 1:2) that the law of non-contradiction is universally valid in every possible world.[91] We cannot serve Him with fallacies. To try to do so is to blaspheme His name, because it implies that He is not true. Any such apologetic would undercut itself at every turn. In every area of endeavor we should give Him the best of which we are capable, not because it is adequate but because He deserves nothing less. This is especially true in apologetics, where we are directly representing Him as Truth and as true: The truth of His existence, the trueness of His character, and hence the truth of His Word, are at stake. Here if anywhere it is critically important that we speak the truth in love, compromising neither the truth nor the love. In the fundamental sense that they both proceed from His character, you cannot have one without the other.

It is beyond the scope of this chapter to teach what the evidence is, what validity in argument is, or what each of the standard methodological approaches to apologetics (classical, evidential, presuppositional) has to offer. (I personally take them as complementary rather than exclusive, and as all belonging in our apologetic toolbox.) The books recommended in the course of this chapter are a good place to start in learning such things; they are aids to the preparedness that Peter commanded us always to have. What is important to the new Reformation we seek is that apologetics be restored to its proper place in theology and ministry and done in the proper spirit, speaking the truth in love. If we can achieve that, Reformation may be at our doorstep indeed.

---

90 C. S. Lewis, *The Lion, the Witch, and the Wardrobe* (N.Y.: HarperCollins, 1978), p. 52.

91 If you question this, try to construct an imaginary world in which contradictory propositions about the same subject can both be true in the same way, at the same time, and at the same place. You will not succeed. Your world will un-world itself.

Thesis 12e:
Apologetics, Like Every Other Aspect of Evangelism, Is Impotent apart from the Convicting Power of the Holy Spirit; and That Is a Reason To *Do* It, Not To Avoid It.

✑

Every person I know of who objects to apologetics as unspiritual makes the point that "You cannot argue people into the kingdom." They sometimes add the claim that nobody has ever been saved as a result of apologetic argument. Well, the second claim is demonstrably false. C. S. Lewis attributed his own conversion to the argument of J. R. R. Tolkien that, when Lewis rejected Christ as a myth parallel to the dying god myth of many pagan religions, he was being inconsistent. What if it had actually happened once?[92] Charles Colson famously attributed his own conversion to the arguments in Lewis's *Mere Christianity*, and countless others give Lewis's arguments a role in either their coming to faith or their preservation and maintenance in faith.[93] It is certainly true that argument *alone* never converted anybody; but that is a very different claim indeed, and one that no apologist need fear.

The first claim—that you cannot argue people into the kingdom—is definitely true. It is also irrelevant. You cannot preach or witness people into the kingdom either, but nobody advocates the abolition of sermons or the repeal of the Great Commission on that ground. Only the Holy Spirit can bring a person through real conviction of sin to saving faith in Christ, and He has ordained certain means through which He normally works in doing so. If we let the New Testament

---

92 C. S. Lewis, *They Stand Together: The Letters of C. S. Lewis to Arthur Greeves*, ed. Walter Hooper (N.Y.: MacMillan, 1979), pp. 427-8. For more information on Lewis's conversion and the role of argument in it, see Roger Lancelyn Green and Walter Hooper, *C. S. Lewis: A Biography* (N.Y.: Harcourt, Brace, Jovanovich, 1974), pp. 101-118, George Sayer, *Jack: A Life of C. S. Lewis* (Wheaton: Crossway, 1994), pp. 217-31, Alister McGrath, *C. S. Lewis: A Life* (Carol Stream, Il.: Tyndale House, 2013), pp. 131-159 (especially important for dating), Donald T. Williams, "G. K. Chesterton, *The Everlasting Man*," in *C. S. Lewis's List: the Ten Books that Influenced Him Most*, ed. David and Susan Werther (N.Y.: Bloomsbury, 2015), pp. 31-48, and most importantly Lewis's autobiography, *Surprised by Joy: The shape of My Early Life* (N.Y.: Harcourt, Brace,& World, 1955).

93 For an evaluation of Lewis's apologetic, see Donald T. Williams, *Deeper Magic: The Theology Behind the Writings of C. S. Lewis* (Baltimore: Square Halo Books, 2016), pp. 216-32.

tell us what they are, we will have to include the written Word, the preached Word, personal testimony, prayer—and apologetic argument. None of the critics of apologetics have the ability to remove apologetics from the list, because they do not have the authority to cut the commandment in 1 Peter 3:15 out of the Bible.

No sinner puts his faith in Christ for salvation without a supernatural intervention by God. The Apostle Paul is very clear about this. "A natural man does not accept the things of the Spirit of God, for they are foolishness to him, and he cannot understand them, because they are spiritually appraised" (1 Cor. 2:14). The natural man does not accept them and hence cannot know them because he is spiritually dead: "And you were dead in your trespasses and sins" (Eph. 2:1). The sinner cannot believe the Gospel, whether aided by rational argument or not, until he is "made alive" (Eph. 2:5). It is not natural for him to do so because the Gospel undercuts his commitment to his own autonomy. It will not let him be his own Lord, nor take any credit for his salvation. Because as a child of Adam the natural man is a constitutional rebel against God's kingdom, he cannot accept the Gospel until a radical change has taken place in his very nature—in his *heart*, in the biblical sense of that word. Apart from the intervention of the Holy Spirit in conviction and calling, he will remain in his sins because dead men cannot even reach out to grab the life preserver.

Alright, then: We are dead in our trespasses and sins and need to be brought back to life. No preacher, witness, or apologist can bring the spiritually dead to life. No wise preacher, witness, or apologist thinks he can. We preach, witness, and present evidence, not because we think any of that can be effective apart from the work of the Spirit, but because He has commanded us to use these means and promised to bless them and work through them.[94] If we are faithful, sooner or later He will give some helpless sinner the ability to respond positively to the Gospel by giving him new life. Apologetics is no exception to this rule. The most brilliant apologist on the planet is just as totally dependent on the work of the Spirit to make his efforts fruitful for the kingdom as the most powerful preacher and the most sincere witness—no more so, and no less. We will be better preachers, better witnesses, and better apologists when we fully realize this truth.

---

[94] For more on the role of the Holy Spirit in conviction and calling and regeneration and His use of means to those ends, see Donald T. Williams, *The Person and Work of the Holy Spirit* (Nashville: Broadman, 1994; rpt. Eugene, Or: Wipf & Stock), pp. 49-79, 210-216.

Our absolute dependence on the Holy Spirit should not discourage us from preaching, giving our testimony, and presenting the evidence for the truth of the Christian faith. Most especially, that discouragement should not be focused on apologetics as if it were somehow uniquely unable to be effective without the Spirit's empowerment in ways not true of the other means through which He works. In fact, the logic should run in precisely the opposite direction. It is because we are absolutely dependent on the Spirit for conviction, calling, regeneration, and new life in Christ to come about that we have a reason to pursue Christian witness and pursue it apologetically.

Conclusion

If the new life sinners need were dependent on my eloquence, my earnestness, or my brilliance or persuasiveness, we would all be lost. But because we have been commanded to preach, testify, and persuade, we persuade men, knowing that our labor is not in vain in the Lord (2 Cor. 5:11; 1 Cor. 15:58). We trust that God in His goodness and His love for lost human beings did not command us to speak and to persuade unless He planned to bless our obedience. We trust also in His wisdom, being granted to see that only when we give up all trust in our own abilities do we have a chance to make arguments that can win people, not just debates; only then can we really speak the truth in love. And so we obey, and so we can obey in hope. And if we can do that, the Reformation we need will be one step closer.[95]

---

95 For essays I've written on apologetic questions that are not published in one of my books in the bibliography, see "Body of Evidence: On Liberal Klingons and the Hard Facts of the Christian Faith," *Touchstone: A Journal of Mere Christianity* 26:2 (March/April 2013): 20-22, "The Justice of Hell?" *Christian Research Journal* 39:1 (Dec. 2015): 46-50, and "Made for Another World: C. S. Lewis's Argument from Desire Revisited" *Philosophia Christi: The Journal of the Evangelical Philosophical Society* 19:2 (2018): 449-54.

Interlude

Apologia

Structured steps within the Dance,
Things which could not be by chance:
Architecture of belief?
Arch of bole and vein of leaf.
Crystal's angles; raindrop's curves;
Bone and sinew knit with nerves.
Flick of wrist, fly-toss, and then,
Break of bubble, flash of fin.
Beyond these sure and certain hints,
A clearer class of evidence:
Broken fever; opened eyes;
Dove descending from the skies.
Footstep firm on slope of wave;
Stone rolled back from Jesus' grave.
Glory growing out of grief?
Architecture of belief;
Things which could not be by chance:
Structured steps within the Dance.[96]

---

[96] Donald T. Williams, *Stars through the Clouds*, op. cit., p. 168.

Commentary, 1 Peter 3:15

We are to keep ourselves in readiness
    Should any ask a reason for the hope
    That is within us and which we confess.
The great Deceiver does not sleep or rest,
    Enticing people toward the slippery slope,
    And so we keep ourselves in readiness.
The Truth is lovely in a silken dress;
    Her servant comes in sackcloth tied with rope,
    A humble penitent who must confess
His great unworthiness, but also stress
    Her grace, the only reason he can cope,
    And thus he keeps himself in readiness.
We are but beggars sharing our success
    With other tramps who also want to grope
    Toward the light with us. And we confess
That ours is not the brilliance we express.
    Christ is the Light; we aim the telescope:
    That's how we keep ourselves in readiness
To justify the great Hope we confess.[97]

---

[97] Ibid., p. 186.

13

Five Theses on Christianity and Culture

The question of the proper relationship of the church to human culture cannot be avoided.

A. Human beings are creative because they are made in the image of the Creator. (We were made in God's image so that we could not only have fellowship with Him but so we would be qualified to represent Him as His sub-regents and stewards on earth.)

B. Culture is the material, social, and symbolic matrix that results from the full range of mankind's creative activity. (It includes business, carpentry, farming, and cooking as well as art, music, drama, and literature; all are seamless products of human creativity.)

C. Culture is not and cannot be spiritually neutral or irrelevant. (It flows from the very heart of human identity as a creature made in the image of God to serve Him as stewards of His earth—or from our rebellion against that identity.)

D. Francis Schaeffer was right to insist that part of Christian discipleship is living out "the Lordship of Christ over the total culture." (Salvation is not just a religious "experience"; it restores us to our role as sub-creators for God's glory.)

E. The Christian subculture in any society should bring salt and light to that society through its own cultural activity, both in creating and consuming culture. (From homemaking to gardening to labor to art and music, the quality of our lives should reflect who we are.)

The Christian church was born out of an ancient Semitic culture into an ancient pagan culture and has survived into a modern secularist and neo-pagan one in the West while expanding into every kind of cultural milieu imaginable across the planet. In the meantime it has been a major player in creating and molding culture, especially Western culture, and has had its influence on whatever culture it has entered. But the situation is complicated in that the influence unavoidably goes both ways. It is not always easy to discern what in contemporary Christendom represents universal and non-negotiable truths revealed by God and what reflects the culture into which those truths have to be incarnated. Another important question: When is that inevitable cultural flavoring a necessary and even positive reflection of the fact that the church has successfully indigenized itself incarnationally, and when is it a corruption of its basic principles?

We have not always done a good job of discerning the answers to such questions. Most people can see that nineteenth-century missionaries should not automatically have tried to get tribesmen to wear Western clothes or switch to Western styles of music. It is not hard to see that American Evangelicalism has been perhaps a bit too much influenced by American pragmatism and consumerism. But where do you draw the line? Not all cultural influence is mere imperialism by the Western church or a corruption of it by pagan or secularist values. Surely the Auca Indians are better off not to have a culture based on vendetta any longer. Well, that is a direct impact of their conversion to Christianity on their culture. And surely current Christians should not wish to jettison Handel's *Messiah* because it uses musical techniques that were developed for the secular opera. (There were some Christians who protested it when it was first performed, because they thought it impious to have the Gospel sung in a secular concert hall instead of a church. They probably would have had a problem with Jesus preaching out on a hillside instead of in the synagogue, if the Sermon on the Mount were not already part of Scripture.)

Handel's Messiah Premiered, Dublin, 1742

The pious found a way to be offended:
> God's Word sung in a public Music Hall!
> It truly was a venue to appall,

Incapable of being comprehended.
> Why, vulgar entertainments there were vended,
> With doors thrown open wide to one and all.

To mix the Gospel with such folderol?
An error that could hardly be amended.

And what would these blasphemers think of next,
> So careless of the Church's reputation?
> Why not associate with sinners? Why,

You might as well proclaim the Sacred Text
> Of God's pure Kingdom and His great salvation
> Out on a hillside underneath the sky. [98]

Figuring out how the church should relate to culture and how it should seek to influence culture without being corrupted by it—figuring out how practically, in other words, for it to be in the world but not of it—is not an easy task. Our culture is complex and all-encompassing, and we are immersed in it in ways we are often not even aware of. The task includes, but is not limited to, how the church and individual Christians should relate to media, education, and the arts. The presence of this chapter in this book indicates that I think American Evangelicals need to do a better job of it, and that no Reformation of that movement can be whole and wholesome otherwise.

It will be easier to achieve that Reformation if we can come to a good theological understanding of what culture is and lay down some basic principles, based on that understanding, that govern our unavoidable participation in it. Why does culture exist? How do the ways of life that human beings create for themselves differ from those of animals? How does the biblical

---

98 Donald T. Williams, *Stars through the Clouds*, op. cit., p. 327.

worldview help us understand such things? And how does all of that help us more faithfully to create, consume, evaluate, and influence culture? Answering those questions will be the task of the next five theses.[99]

---

[99] The foundations for the understanding of culture proposed here are in J. R. R. Tolkien, "On Fairy Stories," *The Tolkien Reader* (N.Y. Ballantine, 1966), pp. 3-84), and Dorothy L. Sayers, *The Mind of the Maker* (N.Y.: Harper and Row, 1968). The place to start for understanding a biblical relationship between Christianity and Culture is Francis Schaeffer's "cultural apologetic," laid out in *The God Who is There* (Downers Grove, Il.: InterVarsity, 1968). Other important works wrestling with issues of Christianity and culture include Abraham Kuyper, *Lectures on Calvinism* (Grand Rapids: Eerdmans, 1931), T. S. Eliot, *Christianity and Culture: The Idea of A Christian Society and Notes towards a Definition of Culture* (N.Y.: Harcourt, Brace, and Company, 1940), H. Richard Niebuhr, *Christ and Culture* (N.Y.: Harper and Row, 1951), Henry R. Van Til, *The Calvinistic Concept of Culture* (Philadelphia: Presbyterian and Reformed, 1959), Clyde S. Kilby, *Christianity and Aesthetics* (Chicago: InterVarsity Press, 1961), Hans R. Roolmaaker, *Modern Art and the Death of a Culture* (Downers Grove, Il: InterVarsity Press, 1970), Francis Schaeffer, *Art and the Bible* (Downers Grove, Il.: InterVarsity, 1973), Leland Ryken, *Culture in Christian Perspective* (Portland: Multnomah, 1986), Andy Crouch, *Culture Making: Recovering our Creative Calling* (Downers Grove, Il.: InterVarsity, 2008), and Donald T. Williams, *Inklings of Reality: Essays toward a Christian Philosophy of Letters* (Lynchburg: Lantern Hollow Press, 2012), and *Deeper Magic: The Theology Behind the Writings of C. S. Lewis* (Baltimore: Square Halo Books, 2016), pp. 201-14. A very helpful practical approach to realizing Christian culture on a personal level is Edith Schaeffer, *Hidden Art* (Wheaton, Tyndale, 1971).

Thesis 13a:
Human Beings Are Creative Because They Are Made in the Image of the Creator.

Why does human culture exist? Why is it different in different places? Why does it have variations even in the same place? My ninth-grade history teacher defined culture as "the learned behavior of man, as he has adapted himself to his total environment." By that definition, every species has a "culture." But all robins make the same style and design of nest, while human beings live in caves, tents, houses, and other structures—and even the houses have an almost infinite variety of designs: log cabin, cottage, shot-house, ranch, Cape Cod, Victorian, neo-classical, Tudor half-timbered, with multiple variations on each of those styles. And while the secular mind emphasizes the continuity—we both build shelters—if a robin started really acting like a human being—making a hundred different styles of nest and, more significantly, making stick and clay statues of famous robins and decorating its nest with them—we should find him, as Chesterton noted, a fearful wildfowl indeed.[100] What is the difference?

Human beings are creative in a way that transcends anything we see in the animal world. We do not, like animals, do things out of instinct and hence do them all the same way. And we do things they don't do at all. Cave men drew pictures of reindeer on the walls of their caves. We have not found any deer drawing pictures of men. It is more than just a matter of intelligence. A monkey might break off a stick to use as a tool for digging termites out of a hill; he might arrange boxes into a pile he can climb to retrieve a banana hung from the ceiling. He surely shows a certain rudimentary intelligence in doing so. But he will not arrange the sticks or the boxes into a symmetrical pattern just so he can sit back and contemplate it, while getting no termites or bananas out of them at all. Birds sing (all the same tune) to look for a mate or mark their territory. "This is my tree! Go find your own!" They do not gather in flocks to listen to a particularly good warbler

---

[100] G. K. Chesterton, *The Everlasting Man* (N.Y.: Dodd, Meade, 1925), p. 22. See this book for a fascinating analysis of why human beings differ from animals in this way; cf. Donald T. Williams, *Mere Humanity: G. K. Chesterton, C. S. Lewis, and J. R. R. Tolkien on the Human Condition*, 2nd ed. (Chillicothe, OH: DeWard, 2018), for more on Chesterton's apologetic.

just because he sounds so cool. So, as Chesterton rightly and aptly concludes, "Art is the signature of man."[101]

It is understandable then that people often confuse culture with the arts. The arts are in fact a salient manifestation of human nature and hence of human culture: We are the only species that has art that exists only for contemplation and enjoyment and has no obvious pragmatic purpose. But it is the same creativity that makes us artists that also makes us unique as a species in science, in agriculture, in industry, in architecture, in homemaking, in politics—all areas in which individual and corporate human creativity generates the kind of world in which we live and affects the way we live in it. Creativity and the culture it generates are central to who we are. In a profound sense, that is what makes us Man.

This radical discontinuity between us and the rest of the animal kingdom demands an explanation, and evolution is not capable of providing it. I am not going to enter into the controversy over precisely how much biological evolution contributed to the origin of our species except to observe that, while it clearly played some role, it cannot be the whole story. With all the physical continuity we have with other animals, we are not in the sum total of our nature just an incremental step further down the same road that they are traveling, but rather represent a right turn and a quantum leap. There is only one adequate explanation for that leap that I have ever seen, and Christians are privileged to have it in their possession—a tremendous advantage if they want to understand and properly relate to human culture. It is in the biblical doctrine of creation, particularly as elaborated by J. R. R. Tolkien in his concept of "sub-creation": We are creative because we were made in the image of the Creator.[102] God's "primary creation" (the universe and us, in His image) leads to our "secondary creation"—of literature and art and music, but first of language itself, and then also of homes and furniture and meals and tools and cities. We through our God-given creative impulses and energy were designed to assist Him in bringing His creation to its full potential, to completeness and fruition—not because He needed assistance, but because in His own creativity and personality He desired graciously

---

101 Chesterton, *Everlasting Man*, op. cit., p. 16.

102 Tolkien, "On Fairy Stories," op. cit. For further analysis of Tolkien's idea and how it relates to the biblical worldview, see Donald T. Williams, *Mere Humanity*, op. cit., esp. chp. 3, and also his *An Encouraging Thought: The Christian Worldview in the Writings of J. R. R. Tolkien* (Cambridge, OH: Christian Publishing House, 2018), esp. chp. 2.

to share with us the joy of making the world. We were to fill the world (with our progeny and also the products of our labor), to subdue it, and to rule it on His behalf (Gen. 1:28). Theologians call this "the cultural mandate."

The creation of culture then is fulfilling to us because it is the expression of our God-given identity: It is who we are. Unfortunately, we rebelled against God in the Garden. As a result, we still rule the world, but for ourselves rather than for Him, and hence often rather badly. But masters of the earth we are still, or try to be, though by its thorns and thistles it does not cooperate with our rule as well as it once might have. Human culture then reflects human identity: We are created in the image of God but fallen, hence both magnificent and wretched, totally depraved in terms of our ability to merit salvation through our own works and yet still retaining the ruins of our original goodness.[103] We still do much that is good (in a temporal, not in a spiritual or salvific sense) because the remnants of our original goodness still inhere in us and because of common grace.[104] But we also do much that is foolish or downright evil. As a result, human cultures, like human beings, are complex mixtures of good and evil. Culture cannot be simply rejected—we could not live without it—but neither can it be uncritically embraced. This applies to all cultures, though some may be more corrupt or more conducive to certain types of goods than others. This is what makes being "in the world but not of it" such a challenging proposition. But it is not a challenge that we have the option to shirk.

Three important conclusions follow from this understanding of the origins of culture. First, culture is significant. It is the central expression of our very identity, flowing from our unique status as cre-

---

103 See Groothuis, *Christian Apologetics*, op. cit., chp. 18, for a fuller discussion of this point.

104 *Common Grace* is a theological term for the way God graciously restrains the full results of sin in human beings and in human societies so that we are not as evil as our Fall would otherwise have made us—He "sends His rain upon the just and the unjust" (Mt. 5:45). It is called *common* grace because all benefit from it, as distinguished from special grace, or saving grace, which applies only to believers in Christ. For the definitive treatment see Kenneth Sealer Kantzer, "John Calvin's Theory of the Knowledge of God and the Word of God." Diss. Harvard, 1950. Calvin does not use the phrase, but well expresses the concept: "Therefore, in reading profane authors, the admirable light of truth displayed in them should remind us that the human mind, however much fallen and perverted from its original integrity, is still adorned and invested with admirable gifts by its Creator.... If the Lord has been pleased to assist us by the work and ministry of the ungodly in physics, dialectics, mathematics, and other similar sciences, let us avail ourselves of it, lest, neglecting the gifts of God spontaneously offered to us, we be justly punished for our sloth." *Institutes of the Christian Religion*, 2 vol., trans. Henry Beveridge (Grand Rapids: Eerdmans, 1975), pp. 1:236-7.

ated in the image of the Creator. That makes culture important and powerful, and it makes us important and powerful as the creators of culture, for good or ill.

Culture is powerful, but its power needs to be seen in the context of the second conclusion: Cultural determinism is eliminated as a valid understanding of how we relate to culture. We cannot say that a person's culture *determines* how he will see the world and what he will do (despite many Post-Modernist analyses that imply that it does, if not stating so outright). Culture, and our "situatedness" in it, is indeed a powerful influence because it flows from the dynamic influence of human creativity. But precisely for that very same reason, we can never hide behind the mantra that "My culture made me do it." We are the creators of culture, and therefore are capable of standing above it. Many may not choose to do so; they may acquiesce in its influence as if it had created them. But if we create culture, or, more accurately, participate in its creation, then it is ultimately subject to our judgment and susceptible to our free actions. Our feelings, beliefs, and acts are influenced by our culture but do not have to be bound by it. Our freedom as moral agents within culture then also flows from the image of God. Creativity means the ability to do things that are not purely the result of antecedent circumstances and influences—the ability to contribute something actually new. We were created in the image of the Creator.

Finally, a "multiculturalism" that considers all cultures as created equal, but is especially suspicious of Western culture because of its historic dominance, is hopelessly naïve. All cultures, being human creations, are complex mixtures of good an evil that have to be evaluated on an individual basis. There is no basis for believing that good and evil are evenly distributed between them, nor that the history of colonialism somehow concentrates it in the West.

Thesis 13b:
Culture Is the Material, Social, and Symbolic Matrix That Results from the Full Range of Mankind's Creative Activity.

⌀

Now we are in a position to give a working definition of culture. The word comes from a Latin root whose most basic meaning is planting, tilling, growing crops. A *cultor* is a planter; *cultura* is tilling; *cultus* means tilling, cultivation. It is for this reason that the very word *culture* is a part of the word *agriculture*. The picture is that of human effort, directed by human intelligence, being expended onto nature to produce a result that nature by herself would not have given us: stalks of wheat or grapevines or olive trees concentrated in ordered rows in a field and growing there in a literally unnatural abundance (an abundance that nature unaided by human action could not have produced) for our convenience, to the end that human beings and human society might flourish.

The picture is very consistent with the biblical account of human beings. We are creators, yes, but only *sub*-creators. Unlike God, we cannot bring something out of nothing. We have to depend on Him for some given material (the natural world) to work with. But we bring forth from those natural raw materials results that nature by herself could not achieve: not primary creation, but real sub-creation. How long we lived as hunter-gatherers I do not know. But when agriculture emerged in human history, it emerged from the divinely imaged nature and creative potential that God had given us. So while the hunter-gatherers surely had culture (they made art and buried their dead with ceremony, for example), with agriculture a new level of culture became possible: what we call *civilization*.

Already in Latin the words *cultor*, *cultura*, and *cultus*, whose literal meanings we gave above, began very early to be used metaphorically to refer to the cultivation or development from their natural state into forms more beneficial (or harmful) to human beings of things other than crops: buildings, cities, arts, governments, religions, Man himself. Once this happens we are on the verge of the definition we would like to use here: *Culture is the material, social, and symbolic matrix that results from the full range of mankind's creative activity.* That is what we speak of today when we refer to a nation or a people or even a smaller group like a school, a church, or a business ("corporate culture") as having a culture. These groups, sub-groups, and institutions have developed a way of doing things, making things, and relating to each other through that doing and making, that characterizes their society. It is inherited but also constantly changing as their creative activity continues to have input, preserving, altering, improving, corrupting, sometimes even destroying that total way of being in the world.

These culture-creating acts are largely unconscious, but sometimes very conscious and deliberate. The resulting cultural matrix grows from the kind of creative activity that is characteristic of human beings because they were created in the image of the Creator. It includes but is not limited to what is sometimes called "high culture": painting, sculpture, fiction, poetry, theater, cinema, music, dance. It includes religion, business, carpentry, farming, cooking, media, and education along with what we call the "fine" arts; it also includes science. All are seamless products of human creativity. You could say it is the mark we leave on each other as we leave our mark on the world.

Now here's the point. We were created to do this. We have to do this. We don't have the option not to participate. It is not a sin to do this. It would be a sin not to do this, if not doing it were possible. Sin or virtue, obedience or disobedience, lies in *the way* we do it. Do we do it for God or for self? In accordance with and reflecting His revealed truth or in rebellion against and suppressing or distorting it? Submissive to His wisdom or insisting on our own folly? Or (almost inevitably) some complex mix of all the above? Sorting all that out is why we need three more theses.

Thesis 13c.
Culture Is Not and Cannot Be Spiritually Neutral or Irrelevant.

Perhaps no one would *say* that culture is spiritually irrelevant. But many Evangelical Christians act as if they thought it were. They would think the idea of the church returning to its historic role as a patron, hence influencer, of the arts, just silly. Meanwhile, they are entertained by music and sitcoms that undermine their biblical worldview and coarsen their manners, blissfully unaware that there is a problem with this. It does not help that the only alternative model they are aware of is the old Fundamentalist rejection of all "secular" culture as inherently evil and corrupting—for example, not using discernment but simply avoiding all public theater and popular music as part of "the world." That was a failure of spiritual responsibility in cultural engagement, an approach just as inadequate as their own. They rejected it (or their parents did—they may not even remember it) without putting any better model in its place. Their unthinking approach contributes greatly to their inability to be faithful to the content or practice of the faith they think they espouse.

Nevertheless, culture is not and cannot be spiritually neutral or irrelevant. It flows from the very heart of human identity as a creature made in the image of God to serve Him as stewards of His earth—or from our rebellion against that identity. Our relationship to culture is thus inevitably complicated. God supports culture because it nurtures His human creatures, who could not live without it. Even the worst and most corrupt cultures contain much that is good by common grace—which no doubt pleases Him. Nevertheless, God also stands in judgment over culture because it is the reflection not only of mankind's identity as created in His image but also of its identity as a rebel against His service.

A seemingly confusing biblical metaphor reflects this dual nature of culture and thus creates a tension for God's people in this complex world. Christians, His redeemed children, are to see themselves as strangers and exiles in such fallen cultures (Heb. 11:13, 1 Pet. 2:11), but they are also to follow in the steps of their Israelite forebears and "seek the welfare of the city where [they] have been sent into exile and pray to the Lord on its behalf," be it Babylon, Nineveh, or Rome (Jer. 29:7). They are neither to identify with human culture nor to stand aloof from it. In other words, this dual role implies that they are to be participating in this foreign culture, not withdrawing from it; but at the same time they should not be finding their primary identity in it, yielding themselves to its influence uncritically, or allowing themselves to be defined by it. They are to be in it but not of it (John 17:14-15).

To navigate this dual role successfully, Christians cannot have an intellectually lazy approach. The path of least resistance is not open to them. They must constantly be exercising *discernment*. That is why Reformation is needed in this area: We *are* intellectually lazy. It is easy to yield to culture; the path of least resistance will accomplish that goal most efficiently. It is relatively easy to convince yourself that you have withdrawn from it. (You will not have, of course, not really.) On neither of those paths is there any spiritual integrity, salt and light, or credible witness to be found.

Where are these things to be found?

Somehow we must be "in" the world and "not of" it at the same time; somehow we must achieve the integration of these two prepositions in one unified lifestyle that becomes the mark of *Christian* culture. But that is difficult. What we often attempt instead is the much easier task of taking one of these prepositions in isolation from the other. It requires no effort at all to be "in" the world; the path of least resistance will suffice for that. And, while it requires more effort, it is also possible to be "not of" the world, up to a point. Here we create our (partially) insulated parallel universe, with borders guarded by ever-increasing lists of Rules. "We don't cuss, drink, smoke, or chew, / And we don't go with girls that do." We create our own little Christian ghetto and withdraw within its borders so we will not be corrupted. We write our own music and books and create our own TV, all of which somehow turn out to be strangely cheap imitations of what the world is doing but without the grosser forms of immorality. But this is a false approach, and Christ makes it clear He does not mean us to take it. He does so both by His prayer in John 17:15 ("I do not ask You to take them out of the world, but to keep them from the evil one") and by His example, hanging out with publicans and sinners and scandalizing the religious conservatives of His day.

We can pursue either of these prepositions in the flesh. We do not have in ourselves either the wisdom or the strength to be "in" and "not of" at the same time. That requires the wisdom and the power of God; that requires discernment and dying to self. And so, of course, it is not to be thought of by half-hearted Christians, and so it is seldom seen. Yet that is precisely what is commanded: not isolated prepositions in the flesh, but the integration of the two prepositions in the Spirit. But how can we do that? Paul provides the answer; "Finally, brethren, whatever is true, whatever is honorable, whatever is right, whatever is pure, whatever is lovely, whatever is of good repute, if there is any excellence, and if anything worthy of praise, let your mind dwell on these things" (Phil. 4:8).

What kind of command is this verse? It is a Positive Command. It is about what we are positively supposed to have our minds dwell on. But in our application of it we have almost universally turned it into a negative command, about what we are not supposed to read, watch, or listen to: "Oh, this is impure, so I'd better stay away from it!" Why have we managed to be so inattentive to what the Text actually says? Because it is easier. It is easier to boycott all movies (or all movies of a certain rating) than to use discernment; it is easier to swear off of "secular" music or "rock" than to listen critically to what the world is actually saying through these media, understand with empathy the cries of its lost voices, but then choose the good, and dwell on that.

I repeat: this verse says not one word about what we cannot read, watch, or listen to. It says not a single word about what we must turn a blind eye to, pretend isn't there, or be ignorant of. It says a lot about what we should nourish and feed our minds on. Contrary to the T-shirt, Nietzsche isn't peachy; he is actually very preachy, and what he is preaching is straight from the Pit. But he has been very influential and he is important, and even in his evil he can teach us some things. Therefore I was not disobeying this passage when I read him, even though he is rightly described by none of the adjectives (except possibly "excellent," in the sense of "outstanding") that the verse recommends. But that is not the kind of thing I feed my mind on constantly. What is? I read Tolkien's *The Lord of the Rings* twice in 1968, the year I discovered it, and have read it annually since as a way of cleaning out the garbage that has collected in my mind from grading freshman essays and reconnecting myself with the values it embodies: with the Good, the True, and with the Beautiful, with the contrast between Good and Evil, with the nature of the Quest, and with the value and significance of Sacrifice.[105] No work speaks more eloquently and powerfully to me of such things. More importantly, I am doing the same thing with Scripture on a daily basis. That is what the verse is talking about.

It is not that there is nothing that is so raw, so evil, so corrupting that we should not expose ourselves to it. There is much that falls in that category, and the increasing decadence of our society can render us appallingly naïve at discerning what it is. But our main strategy for dealing with these problems is too often negative, while the Bible's is positive. Understanding this distinction makes Phil. 4:8 the answer to the dilemma raised by Jesus' words in John 17. How do we live "in" the world without becoming "of" it? We do it through a positive, pro-active program of feeding ourselves on the good. Do not focus primarily on what you cannot read, watch, or listen to. Do not use ignorance as the path to safety. Machen put it well: "Some of modern thought must be refuted. The rest must be made subservient. But nothing in it can be ignored."[106] Rather, the formula is this: Really feed your mind on the Good, True, and Beautiful, as defined by Scripture and exemplified in the best of the classical tradition, and then it will respond rightly to the rest.

---

105 See my book *An Encouraging Thought: The Christian Worldview in the Writings of J. R. R. Tolkien* (Cambridge, OH: Christian Publishing House, 2018) for more on these themes in *The Lord of the Rings*.

106 J. Gresham Machen, *Education, Christianity, and the State* (Unicoi, Tn.: The Trinity Foundation, 1987), p. 57.

Thesis 13d:
Francis Schaeffer Was Right To Insist That Part of Christian Discipleship Is Living Out "the Lordship of Christ over the Total Culture."

If human culture exists as the product of human creativity because human beings were created in the image of the Creator; if culture is the material, social, and symbolic matrix that results from the full range of mankind's creative activity; if culture cannot then be spiritually neutral or irrelevant, so that we can neither ignore it, nor withdraw from it, nor let it influence us uncritically, but must rather engage it responsibly; and if Christ is supreme as Lord of all; then Francis Schaeffer was right to insist that an essential part of Christian discipleship is living out "the Lordship of Christ over the whole of life," which includes the totality of culture.[107] We have not yet understood adequately either the need for such living or the nature of what it asks of us.

When a more or less Judeo-Christian consensus was still dominant in American culture, it was easy for Evangelicals to think of their faith as something that they practiced on Sunday morning. The rest of the week they did not really need to be that different from their neighbors—maybe a little bit more honest and moral, and if they were Fundamentalists, abstaining from alcohol, tobacco, and movies—but otherwise, not radically different. Becoming a Christian or "getting saved" was something they did as part of their religious life. There was no expectation that it would make much difference in how they ran their businesses, how they voted, how they raised their families, or—unless they were Fundamentalists—what kind of recreation and entertainment they would enjoy. Their approach was inconsistent: They were neither consistently withdrawing from culture nor effectively engaging it. Some of them practiced an incoherent hodgepodge of both strategies. Mostly, they were drifting with the culture, which was headed to places that would shock and dismay them a generation later.

---

107 "The Lordship of Christ over the whole of life means that there are no platonic areas in Christianity, no dichotomy or hierarchy between the body and the soul. . . . If Christianity is really true, then it involves the whole man, including his intellect and his creativeness." Francis A. Schaeffer, *Art and the Bible*, op. cit., pp. 7, 9.

Our Evangelical forebears made two mistakes which they have unfortunately bequeathed to many of us. First, they seriously overestimated how deep the Christian influence on American culture was. Traditional morality and the traditional family were in the 1950s being maintained out of habit, while any basis for those things in spiritual or even cultural commitment to their foundations was being hollowed out. Our failure to practice the Great Commission as it was given (see chapter 11, especially Thesis 11b)—to make *disciples* rather than merely converts—meant that the foundations of our Judeo-Christian culture were being undermined even while it looked like we were being successful in reaching people with the Gospel. Too many of our "converts" did not truly become born again, and hardly any of them were being taught the Christian worldview, much less sound doctrine.

The second mistake was a superficial understanding of the Lordship of Christ and its implications for all of life. Christian truth does not exist in an isolated, sealed chamber called "religion." It is true truth *about the world*, because God is the Creator of the world. Therefore Christ is Lord not just of my religion but of my *life*. No distinction that is not arbitrary can be made between "sacred" and "secular" realms of life. C. S. Lewis expressed the truth starkly but accurately: "There is no neutral ground in the universe; every square inch, every split second is claimed by God and counter-claimed by Satan."[108] As J. Gresham Machen put it, "The field of Christianity is the world. The Christian cannot be satisfied so long as any human activity is either opposed to Christianity or out of connection with Christianity."[109]

If what Lewis and Machen said is true, if what the Bible teaches about God, man, and the world is true, it should make a difference in every area of life: how we relate to our family, to our fellow man, to work, to the state, to education, athletics, the arts—everything. Every area of private life, every arena of public life, must now be seen not as something existing autonomously on its own, but as something that exists in relation to Christ: to be redeemed by His grace, informed by His Word, brought into submission to His Lordship, and pursued for His glory. Most of our churches do not even make an effort to teach such things—which means they

---

108 C. S. Lewis, "Christianity and Culture," in *Christian Reflections*, ed. Walter Hooper (Grand Rapids: Eerdmans, 1967), p. 33.

109 J. Gresham Machen, *Education, Christianity, and the State* (Unicoi, Tn.: The Trinity Foundation, 1987), p. 50.

are making no effort to be disciple-making communities.

It is easy to miss the radical relevance of Christian truth to all of life because in many areas there is no difference *on the surface*. The solution to a mathematical equation is the same for a Christian, a neopagan, and an atheist. The solution to which chemical formula of additives to my gasoline will make my car run smoothly and efficiently, or to which medicine will make my body do so, is the same, whether I am a Christian, a Hindu, or a Muslim. The grammar by which I must construct my sentences to make them intelligible and the rhetorical flourishes by which I can arrange them to make them powerful are the same whether I am writing an evangelistic sermon, a promotion for Planned Parenthood, or a translation of *The Communist Manifesto*. There is no particularly "Christian" way of doing any of those things, or a host of other things. But that does not mean there is no difference as to *whether*, *how*, or *why* a Christian should do them.

Two plus two equal four. They do and must equal four and no other number, whatever your religious beliefs or philosophy of life. The Christian and the Non-Christian see the same truth—but they do not (or should not) see it the same way. The Non-Christian says, "Two plus two equal four. I have no idea why. It just seems to work. If I don't take account of this strangely stable fact when I try to balance my checkbook, I will get myself into a heap of trouble eventually, so I just accept it, and then never give it another thought. Whatever." The Christian should look at the same fact very differently: "Two plus two equal four. I can always trust this to be true. And it is thus an awe-inspiring example of the transcendent rationality and trustworthy covenant faithfulness of the beautiful mind of our glorious God, which reminds me to worship Him every time I balance my checkbook. Blessed be He!"

This is not just a matter of the Christian having access to an inspiring emotional penumbra around his facts when he wants it. Seeing all facts as God's facts always makes a practical difference too. Even when we do the same things as Non-Christians, we do them from different motives and with a different ultimate purpose in view. As a Christian, I am not a private individual who has the option of making decisions solely to please myself. I am the servant of Another, bought with a price; I am the steward of the earth and the steward (not the owner) of all my own possessions; I am an Ambassador for Christ. Everything I do, and the way I do it, either advances or thwarts the objectives inherent in these identities. So I do not work just to make a living. I work to *serve* my employer and my neighbor *out of love*. The quality with which I do that is the context out of which my testimony for Christ flows. Martin Luther said somewhere that if you are a Christian cobbler, you accomplish all of this not by putting little crosses on your shoes, but by making really good shoes and selling them for a fair price. Thus you love both God and your neighbor.

A like mentality pervades my approach to every aspect of my life: as a husband or wife, a father or mother, a neighbor, an employee, an employer, a consumer, a citizen, a person just resting and relaxing, I must let my light so shine before men that they will see my good works and glorify my Father who is in heaven (Mat. 5:16). And I do it all not as a burdensome duty but as an expression of the joy of life, of gratitude for my redemption, and of love for God and my neighbor. There is not a single atom of reality or iota of truth about reality that comes into my field of vision that I do not see in relation to Christ.[110]

---

[110] I spoke of this kind of seeing as "wholeness of vision" that flows from "biblical consciousness" in *Inklings of Reality: Essays toward a Christian Philosophy of Letters* (Lynchburg: Lantern Hollow Press, 2012). See that book for more practical advice on how to cultivate wholeness of vision and the Christian culture that should reflect it.

Thesis 13e:
The Christian Subculture in Any Society Should Bring Salt and Light to That Society Through Its Own Cultural Activity, Both in Creating and Consuming Culture.

Everything we do as Christians should reflect our identity as sub-creators, stewards, servants, and ambassadors of Christ. And because we are subcreators, everything we do will make—or mar—culture, in one way or another. As homemakers, family members, gardeners, cooks, workers, voters, participators in social media, consumers of products, patrons of movies, books, music, and plays, members of clubs and of churches, and in a thousand other roles, we never cease to be both creators and consumers of culture. (People underestimate how important our role as *consumers* is. Every purchase we make is a vote that something should be valued, and that more of it should be made.) As people with a different set of beliefs which, however imperfectly, affect our sense of who we are, we will do it in our own unique way (or set of ways, since even the Christian subculture is not monolithic or uniform). Those different ways of life will get noticed as a subset of the larger culture which will interact with it in complex ways. American Christians will have their own ways *of being Americans*, for example; they are not going to live like First-Century Middle-Eastern peasants in the midst of American society. That all this will happen is inevitable. That we will do it well, or even deliberately, or thoughtfully, or intelligently, or faithfully to sound Christian teaching, is not.[111]

Jesus uses two metaphors for His followers' presence in the world that describe the way they are supposed to relate to it and interact with it: salt and light. We are the salt of the earth, so we had better not lose our taste (Mat. 5:13). And we are the light of the world, so we had better not let ourselves be hidden away (Mat. 5:14-15), but rather be seen in such a way that our good works glorify the Father (Mat. 5:16). Salt was valued both as a preservative and as a flavoring. Light

---

111 For a fascinating study of one man who did it well in his generation, see David Stott Gordon, "Sir Philip Sidney: The Faith and Practice of an Elizabethan Christian" (Thesis Trinity Evangelical Divinity School, 1995).

shows the path and shows up both good and evil for what they are (John 3:19-21). So the church's presence in the world should retard its natural slide toward corruption and evil, bring out and enhance the flavor of what is good in it, and keep the way toward grace and truth open and visible to people's eyes so that the Holy Spirit can call them into it.

We do this by preaching the Gospel and sharing our testimony, of course. We should also be doing it by showing the difference following Christ makes in our total way of life. We are still fallen people who sometimes stumble badly, but we should be stumbling on a new path in a new direction. (Remember that Christianity was first called simply "the Way.") That new path is marked by the new identity we have already been given in Christ (restored subcreators, faithful stewards, heavenly ambassadors), and the new direction is toward the full incarnation of that identity that we will receive in its fullness and without compromise when we see Christ face to face. In the meantime, if our work manifests reliable quality for a fair price, if our homes manifest loving hierarchy without oppression (see Theses 9a-e), if our lives manifest creative applications of biblical principles that reveal goodness, truth, and beauty in many ways that can join with the heavens to declare the glory of God (Psalm 19:1), then our preaching of the Gospel will have a credibility and a power that we have not seen in our generation. Then the culture of the Kingdom of Heaven, reaching back into this present evil age in foretastes of the glory that is to come and finding ways to express itself in the idiom of the fallen cultures it invades, will be *seen*. And that may be the most convincing apologetic of all.

Special Section
Christanity and the Arts

I have hesitated long over these next few paragraphs. They are necessary, but I fear that I will not be able to write them so as to avoid some people charging me with elitism. And if elitism is what I am heard as preaching, I will have failed. Elitism lacks the divine humility that should characterize any genuine Christian culture. But bear with me if I sound elitist for the moment. I will try to redeem myself from that charge before the end.

I won't try to assess what kind of Christian subculture we have created in our homes, offices, or workshops. It no doubt ranges from splendid to abysmal, as one would expect. Others are better equipped to speak of those manifestations. Here I am thinking of the face we as Evangelicals and Fundamentalists present to the world with respect to that salient area of human creativity that is often mistakenly equated with culture: the arts.[112] I am afraid it reflects the basic superficiality of our movement, which has often been described as a river a mile wide and an inch deep. What have we given to the world? Southern Gospel; "Praise and Worship"; the "Christian Romance Novel"; paintings of unrealistically pretty landscapes or Victorian villages with Bible verses tacked beneath them; cutesy figurines of angels who could not say, "Fear not!" with credibility if their wings depended on it.

There. I've just offended some of you. Forgive me, and hear me out. Not everything I just listed is always bad or inherently trashy. I like some Southern Gospel myself, when it stays close to its roots in folk music and the Negro spiritual. I don't think less of you if you do too. But nothing I just listed can pretend to be "high" or "serious" art. Why is that a problem? Why do we care if we are not nurturing a bunch of hoity-toity, snotty *artistes* who think they are better than everybody else? Because the very way I just framed that complaint loudly shouts of a prejudice against excellence that is absolutely foreign to, antithetical to, dismissive of, and loaded with antipathy towards our marching orders in Philippians 4:8. "Finally, brethren, whatever is true, whatever is honorable, whatever is pure, whatever is lovely,

---

112 The indispensable works here are Kilby, *Christianity and Aesthetics* (op. cit.), Schaeffer, *The God Who is There* (op. cit.) and *Art and the Bible* (op. cit.), and Rookmaaker, *Modern Art and the Death of a Culture* (op. cit.).

whatever is of good repute, *if there is any excellence, anything worthy of praise*, dwell on these things" (emphasis added). And I framed it in precisely the terms that would be on the lips of too many of us. We should not despise "low" or "pop" culture just for being popular. I don't. It has its place. Neither should we despise the high just for being high. As a whole, our movement does.

It has not always been this way. Conservative, Evangelical, Protestant piety once fostered the epics of Milton and Spenser, the devotional poetry of Donne and Herbert, the music of Bach and Handel.[113] Where is the American Evangelical author who writes anything that is, or can be, appreciated for its literary value by non-Christians who are not already biased in favor of its message? You can think of a few Christians in the Twentieth Century who achieved this feat without compromising their Christian content: G. K. Chesterton, C. S. Lewis, J. R. R. Tolkien, Dorothy L. Sayers, Flannery O'Connor. None of them were American Evangelicals. Why not? You get what you value as a community, as a subculture; you get what you encourage; you get what you reward. One of the reforms desperately needed if we are to give full witness to the Gospel with credibility is a healthier attitude toward culture in general and the arts in particular.

---

113 For a brilliant analysis of how specifically Protestant spirituality once fostered a rich literary culture, see Barbara Kiefer Lewalski, *Protestant Poetics and the Sixteenth-Century Religious Lyric* (Princeton: Princeton Univ. Pr., 1979). For further discussion of these matters, see my *Inklings of Reality: Essays toward a Christian Philosophy of Letters*, op. cit., esp. chap. 10, "Why Evangelicals Can't Write," pp. 207-14.

Conclusion

How do we get there? Not by despising pop culture; not by suddenly running out and trying to be artsier than thou; definitely not by copying the decadent art of the secular culture we live in. We don't want more cacophonic music in our worship services, more incomprehensible poetry in our libraries, more ugly and chaotic paintings on our walls. No, we do it by reforming our attitude toward culture in the terms of these theses. We do it by teaching ourselves and our children to appreciate the best that has been written, sung, and painted in the past, to understand what was good about it, and to value those artistic monuments for what made them great. We do it by teaching ourselves and our children that human culture has value because it flows from human creativity which flows from the image of God, and that, for those so gifted, it is a way of serving God that is cherished by our community. We do it by praying for our children in those terms and supporting them with our attention and our dollars when they try. And then we may be astonished at the Renaissance, Reformation, and Revival that result.

Interlude

The Goal of the Trivium

Commentary, Proverbs 9:1-6

Old mysteries await fresh revelation.
    Such ideas ought of right to be presented
    In royal garments, rich and ornamented,
Befitting their high lineage and station.
Heraldic manuscript illumination
    In Celtic knotwork swirled and brightly tinted
    For metaphors and the meanings they have hinted:
The setting beckons us, an invitation.

What now seems quaint and esoteric lore
    Was once the simple bedrock of our thought:
    First principles and their elucidation.
That's partly what the wondrous words were for—
    Despite our darkness, they can still be caught:
    Faint echoes of the ancient Conversation.[114]

---

[114] Donald T. Williams, *Stars through the Clouds*, op. cit., p. 291.

Commentary, Rev. 21:24-27

The marching orders of the Great Commission:
    Disciple every tongue and tribe and nation?
    The Torah-nurtured culture of the Jews
Was not enough. A richer far rendition
    Was needed for the fuller celebration
    Of God's creation and the happy news
That Christ had come to earth to take our part.
    Every language's enunciation,
    The cadences of every culture's muse,
Their architecture, eloquence, and art—
    And nothing, sanctified, would He refuse.[115]

---

115 Ibid., p. 173.

14
Five Theses on Pietism

We have a deficient and sub-Biblical view of Christian spirituality.

Five Theses on Pietism

A. Pietism, as the word is used here, is the theory that the Christian life consisteth in the multitude and depth of emotions that a person possesseth. (Of course a healthy Christian life should involve an emotional response, because it is for the whole person. But too much popular Evangelical piety in effect *reduces* it to emotion.)

B. Pietism (as a movement) arose as a natural and healthy corrective to the dead orthodoxy of eighteenth-century European state churches. (When those early pietist leaders stressed what they called "heart religion," they thought it included the rigorous use of the mind; they did not throw out the intellectual baby with the dead-orthodox baptismal water.)

C. However, when not rooted in a holistic biblical anthropology and psychology, pietism cannot be healthy, and it has thus contributed to the superficiality, irrelevance, and corruption of American conservative Christianity. (When everything is focused on an emotional response at the "altar," the mind atrophies, the will is paralyzed, and even the emotions eventually become stereotyped and jaded.)

D. Emotions are byproducts of true biblical spiritual life, not the thing itself. (True spiritual life is loving God with all your heart, soul, and mind, and your neighbor as yourself [Mat. 22:37], not just *feeling* like you love them.)

E. Horses should be kept in front of carts. (You will have the right emotional response when your focus is on God, not your feelings.)

"The emotions were made to be servants of reason, to be governed by the judgment, and to be influenced by truth, but they were not intended to decide controversies or to determine what is truth and what error." So wrote Isaac Watts.[116] This would be news to a lot of Evangelical Christians today, but what Watts said in the Eighteenth Century would have been considered simple common sense by the Reformers, the Puritans, and Watts's fellow leaders of the First Great Awakening. How have we got to the place where it sounds radical and unheard of, where the Christian life seems to be about feelings and little else? How have we got to the place where many of us would be far more comfortable taking Darth Vader's advice: "Luke! Search your feelings! [That's how] you know it to be true." That is the story of this chapter and the next five theses, which deal with genuine biblical spirituality as contrasted with one of its most frequently adopted counterfeits.[117]

---

116 Isaac Watts, "The Abuse of the Emotions in the Spiritual Life" (1746), in *A Burning and a Shining Light: English Spirituality in the Age of Wesley*, ed. David Lyle Jeffrey (Grand Rapids: Eerdmans, 1987), p. 70.

117 For the classic work on genuine Christian spirituality, especially as it relates to the emotional life, see Jonathan Edwards, *A Treatise Concerning the Religious Affections* (1746; New Haven: Yale Univ. Pr., 1959). A good and practical modern treatment is Francis Schaeffer, *True Spirituality* (Wheaton: Tyndale, 1971). See also Schaeffer's *The New Super-Spirituality* (Downers Grove, Il/: InterVarsity, 1972), on newer tendencies in his day that have unfortunately continued and been mainstreamed since then. There is also much material relevant to this topic in my *The Person and Work of the Holy Spirit* (Nashville: Broadman, 1994; rpt. Wipf and Stock) and *The Disciple's Prayer* (Camp Hill, Pa.: Christian Publications, 1990; rpt. Wipf and Stock).

Thesis 14a:
Pietism, As the Word Is Used Here, Is the Theory That the Christian Life Consisteth in the Multitude and Depth of Emotions That a Person Possesseth.

God created the whole human being. Christ redeems the whole human being. The Spirit sanctifies the whole human being. Therefore, God deserves the complete devotion of the whole human being. A kind of theology-nerd Christianity that despised emotional responses would be just as incomplete, just as unhealthy, just as dishonoring to the God of wholeness, and just as disobedient to the Christ who commanded us to love God with *all* our hearts, all our soul, and all our minds (Mat. 22:37), as one that despised or denigrated or downplayed the intellect. And such people exist. But they are few and scattered and have a hard time feeling at home in our typical Fundamentalist and Evangelical churches. They need to repent. But they do not characterize the movement, and so they have not received the bulk of our attention in this book. The great reform needed by contemporary Evangelicalism is not learning to be emotional; neither is it that of suppressing emotion, but rather of restoring it to its proper place.

As with many other areas, we have become far too accommodated to the world in this one. Luke Skywalker receives the advice to trust his feelings not just from the evil Lord Vader but also from Obi-Wan and Yoda, who represent the so-called "light side" of the Force. He turns off his targeting computer, trusts his feelings instead of his rational mind, and nails the port on the Death Star. And that act resonates with a supposedly Post-Modern world that has uncritically and unconsciously accepted the elevation of subjective emotion and intuition over reason and fact. This dichotomy ironically flows from the Modernist bifurcation between fact and feeling.

What seemed to have happened in the wake of the Enlightenment was that only science and "common sense" could be trusted to produce real objective truth about the world. Appeals to revelation to justify religious wars in the previous century and a visceral reaction against those memories unfortunately aligned with the birth of modern science to create the impression that only scientific truths could be universal and objective. Values, meaning, and significance then retreated into a private, subjective inner realm of feeling and sentiment (the "heart" in the modern sense of that word) where they could reign unchallenged by cold reason. The price we paid for that retreat was the loss of any ability to claim the status of universal validity or objective truth for truth claims about values, meaning, or significance. But to be protected from challenge by reason is to lose the support of reason. So now everything (meaning, significance) that makes the facts matter has been sealed off from any relation to those facts and survives only by losing its connection to them. We did not at first realize the severe cost of this maneuver.

You can see the effects of the change on religious life in Tennyson's *In Memoriam* (1850).[118] In this great elegy on the untimely death of his friend Arthur Henry Hallam in 1833, Tennyson wrestles with the apparent cruelty of the universe and futility of life. By the time of its publication those issues had been intensified by the general crisis of faith occasioned by the challenges to a literal reading of Genesis precipitated by Lyell's *Principles of Geology* (1833) and leading to Darwin's *Origin of the Species* (1859). So while memorializing his friend, Tennyson is also trying desperately to make sense of what has happened and survive the challenge it all presents to his Christian faith. The sorrow was deep, the suffering intense, the crisis very real, and the wrestling with it agonizing. And the poetry that expresses these things is beautiful and moving. We must be profoundly grateful that Tennyson's faith was in the end preserved. But the way he found to preserve it did not bode well for the healthy grounding of the faith of many in the future.

The poem begins ominously for anyone committed to the integration of faith and reason. It is addressed to the "Strong Son of God, immortal Love" in whom we "believe where we cannot prove." The admission of an inability to prove is not necessarily problematic in itself, but the faith we are left with seems rather blind and bereft of any rational or evidential support at all: "We have but faith; we cannot know." The little word "but" in that sentence is troubling. How do we justify our stubborn clinging to our faith in Christ as the Son

---

[118] Alfred, Lord Tennyson, *Tennyson's Poetry*, selected and edited by Robert W. Hill, Jr. (N.Y.: Norton, 1971), pp. 118-195.

of a loving God in spite of the seemingly overwhelming evidence to the contrary presented by modern science and harsh experience? The bottom line becomes clear after pages of wrestling.

> If e'er when faith had fallen asleep
>   I heard a voice, "Believe no more,"
>   And heard an ever-breaking shore
> That tumbled in the Godless deep,
>
> A warmth within the heart would melt
>   The freezing season's colder part,
>   And like a man in wrath the heart
> Stood up and answered, "I have felt!"
> (Section 124, lines 9-16)

Well, that settles it. God is love and Christ is real because, despite every indication to the contrary, I have *felt* that it is so. Luke—trust your feelings.

Tennyson gives classic expression to a move that a lot of Christians at the time were making in response to the challenges of Darwinism and negative biblical criticism. Rather than meeting the intellectual challenges head on as if Christian truth were actually *true*, they ceded the head to secularism and sought to protect their faith from outward assault by rooting it in the "heart." The general milieu of mid-Nineteenth-Century Romanticism made that a natural response, but it was a short-sighted one for all of that. They failed to understand that the modern English connotations of heart-language were causing them to misread the Scriptures. (When biblical people wanted to use a body part to symbolize the emotions, they chose not the heart but the bowels; the heart stood for the central core of personality where intellect, emotion, and will find their unity.) As a result, with the best of intentions, they substituted for the holistic, robust faith of the Bible a sadly shrunken version which could not command the respect of thinking people and left the Christians who had it vulnerable to the gradual erosion of the content of the faith they still held.

The fruit of that shift is seen in the Evangelical subculture today in many ways. The equation of faith with feeling has permeated every part of Evangelical religion. Conversion is often seen not as a whole-person response of mind, emotion, and will to revealed truth seen as such, but as an emotional response at the "altar." Sanctification is often seen not as a lifelong process but as a crisis emotional response at the altar. The whole worship service is designed to facilitate that emotional response. The Christian bookstore (one resists the temptation to overuse ironic quotation marks) has very little space for books, and almost none of them are geared to serious Bible study, doctrine, or apologetics. They are almost all Christian self-help or Christian romance novels. Tennyson said he could keep his faith in a loving Christ because he had "felt." And even before the advent of "praise and worship," we sang, "You ask me how I know He lives? / He lives within my heart!" Had we remembered what the heart meant in biblical usage, that would not have been a problem. In our present state of confusion, it is a big one.

Do not misunderstand me. I am not denying that Tennyson genuinely felt the love of Jesus, or saying that you should not feel it, and feel it deeply. I am not even saying that those feelings are not a valid *part* of our justification for believing. Surely anyone who would say that his experiences of grace are not one of the reasons why he believes is either inattentive or dishonest. The problem is the *reduction* of Christian faith to emotion—not the presence of feeling but the absence of reason and evidence as important considerations. Mormons will tell you that the reason they "know" that doctrines clean contrary to the Gospel are true is because they make them feel a "burning in the bosom." That experience does not prove they are right. Neither, alone, do our experiences. Emotions should be enjoyed when they line up with Scripture. But emotions by themselves cannot be trusted. They were never meant to have the almost exclusive role we try to give them.

Thesis 14b:
Pietism (As a Movement) Arose As a Natural and Healthy Corrective to the Dead Orthodoxy of Seventeenth-Century European State Churches.

⌀

How did we get to such a place? Pietism as a movement first arose in the Seventeenth Century as a reaction to the dead orthodoxy in European state churches—initially, German and Scandinavian Lutheranism. It took many shapes as it spread across Europe, some more healthy and orthodox than others. At its best it was a needed corrective to a real problem. What concerns us here is the form it took in England and America when it became what we know as the First Great Awakening, in people like Isaac Watts, George Whitefield, the Wesley brothers, John Newton and Jonathan Edwards—and the transformation that happened to it on its way to the Second Great Awakening.

When the leaders of the First Great Awakening stressed the need for what they called "heart religion," they were making a point that was as needed at the time as it was biblical: A cold and merely formal confession of faith is not enough. We are not saved by a merely formal and outward confession of faith but by *faith* (see chapter 3), and faith puts us in contact with the life-changing power of the grace of God, won by Christ, communicated by the Gospel, and applied by the Holy Spirit. Those men stressed the need for what they called "experimental" faith (we would use the word *experiential*). Without the dynamic presence of Christ in the heart through the ministry of the Holy Spirit, just saying the right words and going through the prescribed motions meant nothing. In bringing this message into English-speaking Christianity they were timely, they were biblical, and they were just plain right.

What is impressive about these men was the balance with which they undertook this reform. They stressed the heart (already the word was taking on its modern sense) but they did not disparage the mind. They stressed the importance of experience *along with* rigorous intellectual engagement with the truth of Scripture, not as an alternative to it. They stressed the absolute necessity of maintaining each side of that equation for the other side to be healthy. As Watts put it, "Those

Christians are best prepared for the useful and pious exercises of their emotions in the spiritual life who have laid the foundations in an ordered knowledge of the things of God." He continued, "Knowledge and feeling should go hand in hand in all the affairs of the spiritual life."[119] Yes, they should.

That balance is seen in the ministries of these men and in their lives as well as their words. Isaac Watts, known today primarily as a hymnwriter, was known in his own day as the author of a standard textbook in logic. (Just try to imagine this being true of any praise-and-worship or hymn writer today!) John Wesley edited a fifty-volume Christian's Library for his mostly uneducated followers which included Milton's *Paradise Lost*. Jonathan Edwards, who stirred the emotions with the warnings in a sermon like "Sinners in the Hands of an Angry God" also preached the sermon "A Divine and Supernatural Light," in which he stressed the need for the Holy Spirit to remove "the prejudices that are in the heart against the truth of divine things" so that "the *mind* becomes susceptive to the due force of *rational arguments*" for their truth, so that the reason should be "sanctified."[120] He is still known as the greatest theologian and philosopher in American history.

These great forebears of our movement were adamant that the "heart religion" they wanted should be consciously urged and sought, but they were equally adamant that it never be sought by the cheap means of emotional manipulation. Edwards stirred up great emotional responses in his congregations, but he never *tried* to stir up emotion for its own sake. He is reported to have spoken in a monotone and stared resolutely at the bell rope in the church's foyer across the heads of his people. Watts wrote,

> It is the business of every sacred orator to raise the affections of men toward the things of God. Let him therefore manage his divine arguments in such a manner as to awaken the fears, hopes, desires, penitent sorrows, and pious joys of the whole assembly in a sublime degree—but in order to secure them

---

119 Isaac Watts, "Abuse of the Emotions in the Spiritual Life" (1746), *A Burning and a Shining Light: English Spirituality in the Age of Wesley*, ed. David Lyle Jeffrey (Grand Rapids: Eerdmans, 1987), pp. 80, 81.

120 Jonathan Edwards, "Sinners in the Hands of an Angry God" and "A Divine and Supernatural Light," *The Works of Jonathan Edwards*, 2 vols., ed. Edward Hickman (Carlisle, Pa.: Banner of Truth, 1974), pp. 7-17, emphasis added. Cf. Donald T. Williams, *Inklings of Reality*, op. cit., pp. 232-5.

from excesses and irregularities of every kind, let him lay the foundation of their faith in clear ideas of divine things, and in a just and proper explication of the holy Scriptures. . . . Let him not begin with their emotions and address himself to them in the first place. He must not artfully manipulate those warm and natural feelings before he has set these doctrines and perceptions of his in a fair and convincing light before the eye of their understanding."[121]

We cannot stress too much that this emphasis was needed in its day, and it is the emphasis that is equally needed today—though perhaps we need a different side of it than the audience that originally heard it did. It was a courageous act to preach "heart religion" in the Age of Reason when people were culturally afraid of overt religious emotion in a reaction to the passions that had produced the religious wars of the previous century. Today in our age of rampant subjectivity, the courageous act would be to stress the necessity of critical thinking and reason as a necessary component of a whole and healthy faith. The wholeness promoted by the leaders of the Awakening is the legacy that was bequeathed to us as Evangelicals. But when the cultural tides shifted in the Nineteenth Century toward finding meaning in subjective experience and fearing reason as the enemy of faith, we clung to half of their message and forgot the other half. Unfortunately, the half we retained cannot maintain the same character apart from its counterpart. Philip Doddridge put it well:

It must be allowed that knowledge and affection in the spiritual life are indeed desirable. Without some degree of the former, religion cannot be rational, and it is very reasonable to believe that without some degree of the latter it cannot be sincere. Yet there may be a great deal of speculative knowledge and a great deal of rapturous affection where there is no spirituality at all.[122]

A return to the *whole* emphasis of our forebears is a reform we desperately need.

---

121 Watts, "Abuse," op. cit., p. 81

122 Philip Doddridge, *The Rise and Progress of Religion in the Soul*, (1745), qtd. In Jeffrey, op. cit., p. 182.

Thesis 14c:
However, When Not Rooted in a Holistic Biblical Anthropology and Psychology, Pietism Cannot Be Healthy, and It Has Thus Contributed to the Superficiality, Irrelevance, and Corruption of American Conservative Christianity.

Pietism (as a movement) arose as a natural and healthy corrective to the dead orthodoxy of seventeenth and eighteenth-century European state churches. Unfortunately, the balance of its original adherents in England was not always maintained as the descendants of the original pietists moved into the Nineteenth Century and were affected by that century's over-reaction to the Rationalism of the Eighteenth. Brown gives an excellent treatment of the movement's subsequent history: "Instead of stressing personal Christianity, at a certain point much of Pietism began to cultivate the Christian personality, and soon found itself more Romantic than Christian. In trying to show that true faith changes lives, segments of Pietism began to stress 'life, not doctrine' and ended by forgetting about doctrine altogether."[123] When not rooted in a holistic biblical anthropology and psychology (i.e., biblical doctrines of human nature), Pietism's emphasis on "heart religion" cannot be healthy. When that emphasis on heart religion is not balanced by an equal emphasis on reason and knowledge that flows from that holistic biblical anthropology, Pietism cannot be healthy. Cut loose from those moorings, it has thus contributed to the superficiality, irrelevance, and corruption of American conservative Christianity.

How do we understand that holistic biblical anthropology? Our re-creation in Christ should restore us to what we were meant to be before the fall, and what we were meant to be was image bearers of God. And that image is best understood with reference to the perfect Image we were given. For Christ Himself is both the "radiance of [God's] glory and the exact representation of His nature" (Heb. 1:3)

---

[123] Harold O. J. Brown, *Heresies: The Image of Christ in the Mirror of Heresy and Orthodoxy from the Apostles to the Present* (Garden City, NY: Doubleday, 1984), p. 381.

as the Son of God, and the perfect template of ideal humanity as the Second Adam and the Son of Man (Rom. 5; see thesis 4b).

Son of Man" as a designation for Christ, then, means one who is the ideal human being, one who exemplifies the essential characteristics of humanity perfectly. As we concluded in our discussion of Christ as the perfect template for restored humanity in thesis 4b, when you look at Jesus you see the perfect image of the Father. You also see s perfect picture in His human nature of what mankind was supposed to be. You see what Adam might have been like had he never fallen. You see the perfect template for human nature as it was designed to be, and as in Christ it will become.

This vision is practical, for it shows us the goal or end at which our sanctification aims. Jesus in His earthly life perfectly kept the Law which is summed up in the Great Commandments: to "love the Lord your God with all your heart, and with all your soul, and with all your mind . . . and your neighbor as yourself" (Mat. 22:37-39). Here *heart*, as we have seen, is not a reference to the emotions, but rather to the whole person seen comprehensively, and the addition of the mind serves to reinforce the point. We are to love God (and presumably our neighbor as well) with our whole self. Any dichotomy between head and heart (in the modern sense) is ruled out. Any Christian life that would emphasize either one over the other is inauthentic and incomplete at best. To accept or even encourage such a life is sin; it is disobedient to the Great Commandment as defined by our Lord. And since on these commandments depend the whole Law and the Prophets (Mat. 22:40), we could reasonably expect that from such a defective, half-souled love, would flow corruption that might eventually affect the whole of life.

What are some examples of how such corruption flows from the pietistic confusion of spirituality with emotion and from its rejection of loving God with the mind as irrelevant if not positively unspiritual? How many times have you heard "I'm just not comfortable with that" or "I had (or did not have) peace about that" as a justification for a decision? Sometimes such decisions are innocuous if not good, but sometimes they are not. I have heard betrayal and back-stabbing justified by such phrases, and the justification reinforced by the claim that "This decision was just *bathed* in prayer!" A counselee once tried to tell me that the Spirit had led her to divorce her husband. Did she have biblical grounds for this divorce on *any* understanding of Scripture on that topic? No. That did not matter because she knew in her "heart" that she was right. A friend recently tried to tell me that his decision to violate a clear command of Scripture was not wrong because it had alleviated his depression and increased his subjective experience of the fruit of the Spirit. That—not any reconsideration of context or grammar—was how he knew the traditional understanding of that commandment was incorrect. I somehow could not find disobedience listed in the fruit of the Spirit in Galatians 5:22, but, as with the counselee, mere facts like that do not faze a person who is operating on a pietistic basis. Such stories can be multiplied endlessly by anyone who has done personal work.

As disturbing as such cases are, what concerns me more is the fact that conducting one's spiritual life in this manner is tacitly, and sometimes explicitly, approved by much of the Evangelical subculture. This is true even when by God's grace it does not cause people to go off the rails as it did in these examples. But even when it does not produce such horrifying results it is still wrong and sinful because it does not give God the worship of our whole person which He deserves and because it treats His objective written Word with less than the respect which it deserves (See thesis 6a). We are asking for the kinds of problems I just referenced rather than helping to protect people from such mistakes. But our half-souled worship is perhaps the bigger problem even when it does not lead to outward scandal. The fact that we don't perceive it so may be the biggest scandal of all.

Now, people who are guilty of the opposite imbalance have a similar problem. When they go wrong, they will come up with clever rationalizations for their disobedience rather than just trusting their feelings. Either way it is sin, even when it does not lead to further sin. But the shallow corrupted pietism we have described here is the *besetting* sin of popular Evangelicalism. And we need to repent of it.

Thesis 14d:
Emotions Are Byproducts of True Biblical Spiritual Life, Not the Thing Itself.

To understand the proper role of emotion in the Christian life, we have to know what emotions are and what they are for. Think about the words *emotion*, *motive*, *motion*, and *motor*. They share in common a Latin root from the verb *motare*, "to move." We say that we are "moved" when we have an emotional experience, and a motor is a machine whose purpose is to move a vehicle. The word motive is the bridge that holds all of this motion together. It is what gets us moving, what gets us up off our posteriors to put some plan that has so far been only a theoretical possibility into action. We could say that motion is the act, the body the motor or engine, emotion the fuel, and motivation the clutch that puts the motor in gear so that the journey gets accomplished. Notice what key piece of this puzzle is left out by our words containing the common root: a *destination*. That has to come from somewhere else: for the Christian, Scripture as understood by the mind and embraced by the heart (in the biblical sense). Our old friend Isaac Watts understood this: "Consider, my friends, what the emotions were made for: not merely for the conscious pleasure of human nature, but to give it vigor and power for useful actions."[124]

Once we have separated the meaning of the heart in biblical culture from that of the bowels (often mistranslated "heart" in modern versions) and are no longer confusing them, it becomes plain that the Bible has essentially the same perspective. It rarely commands us to feel an emotion as such because our emotions are not fully under our control. "Rejoice in the Lord always, and again I say, rejoice!" (Phil. 4:4) probably means something like "Celebrate your position in Christ"—with felt joy as a result. It is clear from "the Love Chapter" that the command to love our brother is not a command to have certain mushy feelings toward him, but rather a command to be patient with him and kind to him, not to brag or be arrogant toward him or selfish with regard to his interests or easily provoked with him, etc. (1 Cor. 13:4-7). When one treats one's brother or one's neighbor

---

124 Isaac Watts, "Abuse of the Emotions in the Spiritual Life," op. cit., p. 73.

that way with a good will, loving feelings will normally and naturally follow to accompany those actions. If the feelings already exist, they will help to motivate the actions, but their absence is no excuse for not loving. They are a byproduct of love, not the thing itself. Biblical love is not first a feeling but a way of life.

This understanding of emotions as the byproducts of something else is true about life in general and about the Christian life in particular. Focusing on our own emotions is self-defeating. If you are at a concert by the local symphony and are asking yourself, "Am I having an esthetic experience?" I can pretty much guarantee that the answer will be no. When you have completely forgotten about yourself and your experience or lack of it and are totally absorbed in the music—when you are, as we say, "taken out of yourself"—then and only then will you be deeply moved. You will enjoy a ball game to the extent that you are not (directly) aware of your own emotional state at all—you are living and dying with your team. A Georgia Bulldawg crossing the goal line or an Atlanta Brave sliding across home plate takes up all of my consciousness at such a moment and there is nothing left over for myself as I celebrate *his* victory. We look back on moments like that as our moments of greatest joy.

Why then do we forget this lesson when we get to church? Too many of us are trying way too hard to create moods with music and lighting. Ironically, the very popular praise and worship song that tries to address the problem is itself perpetuating it: "I'm coming back to the heart of worship, / And it's all about you, Lord." But the song actually says very little about the Lord at all; it is all about *us*, and how we feel, how we are "sorry for the thing we've made it." Even when we are not putting all our energy into engineering comfortable emotions with the "worship" service, too many of us are focused on manipulating the congregation into an emotional frenzy that will get a sufficient number of them down to the altar at the end. Is it even possible for an Evangelical young person to give a testimony any more that does not contain the word *passion*? If you want me to worship, don't focus on my emotional response or lead me in a song where I repetitively claim to have one as a way of trying to talk myself into it. Show me the glory of God in the face of Jesus Christ and let my emotional response take care of itself!

A Plea
To Certain Evangelical "Worship" Leaders

What We Think

What elicits deepest feeling?
What promotes profoundest praise?
That were worship whole and healing,
That would set our hearts ablaze!

What We Do

So we focus on emotion,
Turn our gaze within ourselves.
But does that foster true devotion,
However deep the sinner delves?

What We Need

Truth, He promised, is what frees us.
Fill our cup then to the brim!
Stand aside and show us Jesus:
Let our eyes be fixed on Him.[125]

A better, reformed approach to emotion in the spiritual life matters, not only because what we are doing is counterproductive emotionally, but because it sets us up for the problems discussed in thesis 14c. True spiritual life is loving God with all your heart, soul, and mind, and your neighbor as yourself (Mat. 22:37), not just *feeling* like you love them. Feelings are important, but they are a byproduct of something else—ultimately that love for God and for our neighbor, stemming from our vision of the glory of God in the face of Jesus Christ. The degraded, incomplete kind of pietism we practice is self-defeating because it is ultimately self-centered. We need to be God-centered by being Christ-centered. May God enable that reform to take place, to His glory and our emotional health.

---

[125] Donald T. Williams, *Stars through the Clouds*, op. cit., p. 394.

Thesis 14e:
Horses Should Be Kept in Front of Carts.

Emotions are most healthy and best enjoyed when they are not the central focus but the byproduct of something else. True Christian spirituality is not a life focused on our feelings about God but a life focused on our gracious God and His glorious Gospel, the doctrines that reveal them to us, and the practical love of God and neighbor that flows from that focus. It is for the sake of God, first, but also for the sake of a rich and deep inner life itself, that we need to get our focus off of our inner life and back on the God we worship. To emphasize emotion rather than gazing at God, to focus on feeling rather than being devoted to doctrine, is to get the cart before the horse.

This chapter is not anti-emotion; it is not the foe of feeling; its purpose is not to put down Pietism, in its more healthy historic form. Indeed, we owe a great debt to our pietist ancestors. As the Reformation is mediated to the present through the First Great Awakening, historic Pietism and historic Evangelicalism are pretty close to simply being the same thing. It is what Pietism became on the way to the present that is the problem. Harold O. J. Brown captures several aspects of our debt to it well:

> One of the great accomplishments of Pietism was to rescue Protestantism from the dominance of the academic profession and to make faith, devotion, and knowledge of the Bible accessible to ordinary people. Its emphasis on personal Christianity made the Christian life an experiential reality, not merely a theological postulate. It emphasis on the priesthood of all believers and the necessity of faith to be active in love tapped tremendous reservoirs of spiritual energy. . . . Where conservative, biblical impulses in Protestantism have survived, it has almost always been in a Pietistic setting.[126]

But when the emphasis on "heart religion" was divorced from its biblical wholeness and the heart estranged from the head, all the problems we have been discussing ensued. Pietism as it is practiced today is

---

126 Harold O. J. Brown, *Heresies*, op cit., p. 393.

a huge problem indeed. Precisely because emotional experience is the byproduct of something else, and because the same subjective experience can be produced by different stimuli, pious experience cannot play the role we want to give it. "Stressing the necessity of individual religious experience, [Pietism] lost objective criteria for authenticating the validity of such experience."[127] Thus the paradoxical nature of our relationship to Pietism today: "Without Pietism, Protestantism might never have survived the eighteenth century, but with Pietism, it may ultimately cease to be Protestantism."[128]

---

127 Ibid., p. 391.
128 Ibid., p. 292.

Conclusion

What do we need to do? We do not wish to banish the horse or the cart. We just need to get the horse back in front of the cart. "Stand aside and show us Jesus: / Let our eyes be fixed on Him."

Interlude

Counterfeit Spirituality
American Evangelicalism in the New Millennium

> A sanctimonious sobriety
> That masquerades as godly discipline;
> A pathological anxiety
> That claims to be a zeal to flee from sin;
> A stupid, stubborn contrariety
> Presenting itself as love of truth and right;
> Ears that itch for notoriety,
> Eyes not strong enough to bear the light:
> We suffer from the sad satiety
> Of *pietas* degraded into "piety."[129]

---

[129] Donald T. Williams, *Stars through the Clouds*, op. cit., p. 393.

Prescription for a Broken Relationship

The Heart has reasons Reason doesn't know.
    If either from the other looks away,
    There is no way the person can be whole.
Though we must always pay the debts we owe
    And Reason has a voice we must obey,
    The Heart has reasons Reason doesn't know.
Though she may sometimes feel like Reason's foe,
    The Heart must turn to him and sweetly say,
    "As enemies, we never can be whole."
On hearing this, he must not gloat or crow,
    But grace with grace and courtesy repay:
    The Heart has reasons Reason doesn't know.
When we have fallen, shattered bones may grow
    Back crooked; they cannot be left that way.
    We have to break them then to make them whole.
The sad condition of the human soul
    Needs nothing less its conflicts to allay.
    The Heart has reasons Reason doesn't know,
And only what is broken can be whole.[130]

---

130 Ibid., p. 408.

15

Five Theses on the Christian Mind

There is in fact such a thing. There must be such a thing.

A. Anti-Intellectualism is a heresy because it requires us to disobey a part of our Lord's Great Commandment. (We are commanded to love God with all our minds, Mat. 22:37).

B. Study is therefore an essential part of Christian discipleship. (Study is the deliberate, serious, and sustained application of the mind, in dependence on the Holy Spirit and in submission to Scripture, to any given topic or problem in pursuit of knowledge, understanding, and wisdom).

C. Every Christian, because he is a Christian, is called to be a life-long learner. (A disciple is by definition a learner. It is part of our spiritual DNA.)

D. The content, nature, and commission of Scripture require it of us. (As disciples, as stewards, and as ambassadors, we cannot function well without study as defined above.)

E. There are practical steps to the acquisition and wise use of the Christian mind. (Set aside time for it; prepare a strategic lifetime reading list; learn to ask the right questions.)

Evangelical Christianity has not always despised the life of the mind. The Protestant Reformers were among the great minds of their age, as were Puritans like John Owen in England and Jonathan Edwards in America. They were learned men and rigorous thinkers who dedicated their intellectual gifts to the service of God and His people. The leaders of the First Great Awakening continued that legacy. But at a certain point, large segments of the Evangelical movement veered off from the track of their example. It was a well-meaning and understandable but nevertheless foolish response to the secularization of society that began in the Eighteenth Century and seemed to flow from European intellectual elites. As we saw in chapter 14, those believers tried to protect their faith by retreating with it into an inner emotional sanctum which argument could not reach. Harold O. J. Brown describes its results well:

> Despite the fact that virtually all of the revivalists and evangelists were or are personally orthodox, for the most part they changed hearts, not minds, and revived sentiments, not doctrine. Revivalism in the nineteenth and twentieth centuries was a cure for coldness of heart, not for skepticism. . . . The challenge that man's mind had raised was answered by an appeal to his heart. The modern mentality that had undermined the faith was answered with an equally modern sentimentality, rather than a renewal of the Christian mentality.[131]

Thus, five theses at least are needed to address this betrayal of the Christian mind and the sad situation that has resulted from it. The theses flow from Christ's definition of loving God, but equally from no less central a text to Evangelical identity than the Great Commission itself: "Go ye into all the world and make disciples of every creature, . . . *teaching* them to observe all things whatsoever I have commanded you" (Mat. 28:19-20, emphasis added).[132]

---

131 Harold O. J. Brown, *Heresies: The Image of Christ in the Mirror of Heresy and Orthodoxy from the Apostles to the Present* (Garden City, NY: Doubleday, 1984), pp. 419, 424.

132 The classic work on this subject is Harry Blamires, *The Christian Mind* (London: S.P.C.K., 1963). See also John R. W. Stott, *Your Mind Matters* (Downers Grove, Il.: InterVarsity Press, 1972). For further description of what a Christian mind looks like, how the right kind of reading contributes to it, and practical steps to pursuing it, see Donald T. Williams, *Inklings of Reality: Essays toward a Christian Philosophy of Letters* (Lynchburg: Lantern Hollow Press, 2012).

Thesis 15a:
Anti-Intellectualism Is a Heresy because It Requires Us To Disobey a Part of Our Lord's Great Commandment.

☙

Christians hold a set of beliefs about the mind and its uses that has often been hard for them to sort out. On the one hand, it would seem that there could be no greater gift than the mind, and that nothing could be more important. God is a God of truth who cannot lie, and He has made us in His own image (Gen. 1:26). He holds discourse with us and even reasons with us (Is. 1:18). We are, as far as we know, the only physical creature of whom this is true. So we would seem to be expected to act, not out of instinct like the other creatures, but out of understanding. And because our minds were made in the image of that Mind which designed the rest of the physical creation, they should be able to deal with it perceptively, constructively, and responsibly—on their own level, to see and embrace the truth of things; on their own level, faithfully to think their Maker's thoughts after Him.

On the other hand, it would seem that nothing could be more dangerous to Christian faith than the mind. The human mind as it now exists is fallen, twisted and corrupted. Bullied by passion and enslaved by the will's rebellion against its Creator, it is possessed by a sinful indisposition to the truth that makes it incapable, apart from grace, of receiving or embracing spiritual truth (1 Cor. 2:14). So often has it been used to rationalize its rebellion against its Maker that what is now called "human reason" seems most untrustworthy. It becomes easy to see Reason as inherently opposed to Faith and to be suspicious of anyone who puts much stock in it. So Martin Luther infamously called Reason "the Devil's whore." And history seems to confirm these suspicions. It is not from simple Men and Women of Faith, but from Intellectuals, that Secularism and Liberalism have arisen to infiltrate the Church and seduce it from faithfulness to its message. Enough people have gone to university or (even worse!) seminary and lost their faith—or at least their zeal—that we feel justified in thinking that where there is academic smoke there must be secular fire.

But—oh, my—look what we just did! We perceived evidence of a correlation between education and secularism and drew from this evidence a conclusion: the mind and its pretensions to reason are suspect and should not be trusted. But wait a minute. If we did not trust our minds and their thought processes, how could we use them to arrive at and argue for the conclusion that we should not trust them? This is an irresolvable impasse. It seems we have no choice. We *have* to use our minds, and even trust the processes by which they work. We only have the choice to use and trust them honestly, recognizing the risk that we may get things wrong, or the choice to deceive ourselves by pretending that we do not use and trust them—thus doubling the risk that we will not only make even more of the inevitable mistakes, but have no valid means of recognizing or correcting those mistakes when we do. Even if we try to correct our mistaken ideas by quoting Scripture, we have to use our minds, in obedience to the rules of logic, to understand those Scriptural passages, perceive their relevance to the issue at hand, and apply them to it. Christians who reject the use of the mind as "unspiritual" do not have a position that they can—or do—practice consistently. They have actually been known to use their minds quite rigorously for the purpose of thinking up convincing reasons why we should not be using them! And this irony should be a clue that, in spite of the valid evidence that would seem to lead to their conclusion, they have gotten something wrong.[133]

Once we stop to think about it, it is not hard to see where their error lies. We began by presenting two biblical views of the mind: created in the image of God and therefore able to think His thoughts after Him; and corrupt and fallen, incapable of receiving the things of the Spirit. As these views are both biblical, any accurate view of the mind must then be one that somehow encompasses both of them. The suspicious believer acts as if he thought the second of those descriptions could simply overturn or replace the first. At least he is taking seriously the effects of the Fall. But in so doing he forgets both the role and the power of Grace. For Redemption is about beginning the restoration of what was lost in the Fall, and the life of the mind is no exception to this principle. Why should the mind be the only human faculty that is so fallen that God cannot save it, Christ cannot redeem

---

[133] Robert R. Reilly gives a sobering account of how Islam made this mistake and suffers the consequences because Allah, unlike the Christian Trinity, has no Logos inherent in his nature. Historic Christianity has been protected from going down the same path by the prologue to John's Gospel which puts a warning sign at its trailhead—but Christian anti-intellectuals by ignoring it risk more than they know. *The Closing of the Muslim Mind: How Intellectual Suicide Created the Modern Islamist Crisis* (Wilmington, DE: Intercollegiate Studies Institute, 2010).

it, and the Spirit cannot sanctify it or use it?

A fully biblical view of the mind would therefore see the Scriptural view of its fall and corruption as *tempering* the Scriptural view of its grandeur rather than merely *replacing* it. The mind was corrupted, like every other aspect of our nature—not destroyed. It needs to be redeemed, not discarded. This is proved by the fact that God's invitation to come and reason together was addressed to people after the Fall (Is. 1:18), and by the fact that the New Testament describes the renewing of our minds as part of redemption (Rom. 12:2). The mind functions spiritually only when it is saved by God's grace, sanctified by his Spirit, informed by his Word, submissive to his wisdom, and motivated by his love. So we should strive to be sure these things are true of our minds and then *think* with them to the glory of God, not simply reject them and their use out of hand.

Grounded in such a holistic view of biblical teaching on the mind, we would then be able to beware of our propensity to rationalization, but without despising the role of right Reason. We could be suspicious of our own motives and of our conclusions when they seem self-serving, but without succumbing to Post-Modernist cynicism. We could be cautious in our reasoning, but without losing faith in the Holy Spirit's ministry of illumination. And above all we could ask God by his grace to help us obey what our Lord called the greatest commandment: to love the Lord with, among other things, all our minds (Mat. 22:37).

Thesis 15b:
Study Is Therefore an Essential Part of Christian Discipleship.

ℐ

If that is true, then we are ready to look at the role of study in the spiritual life. For those readers who are students, I am not primarily talking about your course work. At this stage in your life, your course work is simply your job. You should therefore approach it in the light of biblical teaching about any work that we are called to perform. To the studies you undertake for your classes apply verses like Eccl. 9:10, "Whatever your hand finds to do, do it with all your might"; 1 Cor. 10:31, "Whether you eat or drink or whatever you do, do all to the glory of God"; and Col. 3:23, "Whatever you do, do your work heartily, as unto the Lord rather than men."

Rather, the question I am addressing in this chapter is this: What will be—what should be—the place of study in your life when you are no longer in the position of being coerced into it by a Professor? What ought the place of study to be in your life, not because you are a student, not because you are an "intellectual," but simply because you are a Christian? Before I can answer that question, I had better explain what this "studying" is that I am talking about. I would define it as follows:

Definition:
Study, as I will be using the word in this essay, is the deliberate, serious, and sustained application of the mind, in dependence on the Holy Spirit and in submission to Scripture, to any given topic or problem, for the purpose of attaining knowledge, understanding, and wisdom. That is a long definition, so let me repeat it: study is the deliberate, serious, and sustained application of the mind, in dependence on the Holy Spirit and in submission to Scripture, to any given topic or problem, for the purpose of attaining knowledge, understanding, and wisdom.

This definition is full of loaded terms. Let me unload some of them. It is "deliberate": something you chose to do and plan to do, not something that just happens haphazardly. It is "serious": It requires mental effort and exertion, and though for some of us that effort is inherently enjoyable, it is not a mere game but is done for a serious purpose. It is "sustained": One devotes time to it and does it on a regular basis. It involves the application of the "mind": that part of you that learns, analyzes, thinks, reasons, deliberates, and ponders. It is done "in dependence on the Holy Spirit": It involves an overt decision not to trust in our own wisdom but rather to pray and ask for His illumination. It is done "in submission to Scripture," which is the grid through which everything is filtered and the plumb line by which everything is evaluated.

It is the application of the mind to "any given topic": we are not talking about Bible study as such, but about the study of anything and everything in relation to the Bible. Bible study *per se* would be a part of our topic, but not the whole. And in our study of all these things we are seeking "knowledge, understanding, and wisdom." "Knowledge" is the possession of facts, of information. "Understanding" is seeing how those facts relate to each other, grasping their meaning in the big picture of the totality of God's universe. And "Wisdom" is knowing how to use that knowledge and understanding in creative and constructive ways for the glory of God, the benefit of our fellow creatures, and the advancement of Christ's kingdom. We have not achieved our purpose until we get there.

That, then, is what I mean by "study" in this chapter: It is the deliberate, serious, and sustained application of the mind, in dependence on the Holy Spirit and in submission to Scripture, to any given topic or problem, for the purpose of attaining knowledge, understanding, and wisdom.

Thesis 15c:
Every Christian, because He Is a Christian, Is Called To Be a Life-Long Learner.

※

Now, if that is what "study" is, we are ready to return to our original question: What ought the place of study to be in your life, not because you are a student, not because you are an "intellectual," but simply because you are a Christian? Given my definition, perhaps my thesis will not seem as outrageous as it might sound to many people. It is this: *No one can be a serious and obedient disciple of Jesus Christ without giving a significant place to study in his life.* Study as I have defined it here is not just something for intelligent people; it is not just something for intellectuals. It is a necessary component of our identity as servants of Christ. For all of us are called to worship a God whom we will never fully be able to understand, to pursue all of the understanding we can get through the study of His revelation in a Book that requires a lifetime to fully absorb, and to serve Him in ways that will make study that Book and its application to life an ongoing need. That is all simply part of what it means to be a Christian.

"God," said Sir Thomas More in Robert Bolt's wonderful historical drama *The Man for all Seasons*, "made the angels to show hi8m splendor—as he made the animals for innocence and the plants for their simplicity. But Man he made to serve him wittily, in the tangle of his mind."[134] No one can be a serious and obedient disciple of Jesus Christ without giving a significant place to study in his life.

So anti-intellectual has the Church become that, even as we have just defined it, many people will have difficulty seeing study as a requirement for all believers, not just when they are in school, but throughout their lives. But at least three considerations make this conclusion inescapable:

---

134 Robert Bolt, *A Man for all Seasons* (N.Y.: Vintage Books, 1960), p. 73.

Thesis 15d:
The Content, Nature, and Commission of Scripture Require It of Us.

✍

(a) The Content of Scripture Commands It.

Scripture has at least three ways of commanding us, in effect, to be lifelong learners. The first is that it gives us, as believers in Christ, the identity of *disciples*. A disciple is by definition a learner, one who learns by imitating his Master. You cannot sign up to follow Jesus without signing up to be his disciple, i.e., his student. The Great Commission (Mat. 28:19) is to make disciples; therefore, to respond to the Great Commission is to become a disciple. And to make a disciple you first have to be one. Therefore, to try to take Christ as your Savior without taking him as your Teacher is as inconsistent and illogical as trying to have him as your Savior without having him as your Lord. The logic is inescapable. No one can be a serious and obedient disciple of Jesus Christ without giving a significant place to study in his life.

In the second place, many passages of Scripture enjoin a careful and thoughtful engagement with the text of Scripture. Now, study as we have defined it means more than this, but it does not mean less; it means at least this much. According to the first Psalm, the person is blessed who delights in the Law of the Lord and meditates on it day and night. That at least involves thinking about it. 2 Tim. 2:15 commands us to study to show ourselves approved as workmen who do not need to be ashamed, rightly dividing the Word of Truth. "Study" in the KJV is not a very accurate translation in contemporary English. The word means "be diligent" in "handling accurately" the Word of Truth. But, ironically, one cannot be diligent in this particular task without "study" in the more technical sense. So the KJV manages to get the right idea after all. No one can be a serious and obedient disciple of Jesus Christ without giving a significant place to study in his life.

Finally, our Lord himself goes out of his way to add study to The Great Commandment (Mat. 22:37). The Old Testament verse he is quoting does not have it, but our Lord quite particularly adds it on his own authority: we are to love the Lord our God with all our heart, all our strength, and all our *mind*. No one can ignore this commandment and claim to be obedient to our Lord. No one can be a serious and obedient disciple of Jesus Christ without giving a significant place to study in his life.

(b) The Nature of Scripture Necessitates It.

Paul tells us in 2 Tim. 3:16 that all Scripture is inspired by God, and that this makes it profitable. "Scripture" is the Greek word *graphe*. It means the writings—literally, ink on parchment or papyrus. That is what was "inspired," or breathed out of the mouth of God. God inspired those writings: those words, in other words, and no others, in that order, in those grammatical constructions written in that language (Hebrew, Aramaic, or Greek) at that particular time in history. This means that when we read the Bible, God says what the words say in the light of their grammar, context, and historical background. These words were written in foreign languages, two to three and a half thousand years ago, in a very different time with a very different culture from our own. It is simply irresponsible to suppose that a casual reading of such a book can give us an accurate understanding of it. Even a simple reader can get the basics, but why would we be satisfied with that? We need the help of those who know Greek and archaeology, the help of commentaries, concordances, and of sound methodologies and the interpretive traditions of the church. Not that these things in themselves will give us true spiritual understanding either. But they are tools the Holy Spirit uses. No one who is too lazy to use them need think he will learn anything from the Lord. And how can we study anything else if we are not willing to be serious students even of Scripture? No one can be a serious and obedient disciple of Jesus Christ without giving a significant place to study in his life.

(c) The Commission of Scripture Requires It.

As we have already seen, the Great Commission requires us to make disciples of all nations. It requires us first to be disciples, that is, learners, and then to help others become disciples, that is, learners. How can we teach others to learn from the Master unless we are doing so ourselves? It is simply not possible.

Scripture uses other pictures of our identity and role as well, and they carry the same implication. We are also called Ambassadors for Christ (2 Cor. 5:20). An ambassador represents his government to that of another country. As ambassadors of Christ we have the authority to speak for him in offering the treaty (or New Covenant) of the Gospel to others and persuading them in his name to accept it. Now, what would you think of a person who was appointed as an ambassador to a foreign land, and who presumed to undertake his assignment without studying its language, its culture, its customs, its history? He would not make a very effective representative unless he knew these things as well as the terms he was authorized to offer to these people, would he? Well, if we are ambassadors of Christ, then that is precisely our position between Christ and the world we were sent to reach.

A third picture Scripture gives us is that we are the Stewards of Creation (Gen. 1). Our Father made the world, designed it, and is redeeming it. He placed Adam and Eve in the Garden of Eden to dress it and keep it—to take care of it for Him. We are still responsible to God for the care of His creation, though now we exercise our stewardship in rebellion and hence often rather badly. Nevertheless, stewards of creation is still our identity and our role under God, and part of redemption is being restored to awareness of that role and to responsible action in it.

This knocks down all the walls. To have God, the Creator, as our Father makes the whole universe our back yard; it makes the whole universe our field of operation. As Machen put it, "The field of Christianity is the world. The Christian cannot be satisfied so long as any human activity is either opposed to Christianity or out of connection with Christianity."[135] History, art, literature, science, law, politics, medicine—whatever the field, whatever the endeavor, Christ has a claim on it and has something to say about it—through us as His representatives. To serve Him thus we must know something about these fields of human endeavor and we must think critically, constructively, and creatively about them in the light of the teaching of His Word. No one can be a serious and obedient disciple of Jesus Christ without giving a significant place to study in his life.

---

[135] J. Gresham Machen, *Education, Christianity, and the State* (Unicoi, Tn.: The Trinity Foundation, 1987), p. 50.

Thesis 15e:
There Are Practical Steps to the Acquisition and Wise Use of the Christian Mind.

The conclusion is inescapable. Every disciple of Jesus, because he is a disciple of Jesus, is called to be a life-long learner. There is no other way for us to fulfill the roles we have been given. Let me therefore suggest some practical steps as we pursue this calling, as we try to make study and the life of the mind an ongoing part of life even after the framework of formal schooling is removed.

(a) Schedule Time for It.

Serious study is not going to happen otherwise. Life will crowd it out. But if you spend just an hour a day reading something you don't have to read for work, something that can deepen your understanding of the biblical worldview and of the world we were sent to reach with it and in which we are called to apply it, the long term cumulative effects will be significant.

(b) Compile a Lifetime Reading Plan.

Not that you will ever finish it—that's not the point. Mine grows faster than I can read the things on it. But if you proceed according to a plan rather than haphazardly, you will get more done, and more significant things done, in the long run. It should include the great classics of the Faith—Augustine's *Confessions*, Calvin's *Institutes*, Bunyan's *Pilgrim's Progress*, Milton's *Paradise Lost*, the works of G. K. Chesterton, C. S. Lewis, J. R. R. Tolkien, and Francis Schaeffer. It should also include some works that support the Enemy. How shall we counter his strategies effectively if we do not know what he is up to? We need first-hand scouting reports. And it should be read critically.

(c) Ask Questions of Everything You Read.

The better the questions you ask, the better the answers you will get. Important and essential ones include the following: How does this fit in with what God teaches us in Scripture? How does it relate to my identity as a person created in the image of God? How does it relate to my identity as a Disciple of Christ, an Ambassador of Christ, as a Steward of Creation? How does it relate to my particular calling as an individual believer? How does it glorify the God of all truth? And what does He want me to do about it?

Conclusion

Every disciple of Jesus, because he is a disciple of Jesus, is called to be a life-long learner. "God has room for people with very little sense," said C. S. Lewis, "But he expects them to use all the sense they have."[136] Matthew Arnold said that the purpose of study was "to see the object as in itself it really is," and on the basis of that vision "to learn and propagate the best that has been thought and said in the world."[137] Unfortunately, without faith in Christ, Arnold gave us no basis on which such lofty goals could be pursued. But the Christian has a greater motive for pursuing them and a greater hope for attaining them. John Milton said that "The end of learning is to repair the ruins of our first parents by regaining to know God aright, and out of that knowledge to love him, to imitate him, and to be like him." And since Christ is Lord of all and His Word is relevant to all, the Christian who is thus learned will be "fit to perform justly, skillfully, and magnanimously all the offices, both public and private, of peace and war.[138]

What is the place of study in the Christian life? No one can be a serious and obedient disciple of Jesus Christ without giving a significant place to study in his life. Every disciple of Jesus, because he is a disciple of Jesus, is called to be a life-long learner. Why? Because this by God's grace may enable us better to obey the Great Commission: to be and make disciples. And by God's Grace it may enable us to obey better a part of the Great Commandment: to love the Lord our God with all our minds. The God of all truth deserves no less.

---

136 C. S. Lewis, *Mere Christianity* (N.Y.: MacMillan, 1960): 75.

137 Mathew Arnold, "The function of Criticism at the Present Time" (1865), in William E. Buckler, ed., *Prose of the Victorian Period* (Boston: Houghton Mifflin, 1958): 420, 440.

138 John Milton, "Of Education" (1644), in Merrit Y. Hughes, ed., *John Milton: Complete Poems and Major Prose* (Indianapolis: Bobbs-Merrill, 1957): 631, 632.

Interlude
The Need for Critical Thinking in the Church

Why is it that the drive to integrate
    Faith and Learning, Heart and Intellect,
    Is treated as a spiritual defect?
When Jesus said the Truth would liberate,
Could he have meant his followers to hate
    The Mind and all its works, or to reject
    Unheard that Truth for fear it might infect?
It is a strange idea to contemplate.

The world is full of charlatans and liars,
    And they can come quite cleverly disguised.
But has your estimate of who conspires
    With them not ever had to be revised?
To love the Lord with all your mind requires
    A certain willingness to be surprised.[139]

---

[139] Donald T. Williams, *Stars through the Clouds*, op. cit., p. 390.

The Roots of Anti-Intellectualism
Commentary, 1 Cor. 1:26

When I was a young and foolish boy,
    I thought intelligence a gift so rare
    That all those who were blessed by it would share
The hunger of the mind for thought, the joy
Of battle on the windy plains of Troy,
    The Big Bang, Quarks—the search for what is *there*,
    The Saint's hope, the Post-Modernist's despair,
Of Hopkins' call: "Have, get before it cloy!"

The church especially would love to trace
    The Father's hand in all He had created.
    It seems that I had underestimated
How far we've let the Enemy deface
    In us the image of the One who made
    In us the very minds we have betrayed.

A short attention span will pad the purse
    Of publishers who ought to be devoted
    To seeing Truth pursued and then promoted.
They take the easy way. And, what is worse,
We justify our treason with a verse:
    "Not many wise," we've quoted and we've quoted;
    "According to the flesh," we've barely noted.
Thus blithely we perpetuate the Curse.

Willing to know the Evil as the Good,
    We bypassed the Instructions on the Tree.
    Not eating from it would have been the key
To all its fruit, if we had only stood.
    We plucked it green, and greedily we ate.
    Now, gorged with garbage, we push back the plate.[140]

---

140 Ibid., p. 387.

16
Five Theses on Christian Education

Christian education should be more than just avoiding the evil influence of the secular Academy. It is positively required by the nature of the Christian mind and the view of Christianity and culture we have seen. It has a critical role alongside church and home in transmitting the biblical worldview to the next generation and also in showing its relevance by applying it to all of life. As Machen said, "While truth is truth however learned, the bearing of truth, the meaning of truth, the purpose of truth" are entirely different to the Christian.[141] Christian education then is not a luxury; it is a necessity if a new Reformation is to make its presence felt.

---

[141] J. Gresham Machen, *Christianity, Education, and the State* (Unicoi, Tn.: The Trinity Foundation, 1987), p. 81.

A. Secular education is an oxymoron. (Every curriculum flows from and reflects an understanding of who man is and what his purpose is. This understanding cannot be spiritually neutral. It will serve true religion or false religion.)

B. You cannot educate a human being unless you know what a human being is and what it is for. (Mere vocational training reduces man to a purely economic, i.e., secular and material, creature.)

C. Human beings were created in the image of God to enjoy Him through fellowship with Him and to glorify Him by serving Him as His deputies and regents in the rule and care of the earth. (We were created to worship and serve God in terms of our position as stewards of the planet; see Theses 13.a-e. In a fallen world this includes the Great Commission; see Theses 11.a-e.)

D. Christian education develops the whole person to glorify God in every area of a whole life; it thus includes, but cannot be limited to, training for employment. (Viewing education in only economic terms is a denial of the *imago Dei*.)

E. Therefore, Milton was right to say that "a complete and generous education is that which fits a man to perform justly, skillfully, and magnanimously all the offices, both public and private, of peace and war." (Christian ladies and gentlemen should be prepared to glorify God in the home, the marketplace, the forum, and the church, as workers and as witnesses, as citizens and as saints.)

The Christian school movement—whether on the primary, the secondary, or the collegiate level—is the stepchild of the church. We give lip service to its importance, but we will not support it on a level at which it can function well. It struggles to pay its faculty a living wage and still remain affordable enough so that it can be a viable option for parents in the real world; but these are incompatible goals. They simply cannot both be met without a constant infusion of cash from outside the tuition structure—whether from endowments or from unrestricted giving. Most Christian schools do not have the endowments and are not going to get what they need in gifts. Qualified faculty members are hard to retain, and when they are retained, they are usually overworked in ways that make it exceedingly difficult for them to advance in their fields.

Nevertheless, despite their constant struggle for survival, Christian schools almost all outperform the public schools when it comes to the basics, the three Rs—not even considering the inculcation of the biblical worldview. We need them to have a much greater impact, but we are not willing to make the sacrifices necessary for that to happen. We talk a good game, but they continue to struggle, and the church is content to have it so. This is a major reason why Renaissance stalls, Reformation is short-circuited, and Revival tarries. How do we get beyond talking a good game and start actually playing one? Understanding these theses about what is at stake could help.[142]

---

142 The foundations of my philosophy of education are found in Baldesar Castliglione, *The Book of the Courtier*, 1528, trans. George Bull (N.Y.: Penguin, 1976), Sir Thomas Elyot, *The Book Named the Governor*, in Hyder E. Rollins, and Herschel Baker, eds., *The Renaissance in England: Non-Dramatic Prose and Poetry of the Sixteenth Century* (Lexington, MA.: D. C. Heath, 1954), pp. 105-115, 587-8, Roger Ascham, *The Schoolmaster* (in Rollins and Baker, op. cit.), pp. 817-40, Sir Philip Sidney, *The Defense of Poesy* (in Rollins and Baker, op. cit.), pp. 605-24, and John Milton, "Areopagetica," 1644, in Merritt Y. Hughes, ed., *John Milton: Complete Poems and Major Prose* (Indianapolis: Bobbs-Merrill, 1957), pp. 716-49, and "Of Education," 1644 (in Hughes, op. cit.), pp. 630-39. For modern treatments, see J. Gresham Machen, *Christianity, Education, and the State* (Unicoi, Tn.: The Trinity Foundation, 1987), Dorothy L. Sayers, "The Lost Tools of Learning" (1948; *A Matter of Eternity: Selections from the Writings of Dorothy L. Sayers*, ed. Rosamond Kent Sprague (Grand Rapids: Eerdmans, 1973), pp. 108-35, Douglas Wilson, *Recovering the Lost Tools of Learning: An Approach to Distinctively Christian Education* (Wheaton: Crossway, 1991), and Donald T. Williams, *Inklings of Reality: Essays toward a Christian Philosophy of Letters* (op. cit.). See also my essays "Repairing the Ruins: Thoughts on Christian Higher Education," *Christian Educator's Journal* 41:4 (April 2002): 19-21, "Loves of Learning: Thoughts on Christian Education," *Christian Educator's Journal* 51:1 (October 2011): 30-32, and "Literature for Wisdom: Donald T. Williams on Reading in the Service of Christian Living," *Touchstone: A Journal of Mere Christianity* 33:4 (July/August 2020): 20-22.

Thesis 16a:
Secular Education Is an Oxymoron.

Let us imagine that we are trying to create a school that will do what our secular, state schools think they are obligated to do: provide an education that is religiously neutral. It will not be Protestant, Catholic, or Orthodox; it will not be Christian, Muslim, or New-Age; it will not even be theistic, animistic, pantheistic, or atheistic. It will maintain a strict neutrality on all such beliefs. And let us imagine that it succeeds in that neutrality, treating all such beliefs even-handedly the same, neither privileging one nor denigrating any. We might be able to imagines such a thing—until we get down to specifics. And then our supposed neutrality will quickly vanish into thin air.

As we design our curriculum, we find that we have to ask what our purpose is. What do we want our graduates to be? Well, surely we want them to be productive workers, able to hold good jobs and provide for themselves. But all the vocational training in the world will not accomplish that goal if they are dishonest, lazy, undependable, and lacking in self-discipline. Employers will not retain them if they cannot trust them. So in order to achieve what we thought was the purely secular goal of vocational training we discover that we cannot ignore virtue. But which set of virtues are we going to inculcate? On what basis? Will it be Christian ethics, or Sharia law, or moral therapeutic deism, or naturalistic utilitarianism? The last option is the only one with even a pretense of religious neutrality. But will a purely pragmatic view of honesty as something that will help you keep your job suffice to keep you from stealing from your employer if you think you can get away with it? Even if we think it will, we have just lost our neutrality. For now we are teaching ethics as if atheism were true.

Do we just want our graduates to be good workers, or do we also want them to be good citizens? Society will surely expect us to do something toward the latter end. So what kind of country are we training them to be citizens of? One that is founded on the idea that all men are created equal and are endowed by their Creator with certain inalienable rights, or one that thinks such ideas are only rhetorical flourishes that were thought useful in the past? One that grounds its concept of rights in the created order or one that grounds it in the will of the majority? Or one that just grounds it in the perceived greater good of the greater number? Or one that has no concept of rights for anyone not favored by those in power? Once again, our goal of religious neutrality has proved elusive. We have to make choices that have religious implications. We don't have the choice not to do so. The only choice we have is whether or not we are going to be honest about it.

Secular education is an oxymoron. It is a contradiction in terms. It cannot really be religiously neutral without implying that it does not matter which religion one embraces, or whether one embraces any. And if religion has no consequences, then it is trivial and unimportant. The harder education tries to be secular, then, the more it becomes secular*ist*. Atheism and naturalism are subtly privileged, in effect, as the only truths that matter. And this privileging is unavoidable.

It is unavoidable because in our supposedly neutral school the secularist message is effectively delivered by the whole structure of the curriculum even if it is never actually verbalized. The very premise of neutrality prevents anyone from saying anything that could possibly contradict it. Even if released time for religious instruction is granted, that instruction is still secluded and segregated from the rest of the curriculum. Science, history, civics, and literature will still have to be taught as if that religious instruction did not exist. One reason Christians lost their influence in the public schools is that they had been lying to themselves about what, by its very inherent nature, public education was capable of being, about the bias that is built into it by its very stance of enforced neutrality.

The full effects of this educational religious "neutrality" were obscured as long as America had a strong Judeo-Christian consensus at the core of its common culture. We could easily pretend that neutrality just meant that the public schools would be non-sectarian. Though they would not be Baptist or Presbyterian or Methodist, they would still uphold ecumenical truths like those at the foundation of the Declaration of Independence. But when the failure of the churches to fulfill their mission of evangelism and discipleship (see chapter 11) had allowed that consensus to erode beyond a certain point, the real nature of the monster that had been created in public education became no longer avoidable.

When I was in high school, in the public schools of Fulton County,

Georgia, as late as the 1960s, we started each day with a reading from the Bible piped over the public address system to every homeroom. Students volunteered to do those readings, and Christians were the ones with the motivation to volunteer. It was a good thing. But today, would we want the same practice restored? Stop and think before you say yes. On what basis could the Koran, the Book of Mormon, the Bhagavad Gita, or even the Red Book of Mao, be excluded, if someone were motivated to read it? The old consensus cannot be restored simply by blindly pretending that it was never lost.

Is public education a necessary evil? Maybe it is. Somebody has to teach the masses basic literacy and math if they are to be employable at all, and Christian schools are not ready to step up to the plate on that scale. But Christians must not continue to be naïve about what secular education is; they must not continue to be naive about the dynamics that drive it to be dishonest about its neutrality even when good and well-meaning people are trying to work in that system. They need to become much more serious about providing an alternative, providing it well, and making it available to larger numbers of people. Otherwise they will not be able to maintain their own distinctive subculture, much less reach the larger culture with the Gospel.

Thesis 16b:
You Cannot Educate a Human Being Unless You Know What a Human Being Is and What It Is for.

✍

One of the reasons why no school can be religiously neutral is that it is impossible to educate a human being apart from some idea of what a human being is, and there is no such concept that is not determined by whether or not we conceive of a human being as created by and related to God—and what kind of God? Are we subject to the inscrutable will of Allah or responsible to the God who is the Father of our Lord Jesus Christ? Or are we trapped in illusion as in the East, or did we just evolve without any purpose at all other than the arbitrary ones we create for ourselves? We will have a very different approach depending on the answers we give to such questions.

The word *education* comes from two Latin words, *e*, out of, and *ducere*, to lead. It means to lead or bring out of the student the powers that lie latent within him—in other words, to help him achieve his potential. Human beings have the native ability to read, write, cipher, and think logically, but they will not realize those abilities unless they are taught. Then there are more complex tasks that are built on the foundation of the basics, which also have to be taught. The ability to add, subtract, multiply, and divide does not automatically make you able to keep the books for a corporation or plot the trajectory of a rocket. The ability to read and write does not automatically make you able to generate an effective political speech or an edifying sermon, and the ability to think logically does not automatically blossom into the ability to combine forensic evidence with principles of the law to achieve justice. There is a host of other ways in which people make a living that require further instruction, both in school and on the job, if they are to be done well or even done at all. Our potential for such things has to be discerned and brought out, or they will never happen.

And what about the time when the graduate is not at work? Here is the place where the question of our nature and purpose becomes unavoidable. Is there more to him or her than just being a cog in an economic machine? Are there other things in life it would be tragic to miss, or not to accomplish, which education ought to prepare us for? Unlike other animals, we cannot learn everything we need to know to be able to participate in and transmit the culture which is the life of our species just from instinct or from our immediate pack. How handicapped would we be, not just for work but for life, if we had never been exposed to the Bible? To Shakespeare? To Bach, Beethoven, and Mozart? To Rembrandt, Van Gogh, and Monet? If *handicapped* seems too strong a word, what about *impoverished*? Will you be able to tell the difference between what Shakespeare and a rap artist can give you without education? Rembrandt and Thomas Kincade? Does it matter?

Can a species be impoverished by missing or not learning to appreciate such things? For most species, the answer is probably not. A cat that is safe, warm, and full will not miss Mozart playing on his master's stereo. But for humanity . . . well, we do seem different somehow. Who are we? Why are we here? What are we for? Any educational system that does not start by asking such questions and insisting on satisfying answers to them is doomed to futility and failure. Any educational system that has the wrong answers will at best fail to bring out the fullness of human potential and will at worst create twisted ideologues who will undermine that potential for others. Before you entrust your children to any educational system, you had better know what its answers are. What are they for believers?

Thesis 16c: Human Beings Were Created in the Image of God To Enjoy Him through Fellowship with Him and To Glorify Him by Serving Him As His Deputies and Regents in the Rule and Care of the Earth.

For Christians, human beings were created in the image of God to glorify Him and enjoy Him forever. We were to be the stewards of His creation, a bridge between the spiritual and material worlds by virtue of being the only creature we know of that fully participates in both. We are creative because we were made in the image of the Creator, and consequently the history of the creativity of our fellow human beings (i.e., culture—see chapter 13) is part of who we are; we are not fully present in the world to the extent that human culture is not present in and to us. We were made in the image of God, but we fell through disobedience and corrupted that image; nevertheless, it is being restored through the redemption wrought by Jesus Christ in those who put their trust in Him. Our purpose is to glorify our Creator and Redeemer by living a full life that expresses our identity as His creatures, that restores our role as stewards of His creation, still beautiful despite its corruption by our fall, and that (most importantly) makes that redemption available to others through the spread of the Gospel. Any Christian education that deserves the name must keep that vision of who we were meant to be front and center at every step of the way.

One of the problems with much of contemporary Christianity that causes it to need reformation is a truncated vision of human nature and human purpose.[143] We retain bits and pieces of the biblical picture but we lack an integrated view of its wholeness. I was a student at a good Christian college in the early 1970s and I have taught at another one for the last thirty-plus years. The students (with some stellar exceptions of course) were marked by American pragmatism on steroids. You would expect Christians to be less utilitarian than their secular peers, but my impression is that they are more so. There

143 Two good sources for restoring that wholeness of vision are Donald T. Williams, *Mere Humanity: G. K. Chesterton, C. S. Lewis, and J. R. R. Tolkien on the Human Condition*, 2nd ed. (Chillicothe, OH: DeWard, 2018) and Edgar Andrews, *What is Man? Adam, Alien, or Ape*? (Nashville: Elm Hill, 2018).

was less of a viable and vibrant intellectual and artistic subculture in either of those Christian institutions than there was in my secular high school. It is not that the faculty were not trying to promote something better—but the Christian subculture would not support it. Most of those not called to full-time ministry were not interested in any course or activity that would not make them more money after they graduated, and most of those who were so called wanted practical skills and had little patience for anything else. The wholeness of a life responding to all of God's creativity with all of ours was not so much missed as resisted like the plague. It is not shocking that in this we resemble the secular society of which we are a part. But it is tragic that our Christian faith does so little to make us different.

We want the education we provide as Christians to move in the direction of wholeness, a wholeness informed by a biblical view of what humanity is. We did not evolve by chance from a purposeless process. We were created in the image of God, and He created us in His image because He had a purpose in mind for us. We would enjoy fellowship with Him while serving Him as the stewards of His creation, finding joy and fulfillment in carrying out our responsibility under Him for the care of the earth and our fellow creatures. We would fill the earth with His glory by exercising oversight and by exercising the creativity we were given by virtue of our existing in the image of the Creator. But we fell into disobedience, and in our revolt lost our fellowship with Him and our awareness of our purpose. Nevertheless, we did not lose that purpose. We still rule the earth, though now in rebellion and hence often very badly. We still exercise our creativity, but now sometimes in ways that are perverse and polluted.

Nevertheless, we are offered by God's grace a redemption that restores those who accept it to our original intended purpose and hence to the possibility of joy and fulfillment (See chapters 2-5). Filling the earth with God's glory now involves preaching the Good News of that redemption to every creature and making disciples of them—fulfilling the Great Commission (See chapter 11). That Commission is not something new, an emergency task added merely as a desperate response to the Fall. It is part and parcel of our original purpose, the form it must appropriately take in the context of our fallen state. It should occur in the context of that creativity which is central to our identity; it is not an alternative to it. This and nothing less than this is the role in the world that Christian education should train and prepare us for.

What would the education we are describing look like? There is a thesis for that!

Thesis 16d: Christian Education Develops the Whole Person To Glorify God in Every Area of a Whole Life.

Education starts with anthropology, the doctrine of man. So Christian education starts with the *imago Dei*, the image of God. It starts in other words with Adam and Eve reigning over the Garden of Nature, representing the Creator in His creation. What possible knowledge about that creation, its nature, and its purpose, could be irrelevant or uninteresting to them?

No one can know everything, and now that there are millions of Adams and Eves, differentiation and specialization are unavoidable in the fulfillment of their task. But God is still the King under whom they govern, and so the universe is their field of operation. And God is (for believers) their heavenly Father, and so the universe is their back yard. Therefore, as the foundation from which they specialize, a well-rounded grounding in general knowledge seems appropriate. They are the lords of the earth, not a niche species. In a complex world that requires analysis and a fallen world that requires discernment of truth from error, they had better be solidly grounded in the tools and methods of critical thinking. In a fallen world that requires discernment of good and evil, they had better be well versed in God's revelation; they should be students and followers of Scripture, understood by the careful use of those tools of critical thinking applied as outlined in chapter six, and elaborated in terms of the biblical worldview. As Eliot put it, "A Christian education would primarily train people to think in Christian categories."[144] As persons created in the image of the Creator to serve him in the context of the culture generated by that creativity, they need to be grounded in the appreciation of and, for those so gifted, the production of the arts. What less could prepare them for the roles they are expected to play?

It sounds very much then as if something very like what we call a "classical education" taught from a biblical perspective is demanded by a Christian understanding of our nature and calling. Such an edu-

144 T. S. Eliot, *Christianity and Culture: The Idea of a Christian Society and Notes towards a Definition of Culture* (N.Y.: Harcourt, Brace, and Company, 1940), p. 22.

cation begins with the Trivium: Grammar, Logic, and Rhetoric. They are together the indispensable tools of thought, the foundation of whatever endeavor we may find ourselves called to pursue.[145] Grammar is the study of the rules of language, of how to say something. Logic is the study of the rules of reasoning, of how to say something valid. And Rhetoric is the study of the rules of presentation, of how to say something well. The more mastery we have of these three skills, the more effectively we can think. We are after all *homo sapiens*, the thinking creature, by virtue of the *imago Dei* the only animal who finds rational thought central to its life and identity. To rule the other animals for God, we have to understand them in ways that they do not have to understand us.

Lest we think this an elitist program unrelated to the practical needs of the church, we should remember that hymn writer Isaac Watts was just as well known in his own day as the author of a standard textbook on logic. A leader as pious as John Wesley recommended to his convert Margaret Lewen a curriculum of the Bible, grammar, arithmetic, geography, logic, ethics, natural philosophy (i.e., science), history, metaphysics, poetry, and divinity (i.e., theology). "And you will then have knowledge enough for any reasonable Christian."[146] Well, yes; it would be a start.

In fact, the practical needs of the church can only be served by an education that is both classical and Christian because the church is the body of Christ, the Lord of Glory, and is made up of redeemed human beings created in the image of God to serve Him in the whole scope of His vast and wonderful world. An education that is *merely* vocational, purely oriented toward making a living, treats man as an economic machine and does not prepare him for the life of a full human being. It is a practical denial of the doctrine of the *imago Dei*. Therefore, there will be no new Reformation in the church until it is committed to an education that reflects these truths—that seeks to develop whole persons who will glorify God in every arena of a whole life.

---

145 For more on the critical importance of the Trivium, see Dorothy L. Sayers, "The Lost Tools of Learning," *A Matter of Eternity: Selections from the Writings of Dorothy L. Sayers*, ed. Rosamond Kent Sprague (Grand Rapids: Eerdmans, 1973), pp. 107-135. See also Douglas Wilson, *Recovering the Lost Tools of Learning: An Approach to Distinctively Christian Education* (Wheaton: Crossway, 1991) and James V. Schall, S. J., *A Student's Guide to Liberal Learning* (Wilmington, De.: Intercollegiate Studies Institute, 2000).

146 John Wesley, "Letter to Margaret Lewen, June 1764," qtd. in *A Burning and a Shining Light: English Spirituality in the Age of Wesley*, ed. David Lyle Jeffrey (Grand Rapids: Eerdmans,1987), p. 246.

Thesis 16e:
Therefore, Milton Was Right To Say That "A Complete and Generous Education Is That Which Fits a Man to Perform Justly, Skillfully, and Magnanimously All the Offices, Both Public and Private, of Peace and War."

How then can we summarize our conclusions on Christian education? We could start with four quotations:

> *In the evening I return to my house and go into my study. At the door I take off the clothes I have worn all day, mud-spotted and dirty, and put on regal and courtly garments. Thus appropriately clothed, I enter into the ancient courts of ancient men, where, being lovingly received, I feed on that food which alone is mine, and which I was born for; for I am not ashamed to speak with them and to ask the reasons for their actions, and they courteously answer me.*
> Niccolo Machiavelli[147]

> *There has never been a great revelation of the word of God unless He has first prepared the way by the rise and prosperity of languages and letters, as though they were John the Baptists.*
> Martin Luther[148]

> *The end, then, of learning, is to repair the ruins of our first parents by regaining to know God aright, and out of that knowledge to love Him, to imitate Him, to be like Him, as we may the nearest by possessing our souls of true virtue, which, being united to the heavenly grace of*

---

147 Niccolo Machiavelli, Letter to Francesco Vittori, 10 December 1513, trans. Alan H. Gilbert. Qtd. in Maynard Mack, et. Al., eds., *The Norton Anthology of World Masterpieces*, 5th Continental ed., (NY: Norton, 1987), p. 1061.

148 Matrin Luther, Letter to Eoban Hess, 29 March 1523; qtd. in Wallace K. Ferguson, *The Renaissance in Historical Thought: Five Centuries of Interpretation* (NY: Houghton Mifflin, 1961), p. 54.

faith, makes up true perfection.
John Milton[149]

And you shall know the truth, and the truth shall set you free.
Jesus of Nazareth[150]

On these four pillars set as cornerstones—the Renaissance Scholar, the Protestant Reformer, the Christian Poet, and, supremely, the Lord of Glory—we may build as on a firm foundation our Christian philosophy of education.

The classical concept of education which inspired men of the Renaissance like Machiavelli involved growing out of the provincialism of one's own time and place to become a citizen of the ages. They heard around them the echoes of a great Conversation as old as the race, in which the great Minds wrestled with the great Questions: Who are we? Why are we here? What is ultimately real? What is the Good, the True, the Beautiful? How do we know? They strove to acquire the intellectual equipment—languages, logic, hermeneutics, etc.—which would enable them to enter into that Conversation themselves, to benefit from the wisdom of the ancients, and perhaps even to make a small contribution of their own for the use of future generations. It was in books that the Conversation took place, and in their own books it would continue when they themselves had faded into dust.

The Christian vision of education is both broader and deeper than that of the ancients. It is more, but not less; it includes the classical ideal while going beyond it. We too seek to join a great Conversation already going on around us. It contains many of the same voices and deals with all of the same questions. But our Conversation is guided by the Voice of Scripture more surely toward the Truth, and it has as its goal not just our own personal enrichment and fulfillment but the glory of God in practical service. Therefore, the greatest service a Christian school can perform is to introduce its students to the Participants in the Conversation so that their lives can be enriched and their service informed by it. It is, in other words, to make them lovers of books[151]: the Bible supremely, the classics of course, and a host of

---

149 John Milton, "Of Education," 1644, in Alexander M. Witherspoon and Frank J. Warnke, eds., *Seventeenth-Century Prose and Poetry*, 2n ed. (NY: Harcourt, Brace, Jovanovich, 1982),p. 389.

150 John 8:32.

151 For, as Milton said, "Books are not absolutely dead things, but do contain a potency of life in them to be as active as that soul whole progeny they are; nay, they do preserve, as in a vial, the

heroes of the Faith who have blazed the trail before us as well.

Both Calvin and Luther recognized the debt that the Reformation—the recovery of the Gospel in its purity—owed to learning. For it was Renaissance Humanist scholars like Colet, Valla, and Erasmus with their battle cry of *ad fontes*, "back to the sources," who had not only recovered the original text of Scripture but pioneered the grammatico-historical exegesis that allowed its Voice to be heard clearly once again.[152] A providential confluence of dates captures the relationship: in 1516, Erasmus the Humanist scholar published the first printed edition of the Greek New Testament, and in 1517, Martin Luther the Protestant Reformer nailed the Ninety-Five Theses to the Wittenberg Church Door. As a contemporary proverb said, "Erasmus laid the egg, and Luther hatched it."

If we wish to preserve, defend, transmit, and intelligently apply the Gospel the Reformation recovered, we would do well then to recapture the educational emphases that made that recovery possible. For, as Luther knew, to acquire as much skill as possible in the languages and literature not only of the New Testament itself but also of the Greco-Roman world from which it sprang is to attune our ears to the message of those John the Baptists who can help to point us to Christ. The proliferation of technical competencies required for entry to the modern marketplace makes it impossible to reproduce literally the classical education of the past. But Evangelical Christians should recognize that their descent from both the Apostles and the Reformers gives them a special motivation for keeping all those classical voices as part of the Conversation heard by the next generation.[153]

Listening to those voices, then, we seek to train whole people for whole lives that give glory to God in every arena of life. We must understand, as Milton reminds us, that they were made in His image, have fallen from it, and are being restored to it by His Grace. As children of the King of Heaven, the whole universe is their back yard. Therefore, they alone have the right to make truthfully the claim of the pagan Terence: "*Homo sum; humani nil a me alienum puto*" ("I

---

purest efficacy and extraction of that living intellect that bred them." In "Areopagetica," 1644, in Witherspoon & Warnke, op. cit., p. 397.

152 For a fuller treatment of these issues, see Donald T. Williams, *Inklings of Reality: Essays toward a Christian Philosophy of Letters*, 2nd ed. (Lynchburg: Lantern Hollow Press, 2012), esp. chp. 4. See also chp. 17 here.

153 For more on what those "classical voices" are, see Louise Cowan and Os Guinness, eds., *Invitation to the Classics: A Guide to Books You've Always Wanted to Read* (Grand Rapids: Baker, 1980).

am a man; nothing human do I consider alien to me"). Hence, before we educate ministers, missionaries, workers for business, or teachers, we educate men and women. Professional competence to pursue their calling they must have, but much more: As Milton also reminds us in the words that encapsulate our final thesis on education, "I call, therefore, a complete and generous education, that which fits a man to perform justly, skillfully, and magnanimously all the offices, both public and private, of peace and war."[154] The Bible, the Liberal Arts, and Professional Skill thus form for Christian educators, in a way that is impossible in the secular academy, a unified and coherent whole which they should understand and articulate as such.

The content of education for Christians is a whole based on the unity of the Truth which flows from the one God, whether revealed in Scripture, in Nature, or in History. With Scripture as the authoritative key and guide, Christian education introduces students to the ongoing quest for that Truth in its fullness, wherever it is found. As Milton explained again:

> Truth indeed came once into the world with her divine Master, and was a perfect shape most glorious to look on: but when He ascended, and His Apostles after Him were laid asleep, then straight arose a wicked race of deceivers, who . . . took the virgin Truth and hewed her lovely form into a thousand pieces, and scattered them to the four winds. From that time ever since, the sad friends of Truth, such as durst appear, imitating the careful search that Isis made for the mangled body of Osiris, went up and down gathering up limb by limb still as they could find them. We have not yet found them all, . . . nor ever shall do, till her Master's second coming; he shall bring together every joint and member, and shall mold them into an immortal feature of loveliness and perfection.[155]

Even the limited, partial, and fragmentary glimpses we have now through a glass darkly can inform, inspire, transform, and liberate, helping us serve the Lord of Truth with the intelligent zeal He deserves.

As servants of the Lord of Truth and Light, Christian educators

---

154 Milton, "On Education," op. cit., 390.

155 John Milton, "Areopagetica," op. cit., p. 411.

will strive to model and teach wholesome values and ideas. But they do not do this by burying their heads in the sand, nor by encouraging their students to do the same. As servants of the Lord of Truth, they are afraid of nothing.[156] They also agree with Milton that they "cannot praise a fugitive and cloistered virtue, unexercised and unbreathed, that never sallies out and sees her adversary, but slinks out of the race where that immortal garland is to be run for, not without dust and heat."[157] The primary reason their students should want to attend a Christian school is not negative but positive; not to escape the evil influence of the secular academy but because the Christian school is the West Point for Christian soldiers, preparing them to make an impact on the front lines of the spiritual and cultural wars that rage around us. There they should learn to say, "Apollyon, beware what you do; for I am in the King's highway, the way of holiness; therefore take heed to yourself."[158]

---

[156] "Though all the winds of doctrine were let loose to play upon the earth, so Truth be in the field, we do injuriously... to misdoubt her strength. Let her and Falsehood grapple; who ever knew Truth put to the worse in a free and open encounter?" Milton, "Areopagetica," p. 415.

[157] "Areopagetica,". P. 402.

[158] John Bunyan, The Pilgrim's Progress, in Witherspoon & Warnke, op. cit., p. 515.

Conclusion

When Jesus said that the Truth would make us free, His primary reference was no doubt soteriological. But if God's purpose in salvation is to restore us to the fullness of our intended status as sub-regents of creation made in His image, then our Lord's dictum has pedagogical relevance as well. Truth seen as a Christ-centered whole frees us to become what we were created to be. Learn to "see God in everything," said John Donne, "and thou needst not then take off thine eye from . . . anything."[159] It is just that theocentric vision that Christian educators have the privilege of imparting as the basis of a life that can test the limits of our potential to glorify our Father in the marketplace of commerce, the marketplace of ideas, indeed truly in all the arenas of life.

---

159 John Donne, "Sermon XXIII," 1640, in Witherspoon & Warnke, op. cit., p. 79.

Interlude

The Hellene And The Hebrew
Commentary, Rom. 12:1 (KJV)

So where does Athens meet Jerusalem?
    Tertullian couldn't find a single place
    And thus condemned the blind and groping race
To groping blindness. Greeks? Well, as for them,
They asked the Questions brilliantly, but slim
    Or none the odds that they would ever trace
    The Answers, which the Jew in every case
Possessed; the Questions never occurred to him.

Separate, they both remain opaque,
    A price we pay for our ancestral treason.
    The unexamined life will never find
A Cross between the two is what can make
    The sacrifice of self an act of Reason:
    To love the Lord your God with all your mind.[160]

---

160 Donald T. Williams, *Stars through the Clouds*, op. cit., p. 297.

17
Five Theses on Renaissance

What is needed for true Reformation and Revival?

Five Theses on Renaissance

A. Renaissance is a recovery of the life of the mind. (If Anti-Intellectualism is a heresy [see thesis 15a], then such a recovery is a necessary prerequisite to Reformation.)

B. God used the historical Renaissance to prepare the way for the Reformation by developing the *ad fontes* ("back to the sources") tradition. ("There has never been a great revelation of the word of God unless He has first prepared the way by the rise and prosperity of languages and letters, as though they were John the Baptists." — Martin Luther, "Letter to Eoban Hess.")

C. In the providence of God, the elaboration of grammatico-historical exegesis by Renaissance humanist scholars in the *ad fontes* tradition made *sola Scriptura* a viabe response to the crisis of religious authority of the time. (The methods of study pioneered by Renaissance scholars, focused on what the text would have meant to its original audience, gave Scripture a renewed ability to speak for itself.)

D. Our day faces a similar crisis of authority, in the church as well as outside it. (The source of meaning has been shifted from the author to the reader, with disastrous results for the ability of Scripture to exercise its proper authority.)

E. We need a new Renaissance to make possible a new Reformation. (Biblical illiteracy must be eradicated from the church and textual faithfulness must become central again to both education and preaching. Neither of these things can happen without the other.)

Though the history of words has mightily obscured this fact, faithful biblical Christianity owes a great debt to humanism—not the secular humanism with which modern Christians are familiar, of course, but a very different kind of humanism that existed in the past: the humanism of the Renaissance. Though contemporary secular humanists share a name and a history with Renaissance humanism, they are very different phenomena indeed. We need to understand the difference to understand our place in intellectual history, and to understand why Renaissance is a necessary prelude to Reformation. How did the same moment in history give rise to two such contrasting and opposed movements as modern secular humanism and Reformation-based conservative biblical Protestantism (i.e., classical Evangelicalism)? The answer to that question will take us on a fascinating historical journey that has crucial relevance for our present crisis.

I speak here of what I call "the other three Rs": Renaissance, Reformation, and Revival. Renaissance is a recovery of the life of the mind, Reformation a recovery of sound doctrine, and Revival a recovery of vital and faithful spiritual life. This chapter will attempt to explain why it was not just a coincidence that the original Reformation broke out when the Renaissance was at its height in Northern Europe. It will attempt to explain how God used the historical Renaissance to set the stage for the historical Reformation, which could not otherwise have occurred with either the clarity or the power it had. I believe we need Him to do the same thing again if real Reformation leading to real Revival is to be possible for our generation.[161]

---

161 For more information on the historical Renaissance and its relation to the Reformation, see Jacob Burckhardt, *The Civilization of the Renaissance in Italy*, 2 vols. (N.Y.: Harper and Row, 1929), Wallace K. Ferguson, *The Renaissance in Historical Thought* (Cambridge, Ma.: Houghton Mifflin, 1948), Paul Oskar Kristeller, *Renaissance Thought: The Classic, Scholastic, and Humanist Strains* (N.Y.: Harper and Row, 1961), Roland H. Bainton, *Erasmus of Christendom* (N.Y.: Crossroad, 1982), William R. Estep, *Renaissance and Reformation* (Grand Rapids: Eerdmans, 1986), Bard Thompson, *Humanists and Reformers: A History of the Renaissance and Reformation* (Grand Rapids: Eerdmans, 1996), and Donald T. Williams, *Inklings of Reality: Essays toward a Christian Philosophy of Letters* (Lynchburg: Lantern Hollow Press, 2012), esp. chap. 4.

Thesis 17a:
Renaissance Is a Recovery of the Life of the Mind.

✍

When I define Renaissance as a recovery of the life of the mind, I am speaking about a cultural shift that needs to take place in the rank and file of Evangelical lay people and pastors today. The choice of this historical metaphor for that shift demands both justification and clarification if it is to be helpful and not misleading. It would be a serious mistake to think of the historical Renaissance as any such recovery in simplistic terms. The old myth of the medieval "dark ages" supplanted by reason and light in the Renaissance was a serious distortion of history. The Middle Ages boasted a high culture that we still rightly admire and from which we can learn much. The age that produced the theology of Aquinas, the poetry of Dante and Chaucer, and the architecture of Notre Dame, Canterbury, and Chartres, was not culturally "dark" or even anti-intellectual in any meaningful sense of those words.

Nevertheless, there were aspects of Medieval culture that in retrospect did not facilitate the growth of healthy, biblical spirituality in either clergy or laity. Rampant illiteracy, a lack of historical consciousness, and a mystical rather than a scientific approach to hermeneutics made it harder than it needed to be for people to hear the Bible speaking for itself in its own voice. So while the darkness of the "dark ages" is often highly exaggerated, the providential breaking down of those barriers did make significant progress possible in art, culture and, science as well as religion. Thus Renaissance—i.e., *rebirth*—was in fact an appropriate name for the period that saw those advances.

It would be equally misleading to talk of a "dark age" of contemporary Evangelicalism. The second half of the Twentieth Century saw what was (perhaps prematurely) called an "Evangelical Renaissance." Evangelicals emerged from cultural marginalization to become a major electoral block that political parties had to take into account. Their churches grew while those of the liberal mainline shrank. They got more post-baccalaureate degrees than ever before and even became a major, positively influential presence in the previously almost completely secular discipline of philosophy, while creating an expanding publishing empire. It was easy to be optimistic about all that growth and apparent health in the 1980s.

Nevertheless, there were aspects of the Evangelical subculture that in retrospect were not signs of healthy growth at all. Evangelicals elected a lot of political candidates but did not achieve their goal of reversing Roe v. Wade. They published a lot of books, but they were mostly romance novels of questionable literary value and religious self-help books with questionable spiritual value. Evangelical *men* who are not pastors read almost nothing. Some of those who are pastors keep an impressive number of theological works in print, but they seem to have very little impact on the culture in the pew, which remains as resistant to and suspicious of serious thought as ever. Meanwhile, many of the Evangelical intelligentsia who pursued higher education were not sufficiently grounded and discipled beforehand to prevent their becoming subtly secularized by their degrees. Their ignorance of classical Evangelical theology (in anything but caricatures) and their accommodation to secular ways of thinking has led to the many deviations from historic Evangelical faith addressed in the previous chapters of this book.

In sum, thinking that is sound and faithful and not just falsely sophisticated is in very short supply. The "Christian Mind" manifested by Evangelical Christianity needs a serious upgrade in quantity, and perhaps even more in quality. In short, despite many surface indications to the contrary, we must say that the Reformation that Evangelicalism needs must begin with Renaissance: if we understand it in the right sense, a recovery of the life of the mind.

Thesis 17b:
God Used the Historical Renaissance To Prepare the Way for the Reformation by Developing the *Ad Fontes* ("Back to the Sources") Tradition.

The parallels between the historical Renaissance that preceded the historical Reformation and the Renaissance we need today are just close enough to be really interesting. In order to explain why, we need to understand how the Renaissance came about.

As the Middle Ages drew toward their close and the modern nation states that had evolved out of Feudalism were becoming bigger and more complex, there arose the need for a new kind of public servant who had to be able to read and write to do his job: ghost writing speeches for the king, negotiating treaties with foreign powers, persuading parliament to pass laws, etc. In Italy they were called *dictatores*—not because they were dictators but because they took dictation. (That is why the heads of government departments in the executive branch are called "Secretaries"—of state, justice, defense, etc.—to this day.) It was a new situation because up until this time almost everyone who could read and write had worked for the church.

These men realized that, aside from giving them basic literacy, their Medieval education—based largely on reading the Bible and church fathers using allegorical exegesis, i.e, looking for supposed secret, hidden, "spiritual" symbolic meanings between the lines of the texts—was not really helping them do their secular jobs. Eventually, some of them realized that if they went back to pre-Christian Greece and Rome, they could find authors who were doing the same kinds of writing they themselves were tasked with. So they started scouring the monastery libraries and digging up neglected copies of the ancient Greco-Roman classics, copying them, editing them, publishing them with the new technology of the printing press, and studying them for pointers about how to write more effective political oratory for their own times.

This was the first intellectual stimulus that led to the Renaissance: a large number of people reading new books (old books, actually, but new to them). The Renaissance was initially a "rebirth" of interest in and knowledge of the old pagan classics. Even more significant than the fact that these early humanists were reading new books was the fact that they were reading them in a new way. If you are reading a speech by Cicero or Seneca to get pointers about how you can be more effective in your own political speech writing, you don't really care about how many hidden symbolic meanings you can read into the text. You want to know the answers to a very different set of questions: What was the historical situation at the time this speech was written? What effect did its author want it to have on its original audience (say, the Roman senate). What did he do in order to achieve that effect? How well did it work? So, for their own purely secular purposes, these early humanists rediscovered and pioneered for their own generation what today we call grammatico-historical exegesis. They were figuring out how to find out what an ancient book had meant to the audience to which it was originally written. Their battle cry, heard across Europe, was "*Ad fontes!*" "Back to the sources!"

You see the *ad fontes* spirit embodied in the context of its relation to Renaissance culture as a whole in Castiglione's description of the Duke's library at Urbino. His palace

> was adorned not only with the usual objects, such as silver vases, wall hangings of the richest cloth of gold, silk, or other similar material, but also with countless antique statues of marble and bronze, with rare pictures, and with every kind of musical instrument; nor would he tolerate anything that was not most rare and outstanding. Then, at great cost, he collected a large number of the finest and rarest books, in Greek, Latin, and Hebrew, all of which he adorned with gold and silver, *believing that they were the crowning glory of his great palace.*[162]

Machiavelli gives us a window on the *ad fontes* spirit and the excitement that humanist study could produce in a letter to a friend:

> In the evening I return to my house and go into my study. At

---

162 Baldassare Castiglione, *The Book of the Courtier*, 1527; trans. George Bull (N.Y.: Penguin, 1976), p. 41 (emphasis added). See David Stott Gordon, "Sir Philip Sidney: The Faith and Practice of an Elizabethan Christian" (thesis Trinity Evangelical Divinity School, 1995), pp. 43-52, for an excellent overview of Castiglione's contribution to the original Renaissance.

the door I take off the clothes I have worn all day, mud-spotted and dirty, and put on regal and courtly garments. Thus appropriately clothed, I enter into the ancient courts of ancient men, where, being lovingly received, I feed on that food which alone is mine, and which I was born for; for I am not ashamed to speak with them and to ask the reasons for their actions, and they courteously answer me.[163]

"They courteously answer me." Humanist scholars had learned to interrogate texts in such a manner that they could with moral certainty uncover their original meaning and be confident that they had done so. Grammar, context, historical context, and rhetorical analysis were the criteria by which one could ask the reasons for the ancients' words and actions and get real solid answers. They were learning a lot of the techniques for textual analysis we covered here in chapter six.

Renaissance Humanism was not in its origins an ideology; it was an educational reform movement. These men were called humanists, not because they believed that man was the measure of all things (that would come later), but because they were interested in the Humanities—the classics. Anyone who wanted to read ancient books in their original languages using grammatico-historical exegesis, and who wanted to reform the educational system to teach that approach because it would better prepare students for public life, was called a humanist. This included people like John Calvin and Huldrych Zwingli. They did not cease to be humanists when they became Reformers. They became Reformers *because* they were humanists first. What was the connection?

It was inevitable that eventually someone would ask, "What would happen if we tried reading the New Testament in the original Greek using grammatico-historical exegesis?" People like John Colet, Lorenzo Valla, and Erasmus of Rotterdam did so, and they were blown away. John Colet taught a course on Romans at Oxford using the new way of reading, and students flocked to it with great excitement. His exposition anticipated many of Luther's points. Erasmus fell in love with the portrait of Jesus in the Gospels, seen afresh with sharper lines and brighter colors, like a restored painting with years of the accumulated dust and grime of tradition removed. He anticipated some

---

163 Niccolo Machiavelli, Letter to Francesco Vittori, 10 December 1513, trans. Alan H. Gilbert. Qtd. in Maynard Mack, et. Al., eds., *The Norton Anthology of World Masterpieces*, 5th Continental ed., (NY: Norton, 1987), p. 1061.

of Luther's points, and edited the first printed edition of the Greek New Testament in 1516.[164] Luther used Erasmus's Greek Testament as his own study Bible and nailed up the Ninety-Five theses in 1517. A coincidence? People at the time didn't think so. It became a proverb with them: "Erasmus laid the egg, and Luther hatched it." Erasmus only partially approved of the chicken Luther hatched. He favored Reformation of the church but never fully grasped the crucial importance of Luther's doctrine of justification by faith alone as the heart of the Gospel. But without the groundwork done by the humanists, there could have been no Reformation.

---

[164] See Bainton, *Erasmus of Christendom*, op. cit., for an insightful study of Erasmus's life and contribution,

Thesis 17c:
In the Providence of God, the Elaboration of Grammatico-Historical Exegesis by Renaissance Humanist Scholars in the *Ad Fontes* Tradition Made *Sola Scriptura* a Viable Response to the Crisis of Religious Authority of the Time.

The great irony of this story is that Renaissance humanists, for their own purely secular purposes, had made common in the European intelligentsia a method of reading that made it much easier for the Bible to speak for itself and cut through the layers of obscuring tradition that had been accumulating over it for a thousand years. They did so at a time when the prestige and credibility of the Papacy was at a low ebb. The memory of the rival popes all claiming to be Christ's sole and unique vicar during the "Babylonian captivity" of the church, the corruption of the Vatican, the secularity of the Renaissance popes who were hard to distinguish from power-hungry territorial monarchs, the ignorance and incompetence of many local priests: All this came together to create a vacuum in the hearts of the faithful, a famine of the Word of God. And so God in His providential rule used Renaissance Humanism to give the Bible its voice back again. That made *sola Scriptura* a viable solution to the problem of religious authority, and that opened the eyes of people like Luther and Calvin to the power of the Gospel. *Ad fontes* made *sola Scriptura* possible, and *sola Scriptura* made inevitable the rest of the message of the Reformation: *sola gratia, sola fide, solus Christus*, and *soli Deo Gloria*, as addressed here in chapters 1-5.

What made the Reformation such a powerful movement for the recovery of the biblical Gospel in its purity and power? God had never left Himself without a witness. John Wycliffe in England and Jan Hus in Bohemia had anticipated a number of Luther's emphases. Wycliffe had translated the New Testament into English in 1380. They found a few disciples (such as the Lollards in England in Chaucer's day), but never had a major impact on the church as a whole. How then were Luther and Calvin able to turn the world upside down?

Between Wycliffe and Luther three things had changed that help to account for the impact of the sixteenth-century Reformation. One was the invention of the printing press, which allowed the message of the Reformation to be distributed quickly and efficiently. A second was the rise of what today we call the Middle Class in the economic boom that accompanied Europe's recovery from the devastation of the Black Death of 1349. These two developments fostered a dramatic rise in the literacy rate, from 5-10% during most of the Middle Ages to around 50% by the time of Luther and Calvin. All of this helped to set the stage. What may have been the most important factor though was the new hermeneutic that had been popularized by the Renaissance Humanists. What did they contribute? An interest in ancient books; the availability of ancient books; wider knowledge of Greek and Hebrew; and above all, they contributed the way of reading that made those ancient texts *open* books. What Luther and Calvin could do that Wycliffe and Hus could not was to explain, through what was now becoming common sense to many of their contemporaries, *why* their reading of Scripture was faithful to its original intent and the Pope's was not. It was no longer just the Reformer's word against the Pope's. People had been given a new ability to judge for themselves.

Luther himself recognized the importance of these contributions of Humanism to the Reformation. As he wrote in a letter to Eoban Hess on 29 March 1523, "There has never been a great revelation of the word of God unless He has first prepared the way by the rise and prosperity of languages and letters, as though they were John the Baptists."[165] "The rise of languages and letters" of course refers to the work of Humanists like Erasmus in making the original text of Scripture available to the eyes and accessible to the minds of educated Europeans once again.

There is one vexing question we need to clear up before we leave this topic. If Renaissance Humanism had such a positive role to play in making the recovery of the biblical Gospel that we call the Reformation possible, how has Humanism come to be the enemy of the Gospel that we see in our own generation? How could the same historical phenomenon have been the ancestor of two such opposite movements as modern secular Humanism and Reformation Christianity? For indeed it was. Francis Schaeffer saw half of that ancestry

---

[165] Qtd. in Wallace K. Ferguson, *The Renaissance in Historical Thought: Five Centuries of Interpretation* (NY: Houghton Mifflin, 1961), p. 54.

clearly. "Renaissance humanism steadily evolved toward modern humanism," which makes "things autonomous" from God.[166] That is the view that many Christians have picked up from him today. It is not so much wrong as incomplete. Here is what actually happened.

Humanism was not initially an ideology; it was an educational reform movement. Anyone who followed the *ad fontes* mentality and wanted to read ancient books in the original language using grammatico-historical exegesis was known as a humanist. This included the Reformers. But as time went on, some Humanists in going back to the sources used Scripture as a plumb line by which to judge what they were reading, and some did not. Those who did not use Scripture as their touchstone picked up from the Greeks a fatal idea. The ancient Greeks had a lot of wisdom, but they were ignorant of the biblical doctrine of the fall of man. They assumed that human nature was either positively good or at least morally neutral—not deceitful and desperately wicked as Scripture teaches (Jer. 17:9). If people chose evil or even lesser goods, it must be because they were confused, they thought. They just needed enlightenment.

You can see the change taking place right before your eyes if you know where to look. By 1534 Rabelais could say in *Gargantua and Pantagruel*, "Those who are free born and well born, well brought up, and used to decent society, possess, by nature, a certain instinct and spur which always impels them to virtuous deeds and restrains them from vice."[167] Those who are "well brought up" are those who possess a humanist education, which brings out this "instinct" they have "by nature." By 1588, Montaigne was even more explicit: "There is no vice truly a vice which is not offensive, and which a sound judgment does not condemn; for its ugliness and painfulness is so apparent that perhaps the people are right who say it is chiefly produced by stupidity and ignorance."[168] If vice comes from ignorance, then the cure for it is not salvation but education.

Now, if you picked this idea of human perfectibility up from the Greeks, it was easy to take the wonderful educational reform you favored, the one that was doing so much good in the world, and think it sufficient to solve all of mankind's problems. And so education was

---

166 Francis Schaeffer, *How Should We Then Live?* Wheaton: Crossway, 2005), pp. 60, 68.

167 Francois Rabelais, *The Portable Rabelais*, trans. Samuel Putnam (N.Y.: The Viking Press, 1946), p. 214.

168 Michel de Montaigne, "Of Repentance," *Montaigne's Essays and Selected Writings: A Bilingual Edition*, trans. Donald M. Frame (N.Y.: St. Martin's Press, 1963), p. 319.

made into an idol. Education logically becomes the new Messiah, even if it is not expressed in such grandiose terms. Once that happens, you are on a straight road to modern secular Humanism as codified in Humanist Manifestos I and II. Those who made that mistake kept the name Humanist, while their fellow Humanists were swallowed up in the Reformation and became known to subsequent history rather as Reformers. So the right use versus the wrong use of the positive contributions of the original Humanists made all the difference. We want to recover that contribution and make sure we make the right use of it this time.

Thesis 17d:
Our Day Faces a Similar Crisis of Authority, in the Church As Well As Outside It.

The first Reformation answered the crisis of authority in the Medieval church by using the contributions of the Renaissance to make the text of Scripture accessible to God's people once again. That allowed the Reformers to recover the biblical Gospel and place our knowledge of it on a sound footing in God's written Word. We face our own crisis of authority today, and we need a new Renaissance to make possible a new Reformation to deal with it. What is the nature of our crisis?

I had an interesting conversation with one of my students at lunch in the cafeteria a while back that illustrates it. Students will often say things to an English professor in the cafeteria that they would not say on their hermeneutics exam while trying to please their Bible professor. This student maintained that the doctrine of the inerrancy of Scripture was *meaningless* because once revelation (which to her was apparently some kind of nebulous personal "encounter" devoid of propositional content) is inscripturated, it becomes language, which is always open to interpretation. Since interpretation is an endlessly open-ended process, one can never finally specify what the propositions are, the truth of which we claim that inspiration guarantees. So we should just let the Holy Spirit change people's hearts through the encounter with Jesus they experience, mediated by the biblical language, without worrying about what is happening to their minds or how they might formulate it into ideas and doctrines later. Meaning is in the eye of the beholder anyway, so we really don't have any other choice.

I replied: Just because it is not always easy to tell what a text means, it doesn't follow that the text has no objectively determinable meaning. Paul makes the *graphe* of Scripture our final touchstone of meaning and truth by saying that the *graphe* are what is inspired and thus profitable for doctrine, etc. (2 Tim. 3:16). The Greek word *graphe* means literally writings—ink on parchment, words on paper. The actual words written by the biblical authors are then what Paul says were inspired, *theopneustos*—actually breathed out of God's mouth.

In inspiration, the Holy Spirit guided the human authors to choose those particular words and no others, in those precise grammatical constructions, in those specific literary and historical contexts, as the ones which could accurately convey what He wanted them to say to us. Therefore, to the extent that we have interpreted the biblical writings accurately in terms of those specific clues (chapter six of this book goes into some detail about how to do that), we can have confidence that we know what God says, and that it is true. To Paul, the text as written (the *graphe*), precisely because it consists of all those specific details, is thus perfectly capable of functioning as the touchstone of meaning. And I think Paul knew more about how Scripture actually communicates than we do.

It is obvious, I continued, that we are powerfully influenced by our assumptions, our backgrounds, our experiences. That is one of the reasons you think we cannot get into the mind of the author, because our assumptions, backgrounds, and experiences are different from his. But an *influence* is not a *determinism*. We also have the ability to step out of our own assumptions, our worldview, and see what the world would look like without them—to try on another pair of glasses, as it were. When you are in the back of the classroom, my eyes would tell me that you have only a pink blob instead of a face. My glasses tell me that you do have a face. Which view is correct? Well, I can test both visions by other senses and by comparing them to what other people see. I can then make a judgment about whether my glasses actually let me see the world more as it really is. That is what I'm doing when I use diction, grammar, and context to tell me what the author really meant; they let me get past the preconceived notions that are my default setting to get me in touch with reality.

To my chagrin, I discovered that, despite my explanations, the idea of "text as touchstone" was completely foreign to this student's way of thinking. To her, and to many of her contemporaries, *a text has no meaning until it is interpreted*. None. The meaning is not in the text waiting for the reader to discover it; rather, it is up to the reader to confer the meaning *onto* the text. Meaning is purely and solely in the eye of the beholder; it exists nowhere else. So since we cannot even discuss truth until we have ascertained meaning, and the text can mean something different to each reader with none of them being finally right or wrong ... you begin to see the problem.

No recital of objective features of the text such as grammar, lexicography, or literary or historical context could budge this student from this conviction. To her it was simply self-evident, and any other way of thinking was just incomprehensible. She made no attempt in that conversation to counter my use of Second Timothy 3:16. She had no alternative interpretation of that passage to offer; she did not think she needed one. The use I had made of the verse, anything I had to say about it, was just lumped into the category of the meaningless because whatever the verse says, it has to be interpreted, so there you go.

This girl had not read any post-modern literary theory and was not using its jargon, but she had absorbed its radical subjectivism from her culture so thoroughly that she did not need to. We can be sophisticated and say with Jacques Derrida that meaning is endlessly deferred in the free-play of language; we can be erudite and question with Stanley Fish whether there is a text in this class; or we can be naïve and object, "Well, that's just *your* interpretation!" It makes no essential difference. The French sophist, the American critic, and the sophomoric student are all ultimately in the same place, on one side of a watershed that separates them from the Christian tradition. At the end of the day, does the text ultimately have authority over the interpreter, or does the interpreter have authority over the text? Does the text through its diction, its grammar, its structure, and its contexts make demands on the interpreter to which he is obligated to submit, or is it just a convenient playing field for his own intellectual gymnastics? That is the watershed choice which faces us. And my student was right to intuit that on the post-modern side of it, the doctrines of the inspiration and authority of Scripture are not so much false as meaningless.

I say that this is the choice we all must make. But our students have increasingly already made their choice without knowing it. Why *wouldn't* my student read Scripture this way? It is how her culture has taught her implicitly, and how secular English departments teach their students explicitly, to read all texts. But it would be different in a Christian school, right? In the case of this young lady, neither her required classes in Bible nor Hermeneutics nor Theology had even minimally confronted her with the awareness that there was even a choice to be made. Her teachers in those classes thought they had, but it had not come through. Students can apparently take all of those classes in a very conservative Christian college, believe that inerrancy is ultimately meaningless, say the opposite on the test to please their professors, and not even be aware of, much less concerned about, the contradiction. And that should concern us greatly.

Why does it matter? It matters because unless meaning resides in the text, unless the reader has the obligation to make a good-faith effort to find the meaning that was put there by the author, then *authority* is inevitably transferred from the text to the reader. Someone other than the author in the text as he wrote it—either the reader herself or some expert to whom she defers—must now tell us what the text is saying. And a text that cannot reach across the gap between the author's mind and mine leaves me trapped inside my own head. A text that can only reflect my preconceived notions back to me cannot correct them. Thus post-modern hermeneutics returns us to the chaos of the Book of Judges, where everyone does what is right in his own eyes.

Now, no matter what you say, even if you still call the Bible the Word of God and think yourself a loyal son or daughter of the church, once you have adopted this view authority has been transferred from the biblical Text to you, the individual. Not only is there nothing to stop you from remaking the text (or the natural world, in the case of the transgender movement) in your own image; you have actually been taught that it is your right to do so, and that so doing is unavoidable. Biblical authors cannot be made an exception to this principle when it rules the mind unchallenged. Readers empowered to create their own subjective meaning rather than exhorted to find the objective meaning left behind by the author are foxes put in charge of the hen house when fallen human nature runs up against the demands of the Law of God.

I say this not to cast blame on my colleagues, the young lady's professors. I happen to know that these men are teaching correct procedures with a good foundation (though this is not the case in every school, even every Christian school). In our case they were teaching the right stuff but had perhaps underestimated the depths of the chasm they were trying to bridge. The bottom line is this: We who teach and preach do need to become more aware of this divide that separates us from many in this generation of Christian young people. We need to make sure that we are not on the wrong side of that divide ourselves, and we need to become much more proactive in trying to overcome it. That is the Renaissance that must pave the way for the Reformation we need.

How can we overcome it? That is the topic of our next thesis.

Thesis 17e:
We Need a New Renaissance To Make Possible a New Reformation.

༄

We need a new Renaissance of faithful reading and interpretation to make possible a new Reformation of faithful thinking and of faithful Christian witness and life based on that thinking. What would it look like? The first Reformation was aided by a renewed interest in reading and a renewed method of interpretation that expected the authors of books, including Scripture, to speak for themselves, wanted to hear the message, and knew how to get at it. They needed to replace an over-thought allegorical approach to texts; we need to replace a superficial and pseudo-sophisticated post-modern approach.[169] They needed to discover grammatico-historical exegesis; we need to rediscover it. How can we get there? Here are a few suggestions.

First, we must not become discouraged about making linear arguments with logical connections. The same post-modern pseudo-sophistication that has undermined our confidence in meaning has had the same effect on our confidence in truth and even reason itself. Linear and logical arguments are no longer popular, but that is simply to say that sound thinking is not popular, because it is hard work. It is still necessary. Reason, in the sense of logic, is ultimately based on the character of God: It is because God is a God of covenant faithfulness who cannot lie that the law of non-contradiction is valid in every possible world. We serve a God of truth and reason who cannot lie, and our speech on His behalf should reflect His character. Besides, logical arguments winsomely delivered can still work beneath the surface in people who ostensibly reject their validity, contributing to the cognitive dissonance that might one day bring them to rethink their mindset.

Then we can proceed by reflecting our post-modern speech partner's statements back to her in ways that are deliberately and obviously inaccurate. "So, what you are saying is that texts have an objectively

---

[169] "Allegories ought to be carried no further than Scripture expressly sanctions; so far are they from forming a sufficient basis to found doctrines upon." John Calvin, *Institutes of the Christian Religion*, 2 vol., trans. Henry Beveridge (Grand Rapids: Eerdmans, 1975), p. 1:291.

determinable meaning that is discernibly present in them whether a given reader gets it or not?" "No, that is exactly what I deny!" Of course, if the speaker is going to be allowed to make that denial, then the statement in question *does* mean what she wanted it to mean and not what I interpreted it to mean. It really did have a meaning of its own prior to and independent of my interpretation. Otherwise there could be no objection to my deliberate misconstrual of it. So her very insistence on that false hermeneutic becomes its inescapable refutation! Critics who tell you that authors cannot communicate their original intended meaning to their readers in their texts are doing quite effectively in their own texts the very thing they claim is impossible for everyone else. Even people who do not believe that logical contradictions are indicators of false claims may be able to realize the *practical* contradiction they have created for themselves. They cannot live by their subjectivist hermeneutic without painting themselves into an intolerable corner. They may want to put you in such a corner, but they will not be willing to live there themselves.

From this realization may come an appreciation for what we might call the hermeneutical Golden Rule: Interpret others as you would have them interpret you.[170] Do you care about what you are trying to say to people? Do you want them to care about what you are trying to say to them and therefore try very hard to find out what it is and get it right? Of course you do. If you say you do not, you are lying. You would not be trying to communicate at all unless you did. Well, then, we have to give the same courtesy to other communicators, including authors, living or dead. We may not have to *reduce* meaning to the author's intention, but we had better make authorial intention foundational to whatever meaning we find, or else we should just shut up.

We cannot expect the public schools to help us in this Renaissance, this restoration of responsible reading to the core of our culture. We can expect many of them to work actively against us. A renewed commitment to Christian education, coordinated at every level—in the home, the school, Christian media, the Sunday School, and the church—is an absolute necessity (see Theses 16a-e). So read the Bible, using the principles from the chapter on hermeneutics applicable to it (Theses 6a-e), and read other worthy literature using those principles applicable to it (6a-b).

---

170 For more on the hermeneutical golden rule, see Kevin J. Vanhoozer, *Is There a Meaning in this Text? The Bible, the Reader, and the Morality of Literary Knowledge* (Grand Rapids: Zondervan, 1998), p. 32.

Conclusion

How do we start a new Renaissance? Read. Read with accuracy and with enjoyment that flows from that accuracy. Start in your own armchair and your own family, modeling, teaching, and encouraging faithful reading. Find and support those Christian teachers, preachers, and writers who are allies in the cause. And pray that God will use these efforts to bring a real Renaissance of Christian reading and Christian culture that will make real Reformation possible.

Interlude

Erasmus and the Egg

"Erasmus laid the egg, and Luther hatched it."
— *Sixteenth Century proverb*

"There has never been a great revelation of the word of God unless He has first prepared the way by the rise and prosperity of languages and letters, as though they were John the Baptists."
— *Martin Luther, Letter to Eoban Hess, 29 March 1523.*

Erasmus, reconnecting with the Greek,
    Gently cleaned away the soot and grime
    That had accumulated on the cheek
    Of Jesus' picture slowly over time.
Astonished at the portrait, he adored,
    Enchanted by the vision of that Face,
    And, editing his Testament, restored
    The primal Scriptures to their proper place.
That humanist could not fully grasp the storm
    He had unleashed, nor fully it condone.
    The base restored, the message must reform
    As well: the Way, by Grace through Faith alone.
The church's wounds were too deep to be patched.
    Erasmus laid the egg that Luther hatched.[171]

---

171 Donald T. Williams, *Stars through the Clouds*, op. cit., p. 309.

The Goal of the Trivium
Commentary, Proverbs 9:1-6

Old mysteries await fresh revelation.
    Such ideas ought of right to be presented
    In royal garments, rich and ornamented,
Befitting their high lineage and station.
Heraldic manuscript illumination
    In Celtic knotwork swirled and brightly tinted
    For metaphors and the meanings they have hinted:
The setting beckons us, an invitation.

What now seems quaint and esoteric lore
    Was once the simple bedrock of our thought:
    First principles and their elucidation.
That's partly what the wondrous words were for—
    Despite our darkness, they can still be caught:
    Faint echoes of the ancient Conversation.[172]

---

172 Ibid., p. 291.

18
Five Theses on Reformation

What would a new Reformation of the church actually look like?

A. Reformation is a recovery of sound doctrine, especially as it relates to the Gospel itself. ("Sound doctrine" here does not necessarily mean full agreement on a complete theological system. It means informed commitment to the contents of the Nicene Creed plus the five Reformation "*solas*" as the basis of Evangelical unity; see Chapters 1-5.)

B. Historically, Reformation was a fruit of Renaissance and a prerequisite to Revival. (The Reformation returned to the Gospel, and the First Great Awakening returned from Dead Orthodoxy to the living faith of the Reformation.)

C. Many so-called Evangelicals are letting the sound teaching recovered by the original Reformers slip through their fingers. (Moralistic Therapeutic Deism is not the Gospel.)

D. These ninety-five Theses represent areas in which a new Reformation is required. (Some are prerequisites to a faith that is truly biblical; others to a faith that is truly healthy and holistic.)

E. The only way to be faithful to the original Reformation is by continuing to pursue the ongoing Reformation of the church. (Because the church is made up of sinners, it is always in need of repentance and grace.)

Well, the reader who has endured this far may justifiably hope that there has been a method to all this madness. I hope so too. We are now attempting to arrive at the bottom line: There needs to be a new Reformation of the church in its Evangelical form, flowing from a new Renaissance, and leading to a new Revival, a third Great Awakening. (We can hope that the third time's the charm!) Central to those needs and the primary focus of this book is Reformation. To achieve the Reformation that the church needs today, we must rediscover our roots in the first one,[173] but we must not be satisfied merely to do so. We must use the nourishment derived from those roots to bring forth the fruit of Reformation in our own generation. Only then can we hope to see real, deep, and lasting Revival.

---

173   If you can only read one book about the original Reformation, I recommend Roland H. Bainton, *"Here I Stand": A Life of Martin Luther* (N.Y.: Mentor Books, 1950). The classic work is J. H, Merele d'Aubigne, *History of the Reformation of the Sixteenth Century* (1846, rpt. Grand Rapids: Baker, n.d.). Also worth reading are Roland H, Bainton, *The Reformation of the Sixteenth Century* (Boston: Beacon Press, 1952), Timothy George, *Theology of the Reformers* (Nashville: Broadman, 1988), and Alister E. McGrath, *Reformation Thought: An Introduction*, 2nd ed. (Grand Rapids: Baker, 1993). On the Reformation in England, see A. G. Dickens, *The English Reformation* (N.Y.: Schocken Books, 1964) and Philip Edgecumbe Hughes, *Theology of the English Reformers* (Grand Rapids: Baker, 1980). A newer study that helpfully relates the Reformation to the Renaissance is William R. Estep, *Renaissance and Reformation* (Grand Rapids: Eerdmeans1986). Also relevant to the Reformation as well as the Renaissance is Bainton's *Erasmus of Christendom* (N.Y.: Crossroad, 1982). And of course there is no substitute for original writings of the Reformers themselves, especially John Calvin, *Institutes of the Christian Religion*, trans. Henry Beveridge. 2 vols (Grand Rapids: Eerdmans, 1975). An excellent reference work is Hans J. Hillerbrand, ed., *The Oxford Encyclopedia of the Reformation*, 4 vols. (Oxford: Oxford University Press, 1996).

Thesis 18a:
Reformation Is a Recovery of Sound Doctrine, Especially As It Relates to the Gospel Itself.

Reformation exists for the sake of Revival; which is to say, it exists for the sake of the Gospel; which is to say, it exists for the sake of the salvation and spiritual health of men and women; which is to say that it exists for the sake of the glory of God; which is to say that it exists for the sake of the right worship of God. Only by seeing Reformation so can we understand the importance of sound doctrine. For doctrine exists, not for its own sake, much less for the sake of argument, but rather for the sake of true salvation, manifested glory, and right worship. Forgetting this, many of us have managed to convince ourselves that theology is irrelevant at best and divisive at worst, and that all we need is "the simple Gospel"—as if there could be any Gospel at all unless the central doctrines about Christ and His Person and His Work were true. Too many theologians have confirmed us in this perspective by doing theology as if it were a mere academic discipline and not the faith-sustaining meat of the church. They have forgotten that it was once possible to define theology as "the science of living blessedly forever."[174] The Reformation we seek will be restorative to us and pleasing to God to the extent that we can restore that older vision of the splendor and the joy of right doctrine.

Doctrine exists for the sake of the Gospel. So it is always taught in the New Testament, and so it was pursued by the church Fathers. In the New Testament, Christ must be confessed as having come in the flesh lest we lose our connection to the Father and be found followers of AntiChrist (1 John 2:22-23, 4:2-3); He must be confessed as risen from the dead lest we believe in vain, be found yet in our sins, and be of all men most miserable (1 Cor. 15:12-19); He must be confessed as saving by grace alone through faith alone apart from works lest men should boast—and lest they be accursed (Eph. 2:8-10, Gal. 1:9). With the Church Fathers, Arianism must be defeated at Nicaea and Chalcedon lest we have a Christ who cannot save; Pelagianism must be con-

---

[174] William Perkins, qtd. in J. I. Packer, *A Quest for Godliness: The Puritan Vision of the Christian Life* (Wheaton: Crossway, 1990), p. 32.

demned lest we trust in our own righteousness rather than His, and so be lost. What is at stake? The souls of men and the glory of God. There is no Gospel, simple or otherwise, unless these things are true. If they are not, we are yet in our sins. It is as simple, and profound, as that.

When theology is healthy as a discipline essential to the life of the church, it focuses on the great truths of God, Grace, Gospel, and Glory. It also has to deal with lesser matters of the Law—for example, the form of church government—but they should always be seen as subordinate to, as servants of, the great Truths, and as having meaning only in so far as they serve them. If our teachers understand the significance as well as the content of their doctrines, they will teach them in such a way that we all understand and feel ourselves to be Christians first, and Lutherans, Presbyterians, Anglicans, Baptists, or Methodists second. The first Reformation, as much as we owe it for the restoration and clarification of the Gospel, failed us in this regard when Luther and Zwingli could not agree to disagree on the precise nature of the Lord's presence in the Communion. By God's grace, let us do better this time!

Because a major purpose of doctrine is to safeguard the Gospel so that it reveals God's glory as it was designed to do (theses 5a-e), and because some other truths are necessary but all truths are secondary to that great purpose, we can understand what we mean by saying that Evangelical Christianity needs a restoration of sound doctrine. We are not looking for complete agreement on a full system of theology but for a theological awakening that puts the biblical Gospel of salvation by grace alone through faith alone in Christ alone to the glory of God alone back in the center of our vision because it, and it alone, is the power of God for salvation to those who believe (Rom. 1:16). We are looking for Evangelical unity, that is, unity around that Gospel and the doctrines that uphold and support it.

A good way of defining that Evangelical center of theological gravity would be to say it means informed commitment to the Nicene Creed and the five *Sola*s of the Reformation. The Nicene Creed still functions as a historic consensus on who God is and who Christ is that has commanded the assent of faithful Christians in all three branches of Christendom for more than a millennium and a half. A God who is the Father Almighty, the Maker of heaven and earth, and who has an only Son our Lord who is God of God and Light of Light, very God of very God, and who was made Man, is the foundation without which there can be no salvation that actually saves. Then the five principles that the Reformers held in common deal with problems and misunderstandings that arose in later centuries, focused on the Gospel itself. The exposition of them in the first five chapters of this book tries to bring out their accurate meaning, their grounding in Scripture, and their crucial relevance. If the Evangelical movement (or a remnant that arises out of its ashes) could rally around that flag once more, it could be a powerful force for the preaching of the Gospel again indeed.

Thesis 18b:
Historically, Reformation Was a Fruit of Renaissance and a Prerequisite to Revival.

※

Reformation, the recovery of sound doctrine, then, does not exist for its own sake but for the sake of the Gospel, for the sake of the God the Gospel glorifies, and for the sake of the lost human beings it saves. A new Reformation has been the focus of this book because a Revival of faithful and genuine Christian life and witness is the real need of the hour, and Reformation is a prerequisite to it that has so far been too much ignored. Why is Reformation a prerequisite to a deep Revival with lasting effects? You cannot return to the biblical Gospel unless you understand what it is. You cannot unleash the power of the Gospel in the church and then in society while the church is living in disobedience because it has allowed itself to be distracted by lesser concerns. So while we are praying and waiting for Revival, we should be working for Reformation.

Chapter 17 laid out how the historical Renaissance prepared the way for the Reformation and how we face in many ways a parallel situation again. So while we wait and pray for Revival, as we are advocating sound doctrine, we must also be modeling a restoration of Scripture to the place it deserves in the church. How? By restoring a proper respect for *all* texts and for reading as a practice by which we can actually receive real messages from the past. The message we receive from Scripture is infallible and the other messages are not; it is authoritative in a way that the other messages are not. But we cannot follow Scripture if we cannot read it; and we cannot read Scripture if we cannot *read*.[175] Before Scripture can rule us again, we need a Renaissance of right reading, of humble appreciation for, and a right relationship to, texts in general. Then we may have a chance to restore Scripture to its rightful place at the head of that army of texts.

We cannot read Scripture if we cannot *read*? Most of us can process letters into words, of course, but too many of us have lost the ability to see interpretation (an essential part of reading) as anything

---

175 For "read" you could substitute the verb "hear." Illiterate people are not exempt from responding properly to God's Word. For more on how to read (or hear), see *Inklings of Reality: Essays toward a Christian Philosophy of Letters* (Lynchburg: Lantern Hollow Press, 2012).

other than a house of mirrors. Just as Reformation is a prerequisite to Revival, a new recovery of grammatico-historical exegesis, a recovery of confidence in the ability of texts to communicate with us, is a prerequisite to Reformation. This is as true for us today as it was for the church in the Sixteenth Century. Back then, allegorical exegesis hindered texts from communicating their original meaning by assuming that every biblical text had a maximally rich plurality of almost endless meanings, in the pursuit of which the actual message could easily be lost. Our own false sophistication assumes that texts have *no* meaning of their own apart from what is supplied by the interpreter. The result is the same: the obscuring of the original meaning of the author—and, in the case of Scripture, of the Author.

How do we recover confidence that God can speak in the text of Scripture and that we can hear? We do it by remembering that we were created in His image, the image of the One who speaks. We do it by having faith in the Holy Spirit's ability to inspire the biblical authors and guarantee that they would faithfully communicate His message. And we do it by trusting with confidence that therefore the hermeneutical principles of chapter six when pursued humbly and in obedience will open our ears to hear and our eyes to see. Then, he who has ears to hear, let him hear what the Spirit saith to the churches!

This is the Renaissance we need. It is the Renaissance toward which we should work whether any further result comes from it or not, simply because it is the right thing to do. This is also the Renaissance whose fruit *might* in God's Providence be the Reformation that may prepare us for the Revival we so desperately need. Let it be so, dear Lord.

Thesis 18c:
Many So-Called Evangelicals Are Letting the Sound Teaching Recovered by the Original Reformers Slip through Their Fingers.

The Evangelical movement is facing a doctrinal crisis. It no longer knows what its theology is. One cannot make such a statement without being accused of broad generalizations, and indeed there are many churches and individuals who are stellar exceptions to the generalization. But people who have done the sociological homework confirm what anyone can hear who just keeps his ear to the ground.[176] Just think of the number of statements now commonplace within the Evangelical fold that would have marked a person as definitely outside of it just a couple of generations ago.

- Martin Luther got Paul's doctrine of justification by faith alone wrong.
- There was no literal historical Adam.
- A person can be saved without explicit faith in Christ, i.e., without hearing the Gospel and coming to believe it.
- Scripture is "inerrant," but the Gospel writers may have made things up and added them to the record as embellishments. (What "inerrant" means in such a scenario is a bit of a mystery.)
- Scripture is not inerrant.
- God is not omniscient (He does not know future contingent free choices of His creatures).
- Male headship in the home was either not taught in Scripture, or Paul did teach it but was wrong to do so.
- There is no distinction between men and women in terms of what offices they can hold in the church.
- God wants all His children to enjoy health and wealth in this life, and these blessings can be "named and claimed" by faith if one practices the correct spiritual techniques.

---

[176] For example, *James Davison Hunter, Evangelicalism: The Coming Generation* (Chicago: University of Chicago Press, 1987). Time has only confirmed what he saw coming a full generation ago. A recent work that confirms his diagnosis and charts the progress of the disease is Stephen Cable, *Cultural Captives: The Beliefs and Behavior of American Young Adults* (Dallas: Probe Ministries, 2012).

What is startling is not that such opinions exist, or even that they are held by increasing numbers, but that the will to regard them as beyond the pale has almost disappeared from large numbers even of those who do not hold them. The Evangelical movement has lost the ability and even the will to police its own borders. It is increasingly difficult even to know where the boundaries are—if indeed there are any left. As Hunter noticed as early as 1987, "There is less sharpness, less boldness, and accordingly a measure of opaqueness that did not exist in previous generations. . . . A dynamic would appear to be operating that strikes at the very heart of Evangelical self-identity."[177] David Wells helps us understand one element of that dynamic. We are simultaneously pulled by the world we live in toward accommodation to modernity and pushed in the same direction by our memory of the rigid Fundamentalist legalism we rightly left behind but against which we are still overreacting (See Appendix I here). "Evangelicalism has reacted against this sense of psychological isolation. It has lowered the barricades. It is open to the world." As a result, "the great sin in Fundamentalism is to compromise; the great sin in Evangelicalism is to be narrow."[178]

Adherents of each of the doctrinal departures listed above will argue that there are good reasons why traditional views needed to be revised. What we now know about Second-Temple Judaism or the human genome or the number of people who have never heard or Greco-Roman biography or the evils of patriarchy make previous views untenable, they say. Yet in each case when we study the issues in greater depth we find that it is not so simple as we were led to believe. We discover that very plausible paths to reaffirming the theology we received from our ancestors with intellectual integrity, or at least withholding judgment on the urgent demand to abandon it, exist. Why then this embarrassingly pitiful eagerness to abandon it? Is the approval of the unbelieving world inside and outside of the church that appealing to us? Have we forgotten the Gospel by which we were saved and failed to understand the essential theological underpinnings that alone can make it work? Or were we never saved by it at all, so that a free conscience able to stand before God clothed in the righteousness of Christ and not dependent on our own works is not

---

177 Ibid., p. 46.

178 David F. Wells, *No Place for Truth, or, Whatever Happened to Evangelical Theology?* (Grand Rapids: Eerdmans, 1993), p. 129.

really all that valuable to us because we have never truly experienced it? The prevalence of preaching that is hard to distinguish from Moral Therapeutic Deism makes one wonder. Combining an emphasis on experience over truth (Theses 14a-e) with our failure to practice the Great Commission in the terms in which it was given and make disciples, not just converts (Theses 11a-e) could certainly be counted on to produce a glut of false "conversions," of people who claim a "born-again experience" without ever having been born again—or at least not born again clearly enough so anyone can tell.

One must not make assumptions about motives in individual cases, but it is hard not to conclude that some combination of such factors has to account for much of our slide as a larger religious community. There are a great number of reforms we need as an Evangelical movement, but central to all of them is recapturing a clear vision of the biblical Gospel and getting it back into the center of our religious life. That is Reformation, the recovery of sound doctrine, in a nutshell.

Thesis 18d:
These Ninety-Five Theses Represent Areas in Which a New Reformation Is Required.

☙

Martin Luther did us a great favor by posting only ninety-five Theses, because that number gave me a convenient place at which to stop. No doubt we can easily think of more areas in which reform is needed, and many more again that might apply only to specific sub-groupings within the Evangelical world. But perhaps my project has been over-ambitious already. At least I hope it is not wholly incoherent. I have tried to put together ninety-five theses stretching across nineteen topical provinces that could let us regain the ground we have lost and maybe capture more solidly a few acres of terrain that we never fully conquered but which would solidify our holdings, being adjacent to the heights we as Evangelicals once claimed.

We started by reconnecting to the five Reformation *sola*s, which give us the formal and material principles of Evangelical faith. We have to learn to relate properly again to the magisterial authority of Scripture and the ministerial authority of Reason, Tradition, Experience, and church leaders, or we have no solid foundation on which to build anything else (chapter 1). Then the Gospel of salvation by grace alone through faith alone in Christ alone, for the glory of God alone, is our *raison d'etre* (chapters 2-5). Evangelicalism took its name from the Gospel of vicarious penal substitution and forensic justification, and needs to remember that it must be preserved intact and proclaimed with power because it alone is the power of God for salvation for those who believe.

Then we moved into other areas that need to be healthy if the Gospel is to be proclaimed with integrity and credibility. Scripture has to be interpreted in ways that allow its original message to be heard and understood with clarity or we cut ourselves off from our marching orders and try to fight blind (chapter 6). The church's ministry, its worship, and its organization are ordained by Scripture to create a community of faith in the context of which the faith in Christ by which we are saved makes sense (chapters 7-9). That community needs to be rightly receptive to the power of the Holy Spirit and not confuse it with forced emotional hype if it is to live out its faith fully and convincingly (chapter 10). It needs, out of the spiritual health flowing from its ministry, worship, and life in the Spirit, to fulfill the Great Commission as it was actually given and make disciples, not just converts (chapter 11). In so doing, it preaches the Gospel as truth that is grounded in reality and can be defended with reason and evidence (chapter 12). In so doing, its activity has the byproduct of offering not just eternal salvation but also temporal salt and light that impacts the surrounding culture to show that the Gospel *is* light and life, both in eternity and here and now (chapter 13).

Meanwhile, in their journey through history Evangelicals have forgotten some important parts of their heritage that impact their ability to live a healthy spiritual life. They need to remember the wholeness of the life lived by their forebears in the First Great Awakening so that they can relate rightly to both their emotions (chapter 14) and to their intellect (chapter 15). They will not be able to maintain and transmit that wholeness or the truths on which it depends without a more serious approach to education (chapter 16). Finally, to bring all of this to pass, they need to experience once again the three great movements of God that alone can get them back on track: Renaissance, a recovery of the life of the mind (chapter 17), Reformation, a recovery of sound doctrine (chapter 18), and Revival, a recovery of vital spirituality in which all of these reforms cease being mere ideas and proposals and actually come to life (chapter 19).

I hope then that my ninety-five theses in these nineteen areas are not just ninety-five random proposals that I happen to favor but represent a coherent whole, a vision that hangs together. I hope it has the unity of the life we should be presenting to the world if we want to proclaim the Gospel with fresh power, the life we should be receiving from the Father if we want to please Him by glorifying His Son. You may not agree with all ninety-five of them—that would be a lot of agreement! But if you find any of them helpful, if any of them strike you as coming with conviction from a higher Authority than mine, then begin where you are, in your home and your church, to implement them. And may Christ be glorified and His church reformed by those efforts! Amen.

Thesis 18e:
The Only Way To Be Faithful to the Original Reformation Is by Continuing To Pursue the Ongoing Reformation of the Church.

✍

One of the slogans of the Reformation that is often forgotten is that the church should be *semper reformata*, always reformed, because it is *semper reformanda*, always reforming. (Those actual phrases were coined a bit later, but the idea is certainly present in the Reformers.) It is a recognition that as a body whose membership on earth is made up entirely of sinners, the church always contains the seeds of its own destruction, seeds which will germinate the very moment it forgets its entire dependence on God's Gospel for its existence, God's Son as its Head, God's Word for its direction, God's Spirit for its power, and God's grace for its health.

It would be a capital mistake then to think that if we could just implement these ninety-five proposals all would be well, the church would march forward victoriously, and we could relax. I think it would be a great thing for the Evangelical movement and its churches and the Kingdom if even a goodly number of them were put on the ground, but that very day the temptation to compromise and corruption would already be at work. And the very next day, even if every reform was still preserved in its full integrity, new problems would come to light that would need to be addressed.

We should not be shocked by this realization. Even if we had living Apostles walking amongst us, we would not be exempt from the necessity of maintaining continual vigilance for Reformation. If we had the Apostle Paul with us today, he would have all he could do to protect some modern Galatia from contemporary Judaizers and some modern Corinth from itself. If John were still with us he would have no difficulty finding seven churches who needed to hear, "Yet I have somewhat against thee." He who hath ears to hear, let him hear. This is what Reformation is all about. And, oh: We do still have them with us, through their writings in the New Testament! And so we must continue to follow them, beginning anew every day.

The very first of Martin Luther's original theses portrayed the

Christian life as one of continual repentance, for indeed the prayer for forgiveness is basic enough to find its place in the Lord's model prayer.[179] We hope for many spiritual victories and many positive gains in sanctification, but neither churches nor individuals will in this life ever completely outlive the need to pray, "Forgive us our trespasses" (Mat. 6:12). Thankfully, if we are faithful to confess our sins, He is faithful and just to forgive us our sins, and cleanse us from all unrighteousness (1 John 1:9). That is what it is to be always reforming.

If ongoing Reformation is to be part of the church's life, two practices must be faithfully maintained: speaking the truth in love and church discipline. Without an ingrained habit of speaking the truth in love, church discipline deteriorates into a witch-hunt for people who do not line up with every jot and tittle of our personal theological opinions. Without a serious commitment to discipline, the love with which we purport to speak the truth will quickly deteriorate into tolerance for every wind of doctrine and eventually heresy. (See Appendix I for further discussion of discipline and the problems associated with it.) If the Fundamentalist movement is replete with instances of the first failure, the Protestant mainline abounds with examples of the second—and too many Evangelical organizations are making up for lost time in catching up with it. In neither case can the church effectively function as the pillar and support of the truth which Paul insists it should be (1 Tim. 3:15).

To maintain its integrity, every congregation, every denomination, every Christian school, college, or seminary, every mission board, and every parachurch organization needs to have a clear doctrinal statement which its officers and teachers are expected to sign annually. The statement should commit it to Nicene orthodoxy and to the five Reformation *Sola*s, and be forthright and open about any denominational or doctrinal distinctives beyond that core of belief that the organization thinks are important. The organization should be upfront about and unashamed of its distinctives, but have a genuinely collegial and cooperative (yea, *loving*) relationship with any group that shares the doctrinal core. Its leadership should exercise continual pastoral oversight to see that its operatives fully embody the spirit as well as the letter of that doctrine. And its lay constituency must

---

[179] John Warwick Montgomery, *In Defense of Martin Luther* (Milwaukee: Northwestern Publishing House, 1970), p. 20.

be diligent to see that these things are being done before they give it their membership, money, or time and labor. (If the constituencies of a number of Christian colleges knew what was being taught in their schools, they would be shocked and horrified.) Mutual accountability is not optional if any of our institutions are to be and remain healthy. None of this guarantees the ongoing Reformation of the church, but these are conditions that make it possible. They should therefore be maintained with diligence. It only requires one break in this chain of accountability for all to be undone.

Conclusion

The program laid out above makes ongoing Reformation possible, but even if all this is done it will not succeed without genuine love for the Lord, His Word, His Gospel, and His people, leading to radical dependence on His grace. Apart from these loves, no one should presume to handle sacred things. We should be asking God to call into ministry, and we should seek to promote into leadership, people of competence and discernment who have those loves deeply and show them infectiously. Then we might see here and now more foreglimpses of the church as she will be when she is revealed at the Marriage Feast: glorious, without spot or wrinkle, washed in the Blood of the Lamb. Even so, come, Lord Jesus!

Interlude
Three Cities:
A Reformation Triptych

Rome
Stained light slanting through the dusty air
    Pointed to the alcove in the nave
    Where in his silent niche the stone saint stood.
Beneath his cool and quiet marble stare
    Passed countless pilgrims marching to the grave;
    He never thought to do them any good.

The contrast, sharp as flesh stripped bare to bone:
    The bone-white marble, impotent to save,
    The flesh flowing past in hopes it would,
Stained red where in his silent niche the stone
    Saint stood.

Wittenberg
Four nails driven deep into the door:
    "The coin into the coffer springs no soul."
    Then, "I can do no other; here I stand."
Because he'd plumbed the Gospel to its core,
    The true treasure of the Church, extolled
    God's grace—for this he had his teaching banned,

Himself, too. In the Wartburg hid for fear,
    Translated Scripture, preached like thunder, told
    Katie he would, the Pope he wouldn't, and
Roared laughing, "I can do no other; here
    I stand."

Geneva
Luther learned the Gospel in his gut
    And taught that Reason was the Devil's whore.
    Calvin fed his mind upon the Book
Until, reformed and sanctified, the slut

Walked saved and singing through the Church's door,
Where all her former thoughts she clean forsook.

The Lord repaired the eyes of one born blind
In Scripture, and he did it one time more:
And fearfully the Devil's kingdom shook
When God fixed Luther's heart and Calvin's mind
Upon the Book.[180]

---

[180] Donald T. Williams, *Stars through the Clouds*, op. cit., p. 311-12.

19
Five Theses on Revival

What is the fruit of Reformation?

Five Theses on Revival

A. Revival is a recovery of vital spirituality. (Revival is not a synonym for evangelism. It restores the church to its proper role and believers to proper seriousness, joy, and devotion; and evangelism is a byproduct.)

B. Revival is a desperate need of the contemporary church, especially its Evangelical wing. (Emotional hype is not spirituality, and more emotional hype is not revival. Worldliness in the church must be eradicated not by guilt but by a true outpouring of the Spirit; see Theses 10.c-d.)

C. Revival cannot be scheduled or arranged by human action however well intentioned, conceived, or executed, but can only come through a strong, supernatural reassertion of God's grace. (Our busyness without that reassertion on the part of a sovereign God produces only busyness.)

D. That strong movement of God's grace can be prepared for by prayer and faithfulness on the part of the Remnant, but it still waits on God's sovereign action. (We should understand what we are praying for.)

E. Historically, a deep and long-lasting revival must be preceded and prepared for by Renaissance and Reformation. (We should not stop praying for Revival, but we should start praying and working for Renaissance and Reformation.)

"We live in an age of small things," lamented D. Martyn Lloyd-Jones of the state of Christian spirituality in his day.[181] Judging by the plentiful lack of lasting effects in many the conversions we think we have recorded, things seem only to have gotten smaller. The need for the kind of Revival we have not seen in many years is obvious to many. We have spent this book arguing that we need something even more basic, a new Reformation. By itself it will mean little unless it leads to revival. But Revival is one of the most misunderstood phenomena in Christian history. What is a true Revival, and how can we best seek it? In our pursuit of Reformation, these are the questions to which we are inevitably led.[182]

---

181 D. Martyn Lloyd-Jones, *Revival* (Westchester, Il.: Crossway, 1987), p. 179.

182 The most paradigmatic revival in history may be the First Great Awakening. The most basic source for it is Alan Heimert and Perry Miller, eds. *The Great Awakening: Documents Illustrating the Crisis and its Consequences* (Indianapolis: Bobbs-Merrill, 1967). A complementary collection of primary source documents with excellent introductions and commentary is David Lyle Jeffrey, ed., *A Burning and a Shining Light: English Spirituality in the Age of Wesley* (Grand Rapids: Eerdmans, 1987). For an eyewitness account by a major player with analysis brilliant and profound, see Jonathan Edwards, *A Treatise Concerning Religious Affections* (1746; New Haven: Yale, 1959). For the history of revival in the Twentieth Century, see J. Edwin Orr, *The Flaming Tongue: The Impact of Twentieth Century Revivals* (Chicago: Moody, 1973). The best summation and application of all that material is D. Martyn Lloyd-Jones, *Revival* (Westchester, Il.: Crossway, 1987).

Thesis 19a:
Revival Is a Recovery of Vital Spirituality.

When I was a boy in what was then rural Georgia, we all thought we knew what a Revival was. It was a week of extra church services with somebody who was not our regular preacher, to which we were urged to invite our unsaved friends and neighbors so they could get saved. It came along every summer as regular as clockwork. It even worked, to a point, because it was competing with only three television channels that were all playing summer reruns. You could sing the hymns with gusto, the preaching would have some good fire-and-brimstone imagery, and the altar call added an element of drama, so it was somewhat entertaining. Some people did get saved, and for this we must be grateful. There is certainly nothing wrong with a church throwing an evangelistic crusade, and the method at the time was not wholly ineffective. But why did we call it a "Revival?" What exactly was getting revived? I did not of course ask that question until much later.

When I grew up and began to study church history, I realized that these evangelistic meetings were called Revivals out of a combination of nostalgia and wishful thinking: nostalgia for great movements of God in the past that had changed the religious and cultural landscape of communities and nations, and hope that if we prayed and invited and preached hard enough we could make it happen again. Our efforts were by God's grace not wholly in vain, but there was no third Great Awakening. If we got a few conversions and rededications and a brief spike in attendance, we persuaded ourselves that there had been one. We had become confused about what we were looking for and where it comes from.

Historically, a Revival is an unusual movement of the Spirit of God in the church which restores a more serious practice of biblical Christianity on the part of people who are already in the church. The sense of sin, the conviction of sin, and the liberation from sin provided by the Gospel become more real to them in an intense way leading to prostration over sin, confession of sin, and exuberant joy over the forgiveness of sin. What is "revived" then is simply a fuller appreciation of the astounding reality of what Christian faith had offered all along.

Regularly scheduled services are typically unable to contain what is happening so that extended meetings and extra meetings result spontaneously. Evangelism of those outside the church results as a byproduct of Revival as outsiders become curious about what is happening inside. The moral tone of the whole community is often raised as a result, not because Christians are picketing, protesting, or boycotting sinful businesses but simply because the demand for their products dries up. In our ignorance today we get things backwards, thinking that if we aim for the effects (extended meetings, evangelism) we will get the cause (Revival). Our desire is noble and our zeal laudable, but our methods are flawed: It just does not seem to work that way.

If we find such a phenomenon as I just described hard to imagine today, that is because we have not seen it on a large scale in our lifetime. Therefore, the historical documentation of actual occurrences of it by Edwards, Orr, Jeffrey, and Lloyd-Jones cited above is indispensable if we are to be convinced that such things have truly been the experience of our ancestors. Many historians believe that the Revival we call the First Great Awakening in England in the Eighteenth Century was so powerful as to save Britain from going through the kind of turmoil that resulted in the Reign of Terror of the French Revolution. Through its sons John Newton and William Wilberforce, the Awakening certainly had the not inconsiderable political fruit of the abolition of the slave trade in Britain. As J. R. Green summarizes it, the Revival

> changed . . . the whole tone of English society. . . . The [established] church was restored to new life and activity. Religion carried to the hearts of the people a fresh spirit of moral zeal, while it purified our literature and our manners. A new philanthropy reformed our prisons, infused clemency and wisdom into our penal laws, abolished the slave trade, and gave the first impulse to popular education.[183]

"The first impulse to popular education?" In a reform typical of that Awakening, Sunday School was invented by Robert Raikes, not as a dispenser of Bible stories but as a ministry to teach literacy to children whose employment in the factories prevented them from at-

---

183 J. R. Green, *A Short History of the English People* (London, 1877-79; qutd. In Jeffrey, op. cit.), p. 23.

tending a regular school. It was held on Sunday afternoon because that was the only time the children could come.

Jeffrey's introduction to the period at the head of his anthology is one of the finest short pieces of historical writing you will ever read.[184] The depressed condition of biblical Christianity in England beforehand reminds one of nothing so much as that of our own day. For our theological liberalism they had Deism and Latitudinarianism, with like effects on the churches. For our drug culture they had demon rum. (The English had always been great beer drinkers, but the recent introduction of stronger distilled liquors had a devastating effect on the lower classes.) And parallel to abortion on demand, they had the slave trade, with a similar moral degradation of the whole of society flowing from arbitrarily declaring one segment of the family of man to be sub-human so it could be deprived of its rights. So the situation, then as now, was seriously a matter of great concern.

While preparations in the prayers of faithful Christians could be found after the fact, nobody at the time saw any such Revival coming. People were actually debating whether Christianity had a future in England. Yet the fruits of that mighty work of God changed the face of England and America, and through them the world. That change included not only the abolition of the slave trade but also prison reform and the ending of child labor so that Sunday School could be repurposed into what we know today. Though they have largely forgotten it, Evangelicals today owe their existence as a movement to the supernatural turnaround that God enabled then.

Two conclusions should be clear from this history. First, nothing less than a similar movement of the Spirit of God can suffice to reverse the compromised condition of the church today. And second, when we say that Revival is a restoration of vital Christian spirituality, we mean a holistic approach to Christian belief and practice that not only involves repentance from personal sin but also applies a robust understanding of and application of the whole counsel of God to all of life—the kind of understanding that can only come from Renaissance and Reformation as we have tried to set them forth here.

---

184 David Lyle Jeffrey, *A Burning and a Shining Light*, op. cit., pp. 1-52.

Thesis 19b:
Revival Is a Desperate Need of the Contemporary Church, Especially Its Evangelical Wing.

⌘

Does Evangelical Christianity in the United States of America need Revival? Objective facts and figures tell a mixed story. While they do not show the precipitous decline that is typical of the mainline, most Evangelical denominations in America are plateaued at best. (Some can show growth, but only by counting their mission churches overseas.) In 2017, for one example, the Southern Baptist Convention, the largest Protestant denomination with an Evangelical bent, saw a marginal increase in average weekly attendance (from 5,200,716 to 5,320,488) but a decrease in membership (from 15,216,978 to 15,005,638). These figures should be taken with a grain of salt because fewer churches reported their statistics than in previous years. More significant, however, may be the decline in baptisms (from 280,773 to 254,122 between 2016 and 2017), given the fact that baptisms have declined for eight of the last ten years, with 26.5 percent fewer in 2017 than in 2007.[185] Also more significant in these numbers is the fact that only one third of *members* bother to show up on any given Sunday. What does that ratio suggest that membership means to the average Southern Baptist? How important can the worship of God and the proclamation of His Gospel and the advancement of His kingdom be to people who manifest such a pattern of church attendance? That one fact alone should signal loudly that we have a serious problem.

Statistics are one thing. Far more concerning are intangible factors that are harder to measure. Only ten righteous men would have sufficed to save Sodom and Gomorrah (Gen. 18:32). So with all of our numbers and activity, where is our influence on American society and culture? We have been fighting the pro-life battle since Roe v. Wade in 1973 and still have hardly any traction on that issue. That court decision galvanized us into political activism—I would say rightly so,

---

[185] Lisa Cannon Green, "Worship Attendance Rises, Baptisms Decline in SBC." *Facts and Trends Newsletter* (June 1, 2018). https://factsandtrends.net/2018/06/01/worship-attendance-rises-baptisms-decline-in-sbc/. Cf. Aaron Earls, "Small, Struggling Congregations Fill U.S. Church Landscape." *Lifewayresearch.com* (March 8, 2019). https://lifewayresearch.com/2019/03/06/small-struggling-congregations-fill-u-s-church-landscape/.

because such an unjust law depriving the most vulnerable members of society of their right to life cannot be ignored, and must be actively opposed, by anyone with any claim to be a good citizen—but did we match our new-found political activism with an equal effort to change hearts and minds by speaking the truth in love? By proclaiming the Gospel in such a way that we made *disciples* whom we taught the implications of the biblical worldview? Apparently not; if we had done so, it is hard to imagine that our political efforts would have been so ineffective. Now the sudden flipping of public opinion on homosexuality and transgender issues over the last decade has caught us off guard and is making its inroads into even (formerly) conservative churches. No one can claim that the influence of the church on the world is growing; the influence of the world on the church is another matter altogether.

Meanwhile, we can now conduct our in-house conversations in front of the world on Facebook, a cursory sampling of which will easily show why the world thinks of us as primarily interested in judgmental, self-righteous, mindless ranting about our own petty squabbles. We've always had a problem with shooting our own wounded, but now social media lets us do it much more immediately, publicly, and dramatically. Then there are the numerous examples of unfaithfulness in doctrine, balance, and practice addressed by the calls to Reformation in previous chapters.

Yes, Evangelical Christianity needs Reformation and it needs Revival, and it is hard to see how either can happen without the other. Reformation is needed to restore the boundaries and forms of faithful content and healthy practice that need to be filled with the restored spiritual life that comes from Revival, and Revival is needed to fill that restored framework with new life. I have presented Reformation as a prerequisite to Revival because historically that is the way it happened, as the gains of the Reformation were consolidated, renewed, and built on by the Puritanism of the Seventeenth Century and the Pietism (the older and healthier strain) of the Eighteenth. In fact, Reformation and Revival may need to come together this time. Without Reformation, Revival will dissipate and flow off into the sand; without Revival, Reformation will lack power and life. May God have mercy on us and send both!

If you think Evangelical Christianity in America is just fine and does not need Reformation or Revival; if you think business as usual is quite sufficient for the needs of the hour; well, then, continue serving the Lord as He gives you the light to do it, and may He bless your efforts. But do not be offended if some of the rest of us are moved ask God for a little more. And if business as usual no longer satisfies . . . please join us. Let us pray.

Thesis 19c:
Revival Cannot Be Scheduled or Arranged by Human Action However Well Intentioned, Conceived, or Executed, but Can Only Come Through a Strong, Supernatural Reassertion of God's Grace.

This thesis would have been considered a truism by Jonathan Edwards and the other participants in the First Great Awakening of the Eighteenth Century. By the Second Great Awakening in the middle of the Nineteenth Century, the assumptions had changed radically. The catalyst behind the change was the greatest evangelist of that age, Charles Grandison Finney.[186] Finney's success as an evangelist, and perhaps more his understanding of his own success, changed the face of American Christianity.

Though they were certainly men of parts who fully consecrated their considerable gifts to the Lord's service, it never seems to have occurred to the Wesleys, Whitefield, or Edwards to attribute the impressive results of their preaching to their own superior skill or methodology or planning. Edwards for example, composed *A Faithful Narrative of the Surprising Work of God*. The word *surprising* and the phrase *work of God* are the keys to how he viewed his own success. A century later, Finney enjoyed a comparable effectiveness in his own evangelistic efforts. He, on the other hand, thought he knew exactly how his success had been pulled off. Revival, he claimed, "is not a miracle, or dependent on a miracle, in any sense. It is a purely philosophical result of the right use of the constituted means."[187] And he proposed to teach us what those means are, the "natural result" of which will be Revival if we use them correctly and God blesses

---

[186] The depth of Finney's influence on Twentieth-Century Evangelicalism can be seen in the uncritical acceptance of his methods by Wheaton College president V. Raymond Edman in *Finney Lives On: The Man, His Revival Methods, and His Message* (N.Y.: Fleming H. Revell, 1951). A good, balanced biography that puts Finney's career in perspective (but could also stand to be more critical) is Charles E. Hambrick-Stowe, *Charles G. Finney and the Spirit of American Evangelicalism* (Grand Rapids: Eerdmans, 1996).

[187] Charles Grandison Finney, *Lectures on Revivals of Religion*, ed. William G. McLoughlin (1835; Cambridge, Ma.: Harvard University Press, 1960), p. 13.

them.[188] Finney basically thought he could reduce Revival to a science. Preach the gospel persuasively, argue for it like a lawyer, preach for decision, call for an immediate response, and you will get it.

The frequency with which he did get a response makes Finney's assumption of the efficacy and sufficiency of his method understandable. That assumption was brought into the Twentieth Century by no less influential a figure than Billy Graham, who wrote on the dustjacket of Wheaton College president V. Raymond Edman's admiring book on Finney in 1951, "To read, study, and pray over this book is an imperative for every Christian worker in such an hour as this."[189] Graham took over Finney's approach and also had, or seemed to have had, impressive results. Graham became the focal point for Evangelical identity in the second half of the Twentieth Century, and so the subtle shift from understanding Revival as primarily something God does for us to something we do for Him was solidified. But while a number of genuine conversions did take place (along with many more that did not manifest the fruit of real faith—see Theses 11c-e), a very important question largely went unasked: Was this really *Revival* as that word has been understood here (Thesis 19a)? When we compare its lasting fruits to the historical accounts of the First Great Awakening, an affirmative answer is not at all self-evident.

The method might be useful at certain times and in certain situations and in the hands of certain gifted people. The evidence that it is *sufficient* even for evangelism, much less for true Revival, is lacking. The claim of sufficiency comports with neither Scripture nor history. Biblically the evidence for total inability and our total dependence on the divine initiative is too strong. The natural man cannot do what Finney thought he could, decide to obey God.[190] "But a natural man does not accept the things of the Spirit of God, for they are foolishness to him, and he cannot understand them because they are spiritually appraised" (1 Cor. 2:14). And true conversion is a supernatural act—a miracle—because we are "born not of the blood, nor of the will of the flesh, nor of the will of man, but of God" (John 1:13). A theology that takes those passages seriously does not, as Finney thought, give the sinner an excuse; rather, it focuses his attention on

---

188 Ibid.

189 Billy Graham, blurb on the dustjacket of Edman, *Finney Lives On*, op. cit.

190 "Religion is the work of man. It is something for man to do. It consists in obeying God." Finney, *Lectures on Revivals of Religion,* op. cit., p. 9.

the only place where there is any hope, on the grace of God alone. A clearer grasp of the Reformation Gospel, including total inability, did not hinder Edwards or Whitefield from being used to reap a great harvest of saved sinners. But somehow we have now convinced ourselves that we cannot preach effectively without the semi-Pelagian assumptions that Finney thought to be the key to his success.

Historically, the evidence for the sufficiency of Finney's measures is no stronger. Lloyd-Jones notes "the tragic blunder of Finney":

> He thought that you can have a revival whenever you like, if you only do certain things and fulfill certain conditions. It is a complete denial of the sovereignty of God. Not only that, it is proved by history to be wrong. I, in my own lifetime, have known numbers of ministers who have taken Finney's lectures on revival and have honestly put them into practice in their preaching and in their churches, and have persuaded their people to do them. But they have not had a revival.[191]

We all know such ministers. Many of us have been such ministers. Finney's book contains a lot of practical wisdom and recommends measures that God has indeed sometimes blessed. Nevertheless, it suffers from the fatal assumption that his measures are in themselves sufficient, an assumption that flows from an inadequate understanding both of the depths of sin and the power of grace. That assumption has drained the Evangelical movement of much of the power that it might have had. It needs to remember that Revival cannot be scheduled or arranged by human action however well intentioned, conceived, or executed, but can only come through a strong, supernatural reassertion of God's grace. That does not mean that we stop acting, or stop acting intelligently, or abandon our good intentions; it does not mean we stop preaching or even stop having crusades; it does not even mean that we ignore all of Finney's sometimes wise advice. It does mean that we would do these things in a different spirit, with the potential for different results when God in His sovereign grace decides to transcend those efforts. Then we might indeed live to see that third Great Awakening that we need so desperately.

---

191 D. Martyn Lloyd-Jones, *Revival*, op. cit., p. 235.

Thesis 19d:
That Strong Movement of God's Grace Can Be Prepared for by Prayer and Faithfulness on the Part of the Remnant, but It Still Waits on God's Sovereign Action.

✠

There is a false dilemma to which our finite minds are subject, and which must be firmly rejected if we are to think profitably about how to parse God's work in salvation and man's response to it. The same false dilemma rears its ugly head in any discussion of Revival. It seems that if salvation is all of grace and not in any sense the result of works, then human beings must be passive puppets in the process whose repentance, faith, and obedience mean nothing. It seems that if the natural man is incapable of receiving the Gospel it hardly matters whether we preach it to him. If he is incapable of repentance, how can we ask him to repent? How can God hold him accountable for his failure to repent? It seems to us that we must either choose what Francis Schaeffer called (divine) sovereignty or (human) significance. It seems to us that we cannot have both of those realities. Yet the Bible teaches both and will neither allow any compromise between them nor countenance the shoving of either under the rug. As Schaeffer once said, "The Bible simply states both and walks away."[192] And so must we.

We cannot explain *how* both doctrines can be true, any more than we can explain how light can be simultaneously a particle and a wave. We still have to accept that photons are somehow both to make our physics equations work. In like manner, we cannot see how our will relates to God's sovereignty because our will is too close to us to be examined and God is too big to be seen. And as it is *our* will we are trying to relate to His, we are standing on one of the very objects we are trying to lift. We believe and trust that the God of truth who cannot lie has a perfectly rational explanation for how we have both His sovereignty and our significance, but we are not in a position in this life to understand it. We still have to accept it to make our theology work. It must be true because somehow we *have* received salvation. We, really we, received, really received, a salvation we could not have

---
[192] The statement occurs, not in any of Schaeffer's books, but in a taped lecture I once heard.

received and would not even have desired to receive if left to ourselves. So we exercise our faith as if it were really ours and then say that even that faith is the gift of God because salvation is all of grace lest any man should boast (Eph. 2:8-10). The Bible states both and walks away, and so must we.

Our belief that salvation is by grace alone apart from works does not stop us from preaching the Gospel and calling on men to repent and believe. In fact, our very belief in God's ability to save by grace alone is what makes that call for response worth making. In just the same way, the humble realization that we cannot engineer a Revival through our own efforts, however well intentioned, sincere, and intelligently adapted to the need they may be, does not stop us from praying. It should not stop us from talking about Revival or calling for it or even from organizing meetings. We cannot cause a Revival to happen, but we can quench the Spirit through our complacency, our pride, our disobedience, or our bad theology. So we try to break up the stony ground and fertilize it and we sow the Seed and water it, knowing that only God gives the increase. He may bring the harvest in spite of our bad efforts as much as because of our good ones. But we make good efforts, not because we are under the delusion that they can ever be good enough to cause Revival on their own or to merit it from God, but because it is that kind of cultivation that the Master of the field deserves from us, His laborers. And when the great harvest comes, we give all the glory to Him.

Thesis 19e:
Historically, a Deep And Long-Lasting Revival Must Be Preceded and Prepared for by Renaissance and Reformation.

We live in the tension between sovereignty and significance because, in a world created by God as the dwelling place of creatures made in His image, that is the only place that exists where we can live. So while we know that our efforts cannot bring Revival, we also know that God may graciously use them to bring it anyway. And while our efforts cannot guarantee that a Revival God sends us will be deep and long-lasting in its effects, God may graciously use them to that end also. So it has typically happened in history, the Renaissance and Reformation we have so often referenced in this study being prime examples as they set the stage for the First Great Awakening.

We have spent many pages laboring to make clear the historical connections between Renaissance, Reformation, and Revival. (See especially Theses 17b-c.). Those connections are a great testimony to the wisdom and Providence of God, for the humanist scholars who gave birth to the *ad fontes* tradition in the Renaissance were not aiming at Reformation in their efforts. Nevertheless, God in His wisdom used those efforts mightily to facilitate the Reformation that the church so badly needed. Working consciously to replicate those conditions today does not guarantee that we will see like results, but it does make those results more likely. And so we make our own efforts in pursuit of Renaissance and Reformation, not because we trust in them, but because we trust in Him.

Conclusion

Understanding this, we do not deceive ourselves into thinking that we can lay the foundation for a deep and long-lasting Revival simply by implementing hard enough and well enough the reforms urged by this book. We pursue them because we are persuaded that they the right things to do, and leave the results in the hands of God. But we do understand that, historically, a pattern emerges in which God has blessed such efforts before. If He does it again, it will be an act of pure grace on His part. It is our part to put ourselves in the place where that blessing is likely to fall, and that place is the path of obedience. And so we work, and so we pray, believing that our labor is not in vain in the Lord (1 Cor. 15:58).

Interlude
The Lord's Work

In the name of the Father,
For the sake of the Son,
By the aid of the Spirit
All that is worthy is done:

All that's a boon to the Body,
Knitting its sinews in love,
Taking the News to the nations,
Born on the wings of the Dove,

For the increase of the Kingdom,
Unto the glory of Grace,
By the means of the Mercy,
Longing to look on the Face.[193]

---

193 Donald T. Williams, *Stars through the Clouds*, op. cit., p. 167.

Excursus I
The Integrity of the Organized Church

The focus of the Reformation sought in this book has been conservative, Bible-believing, Gospel-oriented Protestant Christianity, primarily as it exists in The United States, though with relevance to the same movement as it is found in the Anglosphere in particular and the world in general. In most cases the theses set forth here are simply asking for a return to the best of our history and our Evangelical heritage as it has come down to us from the original Reformation of the Sixteenth Century through the Puritans of the Seventeenth and the First Great Awakening of the Eighteenth. As such they are aimed at Fundamentalists and their Evangelical heirs and mainly represent positions that for most of the history of those movements would not have been considered controversial. Even the one chapter that might be considered an exception to this generalization, the one on Charismatic phenomena, would hardly have been so before the early Twentieth Century. That there is no consensus currently on many of the topics of the other chapters is an indication of how far we have been diverted from that history and that heritage.

My own theological position would be described as basically Reformed. I am a moderate (decidedly non-hyper) Calvinist. But nothing in those chapters requires an understanding that is not classically *Evangelical*. I have argued for no denominational distinctives whatever. The Reformation we seek is not of Calvinists or Arminians, nor of Baptists, Methodists, Presbyterians, Lutherans, Anglicans, or Independents; it is for the *Evangelicals*, the Bible believers who want to be faithful in preaching the biblical Gospel, of all those persuasions. Further theses might well be needed by any of those smaller groupings, but that is not our focus here. Ninety-Five Theses are quite enough to start with!

There is one serious reform that is needed however that splits my target group right down the middle. For that reason it does not fit with the other ninety-five, but without it none of them can be pursued to full fruition. I will therefore deal with it separately here in this appendix. It is what Francis Schaeffer called "the practice of the purity of the visible church."[194] To understand the significance of that phrase we have to begin with some history.

By the 1920s and 30s, most of the mainline denominations in the United States had been infiltrated by theological liberalism to the point of serious compromise. Pastors, seminary professors, and missionaries speaking in the name of their church could deny the inspiration and full truthfulness and reliability of the Bible, the virgin birth and full deity of Christ, the necessity of vicarious substitutionary atonement in His blood, or a literal personal second coming, and either they or people who had no problem with them were in such control of the denominational hierarchy that discipline was not possible. A movement arose to contest this situation: Fundamentalism, so known for its adherence to the five "fundamentals" of the faith. They were the inspiration and authority of the Bible; the deity of Christ; the historicity of the New-Testament miracles, especially the virgin birth and the literal, bodily resurrection of Christ; the necessity of vicarious atonement in Jesus' blood; and a literal and personal future second coming of Christ. You were a Fundamentalist if you believed that these five doctrines were true in themselves *and* that they were essential to the Christian faith. People who did not believe them were not true Christians.

The Fundamentalists' first idea was not to repudiate the denominations but to reclaim them for the Gospel and the historic Christian faith. But by the time they recognized the problem and got organized, the deck was already stacked against them. A pivotal moment was the defrocking of Fundamentalist leader J. Gresham Machen by the Northern Presbyterians in 1936. Rather than exercising discipline, the conservatives found themselves *subject* to discipline for the crime of insisting on faithfulness to the Scriptures and the historic creeds. Machen did not leave; he was thrown out, and so had no choice but to start the Orthodox Presbyterian Church (OPC). After that point many Fundamentalists came to the conclusion that the old denominational structures were not salvageable, and they left to either become independents or start smaller denominations like the OPC that would be faithful to Scripture.

---

194 Francis A. Schaeffer, *The Church before the Watching World* (Downers Grove, Il.: InterVarsity, 1971), pp. 61, 74f; cf. *The Great Evangelical Disaster*, op. cit., pp. 85f, 126.

This exodus precipitated a crisis within the Fundamentalist movement itself. Not all the original Fundamentalists felt called upon to leave and join the "Come-Outers." Some convinced themselves that the situation was not so dire or felt called to stay in and continue trying to witness to the truth where they were rather than abandoning the old denominations completely. Each of these groups naturally felt betrayed by the other. And that division unfortunately led to another one among the Come-Outers themselves. Those who left were known as Separatists. They saw themselves as practicing a biblical principle: "'Come ye out from among them and be ye separate,' saith the Lord, 'and touch not the unclean thing'" (2 Cor. 6:17); thus, they would not be "unequally yoked with unbelievers" (2 Cor. 6:14). But how would they now relate to their fellow Fundamentalists who were (in their eyes) so compromised as to stay behind where they were essentially giving aid and comfort to the Enemy? Would they still recognize them as fellow Christians with whom they could have fellowship, even though they differed on strategy? No, said some. We must not only separate from unbelievers, but also from those who are not as separated from them as we are! Thus arose the new doctrine known as "Secondary Separation" or "Second-Degree Separation." And so the Fundamentalists who had come out tragically found themselves split over how to practice the very act of splitting.

The Fundamentalists who had stayed behind in the liberal churches were derided as "Neo-Evangelicals." The word "Fundamentalist" eventually came to be applied only to the hardline Secondary Separatists, who kept it as a badge of honor, while the Primary Separatists and the Non-Separatists dropped the insulting prefix and became known to subsequent church history simply as "Evangelicals"—reverting to what Gospel-focused Protestants had been called all along. Thus all faithful Evangelicals are (in the original sense) Fundamentalists, but not all Fundamentalists (original sense) are Evangelicals, and no Fundamentalists (modern sense) are. This inability of the original Fundamentalists to find unity even around the Gospel itself is still making life complicated for their descendants today. The negativity, dogmatism, judgmentalism, narrowness, and legalism of the original Secondary Separationists has given Separatism of any kind a bad name. Anyone who stood for theological integrity in the church got tarred with the same secondary-separationist brush. And that may very well be hindering us from pursuing theological integrity in our churches and other institutions in the present.

Schaeffer in the zeal of his hot-blooded youth had cast his lot with the Secondary Separationists. He later came to believe that this had been a mistake.[195] But rather than abandoning biblical separation altogether as many ex-Fundamentalists did, he returned to primary separation and tried to reform it in line with Paul's exhortation to speak the truth in love (Eph. 4:15). In so doing he tried to replace the negative idea of separation with a positive principle: the practice of the purity of the visible church.[196] In this I think he showed great wisdom. He sensed that the primary issue is not separation as such (that is only one possible strategy for dealing with the real issue), but the nature of the church itself. What is it supposed to be? At what point does it become so compromised or corrupted that Christians of good faith can no longer be a part of it without compromising their own testimony? Is a church that cannot or will not practice discipline really still a church? Is theological integrity optional? These are questions, it seems to me, that Evangelicals and Fundamentalists have not adequately faced. We have the scandal on the one hand of people flitting from congregation to congregation based on personalities or programs, and on the other of people squirming even as they continue attending (and tithing to) churches that promote homosexuality and goddess worship and who cannot bring themselves to recognize apostasy when it smacks them in the face. We are hardly acting out of biblical principle in either case.

The New Testament does not give us a lot of obvious guidance in such matters because in most of the First Century there were scarcely any situations where a believer had to decide between two rival congregations (much less denominations) in the same town. There are some hints though that can give us some help toward formulating the principles we need. First, Paul writes to Timothy so that he will "know how one ought to conduct himself in the household of God, which is the church of the living God, the pillar and support of the truth" (1 Tim. 3:15). The church is defined by its relationship to truth; it has a non-negotiable obligation not only to proclaim but to uphold

---

195 See Colin Duriez, *Francis Schaeffer: An Authentic Life* (Wheaton: Crossway, 2008), chp. 5, for an excellent treatment of Schaeffer's change of mind. Duriez is the most insightful biographer of Schaeffer we have.

196 See *The Church before the Watching World*, op. cit., pp. 61, 74f and. *The Great Evangelical Disaster*, op. cit., pp. 85f, 126.

and defend the truth. If it cannot or will not do that, how is it still the church? Then Paul tells Titus that elders should be able to refute those who contradict sound doctrine because they "must be silenced" (Titus 1:9-11). We are not talking about freedom of speech here, but about official spokesmen of the church who need to be upholding the truth on which it stands. Permitting them to continue undermining it instead is not presented as a viable option. Finally, toward the end of the century, John deals in his second epistle with the problem of traveling evangelists who were not "walking in truth" (v. 4). We are not to receive them into our house or even give them a greeting (v. 10). John does not mean we should be rude to them; he is talking about extending the greeting or welcome of the congregation that would accept these people as Christian brethren. For a Christian or a church to treat one who denies the full deity and humanity of Christ (the issue addressed in 1 John) as a genuine fellow Christian and legitimate church worker is to "participate in his evil deeds" (v. 11). And for Paul, those who deny the Gospel of salvation by grace alone through faith alone are accursed (Gal. 1:8).

What must we conclude from these passages? The church has an absolute, binding, non-negotiable mandate to proclaim, uphold, and defend the truth of Scripture and the message of the Gospel. Individuals who undermine and even oppose that mandate are subject to discipline. They must be refuted, recalled to the truth if possible (2 Tim. 2:24-26), and silenced if they prove unrepentant. Those who deny sound doctrine are not to be treated as Christian brothers. In other words, primary separation is mandated by Scripture, as much as a version of it chastened by the failures and excesses of secondary separationism is mandated by history.

These tasks are hard, but they must be done—done with gentleness and love and without rancor, but *done*. And we must reckon with the fact that a congregation or denomination that refuses to do them cannot claim to be a valid instantiation of the church of our Lord Jesus Christ. How can it be "the pillar and support of the truth" and words still have any meaning at all? It cannot therefore claim the loyalty of God's faithful people. As Schaeffer put it, "The church as an organization is not first; Christ is first. Therefore, once Christ is no longer King and Lord in a church, then that church cannot have our loyalty."[197] So there comes a point at which "It may be necessary for

---

[197] Schaeffer, *The Church before the Watching World*, p. 75.

true Christians to leave the visible organization with which they have been associated. But note well: If we must leave our church, it should always be with tears—not with drums playing and flags flying."[198] Thus Schaeffer tried to follow what was right in the original Fundamentalist movement without repeating its mistakes. Perhaps modern Evangelicalism is hindered in speaking with integrity because it is so bent on avoiding the mistakes that it has forgotten what was right.[199]

Schaeffer called this principle "the practice of the purity of the visible church." He chose the word *purity* because he rightly saw this discipline as part of the church's keeping herself faithful to her Bridegroom as the Bride of Christ. It is a good word in that sense, but part of me wishes he had not used it. It is possible to misread it as a counsel of perfection. The church is never going to be "pure" or perfect until Christ comes back. It is always going to have tares among the wheat. It is not some minor disagreement or squabble that should cause us to invoke this principle and consider leaving; it is disloyalty to the authority of Christ in Scripture (Theses 1a-e) and denial of the Gospel of grace (Theses 2a-3e) that should not be tolerated when every attempt at reform has failed. In that sense, a better word would be *integrity*. We will never have perfection or purity in any absolute sense, but we should demand integrity of any congregation or denomination we support, and accept nothing less.

Until we are ready to practice the principle of the integrity of the visible church and pay the price for doing so, we will not see the lasting Reformation on the other ninety-five points that we so desperately need. This is something that our Fundamentalist and Evangelical ancestors were never able to agree on. Let us agree on it now, that Christ may be Head over all things to His church in a way He has not been in our experience before.

---

198 Ibid., p. 74.

199 See Iain H. Murray, *Evangelicalism Divided: a Record of Crucial Change in the Years 1950 to 2000* (Carlisle, Pa.: Banner of Truth, 2000) for an excellent treatment of the history of the transition from Fundamentalism to the divided movement of Fundamentalism and Evangelicalism, and of the consequences of our failure to observe the principle of integrity.

Interlude
The Rise and Fall of Protestant Fundamentalism

Christ's virgin birth, His deity, His cross,
    His Word, His resurrection, His return:
    Could these be given up without the loss
    Of Christian faith itself? was the concern
Of those first known as "Fundamentalist."
    If their descendants' words have proved uncouth
    As if their mind had closed up like a fist,
    At least they started caring for the Truth.
It's one of mankind's greatest tragedies
    Beyond the power of the tongue to tell,
    This hardening of mental arteries
    Within a movement that began so well.
What they forgot should be like hand in glove:
    Truth is not Truth unless we speak in love.[200]

---

200 Donald T. Williams, *Stars through the Clouds*, op. cit., p. 392.

Excursus II

Discerning the Times: Why We Lost the Culture War, and How To Make a Comeback

International Society of Christian Apologetics Presidential Address, 2015

The Culture War is over. We (the Christian Right) lost.

OK, maybe it's not quite over and we're only losing, rather badly. If you quibble over the difference, you will miss the point.

It was a war we were right to fight, for no one who loves his neighbors can be indifferent to how they will be affected by harmful degradations of the culture that surrounds them. But we ought to have fought it very differently. We fought for many of the right things, but often not in a wise, sometimes not in a loving way. We were generally right and we often argued well, but we lost anyway. How did that happen? Why? It happened because we didn't understand where the real battle was until it was too late. We probably don't get it yet. Here's what I mean.

Where The Battle Was

The founding documents of the American republic, from the Mayflower Compact to the Declaration of Independence to the Constitution, are on our side. They really were. Nobody cares. Nobody can even tell. Nobody thinks it matters. We lost the culture war on that score because we lost it earlier on the even more basic front of *hermeneutics*.

We lost, in other words, because we did not pay sufficient attention to changes taking place in our schools and colleges in the way writing and reading are taught. A major shift has taken place there over the last century, one with serious implications for every other issue we deal with. There now, typically, the Constitution—like any literary document studied in our secular schools, including the Bible—no longer has any objective meaning given to it by its authors. It means whatever the "interpretive community" (in the case of the Constitution, five out of nine people in black robes) think they need or want it to mean. That is a huge problem in itself, but we have an even bigger one: Our fellow citizens are fine with this procedure. Why wouldn't they be? It is how they were taught to read themselves.

Many Christian institutions of higher education did not stand against this view with sufficient rigor or energy. Why not? Many Christians either did not understand or just shrugged their shoulders at or even welcomed this change in how we read the world. Some even rejoiced in it as an improvement over the hated "Modernism" they thought had taken over the Christian movement. How foolish! But we allowed it to happen because its earlier manifestations did not seem to be a threat. After all, they were happening in "English," not in Theology or Philosophy, and in the reading of "artistic" works—novels, short stories, plays, poems—rather than "serious" political, legal, or religious texts. And who cares what a bunch of effete aesthetic snobs do with incomprehensible texts that don't matter anyway?

And so in the secular academy the Old Way, the attempt to understand what an author was trying to say to his original audience, believing that what they would have gotten out of his work must be the authoritative starting point for discussing the "meaning" of that work, was abandoned as naïve, unworkable, even perverse. This banishment of authors from their own texts was first crystallized by the "New Critics" of the mid-twentieth century in their concept of the "intentional fallacy": Just pay attention to what the *text* says in itself, they argued reasonably; the author's intention for it, whatever that might have been, is a misleading distraction. (Their emphasis on "close reading" of the text itself was sound. But wait: Did scholars like Wimsatt and Beardsley and the teachers who followed them *intend* for us to focus on the text as a thing in itself rather than as an act of communication by its author? Ahem.)

The aestheticism of New Criticism, its focus on works of art, masked for a while the ideological use that could be made of this new author-free way of reading, not only in other texts but in the literary works themselves. And so most Christian literature professors simply picked up this approach to literary texts with never a thought as to what would happen if some of its presuppositions were applied to other texts. And indeed for a while "close reading" produced genuine insights into the texts as works of literary art. But meanwhile, the exile of the author found its fulfillment in the "death of the author" espoused by current Post-Modern theorists. Now the very distinction between literary texts and other texts has broken down. Now all texts can be mined for their aesthetic value or their ideological usefulness or anything else the critic wants to find in them. The one thing those texts cannot do—are not permitted to do—is allow our ancestors to share with us the wisdom of the past. The "chronological snobbery" C. S. Lewis warned us about now reigns supreme.

The end result is that today if you try to apply the old method, the search for the *author's* meaning (technically called "grammatico-historical exegesis"), to any cultural document, people stare blankly at you as if you were speaking a foreign language. That is one of the major reasons why, even when we had good arguments on the more recognizable issues in what was called the culture war, those arguments had no traction. People simply walked on by as if nothing had happened. To them, nothing had.

Sadly, this blank stare is not limited to "secular" people outside the church. I can tell you that it occurs in many students in conservative Christian colleges. They may tell you something very different when off guard in the cafeteria from what they put by rote on their hermeneutics exam to please their professor. Outside of class, they take it as a self-evident truth needing no support that readers *create* meaning *in*, rather than *receiving* it *from*, the text. Readers; not authors. These students don't know it, but they have picked up by osmosis the epistemological skepticism of Post-Modern hermeneutics. *Readers*, not authors, are the source of meaning. Authors have no authority. Their presence at the moment of "text construction" has no historical or hermeneutical relevance. That would (horrors!) interfere with the freedom of the interpreter. The "free play of the mind in the text" trumps all other considerations. These students don't know any of the jargon, but they have absorbed the assumptions. And few of their professors are equipped to challenge those assumptions. Their more conservative Bible professors can refute the old higher criticism but not the new hermeneutic, and their English professors had to spend their graduate careers pretending to take the chic nihilism of Post-Modern "theory" seriously if they wanted to get their degrees. Not all of them came through that experience unscathed, and many had never been told that any other view was even possible.

Now, no matter what you say, even if you still call the Bible the Word of God and think yourself a loyal son or daughter of the church, once you have adopted this view authority has been transferred from the Text to you, the individual. Not only is there nothing to stop you from remaking the text (or the natural world) in your own image; you have actually been taught that it is your right to do so, and that so doing is unavoidable. Biblical authors cannot be made an exception to this principle when it rules the mind unchallenged. Yes, we have lost the culture war, and many of us have no idea how badly and how deeply! Many of our own children, even the pious ones, are more influenced by the culture at this critical point than by the church or the Christian tradition. Can this influence be unrelated to the fact that according to many studies they are only marginally better than the world in their practice of Christian morality? Readers empowered to create their own subjective meaning rather than exhorted to find the objective meaning left behind by the author are foxes put in charge of the hen house when fallen human nature runs up against the demands of the Law of God.

Where the Battle Is

So we lost. All right, what do we do now? Most importantly, we realize that the battle is never *finally* lost because Christ is sovereign and He is coming back. That guarantees long-term victory. In the short term, since we do not know when He is coming back, we are to be faithful while He tarries and occupy until He comes. Therefore, the battle we have just lost must be followed by another one that we fight more intelligently, with a better recognition of our strategic position. Having lost the battle for faithful reading, we have also lost the cultural privilege and initiative we once enjoyed. We no longer command anything perceived by our peers as moral high ground. We are no longer defending the received tradition; are now trying to come from behind. We are the new Moral Minority. Our position is now much more like that of our brothers in the old Roman Empire, except that instead of being the edgy new challenging Way coming in, we are now the outmoded fuddie-duddies being swept aside. A four-pronged strategy is needed in the situation in which we now find ourselves.

First, we should not do what some are doing, and give up or surrender or try to retreat back into our private religious ghetto. We should continue to advocate biblical positions publicly, even politically, because they are right, wise, good, and the only policies conducive to healthy human thriving in the long run. The unpopularity of biblical positions that are pro-life, pro-traditional marriage, or pro-traditional family is simply an indicator of how badly those views need proclamation and defense. But we can no longer pretend that they are a default setting, or that they are in any way privileged because there was once a consensus in their favor. That situation belongs to an increasingly remote past. Failure to recognize this fact is one of the reasons we keep losing. We're still fighting yesterday's battles.

Second, we must prioritize reading and hermeneutics, and the way they are taught, as keys to our ability to witness effectively to the truth in all other areas. You cannot very well argue that traditional marriage or the sanctity of life should be normative if norms are inconceivable to your audience as anything other than arbitrary impositions of power. Norms cannot be conceivable if meaning (not to mention truth) is by definition in the eye of the beholder. So if you live in an environment where the very act of reading as taught by almost all those who should be our most proficient readers (i.e., English professors) seems to undercut the very concept of determinative meaning and reinforce the absolute sovereignty of the individual, you will have a hard time making norms seem conceivable, much less believable. When truth is nothing more than a fluid miasma of shifting perspectives, the exclusive claims of Christ might be accepted by a few but cannot be taken seriously by anyone.

We therefore need to be much more vigilant against all forms of the Post-Modern "hermeneutic of suspicion" and much more aggressive in making the case for authorial intent as the foundation of textual meaning. Can authors communicate with their readers in their texts? The people who tell you they cannot are saying this in texts in which they are doing, quite successfully, the very thing they deny is possible! The English Professor who believes that they can is now the most needed missionary on the planet, and sending him or her into the secular academy (or even the Christian school) the most strategic mission strategy we can mount.

Sadly, the church herself has become a mission field in this area. Does the Christian college you support have people on its English faculty who piously believe that Deconstruction (for example) is just one more neutral technique to be applied to texts, that it is something Christians should "take seriously" and "learn from?" (Not that I am advocating ignorance of it. People should be aware of the poisons in their cabinet!) You would be surprised at how many do. If you hire such people or contribute to their salaries or send your young people to study under them, you are aiding and abetting the Enemy. It is no exaggeration to say that the result will be more debased definitions, moral relativism, and brutally slaughtered babies.

THIRD, we must recognize the crucial role of the imagination alongside the reason in cultural apologetics. Failure to take seriously the importance of literary art (and all the arts) in the formation of human minds and hearts was one of the reasons we were blind to the shift that took the ground out from under our feet until it was too late. We must not forget that the greatest apologist of the Twentieth Century was the greatest not only because he gave us the rational arguments of *Mere Christianity* and *Miracles*, but also because he showed us what they looked like incarnate in flesh in the Chronicles of Narnia and the Space Trilogy—and most of all because reason and imagination were seamlessly integrated in one unified vision of the wholeness and the wholesomeness of Christian truth. Exhortations to sexual faithfulness, for example, will only be fully effective if they flow from sound arguments for why God's commands really are the expression of His love for us rather than arbitrary prohibitions. And those reasons will only be fully convincing if they are accompanied by compelling portraits of such faithfulness that make it genuinely imaginable as the only path to human thriving and fulfillment.

FOURTH, we must adjust our rhetoric to address the audience that actually exists, not the one that was here two generations ago. We need to stop berating people for departing from a position they no longer remember ever having held, and instead do the hard work of evangelizing and discipling them from scratch. Maybe from less than scratch. They are jaded and cynical about what they think Christianity is, and that is partly our fault—not because we were wrong but because we were (and are) stupid in our approach.

Here's an example of that stupidity: On my way to church I used to pass a billboard proclaiming a meeting in which the Christian Right was going to "take back America." Have we no idea how this message would come across to the multitudes of non-believers who must have read it on a public billboard? It would only reinforce all their worst stereotypes and prejudices about us; it could only put their guard up against us. But even as an in-house communique it did not send quite the right message. We have to *win* back America before we can even begin to think of taking it back.

Conclusion

It's finally about recognizing what the real battle is, something we have not been very good at. If we don't understand that it is too late to preserve the American republic (we have to *restore* it, a very different thing); if we don't understand that we have lost the ability to appeal to the old consensus and we need to stop acting like it is still there; if we don't understand that we need to continue our political opposition to atrocities like abortion or perversions like same-sex marriage but stop putting any hope in it until we do better at the prior job of evangelism and discipleship; if we don't understand that you cannot win the battles for theology, philosophy, and ethics if you lose the battle for philology (literature and reading)—if we don't understand these things, we will be fighting shadows on an empty field the Enemy has already abandoned for juicier prizes.

We have failed in our attempts to preserve the Christian influence that we used to have in American society, and we will not make progress in restoring it until we recognize that fact and deal with the situation we actually face. America might once have been a Christian nation (if you define that concept carefully). But it is a pagan nation now. Until we get serious about evangelism and discipleship, that is not going to change. I'm not saying our political activity should cease; it should continue. But we aren't going to accomplish anything with it until we do better at something much more basic. And that means treating pagans as pagans in need of the Gospel, not as faithless, traitorous Christians in need of shaming. (This is true even when those pagans in their ignorance self-identify as Christians!) Our positions have been correct, but our rhetoric has been scientifically designed to lose friends and alienate people. Well, we are succeeding at that.

Better wise up now than later.

Interlude

The Logic of Post-Modernism

"Logic's nothing but a verbal trick,"
    Post-Modern thinkers often like to claim.
    They work quite hard to make that judgment stick.
All those who don't agree are simply thick,
    Incompetent to play the language game
    Where logic's nothing but a verbal trick.
It's all a plot by Dead White Males to kick
    Non-Westerners and keep them meek and tame?
    Well, that's one way to make their judgment stick.
"Is there a Text in this class?" Don't be quick
    To ask if there's a prof to ask the same,
    For logic's nothing but a verbal trick.
All truth is surreptitious rhetoric,
    For words call only other words by name;
    The will to power makes this judgment stick!
You say it all sounds just a bit too slick?
    Shh! Shh! Don't give the game away—for shame!
    If Logic's nothing but a verbal trick,
What logic then can make *that* judgment stick?[201]

---

201 Donald T. Williams, *Stars through the Clouds*, op. cit., p. 369.

Conclusion

Renaissance . . . Reformation . . . Revival: the recovery, by God's grace, of the life of the mind, of sound doctrine, of vital spirituality: This threefold recovery is the desperate need of the hour. Each of these three recoveries is dependent on the other two if we are to have the complete restoration we need and seek. Without Renaissance it is hard to see how we can muster the knowledge and discernment needed to pursue Reformation. Without Reformation, Revival will dissipate and flow off into the sand. Without Revival, Reformation will lack power and life. Because of that interconnection, our focus on Reformation has forced us to deal with Renaissance and Revival as well. May God give us a vision for all three, a yearning for all three, and some experience of all three as we try to be faithful to the Light in this darkening world. Only He can do so, for this work is too mighty to be accomplished by the arm of flesh.

What then are we to do while we wait for His sovereign action? I urge you to consider a three-pronged plan of attack: Pray; Prepare; Practice.

First, PRAY for Renaissance, Reformation, and Revival. Make it a regular and continual matter of your personal prayers, listed under the rubric of "Thy kingdom come" as you work your way through the outline of The Lord's Prayer.[202] Gather like-minded believers who will make it a matter of corporate prayer. Insert it by example into the prayer life of your church, both in Sunday worship and in prayer meetings. If your church has dropped the practice of having prayer meetings, revive it for the express purpose of making this petition an urgent part of the agenda. And do not grow weary in well doing, but be faithful in this ministry as you continue to grow in understanding of how sorely we need the answer.

Second, PREPARE for Renaissance, Reformation, and Revival. The prayer we have already mentioned is the most important form of this

---

[202] My book *The Disciple's Prayer* (Christian Publications, 1999; reprint Eugene, Or.: Wipf and Stock, 2005) may be helpful in this regard.

preparation, but there is more that can be done. Prepare for Renaissance by living out the lordship of Christ over the total culture as laid out in chapter 13, by following the practical suggestions for the development of the Christian mind in chapter 15, and by supporting and promoting Christian Education as understood in chapter 16. Prepare for Reformation by studying the original Reformation, starting with the sources listed here. Use the 95 theses presented here as topics for study and discussion in a Sunday-School class or Bible-study group. Preach and teach sound doctrine derived from careful exposition and applied faithfully to the whole of life, including the issues of the day. Model Reformation in your own life and ministry. Prepare for Revival by praying and preparing for Renaissance and Reformation and by learning to live, moment by moment, in dependence on the Holy Spirit—as if *Sola Gratia* were actually a practical truth as well as a doctrinal affirmation in the Gospel! In all of this return to the practice of the Great Commission as our Lord gave it: to make disciples, not just converts.

Third, PRACTICE Renaissance and Reformation as the preludes to Revival in the small ways you are able to achieve wherever you are placed. You may not be able to change the culture of American Evangelicalism, anti-intellectual outside the academy and too often pseudo-intellectual inside it, but you can love the Lord your God with all of your own mind, teach your children to do so, and model thinking that is both creative and faithful in your local assembly. You may not be able to reform the Christian world, but you can bring your own life into conformity with sound doctrine and support practical reforms in your own congregation. They may need to be small and incremental at first, for they matter much more when there is real congregational buy-in than when they are imposed. But do *something*. Then when God sees that we are serious in these small ways, perhaps He will grant a power and a momentum to the movement for a new Reformation that we could not have mustered, and perhaps He will enable it to bear the fruit of Revival.

We do this because we live under the Scriptures as our highest, and only infallible, authority. We do it because they teach us that salvation is by grace alone through faith alone in Christ alone, for the glory of God alone. We do it because the Gospel of grace alone through faith alone in Christ alone is the power of God for salvation, and because we have experienced already a taste of the reality of that power in the forgiveness of our own sins, inexcusable though they were. We do it because, having discovered in that Gospel how profoundly Christ first loved us, we love Him in return. We do it because the faint glimpses of the glory of God in the face of Jesus Christ that we have been granted to see already make us long to see more and to share that vision with every creature. We do it because Jesus so supremely and inexpressibly *deserves* all our worship, all our devotion, all our faithfulness, and all our obedience. If we do it for any other reasons than these, we are not doing it.

Let us be doing it. Let us be doing it with confidence in a God who knows what He is doing in history and with absolute trust that when we have done all we can do, it is only to be prepared for His initiative.

Soli Deo Gloria! Amen.

Postlude

The Beneficiaries

But few of wealth or power,
Not very many wise
Will in the final hour
Rise up to claim the prize.

So what of those elected
To gaze upon the Face?
Not perfect, but perfected:
The trophies of his Grace.[203]

---

203 Donald T. Williams, *Stars through the Clouds*, op. cit., p. 188.

Bibliography

Alighiere, Dante. *The Divine Comedy 1: Hell*. Trans. w. intro. by Dorothy L, Sayers. Baltimore: Penguin, 1940.

Allen, Ronald and Gordon Borror. *Worship: Rediscovering the Missing Jewel*. Portland: Multnomah. 1982.

Andrews, Edgar. *What is Man? Adam, Alien, or Ape?* Nashville: Elm Hill, 2018.

Arnold, Matthew. "The Function of Criticism at the Present Time" (1865), in William E. Buckler, ed., *Prose of the Victorian Period*. Boston: Houghton Mifflin, 1958, pp. 420-441.

Ascham, Roger. *The Schoolmaster*. 1570. *The Renaissance in England: Non-Dramatic Prose and Verse of the Sixteenth Century*. Hyder E. Rollins and Herschel Baker, eds. Lexington, Ma.: D. C. Heath, 1954, pp. 817-40.

D'Aubigne, J. H. Merle. *History of the Reformation of the Sixteenth Century*, 1 vol. ed. 1846; rpt. Grand Rapids: Eerdmans, n.d.

Augustine of Hippo. "Reply to Faustus the Manichaean." *Augustin: Writings against the Manichaeans and against the Donatists*. Ed. Philip Schaff. *Nicene and Post-Nicene Fathers*, 1st Series vol. 4. 1887; rpt. Peabody, MA: Hendrickson, 1994.

Bainton, Roland H. *Erasmus of Christendom*. N.Y.: Crossroad, 1982.

----------. *"Here I Stand": A Life of Martin Luther*. N.Y.: Mentor Books, 1950.

----------. *The Reformation of the Sixteenth Century*. Boston: Beacon Press, 1952.

Berkhof, Louis. *Principles of Biblical Interpretation*. Grand Rapids: Baker, 1950.

----------. *Systematic Theology*. Grand Rapids: Eerdmans, 1939.

Blamires, Harry. *The Christian Mind*. London: S.P.C.K., 1963.

Boice, James Montgomery, ed. *The Foundation of Biblical Authority*. Grand Rapids: Zondervan, 1978.

Bolt, Robert. *A Man for All Seasons: A Play in Two Acts*. NY: Vintage Books, 1960.

The Book of Discipline of the United Methodist Church. Nashville: Abingdon Press, 2004.

Brown, Harold O. J. *Heresies: The Image of Christ in the Mirror of Heresy and Orthodoxy from the Apostles to the Present.* Garden City, NY: Doubleday, 1984.

Bruce, F. F. *The New Testament Documents: Are they Reliable?* Downers Grove, Il.: InterVarsity Press, 1960.

Bruner, Frederick Dale. *A Theology of the Holy Spirit: The Pentecostal Experience and New Testament Witness.* Grand Rapids: Eerdmans, 1970.

Burckhardt, Jacob. *The Civilization of the Renaissance in Italy*, 2 vols. N.Y.: Haper and Row, 1929.

Cable, Stephen. *Cultural Captivity: The Beliefs and Behavior of American Young Adults.* Dallas: Probe Ministries, 2012.

Calvin, John. *Institutes of the Christian Religion.* Trans. Henry Beveridge. 2 vols. Grand Rapids: Eerdmans, 1975.

Campbell-Jack, W. C. and Gavin McGrath, eds. *New Dictionary of Christian Apologetics.* Downers Grove, Il.: InterVarsity Press, 2006.

Carson, Donald A. *Showing the Spirit: A Theological Exposition of 1 Corinthians 12-14.* Grand Rapids: Baker, 1987.

Castiglione, Baldesar. *The Book of the Courtier.* Trans. George Bull. 1527; mod. trans. N.Y.: Penguin, 1976.

Chesterton, G. K. *The Everlasting Man.* N.Y.: Dodd, Mead, & Co., 1925.

----------. *Orthodoxy.* Garden City, N.Y.: Doubleday, 1959.

The Chicago Statements on Biblical Inerrancy and Biblical Hermeneutics, available online at http://www.danielakin.com/wpcontent/uploads/old/Resource_545/Book%202,%20Sec%2023.pdf.

Coleman, Robert E. *The Master Plan of Evangelism.* Old Tappan, N.J.: Fleming H. Revell, 1963.

Cowan, Louise and Os Guinness, eds., *Invitation to the Classics: A Guide to Books You've Always Wanted to Read* (Grand Rapids: Baker, 1980.

Craig, William Lane. *Reasonable Faith: Christian Truth and Apologetics.* Wheaton: Crossway, 1984.

Crouch, Andy. *Culture Making: Recovering our Creative Calling.* Downers Grove, Il.: InterVarsity Press, 2008.

Davies, Horton. *Christian Worship: Its History and Meaning.* N.Y.:

Abingdon, 1957.

——————. *Worship and Theology in England*, 3 vols. Grand Rapids: Eerdmans, 1996.

Denney, James. *The Death of Christ*. London: Tyndale Press, 1951.

Derrida, Jacques. "Structure, Sign, and Play in the Discourse of the Human Sciences" (1966). *Critical Theory Since Plato*, by Hazard Adam and Leroy Searle. Boston: Wadsworth, 2005: 1206-15.

Dickens, A. G. *The English Reformation*. N.Y.: Schocken Books, 1964.

Dockery, David S. ed. *The Challenge of Postmodernism: An Evangelical Engagement*. Wheaton: Victor, 1995.

Doddridge, Philip. *The Rise and Progress of Religion in the Soul*. Qtd. in *A Burning and a Shining Light: English Spirituality in the Age of Wesley*, ed. David Lyle Jeffrey. Grand Rapids: Eerdmans, 1987, 178-93.

Duriez, Colin. *Francis Schaeffer: An Authentic Life*. Wheaton: Crossway, 2008.

Earls, Aaron. "Small, Struggling Congregations Fill U.S. Church Landscape." *Lifewayresearch.com*. March 8, 2019. https://lifewayresearch.com/2019/03/06/small-struggling-congregations-fill-u-s-church-landscape/.

Edman, V. Raymond. *Finney Lives On: The Man, His Revival Methods, and His Message*. N.Y.: Fleming H. Revell, 1951.

Edwards, Jonathan. "A Divine and Supernatural Light." *The Works of Jonathan Edwards*, 2 vol., ed. Edward Hickman. Carlisle, Pa.: Banner of Truth, 1974, 2: 12-17.

——————. "Sinners in the Hands of an Angry God." *The Works of Jonathan Edwards*, 2 vol., ed. Edward Hickman. Carlisle, Pa.: Banner of Truth, 1974, 2:7-12.

——————. *A Treatise Concerning Religious Affections*. 1746; New Haven: Yale Univ. Pr., 1959.

Eliot, T. S. *Christianity and Culture: The Idea of a Christian Society and Notes towards the Definition of Culture*. N.Y.: Harcourt, Brace, and Company, 1940.

——————. "Tradition and the Individual Talent." *Selected Essays of T. S. Eliot*. N.Y.: Harcourt, Brace, & World, 1969), pp. 3-11.

Eller, Vernard. *The Language of Canaan and the Grammar of Feminism*. Grand Rapids: Eerdmans, 1982.

Ellis, John M. *Literature Lost: Social Agendas and the Corruption of the Humanities*. New Haven: Yale, 1997.

Elyot, Sir Thomas. *The Book Named the Governor*. 1531. *The Renaissance in England: Non-Dramatic Prose and Verse of the Sixteenth Century*. Hyder E. Rollins and Herschel Baker, eds. Lexington, Ma.: D. C. Heath, 1954, pp.105-115, 587-89.

Erickson, Millard J. *Christian Theology, 2nd ed.* Grad Rapids: Baker, 1998.

Estep, William R. *Renaissance and Reformation*. Grand Rapids: Eerdmans, 1986.

Ferguson, Wallace K. *The Renaissance in Historical Thought: Five Centuries of Interpretation*. NY: Houghton Mifflin, 1961.

Finney, Charles Grandison. *Lectures on Revivals of Religion*. 1835; Cambridge, Ma.: Harvard University Press, 1960.

Gardner, W. H. and N. H. MacKenzie, eds. *The Poems of Gerard Manley Hopkins*, 4th edition. London: Oxford University Press, 1967.

George, Timothy. *Theology of the Reformers*. Nashville: Broadman, 1988.

Gonzalez, Connor. "Training and Discipleship." Unpublished paper, Toccoa Falls College, 2018.

Gordon, David Stott. "Sir Philip Sidney: The Faith and Practice of an Elizabethan Christian." Thesis, Trinity Evangelical Divinity School, 1995.

Graff, Gerald. *Literature Against Itself: Literary Ideas in Modern Society*. Chicago: Dee, 1995.

Graham, Billy. *A Biblical Standard for Evangelists*. Minneapolis: World Wide Publications, 1984.

Green, Lisa Cannon. "Worship Attendance Rises, Baptisms Decline in SBC." *Facts and Trends Newsletter*. June 1, 2018. https://factsandtrends.net/2018/06/01/worship-attendance-rises-baptisms-decline-in-sbc/.

Green, Roger Lancelyn and Walter Hooper. *C. S. Lewis: A Biography*. N.Y.: Harcourt Brace Jovanovich, 1974.

Groothuis, Douglas. *Christian Apologetics: A Comprehensive Case for Biblical Faith*. Downers Grove, Il.: InterVarsity Press, 2011.

Grudem, Wayne. *Systematic Theology: An Introduction to Biblical Doctrine*. Grand Rapids: Zondervan, 1994.

Hackett, Stuart C. *The Resurrection of Theism: Prolegomena to Christian Apology*. Grand Rapids: Baker, 1957.

Hambrick-Stowe. Charles E. *Charles G. Finney and the Spirit of*

American Evangelicalism. Grand Rapids: Eerdmans, 1996.
Heimert, Alan and Perry Miller, eds. *The Great Awakening: Documents Illustrating the Crisis and its Consequences*. Indianapolis: Bobbs-Merrill, 1967.
Henry, Carl F. H. *Confessions of a Theologian: An Autobiography*. Waco, TxL Word, 1986.
----------. *Evangelicals in Search of Identity*. Waco, TX: Word, 1976.
Hillerbrand, Hans J., ed. *The Oxford Encyclopedia of the Reformation*, 4 vols. Oxford: Oxford University Press, 1996.
Hirsch, E. D. *Validity in Interpretation*. New Haven, Ct.: Yale Univ. Pr., 1967.
Hodge, Charles. *Systematic Theology*, 3 vols. 1871-2; Grand Rapids: Eerdmans, 1975.
Hopkins, John, ed. *All Such Psalms of David as Thomas Sternhold Did in his Lifetime Draw into English Meter* (1549); qtd. in Hyder E. Rollins & Herschel Baker, eds., *The Renaissance in England: Non-Dramatic Prose and Verse of the Sixteenth Century*. Lexington, Mass.: D. C. Heath & Co., 1954, 160-63.
Hughes, Philip Edgecumbe. *Theology of the English Reformers*. Grand Rapids: Baker, 1980.
Hunter, James Davison. *Evangelicalism: The Coming Generation*. Chicago: The University of Chicago Press, 1987.
Hustad, Donald P. *Jubilate! Church Music in the Evangelical Tradition*. Carol Stream, Il.: Hope Publishing, 1981.
Jacobs, Alan. "Deconstruction." *Contemporary Literary Theory: A Christian Appraisal*, ed. Walhout and Ryken. Grand Rapids: Eerdmans, 1991: 172-98.
Jeffrey, David Lyle. *A Burning and a Shining Light: English Spirituality in the Age of Wesley*. Grand Rapids: Eerdmans, 1987.
----------. *People of the Book: Christian Identity and Literary Culture*. Grand Rapids: Eerdmans, 1996.
Johnson, Samuel. *Preface to the Plays of William Shakespeare* (1765); qtd. in Geoffrey Tillotson, Paul Fussell, Jr., and Marshall Waingrow, eds., *Eighteenth Century English Literature*. N.Y.: Harcourt, Brace, & World, 1969, 1066-76.
Kaiser, Walter C. *Toward an Exegetical Theology: Biblical Exegesis for Preaching and Teaching*. Grand Rapids: Baker, 1981.
Kantzer, Kenneth Sealer. "John Calvin's Theory of the Knowledge of God and the Word of God." Diss. Harvard, 1950.

Kennedy, D. James. *Evangelism Explosion: the Coral Ridge Program for Lay Witness*, rev. ed. Wheaton: Tyndale, 1977.

Kilby, Clyde S. *Christianity and Aesthetics*. Chicago: InterVarsity Press, 1961.

Kimball. Roger. *Tenured Radicals: How Politics has Corrupted our Higher Education*. Chicago: Dee, 1998.

Kristeller, Paul Oskar. *Renaissance Thought: the Classic, Scholastic, and Humanist Strains*. N.Y.: Haper and Row, 1961.

Koukl, Gregory. *Tactics: A Game Plan for Discussing Your Christian Convictions*. Grand Rapids: Zondervan, 2009.

Kuiper, R. B. *God-Centered Evangelism: A Presentation of the Scriptural Theology of Evangelism*. London: Banner of Truth, 1961.

Kuyper, Abraham. *Lectures on Calvinism*. Grand Rapids: Eerdmans, 1931.

The Lausanne Covenant, https://www.lausanne.org/content/covenant/lausanne-covenant.

Lewalski, Barbara Kiefer. *Protestant Poetics and the Seventeenth-Century Religious Lyric*. Princeton: Princeton Univ. Pr., 1979.

Lewis, C. S. "Christianity and Culture." *Christian Reflections*, ed. Walter Hooper. Grand Rapids: Eerdmans, 1967, pp. 12-36.

----------. *The Lion, the Witch, and the Wardrobe*. N.Y.: Harper Collins, 1978.

----------. *Mere Christianity*. N.Y.: MacMillan, 1943.

----------. *Miracles: A Preliminary Study*. N.Y.: MacMillan, 1947.

----------. "The Poison of Subjectivism" (1943). *Christian Reflections*, ed. Walter Hooper. Grand Rapids: Eerdmans, 1968.

----------. *The Problem of Pain*. N.Y.: MacMillan, 1967.

----------. *Surprised by Joy: The Shape of my Early Life*. N.Y.: Harcourt, Brace, & World, 1955.

----------. *They Stand Together: The Letters of C. S. Lewis to Arthur Greeves*, ed. Walter Hooper. N.Y.: MacMillan, 1979.

Lloyd-Jones, D. Martyn. *God's Ultimate Purpose: An Exposition of Ephesians 1*. Grand Rapids: Eerdmans, 1978.

----------. *Preaching and Preachers*. Grand Rapids: Zondervan, 1972.

----------. *The Puritans: Their Origins and Successors*. Carlisle, Pa.: Banner of Truth, 1987.

----------. *Revival*. Westchester, Il.: Crossway, 1987.

Luther, Martin. *The Table Talk of Martin Luther*. Ed. Thomas S. Kepler. Trans. William Hazlitt. Grand Rapids: Baker, 1979.

MacArthur, Jr., John F. *Charismatic Chaos*. Grand Rapids: Zondervan, 1992.

Machen, J. Gresham. *Christianity and Liberalism*. 1923; rpt. Grand Rapids: Eerdmans, 1981.

----------. *Education, Christianity, and the State*. Unicoi, Tn.: Trinity Foundation, 1987.

----------. *What is Faith?* 1925; Grand Rapids: Eerdmans, 1962.

McGrath, Alister. *C. S. Lewis: A Life*. Carol Stream, Il.: Tyndale House, 2013.

----------. *Reformation Thought: An Introduction*, 2nd ed. Grand Rapids: Baker, 1993.

Menninger, Karl. *Whatever Because of Sin?* N.Y.: Hawthorne Books, 1973.

Milton, John. *John Milton: Complete Poems and Major Prose*. Ed. Merritt Y. Hughes. Indianapolis: Bobbs-Merrill, 1957.

Montaigne, Michel de. *Montaigne's Essays and Selected Writings: A Bilingual Edition*. Trans. Donald M. Frame. N.Y.: St. Martin's Press, 1963.

Montgomery, John Warwick: *God's Inerrant Word: An International Symposium on the Trustworthiness of Scripture*. Minneapolis: Bethany, 1973.

----------. *In Defense of Martin Luther*. Milwaukee: Northwestern Publishing House, 1970.

----------. *The Suicide of Christian Theology*. Minneapolis: Bethany Fellowship, 1971.

Morison, Frank. *Who Moved the Stone?* Downers Grove, Il.: InterVarsity Press, n.d.

Murphree, Jon Tal. *Responsible Evangelism: Relating Theory to Practice*. Toccoa, Ga.: Toccoa Falls College Press, 1994.

Murray, Iain H. *Evangelicalism Divided: A Record of Crucial Change in the Years 1950 to 2000*. Carlisle, Pa.: Banner of Truth, 2000.

Murray, John. *Redemption Accomplished and Applied*. Grand Rapids: Eerdmans, 1955.

Nash, Ronald H. *Life's Ultimate Questions: An Introduction to Philosophy*. Grand Rapids: Zondervan, 1999.

----------. *The Word of God and the Mind of Man: The Crisis of Revealed Truth in Contemporary Theology*. Grand Rapids: Zondervan, 1982.

Niebuhr, H. Richard. *Christ and Culture*. N.Y.: Harper & Row, 1931.

Oden, Thomas C. *Systematic Theology*, 3 vols. Peabody, MA: Prince

Press, 1008.

Orme, Alan Dan. *God's Appointments with Men: A Christian's Primer on the Sacraments*. Athens, Ga.: University Church Press, 1982.

Orr, J. Edwin. *The Flaming Tongue: The Impact of Twentieth Century Revivals*. Chicago: Moody Press, 1973.

Outler, Albert C., ed. *John Wesley*. Oxford: Oxford University Press, 1964.

Owen, John. *The Glory of Christ: The Works of John Owen, vol. 1*. Ed. William H. Goold. Edinburgh: Banner of Truth, 1965.

Packer, J. I. *God Has Spoken*. Downers Grove, Il.: InterVarsity Press, 1979.

----------. *Keep in Step with the Spirit*. Old Tappan, N.J.: Fleming H. Revell, 1984.

----------. *Knowing God*. Downers Grove, Il.: InterVarsity Press, 1973.

----------. *A Quest for Godliness: The Puritan Vision of the Christian Life*. Wheaton: Crossway, 1990.

----------. "Sola Scriptura in History and Today." *The Foundation of Biblical Authority*. Ed. John Warwick Montgomery. Grand Rapids: Zondervan, 1978: 43-62.

Piper, John. *The Future of Justification: A Response to N. T. Wright*. Wheaton: Crossway, 2007.

----------. *Let the Nations be Glad! The Supremacy of God in Missions*. Grand Rapids: Baker, 2003.

Piper, John, and Wayne Grudem, eds. *Recovering Biblical Manhood and Womanhood: A Response to Evangelical Feminism*. Wheaton: Crossway, 1991.

Rabelais, Francois. *The Portable Rabelais*. Trans. Samuel Putnam. N.Y.: The Viking Press, 1946.

Ramm, Bernard. *Protestant Biblical Interpretation: A Textbook of Hermeneutics, 3rd ed*. Grand Rapids: Baker, 1970.

Rapp, Carl. *Fleeing the Universal: The Critique of Post-Rational Criticism*. Albany: State University of New York Press, 1998.

Reilly, Robert R. *The Closing of the Muslim Mind: How Intellectual Suicide Created the Modern Islamist Crisis*. Wilmington, DE: Intercollegiate Studies Institute, 2010.

Ritchie, Daniel E. *Reconstructing Literature in an Ideological Age: A Biblical Poetics and Literary Studies from Milton to Burke*. Grand Rapids: Eerdmans, 1996.

Roach, William C. *Sola Fide: A Primer on Paul's Doctrine of Justifica-*

tion in Romans. Matthews, N.C.: Bastion Books, 2018.

Rollins, Hyder E. & Herschel Baker, eds., *The Renaissance in England: Non-Dramatic Prose and Verse of the Sixteenth Century*. Lexington, Mass.: D. C. Heath & Co., 1954.

Rookmaaker, Hans R. *Modern Art and the Death of a Culture*. Downers Grove, Il: InterVarsity Press, 1970.

Ryken, Leland. *Culture in Christian Perspective: A Door to Understanding and Enjoying the Arts*. Portland: Multnomah, 1986.

----------. *Worldly Saints: The Puritans as They Really Were*. Grand Rapids: Baker, 1986.

Samarin, William J. *Tongues of Men and Angels*. N.Y.: MacMillan, 1972.

Sayer, George. *Jack: A Life of C. S. Lewis*. Wheaton: Crossway, 1994.

Sayers, Dorothy L. "The Lost Tools of Learning." *A Matter of Eternity: Selections from the Writings of Dorothy L. Sayers*, ed. Rosamond Kent Sprague. Grand Rapids: Eerdmans, 1973: 107-135.

----------. *The Mind of the Maker*. 1941; San Francisco: Harper & Row, 1979.

Schaeffer, Edith. *Hidden Art*. Wheaton: Tyndale House, 1971.

Schaeffer, Francis A. *Art and the Bible: Two Essays*. Downers Grove, Il.: InterVarsity Press, 1973.

----------. *A Christian Manifesto*. Westchester, Il.: Crossway, 1981.

----------. *The Church at the End of the Twentieth Century*. Downers Grove, Il.: InterVarsity Press, 1970.

----------. *The Church before the Watching World*. Downers Grove, Il.: InterVarsity Press, 1971.

----------. *The God Who is There: Speaking Historic Christianity into the Twentieth Century*. Downers Grove, Il.: Inter-Varsity Press, 1968.

----------. *The Great Evangelical Disaster*. Westchester, Il.: Crossway, 1984.

----------. *How Should We Then Live? The Rise and Decline of Western Thought and Culture*. 1976; 50th L'Abri Anniversary ed., Wheaton: Crossway, 2005.

----------. *True Spirituality*. Wheaton: Tyndale, 1971.

Schaff, Philip, ed. *The Ante-Nicene, Nicene, and Post-Nicene Fathers*, 38vols. 1887; rpt. Peabody, MA: Hendrickson, 1994.

Schall, James V., S. J. *A Student's Guide to Liberal Learning*. Wilmington, De.: Intercollegiate Studies Institute, 2000.

Shakespeare, William. *Shakespeare: The Complete Works.* Ed. G. B. Harrison. NY: Harcourt, Brace, & World, 1948.

Sidney, Sir Philip. "The Defense of Poesy." 1595. *The Renaissance in England: Non-Dramatic Prose and Verse of the Sixteenth Century.* Hyder E. Rollins and Herschel Baker, eds. Lexington, Ma.: D. C. Heath, 1954, pp. 605-24.

Sire, James W. *Scripture Twisting: Twenty Ways the Cults Misread the Bible.* Downers Grove, Il.: InterVarsity Press, 1980.

Sproul. R. C. "Sola Scriptura: Crucial to Evangelicalism." *The Foundation of Biblical Authority.* Ed. James Montgomery Boice. Grand Rapids: Zondervan, 1978: 103-119.

Stapert, Calvin R. *My Only Comfort: Death, Deliverance, and Discipleship in the Music of Bach.* Grand Rapids: Eerdmans, 2000.

Stewart, Kenneth J. *In Search of Ancient Roots: The Christian Past and the Evangelical Identity Crisis.* Downers Grove: InterVarsity Press, 2017.

Stott, John R. W. *Baptism and Fullness: The Work of the Holy Spirit Today.* Downers Grove: InerVarsity Press, 1976.

----------. *Between Two Worlds: The Art of Preaching in the Twentieth Century.* Grand Rapids: Eerdmans, 1982.

----------. *The Incomparable Christ.* Downers Grove, Il.: InterVarsity Press, 2001.

----------. *Our Guilty Silence.* Downers Grove, Il.: InterVarsity Press, 1967.

----------. *Your Mind Matters.* Downers Grove, Il.: InterVarsity Press, 1972.

Tennyson, Alfred, Lord. *Tennyson's Poetry.* Selected and ed. Robert W. Hill, Jr. N.Y.: Norton, 1971.

Thompson, Bard. *Humanists and Reformers: A History of the Renaissance and Reformation.* Grand Rapids: Eerdmans, 1996.

Tolkien, John Ronald Reuel. "On Fairy Stories." *The Tolkien Reader.* N.Y.: Ballantine, 1966, pp. 3-84.

Trinity Hymnal. Revised ed. Atlanta: Great Commission Publications, 1990.

Van Til, Henry R. *The Calvinistic Concept of Culture.* Philadelphia: Presbyterian and Reformed, 1959.

Vanhoozer, Kevin J. *Is There a Meaning in this Text? The Bible, the Reader, and the Morality of Literary Knowledge.* Grand Rapids: Zondervan, 1998.

Veith, Gene Edward. *Postmodern Times: A Christian Guide to Contemporary Thought and Culture*. Wheaton: Crossway, 1994.

Walhout, Clarence and Leland Ryken. *Contemporary Literary Theory: A Christian Appraisal*. Grand Rapids: Eerdmans, 1991.

Watts, Isaac. "The Abuse of the Emotions in the Spiritual Life" (1746). *A Burning and a Shining Light: English Spirituality in the Age of Wesley*, ed. David Lyle Jeffrey. Grand Rapids: Eerdmans,1987, pp. 70-82.

Wells, David F. *No Place for Truth, or Whatever Happened to Evangelical Theology*? Grand Rapids: Eerdmans, 1993.

Wells. David F. and John D. Woodbridge, eds. *The Evangelicals: Who They Are, What They Believe, and How They Are Changing*. Nashville: Abingdon, 1975.

Wenham, John. *Christ and the Bible*. Downers Grove, Il.: InterVarsity Press, 1972.

Wesley, John. "Letter to Margaret Lewen, June 1764." *A Burning and a Shining Light: English Spirituality in the Age of Wesley*, ed. David Lyle Jeffrey. Grand Rapids: Eerdmans,1987, 244-6.

Williams, Donald T. "Answers for Orual: C. S. Lewis as a role Model for Winsome Apologists," (2016 Presidential Address from the annual meeting of the International Society for Christian Apologetic), *The Journal of the International Society of Christian Apologetics* 10:1 (March, 2017): 5-20.

----------. "Body of Evidence: On Liberal Klingons and the Hard Facts of the Christian Faith," *Touchstone: A Journal of Mere Christianity* 26:2 (March/April 2013): 20-22.

----------, "C. S. Lewis: Defender of the Faith." *Christian Research Journal* 40:2 (March/April 2017): 10-17.

----------. *Credo: Meditations on the Nicene Creed*. St. Louis: Chalice Press, 2007.

----------. *Deeper Magic: The Theology behind the Writings of C. S. Lewis*. Baltimore: Square Halo Books, 2016.

----------. "Defending the Biblical View of Human Sexuality: A Socratic-Question Approach." *Christian Research Journal* 40:4 (July/August 2017): 42-46.

----------. *The Disciple's Prayer*. Camp Hill, PA: Christian Publications, 1999; reprint Eugene, OR: Wipf and Stock, 2005.

----------. "Doubt as a Christian Virtue," *Modern Reformation* 15:4 (July/August 2006): 19-21.

----------. *An Encouraging Thought: The Christian Worldview in the*

Writings of J. R. R. Tolkien. Cambridge, OH: Christian Publishing House, 2018.

----------. "'For the Sake of the Story': Doctrine and Discernment in Reading C. S. Lewis," *Modern Reformation* 18:3 (May/June, 2009): 33-36.

----------. "G. K. Chesterton, *The Everlasting Man*." *C. S. Lewis's List: the Ten Books that Influenced Him Most*. Ed. David Werther and Susan Werther. N.Y.: Bloomsbury, 2015, pp. 31-48.

----------. *Inklings of Reality: Essays toward a Christian Philosophy of Letters*, 2nd ed. Lynchburg: Lantern Hollow Press, 2012.

----------. "The Justice of Hell?" *Christian Research Journal* 39:1 (Dec. 2015): 46-50.

----------. "Literature for Wisdom: Donald T. Williams on Reading in the Service of Christian Living." *Touchstone: A Journal of Mere Christianity* 33:4 (July/August 2020): 20-22.

----------. "Loves of Learning: Thoughts on Christian Education." *Christian Educator's Journal* 51:1 (October 2011): 30-32.

----------. "Made for Another World: C. S. Lewis's Argument from Desire Revisited" *Philosophia Christi: The Journal of the Evangelical Philosophical Society* 19:2 (2018): 449-54.

----------. *Mere Humanity: G. K. Chesterton, C. S. Lewis, and J. R. R. Tolkien on the Human Condition*. Nashville: Broadman & Holman, 2006; rpt. Chillicothe, Oh.: DeWard, 2018.

----------. *The Person and Work of the Holy Spirit*. Nashville: Broadman & Holman, 1994; reprint Eugene, OR: Wipf and Stock.

----------. *Reflections from Plato's Cave: Essays in Evangelical Philosophy*. Lynchburg: Lantern Hollow Press, 2012.

----------. "Repairing the Ruins: Thoughts on Christian Higher Education." *Christian Educator's Journal* 41:4 (April 2002): 19-21.

----------. *Stars through the Clouds: The Collected Poetry of Donald T. Williams*, 2nd ed. Lynchburg: Lantern Hollow Press, 2020.

----------. *The Young Christian's Survival Guide: Common Questions Young Christians are Asked about God, the Bible, and the Christian Faith Answered*. Cambridge, OH: Christian Publishing House, 2019.

Wimsatt, W. K. and Monroe C. Beardsley. "The Intentional Fallacy" (1966). *Critical Theory Since Plato*, by Hazard Adam and Leroy Searle. Boston: Wadsworth, 2005: 1027-34.

Wilson, Douglas. *Recovering the Lost Tools of Learning: An Ap-*

proach to Distinctively Christian Education. Wheaton: Crossway, 1991.

Witherspoon, Alexander M. and Frank J. Warnke, eds. *Seventeenth Century Prose and Poetry*, 2nd ed. San Diego: Harcourt, Brace, Jovanovich, 1982.

Woodbridge, John D. *Biblical Authority: A Critique of the Rogers/McKim Proposal*. Grand Rapids: Zondervan, 1982.

Young, R. V. *At War with the Word: Literary Theory and Liberal Education*. Wilmington, De.: Intercollegiate Studies Institute, 1999.

Index of Names

A
Adam 57, 66, 98, 99-100, 189, 193, 197, 259, 301, 323, 338n, 341, 380
Allen, Ronald 171n, 428
Ambrose of Milan 170, 176
Andrews, Edgar 9, 171n, 428
Aquinas, Thomas 41, 353
Arnold, Matthew 326, 428
Ascham, Roger 332, 428
Aslan 117
Augustine of Hippo 37n, 41, 47, 324, 428

B
Bach, Johan Sebastian 112, 171, 181, 286, 337,
Bainton, Roland H. 23n, 352n, 358n, 374n, 428
Barthes, Roland 136n
Beethoven, Ludwig Von 337
Berkhof, Louis 30n, 5n5, 76n, 94n, 130n, 428
Blamires, Harry 314n, 428
Boice, James Montgomery 30n, 428, 437
Bolt, Robert 152, 320, 428
Borror, Gordon 171, 428
Brandybuck, Meriadoc ("Merry") 235
Brown, Harold O. J. 300, 306, 314, 429
Browne, Sir Thomas 158
Bruce. F. F. 246n, 429
Bunyan, John 324, 347n
Burkhardt, Jacob 352n, 429

C
Cable, Stephen 25, 224, 241, 380, 429
Calvin, John 24, 35, 36n, 41, 45n, 47, 63, 80, 107, 124, 132n, 171n, 271n, 324, 345, 357, 359, 360, 367n, 374n, 389, 390, 429, 432, 437
Card, Michael 179, 181
Castiglione, Baldassare 356n, 429
Chaucer, Geoffrey 210, 353, 359
Chesterton, G. K. 258n, 269,-70, 286, 324, 338n, 429,
Cicero 356
Coleman, Rpbert E. 224n, 429
Colet, John 345, 357
Cowper, William 174, 183
Craig, William Lane 246n, 429
Crouch, Andy 268n, 429

D

Dante 59n, 353, 428
Darwin, Charles 294
Davies, Horton 171,, 429
Denethor 235
Denney, James 55n, 430
Derrida, Jacques 136n, 365, 430
Doddridge, Philip 176, 299, 430
Donne, John 286, 348
Duriez, Colin 412n, 430

E

Edman, V. Raymond 401n, 402n, 430
Edwards, Jonathan 6, 292n, 297, 298, 314, 394n, 396, 401, 403, 430
Eller, Vernard 188n, 430
Elyot, Sir Thomas 332n, 431
Erasmus, Desiderius 345, 352n, 357-8, 360, 370, 374n, 428
Erickson, Millard 30n, 55n, 76n, 94n, 431
Estep, William R. 24n, 352n, 374n, 431

F

Ferguson, Wallace K. 32n, 343n, 352n, 360n, 431
Finney, Charles Grandison 401-3, 430, 431

G

Getty, Keith 179
Getty, Kristin 179
Gordon, David Stott 283n, 356n, 428n, 431
Graham, Billy 224n, 402, 431
Green, Roger Lancelyn 258n, 431
Groothuis, Douglas 10, 21, 246n, 271n, 431
Grudem, Wayne 30n, 55n, 76n, 94n, 188n, 431, 435

H

Hackett, Stuart C. 246n, 431
Handel, George Friderich 286
Herbert, George 169, 286
Hess, Eoban 32, 343n, 351, 360, 370
Hirsch, E. D. 130n, 432
Hopkins, Gerard Manley 151, 328, 431
Hopkins, John 174, 432
Hunter, James Davison 25n, 224n, 380n, 381, 432
Hus, Jan 359-60
Hustad, Donald P. 171n, 432

442

Index of Names

J

James bar Joseph 57-8
James bar Zebedee 98, 131
Jeffrey, David Lyle 24n, 176n, 292n, 298n, 199n, 342n, 394n, 396, 432, 438
Jewel, John 42
John, the Apostle 27, 83, 98, 131, 135, 232, 240, 385, 413
John the Baptist 101, 215,
Johnson, Dr. Samuel 172-3

K

Kaiser, Walter C. 130n, 432
Kennedy, James D. 224n, 433
Kenobi, Obi-Wan 229
Kristeller, Paul Oskar 352n, 433
Kuiper, R. B. 224n, 433
Kuyper, Abraham 267n, 433

L

Lewalski, Barbara Kiefer 286n, 433
Lewis, C. S. 33, 43, 117n, 148n, 159, 193, 208, 246n, 257n, 258, 268n, 269n, 280, 286, 324, 326, 338n, 418, 433
Lloyd-Jones, David Martyn 24n, 112n, 149n, 394, 396, 403, 433
Luther, Martin 6, 11, 23-6, 27, 32, 34n, 37n, 41, 55, 58, 60, 74, 129, 141, 169, 282, 315, 343n, 345, 351, 358, 359-60, 370, 374n, 376, 380, 383, 386n, 389, 433

M

MacArthur, John F., Jr. 207n. 208, 434
Machen, J. Gresham 76n, 278, 280, 323, 330, 332n, 410, 434
Machiavelli, Niccolo 343n, 344, 356, 357n,
Matthew, the Apostle 80, 135
McGrath, Alister 24n, 258n, 374n, 434
McQuilkin, J. Robertson 130n,
Milton, John 16, 49, 286, 326, 331, 332n, 343, 344n, 345-7, 434
Montaigne, Michel de 361, 434
Montgomery, John Warwick 6, 10, 30n, 386n, 434
More, Sir Thomas 152, 320
Moses 56, 95, 115, 208
Mozart, Wolfgang 337
Murphree, Jon Tal 224n, 434
Murray, Iain 232n, 414, 434
Murray, John 55n, 232, 414, 434

N

Nash, Ronald H. 30n, 434

Newton, John 174, 183, 297, 396
Niebuhr, H. Richard 268n, 434

O
O'Connor, Flannery 286
Oden, Thomas 55n, 434
Orr, J. Edwim 394n, 396, 435
Outler, Albert 39, 435
Owen, John 94n, 314, 435

P
Packer, J. I. 6, 24n, 30n, 112n, 130n, 204n, 375n, 435
Paul, the Apostle 34, 42, 55, 56, 58, 59, 60, 62, 69, 77, 81, 83, 84, 90, 99, 104, 105, 113, 133, 135, 138, 139, 141, 142, 149, 154, 206, 208, 214, 216, 217-19, 232, 236, 238, 248, 249-51, 259, 277, 363-4, 380, 385-6, 412-13,
Peter, the Apostle 20, 34, 50, 60, 78, 131, 138, 215, 216, 245, 247, 249, 250, 251, 255, 257, 259, 263
Peterson, Andrew 179
Piper, John 15, 55n, 76n, 188n, 223, 435

R
Rabelais 361, 435
Ramm, Bernard 130n, 435
Rembrandt 337
Roach, William C. 11, 55n, 76n, 435
Rookmaaker, Hans 285n, 436
Ryken, Leland 24n, 268n, 432, 436, 438

S
Sayer, George 258n, 436
Sayers, Dorothy L. 59n, 267n, 286, 332n, 342n, 428, 436
Schaeffer, Edith 20, 268n, 436
Schaeffer, Francis A. 6, 15, 20, 25n, 33, 45-6, 122, 149n, 246n, 265, 267n, 268n, 279, 285, 292n, 324, 360, 361n, 404, 410, 412-14, 436
Seneca 356
Shakespeare, William 173n, 210, 235, 337, 437
Sidney, Sir Philip 283n, 332n, 356n, 431, 437
Simpson, A. B. 181
Sire, James 130n, 437
Skywalker, Luke 293
Spenser, Edmund 286
Sproul, R. C. 30n, 437
Spurgeon, Charles 41
Stapert, Calvin R. 171n, 437
Sternhold, Thomas 174, 432
Stott, John R. W. 94, 149, 204n, 225n, 283, 314n, 356n, 437

T

Talbot, John Michael 179
Tennyson, Alfred, Lord 294-6, 437
Terence 345
Tetzel, Johan 23
Theoden son of Thengel 235
Tolkien, J. R. R. 5, 258, 267n, 270, 277, 278n, 286, 324, 338n, 437, 439

V

Vader, Darth 292, 293
Valla, Lorenzo 345, 357
Van Gogh, Vincent 337
Vanhoozer, Kevin 136n, 368n, 437
Van Til, Henry R. 268n, 437

W

Watts, Isaac 174, 183, 292, 297-8, 299, 303, 342, 438
Wells, David F. 9, 24n, 25n, 224n, 381, 438
Wenham, John 30n, 438
Wesley, Charles 174, 176, 183, 297, 430,
Wesley, John 24, 39n, 41, 174, 297, 298, 342, 430, 438
Whitefield, George 297, 401, 403
Williams, Donald T. 5, 9-11, 19, 21, 26, 27n, 30n, 33n, 41n, 49n, 6n7, 73n, 91n, 108n, 125n, 141n, 144n, 156n, 16n0, 183n, 1808n, 200n, 221n, 242n, 246n, 258n, 259n, 262n, 267n, 268n, 269n, 270n, 288n, 298n, 305n, 309n, 314n, 326n, 327n, 332n, 338n, 345n, 349n, 352n, 370n, 390n, 408n, 415n, 423n, 427n, 438-9
Wilson, Douglas 332n, 342n, 439
Woodbridge, John D. 24n, 30n, 438, 440
Wright 55n, 76n, 435
Wycliffe, John 359-60

Y

Yoda 229, 293

Z

Zacchaeus 80
Zwingli, Huldrych 24, 357, 37

General Index

A
Adam, the Second 13, 57, 67, 83, 93, 98-101, 301,
Anthropology 16, 152, 291, 300, 341
AntiChrist 83, 375
Anti-Intellectualism 16, 152, 313, 315-17, 328, 351
Apologetics 10, 15, 19-21, 33, 244-63, 296, 416, 421
Apostle's Creed 41, 83
Arianism 39, 84, 176, 375
Athens 250, 349
Atonement 57, 60, 70, 77, 87, 101, 103, 176-7, 410
Authorial Intent 135-6, 368, 420

B
Babylon 276
Baptism 78, 86,-7, 157, 234
Beowulf 210
Bible 14, 19, 24, 31, 33-4, 37, 40-43, 44-5, 54, 113, 115, 120, 124, 129-30, 132-4, 136-9, 141-2, 150, 153, 155, 186, 187-9, 195, 224, 238-9, 259, 278, 280, 295-6, 303, 306, 319, 322, 335, 337, 342, 344, 346, 353, 355, 358-9, 366, 368, 396, 404, 405, 410, 417, 419

C
Canon / Canonical 129, 132, 203, 206-8
Canterbury 353
Cessationism 206-7, 210
Chalcedon 41, 375
Charismatic 14, 19, 38-9, 148, 202-21, 409,
Chartres 353
Chicago Statement on Biblical Inerrancy 24, 30n, 130n, 429
Christ 24-5, 27, 29, 34, 37-9, 41, 44, 47, 48, 53-4, 57, 58, 59-60, 61-4, 68-9, 75, 77-8, 79-81-5, 87, 90, 92-109, 111, 114, 115-16, 121, 123, 124, 129, 132, 141-2, 147-8, 152, 153-4, 155, 161, 176-7, 178, 187-8, 190, 191-2, 195-6, 197-8, 199, 202, 206, 208, 212, 214, 215, 220, 223, 226, 232-3, 234-5, 237-40, 242, 243, 245, 247-8, 249-51, 253, 255, 258-60, 263, 265, 276, 279-82, 283-4, 289, 293-6, 297, 300-1, 303-4, 305, 316, 320, 321-3, 325, 326, 336, 338, 342 345, 375-6, 380, 381, 383, 384, 410, 413-14, 419-20, 425-6
Christianity 9, 15, 16, 25, 33, 39, 43, 122, 130, 147, 148, 151-2, 154, 158, 160, 163, 164, 204, 225, 253, 254, 264, 266-8, 280, 284, 291, 293, 297, 300, 306, 314, 316n, 323, 330, 338, 352, 354, 360, 376, 395, 397, 396, 399, 401, 409, 421
Church 10-11, 19-20, 23, 25-6, 29, 33, 35, 38, 40-42, 43, 44-7, 54, 59, 66, 74, 78, 79, 87-9, 90, 103, 105, 110, 112, 116, 124, 129, 130, 133-4, 138, 142, 143, 146-65, 169, 170, 171, 172, 174, 175, 180, 182-3, 187, 188-90, 191, 197-8,

204-5, 209, 211, 214, 216, 217-18, 220, 223, 224, 231, 234-5, 237-40, 242, 246, 249, 253-4, 257, 264, 266, 267, 274, 275 284, 304, 315, 320, 323, 327-8, 329, 330, 331-2, 333, 342, 352, 355, 358, 359, 363, 365, 368, 371, 373, 374, 375, 376-6, 377, 380, 381, 383-4, 384, 385-7, 388, 393, 395-7, 398-9, 406, 409-10,14, 418-19, 421, 424

Church Discipline 386, 410, 412-14
Common Grace 271, 275
Communion 86, 88, 147, 157, 160, 376
Constitution 416-17
Context 13, 129, 131-4, 135, 137, 143, 156, 195, 247, 302, 322, 357, 364-5
Conversion 15, 81, 176, 223, 231, 234, 238, 258, 266, 295, 402
Convert 15, 79, 223-4, 228-41, 255, 280, 342, 382, 384, 425
Corinth / Corinthian 204, 216, 218, 250, 385
Culture 10, 11, 15, 19, 45, 116, 129, 150, 159, 264-89, 303, 322, 322, 330, 334-5, 337, 341, 353, 356, 365, 368, 369, 384,, 398, 416, 418,-19, 425
Culture War 416, 418-19

D
Dead Orthodoxy 16, 39, 291, 297, 300, 373
Declaration of Independence 334, 416
Deconstruction 421
Determinism 272, 364
Disciple 36, 80, 229, 231, 234, 236, 237-8, 249, 281, 289, 313, 320-26
Discipleship 19-20, 78, 154, 223, 229, 231, 234, 239, 245, 239,, 252, 265, 279, 313, 318, 334, 422
Doctrine 25, 33-4, 36, 42, 55n, 63n, 75, 82, 84-5, 99, 105, 113, 118-19, 120-21, 129, 137-8, 139, 153, 156, 157, 176, 224, 238n, 241, 270, 280, 296, 300, 306, 314, 341, 342, 347, 352, 358, 361, 363, 373, 375-6, 378, 380, 382. 384, 386, 399, 411, 413 424-5

E
Ecclesiastical 129, 134
Ecclesiology 162
Education 19-20, 274, 278, 280, 316, 330-49, 351, 354, 361-2, 368, 384, 396, 417, 425
Egalitarianism 187-8, 191, 197
Elders 29, 37-8, 189-90, 237, 239, 413
Elitism 285, 342
Emotion 79, 81, 150, 153, 184, 291, 293, 295-6, 298-9, 301, 303, 305-6
Etymology 131
Eucharist 159
Evangelical / Evangelicalism 9, 11, 17, 24-5, 44-6, 55, 87, 94, 148, 150-51, 157, 161, 184, 224, 225, 232 246, 261, 275, 267 280, 283, 286, 291, 292, 294, 295, 302, 304, 305-6, 314, 345, 353-4, 373-4, 376-7, 380-3, 385-6, 393, 398-9, 402-3, 409-10, 414, 425
Evangelical Free Church of America 5

Evangelism 15, 19-20, 113, 222-43, 245-6, 254, 258, 334, 393, 396, 402, 422
Experience 12, 24, 29, 31, 36, 37, 38, 39, 44, 54, 64, 79, 172, 176, 202-04, 210,
    212, 213, 215, 219, 226, 265, 296-7, 299, 302,
303-4, 307, 363, 382, 383-4
Exposition / Expository 14, 69, 133, 147, 155-6, 159, 163-4, 213, 357, 377, 425

F
Facebook 399
Faith 24-5, 27, 31, 34, 37-39, 44, 54-58, 61, 63, 65, 67, 74-90, 92, 94, 100, 104,
    106, 113-14, 116-17, 123, 124, 129, 133, 135, 137-8, 139-40, 150, 152, 153-7, 160, 162-4, 171, 176, 206, 214, 223, 226, 230, 231-33, 235, 237-39, 241,
    244-5, 249, 254, 255, 258-60, 275, 279, 294-6, 297, 299, 300, 306, 314, 315,
    317, 326, 339, 343, 354, 358, 370, 374, 375-6, 379, 380, 383-4, 395, 402,
    404-5, 410, 413, 415, 425
Fall of Man 361
Father 70, 88, 93, 95, 96-7, 98-100, 104, 106, 107, 113, 114, 141, 154, 181, 189,
    193, 213, 228, 234, 253, 282, 283, 301, 323, 328, 336, 341, 348, 375-6, 384,
    408
Feminism 188n
First Great Awakening 6, 24, 175, 176, 292, 297, 306, 314, 375, 384, 394n, 396,
    401-2, 406, 409
Fundamentalism 39, 45, 279, 285, 381, 409-12, 414n, 415
Fundamentals 410

G
Gender 10, 14, 19, 45-6, 186-99
Geneva 389
Gentiles 56, 58, 116, 190, 191, 237
Glory 12-13, 19, 25, 48, 50, 53, 68, 69-71, 93, 95, 97, 105-6, 111-126, 131, 141,
    143, 159-60, 176, 189, 202, 207, 214, 217, 225-7, 233, 262, 265, 280, 284,
    300, 304-5, 317, 318-19, 339, 342, 344-6, 375-6, 383, 405, 408, 425-6
Glossolalia 204, 209, 211
Gospel 17, 24, 25, 26, 27, 38, 42, 43, 54, 61, 62, 65, 67, 68, 69, 70, 71, 79, 80, 81,
    83, 84, 85, 87, 90, 95, 96, 105, 106, 113, 123, 124, 129, 130, 133, 140, 142,
    158, 176, 190, 204-5, 215, 221, 224, 225-6, 227, 230, 231, 235, 239, 250-52,
    254, 259, 266, 267, 280, 284, 286, 296, 297, 306, 323, 335, 338, 345, 358,
    359-60, 363, 373, 375-7, 378, 380-82, 383-4, 385, 388, 389, 395, 398-9,
    402-3, 404-5, 409-11, 413-14, 422, 425-6
Grace 12, 17, 23-27, 48, 52-73, 75-78, 81, 82-85, 86-7, 90, 92, 96, 104, 106, 111,
    113-14, 128, 157, 165, 176, 193, 199, 200, 202, 214, 226, 229-30, 232-3,
    235, 250-51, 263, 280, 284, 296, 297, 302, 310, 315-17 326, 339, 343, 370,
    373, 375-6, 383, 385, 388, 389, 393, 395, 403, 404-5, 406, 408, 413-14, 424-5, 427
Grammar 32, 217, 281, 302, 322, 342, 357, 364-5
Grammatico-Historical Rxegesis 17, 346, 351, 356, 357, 361, 367, 379, 418
Great Commandment 16, 301, 313, 315, 321, 326

Great Commission 15, 222-41, 249, 258, 280, 289, 314, 321, 322, 326, 331, 339, 382, 384, 425, 437

H
Headship, Male 14, 187, 191-2, 193, 380
Headship, Federal 99-100
Heart 54, 73, 77, 80-81, 84, 88, 105, 129, 137, 139-40, 150-51, 155-6, 165, 171, 177, 221, 229-30, 231, 234, 243, 247-8, 251, 254, 259, 265, 275, 291, 294-6, 297-9, 300-02, 303-5, 306, 310, 314, 322, 327, 390
Heart Religion 291, 297-300, 306
Heaven 59-61, 66, 70, 84, 98, 103, 107, 115, 118, 126, 142, 159, 208, 228, 231, 282, 345
Hell 59, 61, 84, 107, 118, 229, 239, 261n
Heresy 152, 300n, 313, 315, 351, 386
Hermeneutics 19, 24n, 30n, 128-43, 156, 195, 344, 353, 363, 365-6, 368, 416, 318, 416, 418, 420
Hierarchy 14, 30, 32, 44, 48, 187, 189-90, 279n, 284, 410
History / Historical 42, 44, 60, 80, 84, 116, 129, 131-4, 141-2, 156, 171-2, 182, 206-7, 210, 224, 250-51, 272-3, 298, 300, 315, 322-3, 334, 338, 342, 346, 352, 353, 355, 356, 357, 360, 361, 364, 365, 367, 374 378, 379, 380, 395-7, 402-3, 406, 409-11, 418
Holy Spirit 21, 34, 38, 41, 57, 64, 67, 78, 80, 104, 113, 116, 122, 135-6, 138, 143, 148, 152, 171-2, 195, 202-21, 228, 232-3, 234, 245, 256, 258-60, 284, 292, 297-8, 313, 317, 316-19, 322, 363-4, 379, 383, 425
Homiletics 130, 156
Human / Humanity 33, 36, 40, 46, 54, 56-7, 62, 66, 70, 83, 93, 98-101, 118-19, 137-8, 139, 150-52, 187, 189-90, 207, 211, 225-6, 234, 243, 253, 261, 264-5, 269-72, 273-4, 275-6, 279-80, 285, 287, 293, 300-301, 303, 310, 315-16, 323, 331, 336-7, 338, 342, 346, 361, 364, 366, 378, 381, 393, 397, 301, 403, 404, 419-21
Humanism / Humanist 345, 351-2, 356-7, 357, 359-62, 370, 406,

I
Image of God / Imago Dei 96, 158, 265, 271-2, 275, 287, 316, 325, 331, 338-9, 341-2
Inerrancy / inerrant 24, 30, 45, 130, 363, 365, 380
Infallibility / infallible 24-5, 29, 31-4, 35, 40-42, 44, 134, 378, 425
Innovation 42
Inspiration 30n, 33, 34n, 139, 156, 363-5, 410
Intellect 150, 153, 247-8, 279n, 293, 295, 327, 345n, 384
Interpretation 37-8, 40, 44, 46, 46-7, 80, 128-43, 363, 365, 367-8, 378
Interpretation, of tongues 218-19

J
Jerusalem 216, 251, 349
Justification by Faith 53-5, 57-8, 63, 61-5, 74, 76, 84, 90, 140, 233, 358, 380, 383

449

L
Lamb of God 93, 101-2, 107
Language 32, 58, 59, 98, 129, 132, 150, 204-5, 21-11, 215-16, 221, 232, 270, 289, 295, 322-3, 342, 361, 363, 365, 418, 423
Lausanne Covenant 24
Legalism 45, 381, 411
Liberalism 39, 315, 397, 410
Lindisfarne 144
linguistic 129, 132
Linguistics 210
Logic 33, 37, 44, 65, 122, 225, 226, 256, 257, 260, 298, 316, 321, 342, 344, 367, 423
Lord's Supper 86-9, 147, 157-60, 376
,Love 30, 56-7, 68, 69, 72-3, 84, 91, 153, 155, 161-2, 177, 179, 181, 189, 200, 206, 212, 217-18. 225-6, 232-3, 248, 251, 253, 255-7, 261, 282, 291, 293-6, 303-6, 309, 313, 317, 322, 326. 343, 349, 357, 386, 388, 399, 408, 412-13, 415, 421, 425-6

M
Magisterial Authority 29, 35, 37, 39, 41-2, 44, 122-3, 130, 137, 143, 174, 239, 383
Man 57, 59, 66, 93, 96, 98-9, 101-2, 103-4, 131, 158-9, 192, 259, 269-70, 273, 301, 320, 331, 338, 341-2, 346, 357, 361, 377, 397, 402, 404
Mayflower Compact 416
Meaning 46, 98, 102, 124, 129, 131-43, 155, 173, 180, 208, 210, 273, 294, 299, 319, 330, 351, 357, 363-6, 367-8, 376, 378-9, 413, 417-20
Mediator 25, 93-4, 103-4, 107
Messiah 98, 105, 132, 266, 267, 362
Middle Ages 170, 353, 355, 360
Mind 19, 47, 78, 91, 114, 135, 147, 149, 150-2, 156, 159, 161, 164, 173, 218-19, 221, 233, 251, 254, 269, 271n, 277-8, 281, 291, 293, 295, 297-8, 301, 303, 305, 312-28, 330, 350, 350, 352, 353-4, 366, 384, 389-90, 418-19, 424-5
Ministerial Authority 29, 37-41, 44, 48, 239, 383
Ministry 19-20, 23, 25, 38, 47, 59, 139, 146, 147, 153-54, 155-6, 158-9, 161-3, 164, 171, 213-14, 215-16, 217, 218, 220, 246, 249-50, 252, 253-4, 257, 271, 297, 317, 339, 383, 384, 388, 396, 424, 425
Mission 26, 156, 164, 203, 213, 223, 225, 238, 334, 386, 398, 421
Modernism 417
Motive 119, 121, 303, 326
Multiculturalism 272
Music 19, 123, 168-84, 265-6, 267, 270, 274, 275-7, 283, 285-66, 287, 304

N
New Covenant 88, 157-8, 323
New Criticism 135, 136n, 417
New Testament 25, 32, 34, 35, 38, 56, 60, 61, 77, 80, 83-4, 86, 94, 96, 99, 105-6,

129, 132, 141, 147, 154, 161-2, 171-2, 203-4, 206, 208-9, 217, 219, 223, 233, 249, 258, 317, 345, 357-8, 359, 375, 385, 410, 412
Nicene Creed 41, 83-4, 238, 373, 376, 386
Ninety-Five Theses 17, 19, 23, 345, 373, 358, 383
Nineveh 276
Notre Dame 353

O
Old Testament 34, 95-6, 98, 101, 129, 132, 141, 171-2, 179, 206, 214, 219, 250-51, 321
Orthodoxy, Christian 84, 224, 386
Orthodoxy, Dead 39, 291, 297, 300, 373
Orthodoxy, Eastern 39

P
Pelagian / Pelagianism 59, 375, 403
Pentecostal / Pentecostalism 39, 202-221
Pietism 19, 290-308, 399
Pope 23, 40, 60, 170, 360, 389
Post-Modern / Post Modernism 272, 293, 418,-20, 423
Preaching 19, 85, 113, 130n, 147, 149n, 155-6, 162-5, 249-50, 260, 266, 284, 339, 351, 377, 382, 395, 401, 403, 405, 409
Ppriest 94, 101, 104
Priesthood 54, 165, 189, 306
Private Judgment 40, 41
Protestant / Protestantism 30, 41-2, 54, 55n, 62, 65, 76n, 148, 161, 174, 176, 286, 306-7, 314, 333, 344-5, 352
386, 398, 409, 415
Public Schools 257, 332, 334, 368
Puritan / Puritanism 24, 292, 314, 399, 409

Q
Quadrilateral 39

R
Readers 132-3, 136, 150, 318, 366, 368, 418-20
Reading 40, 43n, 47, 131-2, 136, 143, 322, 324, 335, 355-7, 359, 360, 367-9, 374, 378, 417, 418-22
Reason 2021, 29, 31-3, 36-9, 41, 44, 91, 137, 292-6, 298-9, 300, 315-17, 349, 353, 367, 383-4, 389, 421
Reformation 19, 23-6, 30, 31, 33, 35, 39, 40, 48, 52, 54, 65, 71, 85, 87, 89, 94, 105-6, 112, 124, 130, 136, 138, 140, 142-3, 170, 174, 198, 2-5, 211, 217, 220, 225, 227, 238, 240, 246, 248, 257, 261, 267, 276, 287, 306, 330, 332, 338, 342, 345, 350, 351, 352, 354-5, 357, 358,-60, 362, 365, 366, 367, 369, 372-90, 392-3, 394, 397, 399, 403, 406, 409, 414, 424-5
Reformers 24, 31-2, 35, 42, 59-60, 65, 107, 124, 225, 292, 314, 345, 357, 361-2,

363, 373, 374n, 377, 380, 385
Regeneration 53, 64, 78, 176, 223, 231-3, 237, 259n, 260
Renaissance 19, 24n, 33, 287, 332, 344-5, 350-72, 373-4, 378-9, 384, 393, 397, 406, 424-5
Repentance 78, 135, 154, 214, 254, 293, 302, 361, 373, 386, 397, 404
Resurrection 54, 75, 78, 83, 84, 88, 107, 116-17, 151, 246n, 250-51, 410, 415
Revival 19, 25, 39, 287, 332, 350, 352, 373,, 375, 378-9, 384, 392-407, 424,-5
Rhetoric 142, 150, 151, 421-3
Tighteousness 53, 54, 56-8, 59, 63, 67-8, 77, 88, 99-100, 129, 139, 155, 233, 247, 376, 381
Roman Catholicism 30, 35, 39-41, 59, 84, 157
Rome 23, 40, 85, 251, 276, 355, 389

S
Sacrament / Sacramental 14, 53-4, 59, 75, 78, 86-7, 147, 149n, 157-9, 161, 163-4
Salvation 23-5, 48, 53, 54-5, 56-8, 59-60, 61-4, 65-8, 69-70, 71, 75-6, 77-8, 79-81, 82-4, 86-7, 89-90, 99, 105-07, 110-11, 113-14, 115-17, 118-19, 120-21, 122-4, 132, 143, 155, 214-15, 223, 225-7, 232, 233-5, 237-8, 241, 259, 265, 267, 271, 348, 361, 375-7, 383-4, 404-5, 413, 425
Sanctification 53, 57, 64, 65, 100, 140, 204, 223, 231, 233, 237, 301, 386
Scripture 24-5, 28-48, 67, 75, 94, 124, 128,-34, 137, 139-40, 141-3, 155, 158, 165, 171, 174-5, 187-8, 190, 193, 197-8, 203, 206-7, 213-14, 219-20, 239, 246, 266, 278, 296, 297, 301-2, 303, 313, 316, 318-19, 321-3, 324, 341 344-6, 351, 360-61, 363-5, 367, 377, 378-9, 380, 383, 389-90, 402, 410, 413-14
Second Adam 67, 83, 93, 98-100, 101, 301
Secular Education 331, 333-5
Separation / Separatism 411-13
Sin 23, 54, 55n, 56-7, 61, 63, 65-7, 69, 78, 83, 88, 93, 96, 99-100, 101-2, 103-4, 116-17, 124, 132, 147, 153-4, 163, 164, 177, 198, 214, 225, 253, 258, 271, 274, 301-2, 309, 381 395, 397, 403
Sitz im Leben 135
Son of God 65, 93, 101-2, 103, 153, 225, 294, 301
Spirituality 24n, 152, 153-4, 156, 160, 163, 164, 204, 286n, 290, 292, 298n, 299, 301, 306, 309, 353, 384, 393, 394, 395, 397 424
Study 45, 130, 135, 140, 172-3, 202-3, 296, 313, 318-19, 320, 321-3, 324, 326, 381, 395, 402, 425

T
Teaching 35-6, 38-9, 44-6, 54, 84, 105, 129-30, 139-40, 147, 155, 161, 170, 171, 173, 198, 199, 213, 217-18, 228, 231, 234, 236, 249, 283, 287, 314, 317, 318, 323, 333, 366, 369, 373, 389
Theology 23, 34n, 44, 54, 57, 59, 61, 68, 84-5, 87, 130, 133, 148n, 158, 176, 204-5, 206, 210, 217, 242, 246, 293, 342 353-4, 365, 375-6, 380, 381, 402 404-5, 417, 422
Toccoa, Ga. 148
Tongues (cf. Glossolalia) 38, 195, 203-21

Tradition 29, 31-6, 37-44, 148, 357, 359, 365, 383, 406
Transubstantiation 158, 160
Trinity / Trinitarian 113, 189, 193, 316n
Trivium 288, 342, 371

V
Virgin Birth 116, 410, 415

W
Wittenberg 23, 345, 389
Works 23, 27, 53-70, 75, 77-8, 83-4, 106, 231-2, 234-5, 271, 282, 283, 375, 381, 404-5
Worship 73, 86, 88-9, 95, 105, 110, 112, 113, 120, 123, 141, 147, 152, 157-60, 161-3, 168,-84, 202, 218-19, 223, 225-6, 235, 281, 287, 296, 298, 302, 304, 305-6, 320, 331, 375, 383-4, 398, 424, 426

Y
Yahweh 95, 113

Scripture Index

Gen. 1	323	Is. 6:5	95
Gen. 1:26	98, 315	Is. 42:8	69
Gen. 1:26-7	98	Is. 48:9-11	69, 114
Gen. 1:28	271	Is. 59:2	66
Gen. 3:9	196		
Gen. 12:3	98	Jer. 13:23	66
Gen. 15	133	Jer. 29:7	276
Ex. 3:12	113	Dan. 1:13-14	98
Ex. 7:3-5	113		
Ex. 9:16	113	Mat. 5:13	283
Ex. 12:5	101, 113	Mat. 5:14-15	283
Ex. 19:16-25	115	Mat. 5:16	70, 282, 283
Ex. 20:4-6	95	Mat. 6:12	386
Ex. 24:9-18	115	Mat. 11:28	103
Ex. 33:18-23	115	Mat. 13:18	137
Ex. 40:34	113	Mat. 15:6	137
		Mat. 16:28	131
Lev. 22:21	101	Mat. 17:2	103
		Mat. 20:25-28	190, 191
Deut. 4:12	96	Mat. 22:35-38	150
Deut. 13:1-5	37	Mat. 22:37	251, 291, 293, 301, 305, 313, 317, 321
Deut. 18:20-22	37		
Deut. 25:2	99	Mat. 22:37-39	301
		Mat. 22:40	301
Judges 21:25	41	Mat. 24:35	138
		Mat. 26:28	88
1 Sam. 9:16	105	Mat. 28:16-20	228
		Mat. 28:19	224, 314, 321
1 Kings 8:10-13	115	Mat. 28:19-20	224, 314
Ps. 1	321	Mark 1:15	78
Ps. 19:1	113, 116, 284	Mark 4:41	103
Ps. 33:3	171-2	Mark 10:15	103
Ps. 79:9	113	Mark 16:16	78
Prvb. 9:1-6	288, 371	Luke 16:17	34
		Luke 22:19	88
Eccl. 9:10	318	Luke 22:26	187
Is. 1:18	315, 317	John 1:1	96, 103
Is. 6:1f	115	John 1:13	232, 402

Scripture Index

John 1:14	96, 103	Acts 24:10	251
John 1:18	95	Acts 26:26	251
John 1:29	101	Acts 28:24	251
John 3:3	232		
John 3:13	31	Rom. 1:16	61, 123, 376
John 3:16	54, 113	Rom. 1:20	116
John 3:19-21	284	Rom. 3:20	53, 56
John 3:30	216	Rom. 3:22	77
John 4:9	133	Rom. 3:24	53, 56, 60, 63
John 4:34	189	Rom. 3:26	77, 100
John 5:19-23	189	Rom. 3:27	61
John 8:32	344	Rom. 4:2	61
John 10:30	189	Rom. 4:3	68, 77
John 13:1-16	191	Rom. 5	72, 77, 93, 218, 301
John 13:12-16	191	Rom. 5:1	77
John 14-16	213f	Rom. 5:5	218
John 14:6	257	Rom. 5:8	72, 93
John 14:9	97	Rom. 6:1	60
John 14:16-18	213	Rom. 6:3-7	78
John 14:26	213	Rom. 6:23	56
John 15:26-7	213	Rom. 8:15	104
John 16:13-16	213	Rom. 10:9	54, 75, 77, 106
John 16:14	203	Rom. 10:9-10	84, 234, 254
John 17:1	113, 114, 115	Rom. 10:14-15	226
John 17:12	99	Rom. 12:1	349
John 17:14-15	276	Rom. 12:2	317
John 17:15	276	Rom. 14:23	67
Acts 1:3	250	1 Cor. 1:26	328
Acts 2:17-21	215	1 Cor. 2:14	259, 315, 402
Acts 2:22-36	215	1 C0r. 5:17-19	83
Acts 2:36	250	1 Cor. 10:31	318
Acts 2:38	78	1 Cor. 11:3	190
Acts 2:47b	223	1 Cor. 11:23-26	157
Acta 9:23	250	1 Cor. 11:26	87
Acts 9:29	250	1 Cor. 12:3	217
Acts 10:44-48	78	1 Cor. 12:7	217
Acts 16:30-31	77, 105	1 Cor. 12:13	223
Acts 17:2-3	250	1 Cor. 12-14	216
Acts 17:11	35, 40	1 Cor. 12:30	217
Acts 17:17	250	1 Cor. 13:2	218
Acts 17:31	250	1 Cor. 13:4-7	303
Acts 18:4	250	1 Cor. 13:10	203
Acts 18:28	251	1 Cor. 13:12	126
Acts 19:8	251	1 Cor. 14	161, 180, 203
Acts 22:1	251	1 Cor. 14:1	218

455

1 Cor. 14:1-4	218	Eph. 2:16-22	237
1 Cor.; 14:14	218	Eph. 4:11	35, 153
1 Cor. 14:18	218	Eph. 4:12	249
1 Cor. 14:19	218	Eph. 4:15	248, 412
1 Cor. 14:26	161	Eph. 4:22-24	233
1 Cor. 14:26-33	218	Eph. 5:18-21	195
1 Cor. 14:29	219	Eph. 5:19-20	171
1 Cor. 14:33	219	Eph. 5:21	14, 187, 188
1 Cor. 15:3-4	54, 84	Eph. 5:21-24	188
1 Cor. 15:6	251	Eph. 5:22	14, 187, 188, 195
1 Cor. 15:8	251	Eph. 5:23	190
1 Cor. 15:12-19	375	Eph. 5:25-28	192
1 Cor. 15:17	83		
1 Cor. 15:58	261, 407	Phil. 1:9-10	171
		Phil. 2:10-11	106
2 Cor. 3:18	233	Phil. 4:4	303
2 Cor. 4:3-6	115	Phil. 4:8	277, 278
2 Cor. 5:11	261		
2 Cor. 5:17	81, 232	Col. 1:28	147, 155, 249
2 Cor. 5:20	323	Col. 2:9	97, 103
2 Cor. 6:14	411	Col. 3:16	161
2 Cor. 6:21	101	Col. 3:23	318
Gal. 1:6-7	84	1 Tim. 1:4-5	129, 139
Gal. 1:8	413	1 Tim. 2:4	93, 94
Gal. 1:9	375	1 Tim. 2:5	104
Gal. 2:16	84	1 Tim. 2:12-14	193
Gal. 2:21	53, 68	1 Tim. 3:2	35
Gal. 3:24	141	1 Tim. 3:15	238, 386, 412
Gal. 3:28	190	1 Tim. 5:17	190
Gal. 4:4	142	1 Tim. 6:15	93, 95
Gal. 5:2-4	75		
Gal. 5:22	233	2 Tim. 1:13-14	148
Gal. 5:22-23	233	2 Tim. 2:15	321
		2 Tim. 2:24-26	413
Eph. 1:5	60	2 Tim. 3:15-17	155
Eph. 1:10	142	2 Tim. 3:16	34, 129, 138, 139, 156, 322, 363
Eph. 1:12	69, 111, 214		
Eph. 1:14	69, 111	2 Tim. 3:17	249
Eph. 1:20	104		
Eph. 1:22-23	237	Titus 1:2	257
Eph. 2:1	64, 232, 259	Titus 1:9-11	413
Eph. 2:1-5	64		
Eph. 2:5	259	Heb. 1:1	137, 141
Eph. 2:8-10	62, 375, 405	Heb. 1:1-3	141
Eph. 2:10	60, 69, 237	Heb. 1:3	93, 97, 300

Heb. 4:15	101		
Heb. 4:16	104	James 2:18-24	57
Heb. 7:25	104		
Heb. 9:22	93	1 John 1:9	386
Heb. 10:24-5	147	1 John 2:22	75, 375
Heb. 10:25	240	1 John 2:22-23	375
Heb. 11:6	67	1 John 4:2	83
Heb. 11:13	275	1 John 4:2-3	83
		1 John 4:20	240
1 Pet. 2:11	275		
1 Pet. 3:8	247	2 John 1:4	413
1 Pet. 3:15	15, 20, 245, 246, 247f		
1 Pet. 3:16	247	Jude 1:3	249
2 Pet. 1:19-21	138	Rev. 21:24-27	289
2 Pet. 3:16	34		

Index of Latin and Greek Terms

A
ad fontes 17, 345, 351, 355-6, 359, 361, 406
allos 213
analogia fidei 13, 129, 137, 143
apologia 15, 20, 245, 247-8, 251, 262

C
cultor 273
cultura 273
cultus 273

D
ducere 336

E
evangelium 224

G
graphe 34, 156, 322, 363-4

H
heteros 213

I
imago Dei 332, 342-3

K
kyrios 95, 105

L
logos 96, 316n

M
magisterium 35
motare 303

P
parakletos 213

S
semper reformanda 10, 25, 385
semper reformata 385
sola fide 12, 25, 55, 74-90, 124, 359
sola gratia 12, 25, 52-73, 76, 85, 106, 124, 187, 359, 425
sola scriptura 12, 25, 28-48, 52, 124, 351, 359
soli Deo gloria 13, 21, 25, 71, 110-124, 226, 359, 425
solus Christus 13, 25, 92-109, 124, 359
summum bonum 95

T
theopneustos 34, 363

www.ingramcontent.com/pod-product-compliance
Lightning Source LLC
LaVergne TN
LVHW021650060526
838200LV00050B/2288